The English Musical Renaissance
1840–1940

MANCHESTER
UNIVERSITY PRESS

Music and society

Series editors   Peter J. Martin and Tia DeNora

Music and Society aims to bridge the gap between music scholarship and the human sciences. A deliberately eclectic series, its authors are nevertheless united by the contention that music is a social product, social resource, and social practice. As such it is not autonomous but is created and performed by real people in particular times and places; in doing so they reveal much about themselves and their societies.

In contrast to the established academic discourse, *Music and Society* is concerned with all forms of music, and seeks to encourage the scholarly analysis of both 'popular' styles and those which have for too long been marginalised by that discourse – folk and ethnic traditions, music by and for women, jazz, rock, rap, reggae, muzak and so on. These sounds are vital ingredients in the contemporary cultural mix, and their neglect by serious scholars itself tells us much about the social and cultural stratification of our society.

The time is right to take a fresh look at music and its effects, as today's music resonates with the consequences of cultural globalisation and the transformations wrought by new electronic media, and as past styles are reinvented in the light of present concerns. There is, too, a tremendous upsurge of interest in cultural analysis. *Music and Society* does not promote a particular school of thought, but aims to provide a forum for debate; in doing so, the titles in the series bring music back into the heart of socio-cultural analysis.

The land without music: music, culture and society in twentieth-century Britain   *Andrew Blake*
The imagined village: culture, ideology and the English Folk Revival
   Georgina Boyes
Music on deaf ears: musical meaning, ideology and education
   Lucy Green
Sounds and society: themes in the sociology of music   *Peter J. Martin*
Popular music on screen: from the Hollywood musical to music video
   John Mundy
Popular music in England 1840–1914: a social history   2nd edition
   Dave Russell

Further titles are in preparation

Meirion Hughes and Robert Stradling

The English Musical Renaissance
1840–1940   Constructing a national music

SECOND EDITION

Manchester University Press
Manchester and New York

distributed exclusively in the USA by Palgrave

Copyright © Meirion Hughes and Robert Stradling 1993, 2001

The right of Meirion Hughes and Robert Stradling to be identified as the authors of this work has been asserted by them in accordance with the Copyright, Designs and Patents Act 1988.

First edition published 1993 by Routledge

This edition published 2001 by
Manchester University Press
Oxford Road, Manchester M13 9NR, UK
and Room 400, 175 Fifth Avenue, New York, NY 10010, USA
http://www.manchesteruniversitypress.co.uk

Distributed exclusively in the USA by
Palgrave, 175 Fifth Avenue, New York,
NY 10010, USA

Distributed exclusively in Canada by
UBC Press, University of British Columbia, 2029 West Mall,
Vancouver, BC, Canada V6T 1Z2

British Library Cataloguing-in-Publication Data
A catalogue record for this book is available from the British Library

Library of Congress Cataloging-in-Publication Data applied for

ISBN 0 7190 5829 5 *hardback*
   0 7190 5830 9 *paperback*

This edition published 2001

10 09 08 07 06 05 04 03 02 01   10 9 8 7 6 5 4 3 2 1

Typeset in Great Britain
by Northern Phototypesetting Co Ltd, Bolton
Printed in Great Britain
by Bookcraft (Bath) Ltd, Midsomer Norton

Contents

Plates

'HARMONY: or THE PRINCE OF WALES'S ROYAL MINSTRELS', from *Punch*, 11 March 1882

Royal involvement in the English Musical Renaissance, see pp. 19–31

For our sons: Rob, Ed, Nick and Tom

Preface and acknowledgements

In this second edition, although various emendations and additions have been made, the dialectical content remains fundamentally unaltered. We would like, however, to draw the reader's attention to the fact that the book reaches back further into the nineteenth century than did its predecessor, and incorporates a wholly new section on the importance of Mendelssohn and his relationship with the music press in the construction of the English Musical Renaissance. Furthermore, in the preparation of this edition we have revised the text in the light of developments in English music scholarship and wider trends in musicology. Because of the critical reception accorded the first edition, we have taken the opportunity to append a 'Postlude' in which we seek to defend, and to explain, the intellectual position adopted in 1993.

We would like to thank Liz Bird, Cyril Ehrlich and the late Arthur Jacobs for their interest, intellectual stimulation and support since the publication of the first edition of this book. The second edition would have not been possible without the commitment of Matthew Frost at MUP.

Note on citations

The method adopted is basically the Harvard (author: year) system, but with various modifications made in order to accommodate the demands imposed by an unusually wide range of generic source material. This includes manuscript letters and other archive memorabilia; newspaper reviews and music features; LP and CD sleevenotes and disc 'liner notes'; broadcast television and radio documentaries, interviews and other 'talk' features.

Unpublished archival sources

Manuscript citations are designed to match the Harvard system: the archive (acronymic) is followed by the collection title's initial, volume (box or file) number, folio (page) numbers – where available – and, in six-figure form, the date (where known) of the document.

Thus BLMC A/5325/32: 020234 = British Library Manuscripts Collection, Additional Series, volume 5325, folio/page 32: 2 February 1934; and FWLC GT: 181088 = FitzWilliam Library, Cambridge, Barclay Squire's correspondence with Goring-Thomas: 18 October 1888.

Published sources

In all citations of books and articles, the year of earliest appearance (where known) is given first; the year given after the oblique is that of the version used by us.

Items cited from the *Radio Times* and the *Musical Times* are entered in separate sections under 'Sources'.

Radio and television programmes

Broadcast material is referenced by the name (where known) of the
writer or producer, followed by the channel (abbreviated) and, in
six-figure form, the date of the broadcast.

Thus Jones BBC R3: 130887 gives Jones as the writer/producer
(or, occasionally, as the subject of interview), broadcast on BBC
Radio 3: 13 August 1987.

Disc 'notes'

LP and CD notes are referenced by author, date (where known),
record company and disc number.

Thus Brooke 1969: Hyperion AGRB 702 refers to Brooke's
sleeve-notes (or insert text, if a CD) for Hyperion's recording of the
work in question.

Abbreviations

BBC	British Broadcasting Corporation
BBC R3	BBC Radio 3
BBC R4	BBC Radio 4
BBCC	BBC Written Archives Centre, Caversham
BLMC	British Library Manuscripts Collection
BLMC A	British Library Manuscripts Collection, Additional Manuscripts
BLMC E	British Library Manuscripts Collection, Egerton Manuscripts
BLMC L	British Library Manuscripts Collection, Loan Collection
BNOC	British National Opera Company
BRBC	Bristol University Barter Collection
BRBC DM	Bristol University Barter Collection, box no.
BUBM	Birmingham University Bantock Manuscritpts
BUBM F	Birmingham University Bantock Manuscripts, file no.
CBSO	City of Birmingham Symphony Orchestra
DNB	*Dictionary of National Biography*
EBCB	Elgar Birthplace Collection, Broadheath
FWLC	Fiztwilliam Library, Cambridge
FWLC BS	Fiztwilliam Library, Cambridge, Barclay Squire Papers
HWRO	Hereford and Worcester Record Office, Worcester
ISCM	International Society for Contemporary Music
LPO	London Philharmonic Orchestra
LUBC	Leeds University Brotherton Collection

MT	*Musical Times*
NTS	National Training School
Oxf.Bod	Bodleian Library, Oxford
Oxf.Bod. EL	Bodleian Library, Oxford, English Letters
PROK	Public Record Office, Kew
PROK PREM	Public Record Office, Kew, Prime Ministers' Papers
RAM	Royal Academy of Music
RAMA	Royal Academy of Music Archives
RAMA PAM	Royal Academy of Music Archives, Pamphlet Collection
RCM	Royal College of Music
RCMA	Royal College of Music Archives
RCMA NTS	Royal College of Music Archives, National Training School Minutes
RCMA PAM	Royal College of Music Archives, Pamphlet
RMCM	Royal Manchester College of Music
RNCM	Royal Northern College of Music
RPS	Royal Philharmonic Society
RT	*Radio Times*

Introduction

> They had no vision amazing
> Of the goodly house they are raising;
> They had no divine foreshowing
> Of the land to which they are going.
>
> (O'Shaughnessy, *The Music Makers*, 1874)

In researching and writing the original edition of this book, the authors experienced constant stimulation of their own arguments from the metaphorical language of Arthur O'Shaughnessy's ode. For us, its role as a signifier was both complemented and enhanced by the musical setting made by Sir Edward Elgar, in which so many of O'Shaughnessy's abstract poetic formulations are constrained to refer concretely to the role of the 'great composer' in the construction of a 'national music'. In particular we adopted the phrase 'the goodly house' to mean the Musical Renaissance itself, as a conscious and official project, with a finite and defined content, and often (though not always) with a local habitation and a name – the area of South Kensington which embraces the Royal College of Music and the Albert Hall, resting on the foundations (as it were) of the Great Exhibition of 1851. It is in this sense that the phrase is used throughout what follows.

That music and politics are intimately connected on many levels, especially in their mutual enhancement of meaning, is now widely accepted. Not too long ago an outrageously heretical proposition, during the 1990s it became almost an orthodoxy of music writing. Its move into the establishment was acknowledged by the BBC's dedication of a recent Proms Season to celebrating 'the tangled relationship between music and politics' (BBC 1998: 13). Given the discourse of 'virtual politics' in the new millennium, political parties think as carefully about the 'music logo' which accompanies their media appearances as about their more tangibly representational images. Music as a fund of national, as distinct from mere party, propaganda is a case even less in need of demonstration. Even a decade ago Minister for the Arts, Timothy Renton, announced the arrangements for a 'National Music Day' (28 June 1992) with the words: 'We *should* blow our own trumpet. The Germans used to refer to us as "the land without music", but now I suspect we have more music than anywhere else in Europe' (BBC R4: 240991). Nor does it come as a shock to discover that the idea was put to the Government by Mick Jagger, rock relic and erstwhile scourge of the establishment.

There remains reason for apprehension in that, while almost everyone outside the industry is aware of music's political dimensions, many inside it – above all, music historians – are apt to reject claims that 'Great Music' can ever be heard (or 'read', it makes no difference) in political terms. In order to maintain this position, they need to deny that music contains any linguistically coherent discourse. Indeed, it is still not unusual to encounter the neo-platonic argument that music is great precisely in proportion to its freedom from 'extra-musical' considerations. Even today, elitist and exclusivist nostrums of this kind, most rigorously derived from the work of the great musicologist and apostle of analysis, Heinrich Schenker, retain enormous influence. Because this book rejects such arguments in principle, we still feel the need to recapitulate in advance George Orwell's warning that 'the opinion that art should have nothing to do with politics is in itself a political attitude' (Orwell and Angus 1970: I, 26).

The belief in a rigidly autonomous discourse is bipartite. It has an extrinsic, or social, aspect – summed up by Frank Howes, *The Times*'s critic and lifelong supporter of 'national music' in England, in describing the task of the music historian: 'It is with music pursued consciously as an art, enjoyed for its own sake and regarded as an independent sphere of the human spirit, that we primarily have to deal' (Howes 1966: 23). But this proposition derives directly from the second aspect, the intrinsic autonomy of 'the music itself' – both in its permanent semiotic appearance (the score) and in its ephemeral physical manifestation (the sound) – maintained most famously by Stravinsky. It is our contention that these dogma are equally untenable manifestations of a cultural bloc – a rebarbative formation defending the imperial parameters of a system which has enormous vested interests at stake. These interests are variously commercial, social and academic – and on all counts, therefore, undeniably political.

The proposition advanced by Howes permits the history of Western music to order itself on the basis of intangible and unaccountable rules based on a dubious fringe aspect of philosophy known as 'aesthetics' relating to the consideration of the intrinsic 'value' of a (self-projecting) work of art. The resulting *mirabile dictu* is applied with oracular definitiveness to the standards of production (of composers) and performance (of executants). So-called 'aesthetic' judgement is both necessary and sufficient explanation for the position of every stone in the pyramid of the serious music industry, from the admission of a new member at its base to the apotheosis of the Great Composer at the pinnacle. Because allegedly intangible and ineluctable, these rules possess no set morphological character. They are truly sphinx-like in their inscrutability, reflecting the preconceptions of a masonic order. They are mobilised not only in the assessment of any contemporary 'creative' work but in the constant categorisation, labelling and re-labelling of musical forms and modes – Classical (or Serious), Light, Jazz, and so on down the line to Grunge or Gangsta. They are also infallible, because retrospectively self-correcting. History is rewritten – for example, in the case of Mahler, whose music was for fifty years regarded as not merely bad but positively corrosive. Once left outside in the desert sands, Mahler was transposed to the pyramid's top with a flourish of Mozart's magic flute, and without the ghost of an admission that the almost universal depreciation of this composer was in any way socially constructed. Sarastro's word is law.

This system is operated by a self-appointed and self-perpetuating oligarchy, and has a powerful input into the contemporary government of the whole musical world, through the appraisal of individuals, fashions, styles, idioms, genres, academic curricula and performance repertoires. Its judgements have essentially diachronic and spiritual characteristics – though the object of appraisal may have been moulded by nurture, the raw material is a product of nature, immanent and unchanging. Once decided, they are imposed on the consuming public through what for over a century was known, quite candidly, as 'the training of taste', operating through

concert programming, press treatment and organised 'music appreciation' (Howes 1966: 343–7). The resultant structures, at their
most blatant, allow successful campaigns for national music which
support and advance a homophonic, chauvinistic collectivism to
operate behind the screen of 'objective' appraisal; at their worst,
they enable defenders to claim that such appraisal is motivated by
the spirit alone, and that the greatest of its attributes is its political
virginity. This book is motivated largely by the need to examine this
apparent parthenogenesis.

Frequent attacks have been made on the system; its survival, like
that of the Catholic Church or the capitalist world economy seems
to be evidence of anthropological inevitability. Its methods of
assessment have (of course) come in for continual scrutiny. Around
1920, for example, the composer and suffragist Ethel Smyth adopting the role of Queen of the Night expostulated: 'For an English
composer, success depends entirely upon being taken up by the
Machine. 1 always felt that the public liked my work when they got
the chance to hear it ... but it was frowned upon by the Faculty'
(Anon. BBC R3: 060486)

At the same time, a new, professedly iconoclastic magazine
announced:

> The Sackbut will have no rigid 'policy', no axes to grind, no cliques,
> coteries or societies to support, and above all, will put no ban on the
> free expression of opinion ... Its aim will be [to regard] music not as
> an isolated phenomenon, existing in its own separate sphere under its
> own laws, but as an integral and essential factor of modern life. [The
> music lover will learn that] music is not the mystery that many of its
> professors and pseudo-critical jargon-mongers would have him
> believe. (Heseltine and Gray 1920–22: 7–8)

Today, it is true, most musicologists would agree with Philip Heseltine (Peter Warlock). But even as he wrote – often the tendency
where free expression of opinion obtains – he was being undermined from within his own editorial board. For only five pages later
(p. 13), his friend Cecil Gray argued, *per contra*, that

> Nothing matters save the work of art itself ... With the march of time,
> the very aspect of a work may change ... only the purely spiritual qual-
> ity remains, and it is this alone which should concern the critic. [As
> Hanslick argues] criticism should concern itself with the beautiful
> object, not with the perceiving subject.

For Gray, as for Eduard Hanslick and Matthew Arnold before him (and many since), the most dangerous threat to the eternal and stable unities conveyed by Art are the ephemeral and volatile divisions introduced by politics. In conventional music history, there is a reluctance to admit that Great Composers, even in their most uncharacteristic works, forwarded a political purpose, especially where any such purpose is seen as undesirable from our present moral perspective. A relevant example of this is modern treatment of Elgar, who is approaching the status of Shakespearean icon and thus – despite the strong evidence on all counts – simply cannot be associated with imperialism, jingoism, militarism; even worse, with selfish careerism. An adjacent example outside our present patch is the recent controversy over Shostakovich, in which several commentators refused to accept that he was capable of writing sincere works which reflected the positive achievements of the Soviet system. From wherever the shifting and relativist perspective of the commentator has derived, the Great Artist must be seen as having the absolute veracity of the seer. Vaughan Williams's *Symphony No. 4* was widely rejected when first heard in 1935, not least because (for many) it seemed to betray the deepest ideals of English music that its composer had sanctified. After the war, however, it could be said that 'This is one of the greatest contemporary symphonies, and a complete vindication of the now more widely accepted view that the creative artist has, either consciously or unwittingly, the faculty of sensing and portraying impending events' (Dannatt 1947: 84). More than most other branches of history, the history of music is still subject to the kind of promiscuous revisionism practised professionally by Winston Smith in Orwell's *Nineteen Eighty-Four*.

The artist's supposed insight into moral realities which others perceive only years later is one aspect of his detached other-worldliness. Another, celebrated as a well-nigh universal trope in biographical literature, is that Great Composers almost by definition are above the common aspirations of humanity. Indeed, such writings almost invariably assert that these geniuses never themselves stooped to court worldly success. The strong implication in much of our relevant reading is that this was a special feature of English composers, in whom an appealing modesty and reticence were linked to effortless 'natural' greatness. Hundreds of writers must have believed, or at least expected their readers to believe, this demonstrable and risible absurdity. In the course of our researches, we have failed to find a single exception to the exact opposite of this rule – that all composers sought strenuously to procure 'recognition', while some did so obsessively. Yet this important social fiction is sedulously preserved, and is especially important in cases of rejected figures. With the 'neglected' composer Havergal Brian, it took a carefree outsider like Kenneth Eastaugh (then on the staff of the *Daily Mirror*) to puncture this shibboleth, when he demonstrated that the stereotype was 'a portrait that Brian himself created and encouraged' (Eastaugh 1976: v).

Since acknowledgement was crucial to the artistic psyche constructed by bourgeois society, and the obstacles to its achievement so numerous and imponderable, all this is not surprising. As Frank Bridge, another victim of the aesthetic tastes of the interwar period, protested, in language which surely voiced the feelings of many:

> The fact is – whatever my shortcomings – that I have been bitterly hurt at the almost complete indifference shown to my existence in London music ... I realise how much alone I am when I observe the contentment with inferior standards and the degradingly necessary wire-pulling to obtain the recognition which means one's livelihood. (Hindmarsh BBC R3: 290788)

The almost frenetic atmosphere of the early English Musical Renaissance constructed and mediated a national need for Great Composers. From the physical resources it created, it launched a search which placed enormous emphasis on the transcendental promotion of being which society would accord to those who pleased and served it in this capacity. The mighty transfiguration of the first 'Musical Bard' to be discovered and recognised nationally, Sir Edward Elgar, was evident for all aspirants to admire. For many, the call was irresistible. Young Billy Brian changed his name to Havergal because it sounded more artistic, while contemplating Great Art, he said, made him 'grind my teeth with a determination that come what will I'll do something equal for English music' (Eastaugh 1976: 40–3). Composers died early deaths from overwork (Hurlstone, Coleridge-Taylor, Bainton), or went mad in their desperation to succeed (Gurney). Others endured existences of continual frustration and disappointment, like William Fenney, the young starlet who dazzled Bantock's composition classes before the Great War, who lived to attract the ironic pity of Cecil Gray, and died in an Epsom bed-sitter so alone that his body was not discovered for days (Gray 1948/85: 162–3; Foreman 1987: 298–9).

Let us turn to the second – a complementary, and more rebarbative – aspect of music's autonomy – the *intrinsic* signifier. The unique autarky of musical discourse, of 'the notes themselves', is held to privilege the medium. Its more recalcitrant advocates seem to pose as a species of monoglot worker-wasps or bumble-bees who emerge from the hive to amaze with their noise, colour and flight patterns. Yet all aspects of music and musicology are – and can only be – communicated through the constant use of ordinary verbal language. Harmony and counterpoint, tempo, dynamics, expression, mode of execution, as well as appreciation and assessment, all rely absolutely on non-musical description and instruction. The cabbalistic semiology of the notes on the page is always in need of translation, and though it may serve to maintain a modicum of mystique, not a single note can be articulated without the interposition of language. We do not deny the theoretical possibility that music may communicate to some individuals in verbally unmediated ways, though in this respect, unlike other intelligent mammals, they are only receivers not transmitters. This is a process which is, by definition, and *sui generis* meaningless to others: it may be of interest to philosophers, but it makes little demand on our attention.

We cannot leave this subject, however, without advancing some views on one important area of debate. The ability of folk-based Art Music to communicate its regional–national affiliations without the intervention of language is (paradoxically) one of the most common assumptions of all writing and talking about music. Music lovers who have no experience of Transylvania beyond the vicarious agency of Dracula movies are constantly assured that they are hearing its accents in the music of Bartók. But this assurance rests upon a circular argument, for the listener cannot otherwise be possessed of the information with which to appraise precise ethnic origins, and will make the 'correct' identification only once that information is possessed. Such blind preparation can lead to bizarre absurdities. In a BBC TV film on Bartók, Ken Russell used dancing Transylvanian peasants to illustrate the *Concerto for Orchestra* – unfortunately at the exact point in the score at which a tune from Shostakovich is being parodied. And even these objections leave aside the whole question – far from having been settled by ethnomusicologists – of whether any music is capable of a geographical typology, even of an imprecise nature.

Two suitably esoteric examples cropped up on a single day of Radio 3 broadcasting (190889):

> The music [of Guy Ropartz] gives off the authentic flavour of Brittany – indeed its last movement is based on a Breton folk tune.

> Nielsen's music utilised a great deal of material from his island home-land of Fünen … which is why it sounds so Danish.

G. B. Shaw sent such ludicrous propositions packing a full century ago: 'Grieg's music does not remind me of Norway, perhaps because I have never been there' (quoted in Banfield 1981b: 472). These observations represent, surely, 'training of taste', not in music but in politics. They rely entirely on a premediated structure of receptivity. Cecil Sharp knew well enough that England needed to establish folksong in schools before it could be possible for a Vaughan Williams to establish a national music in the country at large. Yet half-a-century later Frank Howes was – if with some desperation – assuring his readers that the music of his friend Edmund Rubbra

> is wholly English, negatively because not a trace of foreign influence, neither French impressionism nor serialism from Central Europe is to be found in it, positively because of its roots in Elizabethan polyphony, and generally because that is what it sounds like … In the last resort the quality is not to be specified, demonstrated and proved, but must be perceived. (Howes 1966: 260–2, our emphasis)

Moreover, both verbal and non-verbal discourses are inscribed with a frankly political vocabulary. In the latter we have the bar line and the stave present as elements of discipline and punishment – placed in a vertical aspect they appear as the fasces of the Roman tribune and the fascist state. The physical appearance of minims and semi-demiquavers: the former larger, usually set in splendid isolation, and expressive; the latter usually crammed together in phalanx-like processions of soldiers or workers, playing a supportive and/or tran-sitional role. The hierarchy of importance is obvious. In the former we have scales, dominant and subdominant, major and minor, tonic and supertonic, harmony and dissonance – a veritable Nietzschean social order. It is no accident that class relations are often expressed in the metaphor of music – 'take but degree away, untune that string'. The language of music criticism is riddled with political ter-minology – radical, revolutionary, conventional, conservative, and so on. If the sobriquet 'classical music' means anything in sociological reality, it is that what it describes is meant to be 'classy', and thus belongs to those with 'class'.

Part I

The history and politics of Renaissance

1

Renaissance and reformation (1840–94)

The less we compose at present the better: there is good music enough written to serve the world for ever. (Ruskin 1877: v)

A land too musical?

In general Victorian England had a low opinion of Art Music. The dominant ethos of the age was practical and empirical, with the arts deemed at best 'luxuries', at worst tainted with eighteenth-century decadence and aristocratic excess. Consequently, they had been in retreat since the end of the Georgian era. The early decades of Victoria's reign was characterised by 'utilitarian' thinking – as set out by Jeremy Bentham and J. S. Mill. The generation before 1860 witnessed the apogee of the British industrial and financial bourgeoisie and its values of business success, thrift, social conformity and practical action. 'Useful' knowledge predominated over the 'pure' intellect; what Matthew Arnold identified in *Culture and Anarchy* as 'the tyranny of practice and utility' was all pervasive (Houghton 1957: 118).

In a culture where art was seen as having a mostly decorative and functional role, the position of music was difficult. Romanticism, with its love of the beautiful and imaginative, was tainted with notions of social upheaval and even of revolution. Ruskin made this connection explicit in his essay 'Queen of the Air' (1869):

Of all the arts [music] is most directly ethical in origin, [and] also the most direct in power of discipline: the first, the simplest, the most effective of all instruments of moral instruction; while in failure and betrayal of its functions, it becomes the subtlest aid of moral degradation. Music is thus in her health the teacher of perfect order, and is the voice of the obedience of angels ... In her depravity, she is also the teacher of perfect disorder and disobedience, and the *Gloria in Excelsis* becomes the *Marseillaise*. (Ruskin 1869: 59)

Many shared his conviction that music, with its dangerous emotional appeal, could herald the call for radical change. Thomas Carlyle, in *Past and Present* (1843), went so far as to define the national symbol, 'Mr Bull', in terms of his ability to control his emotions. His virtues were presented as: 'toughness of muscle, toughness of heart, candid openness, clearness of mind ... and a mastery of the passions' (Carlyle 1843/1909: 165). For Carlyle, music was not only potentially subversive, but actually quasi-effeminate.

These suspicions stemmed partly from the conviction that civilisation was under threat. The mid-Victorians perceived moral and political challenges from several directions, not only from music and the arts, but from science and rational philosophy – paradoxically the very foundations of Victorian success. The upheavals of the Industrial Revolution, and especially the growth of urban populations, created apprehension about the traditional bases of society, not least about the future of Christianity – upon which the nation's moral order was deemed to depend. In such a climate it was not surprising that music was left to slumber largely undisturbed.

All this bred pessimism, reinforcing the conviction that music was not a strong feature of the arts in England, which were distinguished mainly by literature. Moreover, music was seen as essentially alien: to the English mind, foreigners composed music, and had a monopoly of its performance. With the increasing fame of Liszt and Wagner in the 1850s, music became ever more 'foreign' and politically suspect. Henry F. Chorley (1808–1872), the *Athenaeum*'s long-serving music critic, made a direct link between the 'Year of Revolutions' of 1848 and the malign influence of the new music: 'the ferment brewing around us has produced Wagner and all his horrors ... The waters are out, there is no calling back' (Chorley 1854: II, 369–70).

The Victorians, of course, had a thriving musical culture – but mainly a closeted and/or private one. The urban masses had musichalls, but these were tainted, in the middle-class mind, with drunkenness and vice. The middle classes themselves indulged in domestic music-making, and the 'piano in the parlour' created a huge market for music publishing. The Anglican Church gave music a low priority. A combination of disinterest and under-investment left Church music in an unattended state. In the provinces, the choral festivals thrived; but they reflected a deep conservatism which kept Handel in great demand. The upper classes took their music as and when required; generally at the Philharmonic Society Concerts and at the Italian opera in London. But the hunting, shooting and empire-building priorities of the gentry precluded any serious interest.

At every level of education, music was virtually non-existent, although many thinking people recognised that, properly inculcated, it could be a force for social improvement rather than subversion. The mid-Victorian approach to the problems of industrial society was notoriously haphazard. *Laissez-faire* values tended to support indifference over music, and it stayed very much in the market-place. There was a complete lack of intervention on the part of government (at local and national levels) to alter this situation. Other areas of the arts enjoyed government funding for example, the British Museum and the National Gallery – alongside these music appeared a poor relation.

The most important performing traditions were still based firmly on Handel. This German composer – 'anglicised' in his lifetime – had since his death been thoroughly assimilated into the national culture. Indeed, this process of building a national institution around his works and fame was still continuing even in the generation immediately preceding the music revival. For example the Handel Society was formed in 1843 and the most popular of all the festivals of his music was established, as late as 1859, at the Crystal Palace. Handel's output – particularly, of course, his choral works – seemed to radiate magnificence and beneficence to the mid-Victorians; and his character-image was progressively adjusted to make him appear an archetypal Victorian Englishman – large-scale, biblical, positive, patriotic. George Grove later summed it up:

> There is something expressly English in Handel's characteristics. His size, his large appetite, his great writing, his domineering temper, his humour, his power of business, all are our own. So was his eye to the main chance ... In fact he pre-eminently belongs to England ... Abroad, he is little known, and that mostly as a curiosity. (Grove 1890: 542)

Above all, perhaps Handel was perceived as pre-eminently a Christian composer famed for his powerful oratorios and renowned for his charitable works and social conscience. The music of the 'Great Saxon', as Grove once called him, was therefore an unimpeachably

moral force, with *Messiah* as the rock upon which the choral life of
the nation had been built.

Despite the durability of the Handelian choral tradition, the
notion that music was inherently immoral continued to be widespread among the middle-classes. This ethical doubt proved to be a
major barrier to musical progress. Although many writers tried to
address the issue in the musical press it was not until 1871, and the
Reverend H. R. Haweis's *Music and Morals* (1871), that the subject
was tackled head on and at length. This extraordinary volume
became the first line of defence for those seeking to bring Art Music
into the mainstream of Victorian civilisation. *Music and Morals*, one
of the ur-texts of the English Musical Renaissance, not only passionately advocated music as a force for moral and social good, but
also promoted the idea of an English national school of music as an
essential aspect of cultural well-being. Haweis set out to convince his
readers that music was not in itself corrupting, but on the contrary
it could and should be harnessed for the 'healthy' development of
the individual in a 'healthful' society (1871: 42–3). The moral (or
immoral) content of music was determined by the creative artist: his
was the ultimate responsibility, since '[the composer's] profession,
rightly exercised, does not lead to the unbalanced excitement of
sensuous emotions, which is certainly highly prejudicial to both
moral and physical health – but to the orderly education and
discipline of emotion ...' (p. 87). Thus the composer moved to cen-
tre-stage, a development which ensured that the 'life and works'
biography would remain at the heart of musicology for generations
to come. Haweis stressed that all music should have regard to the
'moral health of society' and that there was no better exemplar than
German music, most especially that of Mendelssohn, which, for
him, combined the most intense emotion with the 'highest control'
within a moral and philosophical framework.

Haweis's conclusions on the condition of music in England made
for gloomy reading. In contrast to other nations, the English lacked
(as he expressed it): 'true art feeling, and true religious feeling, and
musical taste; however improving and improvable, the English are
not, as a nation, an artistic people, and *the English are not a Musical
People*' (pp. 124–5). Music in England, he asserted, had always been
an 'exotic' pursuit, and there had never been a proper indigenous
school of music. The history of English music was rather a catalogue
of foreign influences, Haweis even deemed the 'Golden Age' of

Tallis and Byrd a sham and Purcell as 'largely French' and was adamant that

> English composers did not write for the people, the people did not care for their music. The music of the people was ballads – the music of the people is still ballads. Our national music vibrates between 'When other lips' and 'Champagne Charley' ... this will be so until music is felt here, as it is felt in Germany, to be a kind of necessity – to be a thing without which the heart pines and the emotions wither – a need, as of light, and air, and fire. (pp. 492–3)

Despite this damning assessment of England's musical past, Haweis was prepared to concede that there had been hopeful developments in recent decades: the re-invigoration of concert life, the huge expansion of piano ownership; and the enduring influence of Mendelssohn. As for the future, he had mixed feelings: England, he felt, desperately needed to evolve musically, so that music, for the first time, could fulfil its 'high mission' in the moral and cultural life of the people. This could not be left to chance:

> We must not be content with foreign models ... but we must aim at forming a real national school, with a tone and temper expressive of England ... When we have a national school of music, and not before, we shall have high popular standards, and the music of the people will be as real as an instrument of civilisation in its way, and as happily under the control of public opinion, as the Press, the Parliament, or any other of our national institutions. (pp. 573–4)

All in all, Haweis's *Music and Morals* was a seminal text. Alongside other developments in the 1870s, both at home and abroad, it should be regarded as a turning-point in the cultural climate of Victorian Britain. It provided that powerful moral defence of music that had for so long been absent. Not only *could* England become a musical nation, but it *should* be so. Haweis was determined that Art Music was no longer to be stranded in the squalor of the music hall or in the aristocratic decadence of the opera house but, for the first time, enjoy a place at the heart of a wholesome national culture. It is an index of the deep-seated prejudice against Art Music in England that such a prolonged and bitter debate about the morality of music occurred in no other European country. Yet *Music and Morals* offered a conservative and quintessentially Christian vision of England's musical future. Central to this vision were the works of Mendelssohn which, Haweis believed, could win the battle for the

Victorian middle classes in the parlours, choir-practice rooms and
the new urban concert-halls:

> [Mendelssohn] had the highest conception of the dignity of art and the
> moral responsibility of the artist.. In this age of mercenary musical
> manufacture and art degradation, Mendelssohn towers above his con-
> temporaries like a moral lighthouse in the midst of a dark and troubled
> sea … In a lying generation he was true, and in an adulterous genera-
> tion he was pure … (Haweis 1871: 92–3)

It was Mendelssohn as creative artist, moral exemplar and 'lighthouse', who would recuperate Art Music into England's cultural
mainstream. It is, of course, an open question as to how far Haweis's
analysis of England's musical future was to influence the nation's
composers. Yet it is surely an index both of society's persistent moral
reservations towards music that *Music and Morals* went through
twenty editions and remained in print until 1906.

Elijah of 'true art'

> To the noble artist who, surrounded by the Baal-worship of corrupted
> art, has been able by his genius and science to preserve faithfully, like
> another Elijah, the worship of true art … (Prince Albert to
> Mendelssohn: 230447, quoted in Benedict 1850: 53–4)

Thus did the Prince Consort inscribe his libretto of *Elijah* to
Mendelssohn, as a souvenir-gift of the oratorio's first London performance. The queen's husband was not alone in his enthusiasm for
the German composer since, by 1847, early-Victorian England had
long since settled for Mendelssohn with relish. There were many reasons for the lionisation of the Leipzig composer by musical England.
He had all the commodious talents and social graces, looks and fine
manners which the early Victorians associated with the 'Romantic
Artist'. He also possessed an effortless command of the English language. The composer was also perceived as having a fondness for the
landscape and literature of Britain – as evidenced by two early works,
the *Midsummer's Night's Dream Overture* (1826) and the *Hebrides
Overture* (1830) – as well as a genuine interest in the musical life of
the nation. In addition, Mendelssohn's artistry and personal charm
had made a deep impression on the young Queen (as well as her
Consort) so that the composer was soon regarded by the musical
public as having gained the accolade of the new Victorian court.

Beyond personality and talent there were however, other reasons for Mendelssohn's unusual hold on the English musical public. In particular, the composer quickly came to be regarded as an ethical exemplar, in both his life and music. To begin with, Mendelssohn's conversion to the Protestant faith was a boon in a society which was still instinctively anti-semitic, while his private life provided a picture of domestic harmony and strenuous creativity in an age which put great store on family values, hard work and Christian piety. Furthermore, his wealthy banking-family background went down well in a society which celebrated commercially acquired wealth and which viewed material success as a mark of divine favour. In his music, too, Mendelssohn showed himself to be deeply in sympathy with his English public; his choral works, in particular the oratorios *St Paul* (1836) and *Elijah* (1846), the latter commissioned by the Birmingham Festival, enjoyed huge popularity, and provided generations of amateurs on the choral festival circuit with an uncomplicated and sincerely felt Christianity expressed in a contemporary Romantic idiom. The appeal of *St Paul* most especially, may be said to have transformed the musical destiny of England. At the opposite end of the musical spectrum in terms of genre, Mendelssohn also secured great success with his piano miniatures (*Songs Without Words*) for the Victorian parlour, which the Novello publishing house ensured were never out of print. In all, Mendelssohn was a composer who had unique artistic and moral contact with Victorian bourgeois culture.

Mendelssohn's impact on England's musical life really began with the English premiere of *St Paul* at the Liverpool Festival of 1836. This occasion was probably instigated by Sir George Smart (1776–1867), resident conductor of the festival and erstwhile patron of Weber, who brought the work to Merseyside after its successful premiere at the Lower Rhine Festival. Smart was a powerful figure in musical life, and his backing for *St Paul* ensured considerable interest in the premiere. Yet there was more to Mendelssohn's (and *St Paul*'s) success than Smart's patronage. The composer's popularity was much more the result of a conjunction of forces that was to shape the development of music in England for the remainder of the nineteenth century. First, there was the increasing importance of music critics and criticism in the mainstream of an expanding journalistic profession; second, the rise of the Novello music publishing company and its commercial decision to promote Mendelssohn as its main 'house' composer; and, third, the evangelical revival sweeping through British Christianity in the 1830s, which quickly appropriated the 'moral' (yet excitingly contemporary) Mendelssohn as its musical cynosure.

The chief element in the Mendelssohn breakthrough of 1836 was the role of the press, that single most important medium for the communication of ideas. Music criticism established a secure place within the journalistic culture in the 1830s and 1840s, with the national dailies the *Morning Post* and *The Times* leading the way in covering important musical events as a matter of course. Among the influential literary journals, the weekly *Athenaeum*, with an estimated circulation of 18,000, featured a pioneering music column from its inception in 1828 (Sullivan 1984: 21). Of equal importance was the evolution of a commercially viable musical press, with the foundation of the *Musical World* by the Novello publishing house in 1836. Whereas the national papers and journals had the edge in terms of sheer circulation, it was the fledgling musical press that had the scope for in-depth comment on musical subjects. The *Musical World*, issued weekly at a modest 3d, was the first journal of its kind to combine coverage of musical matters with topics of general interest. The press was becoming became *the* crucial channel in which composers' reputations were projected and their music promoted. It is no exaggeration to say that the Victorian public often first 'heard' a composition in the music reviews' column of a newspaper or periodical.

Within the evolving journalistic culture of the 1830s, individual critics were given scope to express their own opinions and project their own musical affiliations. Accordingly, it was they (and not their editors) who could make or break a composer's reputation. One of the most prominent Mendelssohnians was the hymnodist Henry J. Gauntlett (1805–76), who wrote for the *Morning Post* (as well as the *Morning Chronicle* and *Musical World*) and who was to soon become a personal friend of the composer. In contrast, Charles Kenney of *The Times* was a reluctant convert to the Mendelssohn cult, although he too eventually joined the composer's supporters in Grub Street. In 1836 the *Athenaeum* appointed as its chief critic Henry Chorley, a journalist who was determined to place music in the mainstream of intellectual and artistic life. Chorley regarded himself as a critic–patron, one who bestowed and withheld his patronage with equal fervour. Over a career spanning thirty years,

Chorley was to become an ardent and loyal champion of the Leipzig composer, and judged other composers largely on their relationship with Mendelssohn. Chorley and his colleagues were immediately attracted to *St Paul* because of the way in which the oratorio combined clear reverence for the past with a powerful Romantic sensibility suffused by Christian conviction. Furthermore, by dispatching *St Paul* to the Liverpool Festival in an English translation by his friend Karl Klingemann, the composer had signalled a clear intention to work with the grain of England's existing choral tradition. Chorley, as we shall see, was not alone among critics in seeing Mendelssohn as a Pauline missionary who would bring England to musical salvation.

The role of the house of Novello was vital in promoting and projecting Mendelssohn's career in England. The composer became a friend of the Novello family on his first visit to England in 1829, and it was a connection that deepened over the following years. The firm's commercial relationship with Mendelssohn began with the publication of a collection of *Songs Without Words* (Op. 19). A crucial breakthrough came in 1836, when Novello snapped up the English copyright of *St Paul* (almost before the ink was dry on the pages) and decided to place its considerable commercial weight behind the new oratorio. Novello not only published *St Paul* both in full and piano score in time for its Liverpool premiere, but established the *Musical World* to advertise the firm's wares – with Mendelssohn's new oratorio to the fore. The fact that, despite the *Musical World*'s immediate success, Novello decided to sell it within a year tends to confirm the view that the company regarded its new journal as mainly an advertising vehicle for *St Paul*. Novello had established *St Paul*, and *St Paul*, in turn, had assured Novello's commercial future (Hurd 1981: 40–1).

Mendelssohn's meteoric rise in English musical life was due also to the evangelical revival of the 1830s and 1840s. A broad consensus had emerged about the parlous state of British Christianity, which was perceived to be under attack from the twin processes of urbanisation and industrialisation. It seemed that the very fabric of civilised society was under threat, and the idea of launching an all-encompassing mission to win back the 'heathen at home' seized the imagination of millions of Christians. The evangelical movement, which had for so long been the preserve of nonconformists, quickly found its influence spreading to the Anglican and the (newly emancipated) Catholic communities, so that it became 'the strongest force in British religious life' (Chadwick 1966: 5). Huge new investment – public and private – was put into church and chapel construction: for example, in the 1830s alone, the Church of England received a colossal £1.5 million in state aid for its building programme. Mendelssohn and his music rode the evangelical tide, to the extent that with *St Paul* the composer became the standard-bearer of the revival. He had, after all, put much of his own personal conversion to Christianity into the oratorio, and, to many, *St Paul* came to express their own hopes for the nation's re-conversion. In another sense, too, *St Paul* may also be said to have started the 'conversion' of England to what the *Musical World* referred to, perhaps paradoxically, as the 'most divine and humanizing of the arts' – music (*MW* 020936).

In 1836, therefore, England was ready for 'Mendelssohn', and *St Paul* was accordingly promoted in national newspapers and journals as well as in the musical press. In particular, the successful *Musical World* was effusive, giving the oratorio a feature article (written by the librettist Klingemann) in which it was praised for its 'calm grandeur and pure beauty' as well as for 'pure expression of nature and truth' (*MW* 170636). Already in Klingemann's piece, with its emphasis on the purity and 'truth' of *St Paul*, we can see the appeal of the moral and Christian dimensions of Mendelssohn's art for the soon-to-be Victorians. In the wake of the Liverpool premiere, the press reviews proclaimed the masterpiece status of *St Paul*: *The Times* (101036) greeted it as 'a work of considerable genius and erudition'; Gauntlett in the *Morning Post* (101036) described it as of the 'highest excellence' and possessing 'infinite grandeur'; the *Musical World* (141036) recommended the oratorio to its readers as the 'reflective outpourings of a young and healthy mind'. Yet it was Chorley of the *Athenaeum* who had the shrewdest grasp of the potential of *St Paul* for the future development of music in England: 'as regards the future, it is to Mendelssohn that we have to look for works, not merely of the subtlest intellectual refinement, but also of the brightest genius' (Chorley 1836). *St Paul* thus entered the musical bloodstream of the nation, whilst the critics' relationship with the composer went from strength to strength.

Mendelssohn continued to count on his many sources of support in the years after 1836. Novello certainly backed him to the hilt, and reinforced its leading position by securing the copyright for another set of *Songs Without Words*, along with the *Piano Concerto No. 2*, the *42nd Psalm* and the *Symphony No. 2* ('*Lobgesang*'). In addition, Mendelssohn's links with English Christianity were strengthened, not only with music specifically written for Anglican worship (including his *Magnificat*, *Nunc Dimittis*, *Te Deum* and *Jubilate*), but with the 'Wedding-March' (from the *Midsummer Night's Dream* music) – to the strains of which untold thousands of Victorian couples left the altar. The composer's standing among Christians was further bolstered by the hymn *Hear My Prayer* (with its 'O for the Wings of a Dove' setting) and the carol 'Hark the Herald-Angels Sing', the latter a setting of a text by the Rev. Charles Wesley – one of the founding-fathers of the evangelical revival. There can be no better index of the influence that Mendelssohn had on Victorian musical life than his account of a visit to Buckingham Palace in 1842 – when the composer played the chorus 'How Beautiful Are the Messengers' (from *St Paul*) on the palace organ, with Prince Albert pulling out the stops (Radcliffe 1990: 39).

The convergence of taste between the critics and the wider musical public ensured that Mendelssohn's classical Romanticism became the tradition with which English Music could move into the future. Although this represented – in the context of developments on the Continent – a conservative agenda, for the majority of music lovers it provided a comfortable blend of the past with the best of the present. In return for the critics' backing Mendelssohn cultivated close relationships with several of those who promoted his music. One of the composer's oldest contacts was James W. Davison (1813–85). Their friendship went back a long way – to the critic's first visit to Germany in 1836, when he attended the first ever performance of *St Paul* at the Lower Rhine Festival (Reid 1984: 14). Davison returned to England a 'Mendelssohn militant', and through his writings (mostly) in the *Musical World* – and in *The Times* after 1846 – he remained a loyal supporter of the composer (p. 15). In Chorley, to whom the composer was introduced in 1839, he secured another immediate and fervent disciple. Directly after his first meeting with Mendelssohn, Chorley, who had ambitions as a librettist, proposed several collaborations to the composer. Despite the fact that these ideas suffered polite rejection, the two men remained on close terms during the 1840s, a contact which Chorley cherished for the rest of his days. Mendelssohn also maintained a good relationship with Gauntlett during his frequent trips to England, taking an interest in Gauntlett's work as a collector and editor of hymn-tunes. Given his staunch support over the years, Gauntlett must have been overjoyed when the composer asked him to play the organ part in *Elijah* at the work's premiere.

The premiere of *Elijah*, specially commissioned for the Birmingham Festival of 1846, served to confirm Mendelssohn's complete domination of English musical life. The performance met with the composer's complete approval, as did the ecstatic response of the 2,500 strong audience – which had demanded eight numbers encored. The critics reported the occasion with relish, Davison, *The Times*'s new critic, leading the way:

> The last note of *Elijah* was drowned in a long continued and unanimous volley of plaudits, vociferous and deafening ... Never was there a more complete triumph – never a more thorough and speedy recognition of a great work of art. *Elijah* is not only the 'chef d'ouevre' of Mendelssohn, but altogether one of the most extraordinary achievements of human intelligence. (*The Times* 270846)

Gauntlett's extensive report for the *Morning Post* (270846) declared that *Elijah* combined 'ancient grandeur' with the 'passionate beauty of the present day', summing up the occasion as 'an event of the greatest interest in the annals of musical art'. Chorley, not to be outdone, gave the oratorio a prominent review in the *Athenaeum*, in which he declared that *Elijah* was 'a great work by a great man' (Chorley 1846). The adulation of the critics seemed to know no bounds: repeatedly Mendelssohn was hailed as the prophet of the new music, the *only* composer who possessed the moral and artistic authority, and the sheer popularity, to lead England out of the musical wilderness. In the space of ten years Mendelssohn had brought musical Romanticism to England, a safe, reassuring and 'moral' version of Romanticism, representing stability in an age of political turmoil at home and revolution abroad. In both his music and performing manner he was judged to be free from the egoism and erotic overtones of the virtuoso cult, while gaining respect as a scholar who had rediscovered and rehabilitated the music of J. S. Bach.

When Mendelssohn died suddenly in November 1847, his passing was viewed as a catastrophe for English musical life. The obituaries which followed eloquently (and at times hysterically) expressed a deep sense of personal and collective loss. Davison was among the first to respond to the grim and unexpected news from Leipzig:

The greatest musical genius in the world has left us. Mendelssohn is dead ... his death is music's eclipse and all eyes are sensible to the 'dunnest cloak' that ever misfortune threw athwart the bright day of art. [...]
In the face of the great masters of all times, he founded a new school, which having truth for its basis, and knowledge for its superstructure, will live while music lives.
[...]
It was amongst us he found his fondest admirers, and it was our writers, who labouring in his golden wake, first rendered his school a great model for composition. (Davison 1847: 718–20)

Here is the inescapable sense that Mendelssohn had brought moral credibility and artistic distinction to English musical life, alongside a proud recognition of the role which English critics had played in the construction of 'Mendelssohn' as the future model for English composers. After all, he had legitimised music as had no other and positioned the art as a civilising force in early-Victorian society. Chorley in the *Athenaeum* agreed, writing of Mendelssohn as 'the greatest of modern musicians [who was] anxious to employ his art as an instrument of peace, brotherly love, and progress' (Chorley 1847). The *Musical Times* framed the composer's death as a national tragedy, almost naturalising him in the process, by declaring that 'the personal influence of Mendelssohn on the progress of music, especially in England, cannot be replaced ... He was the adopted son of England' (Anon. 1848). The grieving went on for years, and many critics who lived through the Mendelssohn decade remained inconsolable. Chorley, who had touched the mantle of the prophet, could still write in the 1860s, his infatuation and grief undimmed: 'no musical artist, creative or executive, [can] be compared to ... Mendelssohn as regards love, hope, joy, success, prosperity, intellectual cultivation, immediate recognition, – all that makes heaven on earth' (Chorley 1860).

The extent of Mendelssohn's impact may be appreciated in a species of quest for an English replacement. This hunt for a native 'Mendelssohn' took many forms, the most striking of which was a search for an English oratorio. Festival commissions in the 1850s revealed a willingness on the part of committees and choral societies to take risks in order to give young native composers a chance. Charles Horsley (with *David*, 1850), William Bexfield (*Israel Restored*, 1852) and Henry Leslie (*Immanuel*, 1854) all set out for the grail of the 'great' English oratorio, and all ultimately fell by the wayside. We shall see how the need for English composers to prove themselves in the oratorio form continued for fifty years, with Arthur Sullivan and Hubert Parry (among others) searching in vain for international respect. It was not until Elgar's *Dream of Gerontius* (1900) that an English oratorio could claim a place in the repertoire alongside those of Mendelssohn.

The profound sense of loss which followed Mendelssohn's death resulted in a spate of hagiographies. Perhaps the most distinguished of these was by composer–conductor Sir Julius Benedict (1804–85), Weber's pupil and friend, whose *Sketch of the Life and Works of the Late Felix Mendelssohn-Bartholdy* (1850) created a template to be employed by several others. Benedict's line was uncompromising – that Mendelssohn, with his intellectual and moral qualities, was heir to the great Austro-German tradition: 'All at once … the great gap left by Beethoven seemed literally to be filled up' (Benedict 1850: 13). The notion that Mendelssohn had somehow given his life for music was assiduously cultivated – a martyrdom which stemmed from love of his art: 'His one absorbing aspiration through his life was the promotion of his divine art; which, beyond all else, he cherished and worshipped, as well as sanctified by the purity of his life' (Benedict 1850: 60). Benedict stressed that the composer had been taken into the domestic circle of the Royal Family and enjoyed the unique patronage of the Queen and her Consort. The idea that the composer was the prophet–apostle of music Benedict cleverly conveyed in the anecdote concerning Prince Albert's inscription in the *Elijah* libretto presented to Mendelssohn, already cited above. For the Prince Consort, Mendelssohn had clearly *become* 'Elijah', the prophet who, despite the odds, could convert the Queen's subjects to a love of Art Music; England would thereby be 'saved', its people made happier and its political underpinnings made more secure. This, too, was Benedict's judgement, and it became a line reiterated in the hagiographies that continued to appear to the end of the century. George Grove, for example, reinforced the Mendelssohn legend in a magisterial article in his *Dictionary of Music and Musicians* (1879–89); as, indeed, did Elgar's friend Frederick G. Edwards, the editor and critic who, as late as 1896, wrote a loving account of the composer's final creative phase, *The History of Mendelssohn's Elijah*.

Mendelssohn-worship even found expression in mid-Victorian fiction. The romanticisation of the composer's life is best seen in the

novel *Charles Auchester* by Elizabeth S. Sheppard, which appeared
in 1853. This extraordinary work, published through the good
offices of Disraeli, goes far beyond a mere sentimentalising of
Mendelssohn's life. The novel seeks to publicise the composer's cultural mission in England: the conversion of the English to idea of Art
Music as a moral and spiritual experience. Sheppard's sub-text is
that Mendelssohn's legacy is the best and brightest hope for making
England into a musical nation. The future prime minister, clearly
a devot of the Mendelssohn cult, endorsed the novel on its title-
page, where he observed that, 'were it not for Music, we might in
these days say, the Beautiful is dead' (Middleton 1911). The narrative tells how the eponymous Charles gets a musical education, and
how in Germany he comes into the presence of the Seraphael–
'Mendelssohn' figure. Sheppard closely follows the facts of Mendelssohn's life as well as the traditions and myths that were accumulating around the dead composer, and towards the end contrives to
present Seraphael as a Christ-like presence, prepared to sacrifice
himself for his art so that others might truly 'live'. (The name 'Seraphael' itself, a none-too-subtle compound of 'seraph' and
'Raphael', connects the divine with the artistic, the metaphysical
with the musical.) As overwork and bereavement cast their shadows
over him, Seraphael acknowledges his Pauline destiny: '"I should
rather be a martyr than a saint ... Shall I die young and not be
believed to have died for music?"' (Sheppard 1853: III, 252–3).
Though it is impossible to gauge the impact that *Charles Auchester*
made on its readers, Disraeli was certainly impressed, writing to the
author: 'no greater book will ever be written upon music ... that
divine art' (Middleton 1911: vii).

Although the Mendelssohn factor was to remain central to the
development of English music throughout the second half of the
nineteenth century, many conservative attitudes about the nature
of music and its place in the national culture remained deeply entrenched. Meanwhile, elsewhere in Europe, music was undergoing
rapid change; and the 'Music of the Future' was soon to make
Mendelssohn sound like a composer from a past era.

By the mid-1860s, the notion that musical success could be a
source of national pride was gaining ground, yet this, in itself, made
the fact that England had yet to produce a composer of international
stature all the more painful. There were figures – like William Sterndale Bennett (1816–75) and George A. Macfarren (1813–87) – who

had achieved some standing; but they were honoured more for academic eminence (both were principals of the Royal Academy of
Music) than as creative musicians. The Victorian expectation of
native composers being what it was, it is hardly surprising that
neither Bennett nor Macfarren could convince the public of his
'Great Composer' status. Both men lived at a time when the only
'respectable' English musicians were professors.

One index of the changing value accorded to music in Victorian
society was the increasing number of honours – both official and
semi-official – which musicians received. For much of the nineteenth
century such recognition was virtually non-existent, with Henry
Bishop being for many years the only recipient of a musical knighthood (1842). This situation began to change perceptibly around
1870, however, with knighthoods being awarded to the Italian-born
conductor Michael Costa and to the composers Sterndale Bennett,
Julius Benedict and John Goss, within a three-year period
(1869–72). Bennett's biographer commented that these honours
were 'proof of Queen Victoria's desire to encourage and advance the
musical profession in England' (Bennett 1907: 409).

The emergence of Arthur Sullivan was dependent upon a subtle but
important shift in this spirit. For a remarkable ten years it appeared
that, in Sullivan, England had found a significant talent. A brilliant
student at the Royal Academy of Music (RAM), Sullivan spent three
years (1858–61) at the Leipzig Conservatorium, the very heart of the
Mendelssohn tradition. With this training, and an increasingly
important array of patrons –including the Queen and other members
of the Royal Family – Sullivan scored a string of triumphs. He produced a sequence of successful Art Music pieces – from incidental
music to *The Tempest* (1862) to the cantata *Shore and Sea* for the
opening concert of the new Royal Albert Hall (1871). Before he was
30, Sullivan had secured a reputation in England which rivalled that
of Mendelssohn. At this point, however, he began to concentrate on
composing music for the theatre, the financial rewards of operetta
proving impossible to resist. Yet it must be emphasised that he continued to write 'serious' music, and himself saw no incompatibility
between writing for the 'respectable' music-theatre and meeting the
demands of being the nation's greatest composer.

While Sullivan occupied the limelight as a creative musician,
behind the scenes the physical infrastructure was being moved into
place. The foundations of the English Musical Renaissance were

firmly set in the ideology which informed the Great Exhibition of 1851. The inspiration for the Exhibition came from Albert, the Prince Consort. Its success was such that South Kensington was thereafter designated for the development of permanent institutions which would further the general aims of the Exhibition, and thus 'extend the influence of Science and Art upon Productive Industry' (Sheppard 1975: 49). Prince Albert involved a number of individuals and bodies in this grand design – including Gladstone and Disraeli, who were expected to provide state backing for the project. The 'most energetic of South Kensington's creators' was Sir Henry Cole, a civil servant with enormous organisational talent who acted as chief executive for the project (p. 49).

A constitutional and patriotic effort

Henry Cole (1808–82) spent a long life in public works. He was a man who found his *métier* in the expanding government departments of the early industrial age. His career began in the Record Commission (now the Public Record Office), and later he helped to introduce the Penny Post. In the 1840s, his talents were devoted to the administration of the railways, where he introduced the uniform gauge. During 1849–51, Cole's energies were concentrated on the Great Exhibition. From the beginning he was in constant touch with Prince Albert, assisting at every stage of planning and execution, sitting on both the relevant Royal Commission and the executive committee. At its successful conclusion, Albert wrote to him: 'You have been one of the few who originated the design, became its exponent in public, and fought its battles in adversity' (Cole 1884: I, 203).

The South Kensington scheme was basically of German derivation – heavily based on the exemplar of Munich, it was a site to enshrine the fusion of art and science, a comprehensive centre of knowledge which would have a direct utility for education. Land was acquired close to the original Exhibition area, and the whole scheme took shape over the following decades (Sheppard 1975: 177ff.). A place for a 'music school' had always been integral, being mentioned by the Prince himself in 1853. Shortly after Albert's death in 1861, Cole and the Exhibition commissioners decided the time was ripe to implement the idea.

In 1866, Cole took the first steps towards the creation of a music academy in South Kensington. Only two years earlier, the ailing

RAM had received its first-ever government grant – £500 a year – and Cole judged this a good moment for his initiative. The scheme was linked to an ambitious idea for a 'chorus hall', or 'amphitheatre', to be known as the Royal Albert Hall. As vice-president of the Society of Arts, Cole set up a committee with a wide-ranging brief to investigate the 'state of music education at home and abroad' (Royal Society of Arts 1867). This influential body persuaded Alfred, Duke of Edinburgh (Albert's second son and the Society's president), to be its chairman.

A national institution was envisaged, equal to the best in Europe, which would provide – first and foremost – a training for performers, but also a music education for those who wanted to teach. It was to be a professional 'conservatorium'; but, in typically Victorian fashion, Cole stressed the importance of what it might offer to the individual. For him, making the most of 'the gifts of Heaven' went alongside cultural and social utility. He summed up his feelings in a deposition before the committee:

> I think music is to be encouraged in order not that any special class, but that the country at large, may derive benefit and pleasure from it … As almost all civilised governments of the world have thought it good state policy to devote some portion of their revenues to the encouragement of musical education, so I think the time is come when our own government may be fairly asked to do the same without stepping beyond its functions. (Cole 1884: 24–5)

At this stage, plans relied on a take-over of the existing Royal Academy of Music, which was to be used as the core for a much-enlarged institution. Cole felt that the RAM had a number of advantages (apart from its government grant) to recommend its merger in the new institution. It already had a royal charter, the Queen was its patron, and it had a tradition of aristocratic support. However, from evidence given to the committee, it is clear that William Sterndale Bennett (the principal) and his staff were not prepared to accept the extensive changes that a merger would require. Furthermore, the RAM had a history of financial trouble, exacerbated by mediocre management; it was firmly set in its ways and its buildings in Tenterden Street were in urgent need of renovation. As early as 1851, application was made for a gift of land from the Exhibition commissioners in order to move to a new site in South Kensington. On top of this, falling prestige had reduced student numbers to a critical level.

Several years of fruitless negotiation followed the 1867 report, while the RAM lurched from one crisis to another. On one occasion it was forced to close for a term, and the professorial staff took salary cuts to stave off permanent closure. By the end of 1868, only sixty-six day-students remained, as the Disraeli Government cut off its subvention. Bennett, determined that the RAM should survive and remain independent, went on the offensive. In May 1868, he publicly attacked Cole as the 'national music-master', ridiculing the idea of a 'gigantic music-school in Hyde Park', and declaring the Royal Society of Arts' report a 'deception' (Bennett 1907: 373–4). Salvation came with the General Election of 1868, when the Liberals were returned to power, and restored the Academy's state subsidy.

Despite this setback, the passing of the Education Act of 1870 – for which Cole had lobbied hard – gave his proposed project a new impetus. The Act marked a watershed in the involvement of the State in the provision of education: for the first time, there were specific provisions for the teaching of music in elementary schools. Cole seemed to have things close to fruition, but Bennett was obdurate, and his knighthood conferred a new prestige upon the RAM – and that effectively marked the end of Cole's take-over plans. Although he continued to court Bennett – for example, with ideas of sharing accommodation in the new Royal Albert Hall – by 1873 Cole and his royal supporters had decided to go it alone and set up a 'National Training School of Music'.

The intellectual background to the Education Act deserves some consideration. The grip of mid-Victorian mores was beginning to slacken, as writers and artists began to challenge the alleged philistinism and mediocrity that had dominated the artistic life of the nation for two generations. Out of these changing perspectives on art, and the relationship between art and society, what was to become known as the 'English Musical Renaissance' was born. There were two seminal texts in its formation: Jakob Burckhardt's *The Civilization of the Period of the Renaissance in Italy*, published in German in 1860 and translated into English in 1878; and Walter Pater's *Studies in the History of the Renaissance*, published in 1873. These two books sounded the death-knell of the 'high' Victorian view of the arts. A new aesthetic was being born.

It was Walter Pater (1839–94) – art-historian, critic and Oxford don – who coined the rallying cry of his generation: 'Art for art's sake.' He introduced Burckhardt into English intellectual life; and although Pater's book is devoted to critical studies of various specific worthies of the Italian Renaissance, it is nothing less than a call to arms for another 'renaissance', in England, in the 1870s. The call duly received its response: 'renaissances' sprouted and flourished as Pater's work inspired a whole generation. The English Musical Renaissance was thus one of the several 'rebirths', or 'resurrections'.

Although Pater said little specifically about music, the sweep of his thought was not lost on those who yearned for a musical revival. He identified many results of the 'original' Renaissance, chief amongt which was 'an outbreak of the human spirit' (Pater 1873: xi–xii). Three other aspects were of paramount importance: a love of the intellect for its own sake; a commitment to the imaginative; and, as he put it, 'a more liberal way of conceiving life'. In its realism and appeal to experience, Pater argued, the Renaissance was close to the modern spirit. Art had an authentic power to embrace humanity in a 'new, striking, rejoicing way'. The connection with Pater's own society was specific: 'and what does the spirit need in the face of modern life? The sense of freedom.' Victorian artistic values were confronted head-on in the notion that life was too short for compromise; the individual should never settle for less than 'the poetic passion, the desire of beauty, the love of art for art's sake' (pp. 2, 186, 205, 213).

Pater's domestic challenge to the Victorian aesthetic order was found shocking by many. Even greater shocks were delivered to Victorian complacency by a number of dramatic political shifts which overturned long-held assumptions about international relations. Between 1866 and 1871, the fifty-year-old European balance of power was thoroughly upset. Having defeated Austria and France, Germany emerged as a united nation and the dominant power on the Continent. Germany had suddenly acquired the political and military clout to complement its cultural – and especially musical – influence. Simultaneously, another major musical people achieved political nationhood. Italian composers and musicians generally had played a key role in the fight for independence; Verdi, in particular, had demonstrated the political power of music. It must have seemed to Cole and his backers that England more than ever needed a vibrant and successful musical culture of its own – and what better starting-point than the proposed conservatorium on continental lines?

Cole launched the National Training School (NTS) 'by voluntary effort' under the auspices of the Society of Arts. There was an assumption that within five years the institution would be transferred to 'the responsible management of the State' (RCMA NTS 18a: 290573). It was to recruit students from all social classes by competitive selection – the essential qualification was the promise of excellence. The land for the NTS – adjacent to the Royal Albert Hall – was donated by the Exhibition commissioners. The building itself was paid for by a London builder, Charles Freake, to a design by Henry Cole's son Lieutenant H. H. Cole of the Royal Engineers. Scholarships were funded by subscriptions from counties, towns, public bodies, businesses and private individuals.

The NTS opened in 1876, with (the soon-to-be-Sir) Arthur Sullivan as principal. However, Cole disapproved of the latter development. 'I have the strongest conviction that Mr Sullivan's appointment on several grounds is undesirable', he wrote to the Duke of Edinburgh (RCMA NTS: 110176). Yet, in addition to his theatrical career, Sullivan was already a professor at the RAM. Indeed, he had been reluctant to accept the NTS post without 'increased dignity' – to the tune of an annual salary of £1,000 (RCMA NTS: 010176). Cole opposed this; not only on grounds of expense, but because he doubted the extent of Sullivan's commitment. But the Duke – a close friend of the composer – overruled him. A compromise was quickly found, whereby the principal would receive £480 plus 'instruction fees'. All this emphasises the central role which Sullivan enjoyed in English music, together with the intimate royal influence in the affairs of the South Kensington conservatorium.

The NTS was a modest institution by continental standards. It had an initial intake of only fifty students, and a total of fourteen staff, employed on a part-time basis. During its brief existence it received none of the government funding in which Cole had placed so much faith. Already by 1878, the project seemed to have no future. It was at this juncture that Cole managed to stimulate a further phase of royal interest – as the Prince of Wales and the Duke of Albany joined their brother, Edinburgh, in backing the scheme (Colles 1933: 4). The royal connection was to prove decisive in the metamorphosis of the NTS into a new existence as a Royal College of Music. In 1880, a new charter for the College was drawn up; and, in July 1881, Henry Cole being too old for a major new fund-raising effort, the Prince brought George Grove (1820–1900) on to the College Council to spearhead the campaign. Grove's involvement in the project was to prove a turning-point in the history of music in England.

Grove's first career was as an architect and railway engineer. He was much involved in the Great Exhibition and, having moved the structure from South Kensington to Sydenham, he became secretary to the company which managed the Crystal Palace on its new site. But he had a parallel career as a scholar and man of letters, being engaged in several projects, including the *Dictionary of the Bible* and the editorship of *Macmillan's Magazine* (1868–83). Grove's responsibilities at Macmillan included advising on literary projects: indeed, it was possibly on his recommendation that they took up Pater's *Studies* – an extraordinary conjunction, given the influence of both men on the soon-to-emerge Musical Renaissance. As a measure of his standing as engineer and literary figure, Grove was elected to The Athenaeum in 1871.

Although Grove was not a practising musician, he had many distinguished friends and contacts in the musical world. He used his position at the Crystal Palace to promote orchestral music, and, in 1855, he appointed August Manns to the conductorship, under whom the Saturday Concerts ran until the end of the century. Grove also played a major role in establishing the Handel Festival at the Crystal Palace in 1859. The event quickly became the London 'Festival', known for employing huge choral forces typical of Victorian gigantomania. But his greatest contribution was the *Dictionary of Music and Musicians* (1879–89), a project in which he combined his talents as editor and writer with his passion for music. The 'Prospectus for the Dictionary', announced in January 1874, stated that the 'immense progress' made by music in England since 1850 justified such a work (Graves 1903: 205–6). There is, however, much more to the *Dictionary* than a fulfilling of scholarly needs: it is a powerful anglocentric document which gives English musical culture an extraordinary coverage and bias within the overall format. The 1874 'Prospectus' was nothing less than the first 'manifesto' of the English Musical Renaissance.

Part of the inspiration for the *Dictionary* came from the Franco-Prussian War and the European crisis of 1870–71. Grove's evangelical background led him to loathe war, and especially distressing was a conflict between two of the most civilised states in Europe. He admired both countries and supported the goal of a united Germany; but a catastrophic war was far too high a price to pay to achieve this end (BLMC A54793/54: 210770). Grove was also dismayed by the political and social consequences of the war in France, especially the popular revolution of the Paris Commune (Graves 1903: 193). In common with many others', Grove's image of Germany was permanently changed by these events. The Germans had hitherto been considered a hard-working and civilised people who were both musically supreme and politically divided. After 1871, other traits were perceived in the German national character: ruthlessness, military prowess and the politically threatening identity which Bismarck so successfully fashioned.

Many German musicians fully shared in the upsurge in nationalist feelings. The war of 1870 even managed to bring Wagner and Brahms together – in their shared triumphalism at France's defeat. Ferdinand Hiller, one of the most eminent music historians in Germany and a regular contributor to *Macmillan's Magazine*, was swept along on the same tide. In his essay 'Quasi Fantasia', a contribution to the Beethoven Centenary Celebrations, Hiller (1870) made clear the new political importance attached to music. He pictured the great representatives of the German music tradition as having shown the way forward for the whole nation. It was they, as much as any politician or military figure, who opened the doors to national unity. He even went on to make an explicit connection between Beethoven's music and Germany's great future. In an extraordinary passage he proclaimed:

> And Haydn, and Weber, and Schubert, and Mendelssohn! What a propaganda have they made for the fatherland! That they speak a universal language does not prevent their uttering in it the best which we possess as *Germans* – I can wish for the nation nothing better than it should resemble a Beethoven symphony – full of poetry and power; indivisible, yet many-sided; rich in thought and symmetrical in form; exalted and mighty! (Graeme 1870: xx)

In this atmosphere, music *in* England was no longer enough: there had to be an English Music, too. Such matters could no longer be taken lightly. A Music for England became a political priority, an extension of competing nationalisms.

The first edition of the *Dictionary of Music and Musicians* (Grove 1879–89) provides important insights into Grove's priorities. The selection of subjects and the length of the entries, as well as his choice of contributors, reveal much about Grove and the state of English musicology in the 1870s. Its compilation demonstrates that the editor believed in leading from the front. He wrote much of it himself, including several of the longest articles – on Beethoven, Schubert and Mendelssohn – as well as a great number of the shorter entries. But equally noteworthy is the profusion of Grove's own articles on English music and musicians of his own day – including Parry, Stanford and Sullivan, and even Prince Albert. In this respect, the Renaissance was already inscribing itself: Parry and Sullivan were not only featured in, but were themselves contributors to, the first edition. A signal omission is any entry on Grove himself – modesty clearly prevailed. He was, however, accorded a place in the (Edwardian) second edition (Fuller Maitland 1904–10).

English composers before 1850 were given unparalleled exposure in the *Dictionary*. Grove allocated the bulk of the task of publicising English music as never before to William Husk, who ranged far and wide for his material, clearly intending to rewrite the history of English music. He wrote up everyone he could find from earlier epochs: Luffman Atterbury, George Aspull, Charles Stroud, Andrew Ashe; while Purcell had a longer entry than did J. S. Bach. The objective was to show that England had been a musical nation and that contemporaries could with confidence set about building a Musical England in modern times.

Grove drew on writing talent both at home and from abroad. The Viennese academic Ferdinand Pohl covered Haydn and Mozart, while the Berlin scholar Philip Spitta wrote at length on Weber and Schumann. The 'progressive' school was covered by two London-based Germans: Francis Hueffer, on Liszt, and Edward Dannreuther, on Wagner. But Grove relied most heavily on English expertise. It was really a blend of established eminence and youthful talent: Ebenezer Prout, Rockstro and Hullah rubbed shoulders with Barclay Squire, Fuller Maitland and Hubert Parry. The last-named contributed dozens of weighty articles, for example on 'Symphony', 'Sonata', 'Suite' and 'Harmony'. The *Dictionary* is, in fact, a fascinating weave of contributions from older Victorian scholars with those from the new men who were to form the elite of Grove's musical revival.

Grove's second legacy to English Music was in his work for the Royal College, a cause which this ex-builder of lighthouses made into the guiding beacon of the Renaissance (Plate 1). Once, on the Prince of Wales's fund-raising team, he ran a campaign of national publicity. Indeed, it has not been fully realised by historians that Grove himself drafted the key speeches to be given by the royal supporters who stumped the country. His own annotated copies, kept in the Royal College of Music Archive (RCMA) reveal his single-minded determination in preaching the need for revival (RCMA PAM xxii B 20 (1): 'Music in England. The Proposed Royal College of Music' [1882]). To these tasks he brought a new and urgent nationalism which went far beyond Cole's outlook, at once more gentle and internationalist. The addresses also look to the future, a future in which the Royal College would have the crucial role as the powerhouse of music reform. There were altogether three grand public occasions when the royal patrons put forward the case.

The first great fund-raising gathering took place on 12 December 1881 at the Free Trade Hall in Manchester. There were three princes present – the Dukes of Edinburgh and Albany, and Prince Christian – and the audience comprised the great, the good and the wealthy of the industrial north. The Duke of Edinburgh opened the proceedings by setting out the intention 'to enlist sympathy on behalf of music', and in favour of the creation of a 'Central Public Institution' which would rank with 'national conservatories on the continent' (1882: 3). The centrepiece of the meeting was a long address by the Duke of Albany – a ringing appeal for the public to fund the future development of English Music. The speech concentrated on three

1 Grove lights the way for the Musical Renaissance: the lighthouse at Morant Point, Jamaica, built by George Grove in 1842

themes: the social and moral value of music; the history of music in
England; and the best means to build on the nation's inheritance.
The social benefits were stressed at the outset – music would be 'a
civilising element, a refining and elevating influence in common life;
one of the best bonds of the family circle' (1882: 5). The new College would aim for the highest standards, offering an education to a
university degree level. It is significant that Grove's campaign, at this
meeting as elsewhere, constantly reiterated the educational priority
of the planned conservatoire – an attempt to dispel doubts about its
'utility' (and that of music itself) to the individual and to society.

The Duke went on to identify some of the reasons why England
was still generally regarded as unmusical. The dominance of foreign
music and musicians, and the lack of a presence in the provinces
were mentioned. In Albany's voice, Grove tackled the profound cultural issue which had crippled music for generations: 'ignorance of
music ... on the part of men of the greatest intellect, culture, and
position', who put music on a par with dancing. To counter this prejudice, and to construct a genuine prestige for music, it had to be
made available to the people, who must be given every opportunity
'to take a deep and intelligent interest in this greatest of all civilisers'
(1882: 9–10).

In the most extraordinary section of his speech, Albany/Grove
asserted that the English were a musical people, since in earlier times
they formed the first and greatest musical nation in Europe.
Supreme evidence of this was the thirteenth-century song 'Sumer Is
Icumen In':

> [T]his tiny glee, which is the germ of modern music, the direct and
> absolute progenitor to the oratorios of Handel, the symphonies of
> Beethoven, the operas of Wagner is a purely English creation, dealing
> with English sights and sounds – the cuckoo, the blooming meadow ...
> the pastures of Berkshire. (pp. 11–12)

The whole German musical tradition – therefore – is 'English' in
essence; and, more, it has within itself the quiet and certain peace of
the landscape of the Home Counties. Thus Grove at a stroke dis-
possessed Germany's musical culture of its 'Germanness'. Hence-
forth, the Germans could boast only that their music was originally
'Made in England'.

The Duke's speech continued in a slightly less controversial vein.
English musical leadership, he asserted, lasted until the middle of the

seventeenth century. The damage inflicted on music by the Puritans was never properly made good, and the eighteenth century's preoccupation with commerce threw national energy into channels other than art. The presence of Handel in England marked the onset of domination by foreigners, and especially by Italian opera, in musical life, a development which peaked around 1850. Despite these crippling problems the flame of English Music was kept alight in small and unobtrusive ways: the cathedrals, the glee-clubs and in ballad operas – and, in a strikingly dynastic image, the Duke asserted that 'the succession has never failed' (pp. 14–16).

Albany/Grove then turned to present conditions. For some years there had been hopeful signs: the expansion of concerts in London, developments in music publishing, improvements in the provincial festivals. But this was hardly enough, and especially when compared with Germany – always Germany, the obsessive point of comparison, and the object of so much competitive envy in the discourse of English Music. As the Duke opined: 'It only wants the same use of the same means and the patient expenditure of the same time that have been so successful in Germany, to enable us to rival the Germans.' The key to German success was planning in education: specifically, universal elementary instruction, backed up with conservatoires which would nurture the gifted young. The result of such provision was a 'thoroughly musical people', for whom music was 'a daily, necessary and regular element of life' (pp. 18–20).

The Manchester gathering closed with two further contributions from the royal patrons. Prince Christian reminded his audience of the abortive negotiations between the National Training School and the Royal Academy, and hence the inevitability of having to establish a completely new institution. The Duke of Edinburgh reiterated music's importance to the poor , and stressed the proposed College's democratic ideal: 'To have music, then, in perfection, you must search through every class of society, and pick up a diamond, however rough it may be, where it is to be found' (p. 29). There is almost a reflection of a kind of 'cultural conscription' in Grove's outlook. In Europe, state funds were forthcoming for such institutions, and so should they be in England – but in the meantime public support was crucial.

A second fund-raising convention met at St James's Palace in February 1882. Called by the Prince of Wales, it commanded even more prestige than the Manchester occasion. It was intended to be a

national meeting, 'to bring together representatives of counties, the
Church, heads of education ... [with] every person prominently concerned in music ... [and] the heads of social life' (Grove 1883:
11–12). The Prince's speech, with Grove's ideas evident in every
line, was a reworking of Albany's at Manchester, but had some different points of emphasis. The civilising potential of music was given
the heaviest stress, along with its capacity to bind together all classes
in society. The College

> will be to England what the Berlin Conservatoire is to Germany ... the
> recognised centre and head of the musical world ... why is it that Eng-
> land has no music recognised as national? [Because] there is no centre
> of music to which English musicians may resort with confidence ... To
> raise the people you must purify their emotions and cultivate their
> imaginations ... no excess in music is injurious. (pp. 17–18)

Speeches followed from eminent supporters, such as the Archbishop
of Canterbury and Prime Minister Gladstone and the Lord Mayor of
London, with the latter stressing the need for 'a constitutional and
patriotic effort' (p. 28) (see title page illustration).

Two further gatherings were held in March 1882. The Lord
Mayor hosted a meeting intended to canvass contributions from the
'influential gentlemen connected with the colonial Empire'. The
Duke of Connaught claimed that, in the RCM campaign, 'our
objects are not metropolitan, are not provincial, but national and
imperial'. The College would be 'a source or reservoir from which
music may circulate throughout the whole body of the Empire' (pp.
38–9). Later in the month, at his London residence of Marlborough
House, the Prince of Wales put forward the RCM as an institution
which would enhance 'colonial co-operation and sympathy' to the
overall benefit of national unity; furthermore, 'by inspiring among
our fellow-subjects in every part of the Empire these emotions of
patriotism which national music is calculated to evoke ... [m]usic
can benefit and provide for the leisure hours ... elevating enjoyment
[and would] strengthen a common love of country' (pp. 41–2).
There could hardly have been a more emphatic statement of both
the power of music and its political significance. By the 1880s, it
seemed, the Empire had come to need English Music as much as it
did the Royal Navy.

Grove's missionary zeal had produced a manifesto, proclaimed in
royal accents, for the renaissance of English Music. Its political

dynamic is unmistakable. The product of years of reflection and of work in compiling the *Dictionary*, it employs a stridently patriotic, even chauvinistic, vocabulary. Grove drew on history, and on social and educational issues in the Victorian present, to justify the creation of a Royal College. Grove's was a seminal influence in the history of English Music. He launched a revolution from above, with the royal brothers themselves as its willing figureheads. He set a programme and a vision which has dominated his country's musical culture, arguably down to the present day.

The house that Grove built

Grove's efforts on behalf of the Royal College were ultimately successful. His fund-raising campaign had been a barnstorming performance on a national scale. Admittedly, when the dust settled, he had managed to reach only £110,000 from the target figure of £300,000, yet this – joined with the gifts of land and building – was sufficient to enable the College to open its doors in May 1883. He was duly appointed director of the new institution; the Queen agreed to become its first patron and the Prince of Wales its first president. On the day of the opening ceremonies Grove's knighthood was announced.

Grove understood that the College's success would to a large extent depend on his academic appointments. He certainly put a great deal of his musical 'philosophy' into selecting his team. The broad approach – as with the *Dictionary* – was to combine established eminence with youthful promise. Slight regard was paid to continuity of personnel from the NTS. Ultimately, only three of the latter survived, among them Frederick Bridge, who was retained with two professorships – of organ and counterpoint. Bridge – despite apparently impressive credentials, involving Oxford, Windsor and Westminster Abbey – was generally recognised as an indifferent talent. His success was entirely due to pressure on Grove from the Prince of Wales to retain his services (Bridge 1921: 256). The most notable missing figures were Sullivan, who declined Grove's offer, and John Stainer, who had been the School's principal in its last year. Grove also approached the violinist Joachim, the conductor Charles Hallé, and Frederic Cowen – apart from Sullivan the most successful English composer – but all without success. He did, however, secure Jenny Lind-Goldschmidt as professor of singing, as well as the famous piano virtuoso Arabella Goddard.

Grove therefore had at his disposal a new centre of excellence which would not only attract the best students, but would encourage the private and state funding that the College needed in order to prosper. Five of the professorships were placed in the hands of three men: Parry (composition and music history); Stanford (composition and orchestra); and Walter Parratt (organ). In Parry and Stanford, Grove had recruited two of the brightest talents. This trio made up an inner Grove 'group'; they shared a vision of the future in which a musical establishment would be constructed along contemporary lines. They were committed to Grove's goals – more and better music in England, more and better English Music.

On the face of things, Parry was an unusual academic. He was educated at Eton and Oxford, but spent six years in the City before turning to music. Parry's social credentials recommended him, since a more 'gentlemanly' image was needed, and as the Earl of Pembroke's brother-in-law he was a decided asset. Grove had, of course, employed him on the *Dictionary*; but when he was recruited to the RCM, he had yet to prove himself as a composer. His *Scenes from Shelley's 'Prometheus Unbound'* (1880) had impressed Grove and Stanford as a truly contemporary piece, but made little impact with critics and public. However, as the South Kensington Renaissance gathered momentum and as (in time) Parry succeeded Grove as its guiding light, the premiere of Parry's work acquired a mythic place as 'a definite birthday for English Music' (Walker 1907: 300).

In contrast to his colleague, Stanford already enjoyed a national reputation. His career was based in Cambridge University and its Musical Society, which he had made a focus for the promotion of 'modernism' in the 1870s. By the time he began teaching alongside Parry, Stanford had a proven record in composition, having written two symphonies and secured an opera premiere in Germany. Bach, Beethoven, Schumann and Brahms were Stanford's heroes, whereas he found Liszt and Wagner mostly uncongenial. Perhaps his most striking contribution, in terms of future developments, stemmed from his belief in the significance of folk-music. For Stanford, folk-song had a special importance in any national scene, and he was a lifelong advocate of establishing its rightful place in English Art Music. As early as 1889, he argued the essential connections between 'national music' and 'folk-music': 'Without the foundation of such music no healthy taste can be fostered in the population. From all times it has been the germ from which the great composers have come ... The greatest composers have sprung from the heart of the people' (Stanford 1908: 53).

Walter Parratt was the third member of Grove's inner circle. Trained as an organist of the old school, Parratt may have seemed a rather unlikely radical. Yet, despite his connections in the church-music establishment both at Oxford and at the Chapel Royal – he eschewed Mendelssohn and Gounod in favour of the progressives in his field, Franck and Reger, and was among the first to spot Elgar's talent. He was the first of the RCM professors to be knighted (1892); and, when he was made Master of the Queen's Musick, in 1893, he brought the court and its patronage within the orbit of the College and the Renaissance. Of his activities at the RCM, his biographers remark: 'It meant work by which he was to influence the world of British music more powerfully than was possible in any other way or place' (Tovey and Parratt 1941: 72).

Grove's tenure as director at South Kensington lasted until 1894. During this time, the financial position of the RCM was strengthened, and the pressing question of better premises was resolved by the generosity of a Sheffield industrialist. Samson Fox was the embodiment of Victorian entrepreneurial success: the son of a weaver, he made a fortune by inventing a new steel process. Given that the RCM had never secured enough original funding, Fox transformed its prospects when, in 1888, he offered the Prince of Wales the sum of £30,000 for a purpose-built conservatorium (Plate 2). By 1894, when the new building was completed in Prince Consort Road, Fox had donated a total of £46,000, meeting every expense out of his own pocket – generosity on a staggering scale. At this time, there was still no sign of the much-anticipated state subsidy and the RCM could only survive by attracting such 'new money' (Young 1980: 198). In contrast to this private largesse, state support for the RCM was niggardly. Although an annual grant of £500 was awarded in 1892, this remained static for over half a century, and may be contrasted with the state subsidy of the Paris Conservatoire in the 1890s which averaged £10,000 (equivalent) (Barty-King 1980: 60).

One of Grove's most important tasks was to repair relationships with the RAM. This he accomplished through personal friendship with its new principal Alexander Mackenzie – aided by the fortuitous circumstance of the two men being neighbours in Sydenham. Well-known as a composer both at home and on the Continent, Mackenzie succeeded the arch-conservative Macfarren in 1888, and proved a

2 The Goodly House (Mark II) – Samson Fox's folly: the Royal College of
Music (1894)

staunch ally of the Renaissance from the outset. It was vital for English
Music to be seen to be free of schism, and for its two conservatoria
to progress in harmony and in the spirit of co-operation, since funding, political support and international prestige depended on it.

The most obvious sign of the new partnership between the RCM
and the RAM was the establishment of the Associated Board, a body
designed to administer national examinations on behalf of the two
institutions. It was underpinned by a genuine warmth between
Grove and Mackenzie, which can be gauged from their speeches at
the Board's annual dinner in 1892. Mackenzie announced that:

> Sir George Grove and I have been feeling like a couple of musical Jack
> Horners tonight, rubbing our hands and saying mentally, 'Oh! what
> good boys we have been' ... I am perfectly certain that our united
> endeavours must flourish. [Grove responded:] We are at the head of
> music in this country – there can be no doubt about that ... we have
> common work and a common end, common sympathies and common
> ideals. (RCMA PAM xxii B 10(3)113–15: 140792)

The RCM could not afford to rely solely on its reputation as a
teaching institution, but needed to distinguish itself in every area of

musical endeavour. The heaviest burden fell on Parry and Stanford – and not only as professors of composition. Stanford's responsibility for the College orchestra put him in a pivotal role – to develop a tradition of orchestral playing and conducting. For his part, Parry needed to deploy his scholarship not only for the benefit of his students but in continuing the work of Grove's *Dictionary* in the vital task of interpreting English Music History – from the new perspectives of the South Kensington revival.

The greatest obstacle to change and renewal was perceived to have been the choral festival tradition. Outside London's concert life – the Philharmonic Society, the Monday 'Pops' and the Crystal Palace orchestral concerts – the festivals were the backbone of musical England. There were five great triennial institutions: the Three Choirs' Festival, held cyclically at Worcester, Gloucester and Hereford, dating back to 1724; Birmingham (1768); Norfolk and Norwich (1824); Leeds (1858); and London's Handel Festival founded in 1859. All were conceived originally as charitable events, and were therefore interested in making a profit. For example, the Norfolk Festival of 1863 made a surplus of £1,270 on receipts of £5,270 (Legge and Hansell 1896: 179). Their financial imperatives made the choral festivals very conservative, inculcating a concern for 'safe' programming, with few incentives to experiment with untried composers.

In addition, the hegemony of Handel, Haydn and, increasingly, Mendelssohn in the field of oratorio was a major barrier to modernisation. Nothing had changed since 1868, when the programme for the Third Handel Festival had declared: 'Handel! ... Warriors march to his defiant or triumphal strains – Kings, Queens and Princes are christened and crowned, married and buried to his everlasting hymns, while Musicians with one accord proclaim him The Master of Music' (RCMA PAM xxii C 36 (6)).

This ethos was constantly reinforced by musicians like Sullivan, Gounod – and even Dvořák – who accepted the fact that a successful oratorio was a lucrative proposition. However, the *Daily Telegraph*'s critic Joseph Bennett (1831–1911) quickly discerned the direction of the revivalists' thinking . As early as 1877, he sounded an alarm:

Handel has been an institution for 150 years, an all-embracing, well-nigh absolute influence... A musician of the people with a passion for

imperial grandeur [Yet he] is out of fashion among the mass of connoisseurs ... But it may be said that the estrangement from him of
musical society is ominous of a more complete catastrophe. (Bennett
MT 1877)

Such was the strength of the Handel public that the Renaissance
leaders were for a time obliged to pander to its predilections. If they
wanted to gain necessary hearings and influence, works in the choral
tradition had to emanate from South Kensington, at least for a time.
Receiving a commission to write the oratorio *Judith* for the Birmingham Festival of 1888, Parry wrote to Dannreuther: 'The Birmingham people stood out for a regular oratorio. I hope you won't
swear! ... I caved in, but with a mental reservation that there should-
n't be much of religious or biblical oratorio beyond the name'
(Oxf.Bod. EL e.117/153: 201087).

By the 1880s, two specific revivals were in full swing within the
general phenomenon – those of J. S. Bach and Henry Purcell. These
were to provide South Kensington with the material to re-energise
the choral tradition. The roots of the Bach revival went back to
Mendelssohn, and to the formation of the Bach Society in 1849. With
the proliferation of Bach choirs, his music found a permanent place
in the musical life of the country. Stanford and Parry seized upon the
Bach revival for several reasons. They firmly believed in the unique
aesthetic and ethical qualities of Bach's great choral works. But also
his personality – his sincerity, integrity and devotion to his art – provided a strong appeal. Above all, for Parry, Bach was the originator of
that 'Darwinian' process, the pure evolutionary current that led,
through Beethoven, to the contemporary genius of Brahms.

The Purcell revival started with the founding of the Purcell Society in 1876. In many ways, the idea of an English equivalent of Bach
lay behind it – the desire for a national composer of the Baroque age.
Therefore it was both complementary to and competitive with the
Bach revival. The personnel of its committee, including Sterndale
Bennett, Macfarren, W. H. Cummings and Prout, reflected its roots
in the RAM and the Novello publishing house. In any event, the
Renaissance seized upon this new champion not least because in Purcell they cherished an English musician who could compose serious
opera – a profound genre which anticipated any German equivalent.
Stanford's edition of *The Fairy Queen* appeared in 1892; a decade
later Parry, in a volume of the *Oxford History of Music*, made the
extraordinary claims that 'Purcell's work covers more ground than

that of any other composer this century ... The most brilliant moment in the history of 17th century music remained outside the general evolution of European art. The style was too individual and uncompromising to appeal to foreigners' (Parry 1902: 306–7).

Stanford and Parry were committed to the Schumann–Brahms tradition and for them this was the direction in which English Music had to progress. The former enjoyed a long friendship with Joachim and had avidly promoted Brahms since his student days. The latter's musicianship had been formed by a long association with the Wagnerite Edward Dannreuther – but like Stanford, he found the later Wagner impossible to accept. Neither man had much sympathy with Wagner's more 'advanced' techniques; still less were they enamoured of his philosophy and the theories which informed his music. Least of all did they wish to infect the English Renaissance with the bitterness of the debates between the 'Brahmins' and the 'Wagnerites', which had for some years divided German musical life. To the Renaissance mandarins, it was difficult enough to get English Music moving after generations of relative stagnation, without importing potentially disabling controversies. Grove was in full sympathy with his two professors in this. He was a worshipper of the German 'classics' up to Schumann; and, when Brahms arrived, he was prepared to embrace him, too.

The years of Grove's leadership saw a steady stream of compositions from South Kensington, and the 1880s witnessed a remarkable succession of choral and orchestral works. From Parry, there were four symphonies, including his popular English (1889), the oratorio *Judith* and his Milton setting *Blest Pair of Sirens*. From Stanford, *The Revenge* (1886), the *Elegiac Ode* (1884) and the ('Irish') *Symphony No. 3* of 1887, which secured him an international reputation through its hearings in Germany under Richter and von Bulow. Perhaps the first sign of outstanding artistic success came with the all-Stanford concert given in Berlin in January 1889, including the specially commissioned *Symphony No. 4*, an unprecedented event for a British composer. This 'export' of music to the Reich was one of many reasons why the RCM could be proud of its young professors in these early years.

The goal of unity in aim and action was thus as nearly achieved as possible by 1890. The two main institutions had established a close collaboration, and internecine squabbles over fundamental values had been avoided. Within the RCM, however, despite their cordial partnership, Stanford and Parry failed to agree on one important area. Parry loathed opera, calling it 'the shallowest fraud that man ever achieved in the name of art: its invariable associates are dirt and tinsel' (Graves 1926: II, 213). Stanford, on the other hand, thought opera essential, and championed it in the South Kensington context (Stanford 1908: 1–22). Most musicians seemed to be on Stanford's side in this debate. Opera was seen as a weapon – perhaps the best weapon – with which to defeat foreign domination. After all, according to the Renaissance view of English music history, it was Handel's importation of Italian opera which had perverted the whole course of national musical development. Therefore, opera should now take the lead in restoring its well-being.

Stanford was already a successful opera composer before joining the RCM. *The Veiled Prophet* (1878) was premiered at Hanover in 1881, and *Savonarola* was given in German under Richter at Covent Garden in 1884. He remained a passionate lobbyist for RCM commitment to opera, to the extent that even Parry felt it best to have a go – with his *Guenever* (1886). Dannreuther thought it 'the real English Opera for which we have waited so long' (Graves 1926: I, 266). But despite a German translation and discussions with the Mannheim Theatre, even Dannreuther failed to save *Guenever* from oblivion.

By the end of this decade a powerful start had been made on raising the profile of English Music at home and abroad. It was vital to establish a creative 'English School', comparable with those of other nations – perhaps the best example being Russia, with Glinka, Balakirev and the *kutchka* (or 'mighty handful'). At the other extreme, and thus rather more embarrassing, even little Norway – which technically was not an independent state at all – had Nordraak and Grieg to fly its musical flag. The English Renaissance conforms in so many respects to such parallel phenomena that it must (to some extent) be viewed in the same light. Joseph Bennett of the *Daily Telegraph* wrote that 'the turn of musical England is at hand ... [Four composers] have the immediate future in their hands ... [and they] must conserve everything distinctly English' (Bennett *MT* 1884: 326). This comment, coming in the year following the foundation of the RCM, was the first to group together composers, in effect to form a 'school'. The four were Cowen, Goring Thomas, Mackenzie and Stanford. Parry was soon to join them; and indeed, to assume the leadership.

Though not on the staff of the RCM, Mackenzie, Arthur Goring Thomas and Frederic Cowen were regarded by Grove and his team as being associated with them in their great cause. The group can be regarded as a 'British *kutchka*' – Mackenzie himself stressed the 'British' against the 'English' affiliation – which was the focus of change and achievement. One of the most striking qualities of the South Kensington Renaissance was its 'team spirit', the collective sense which proclaimed itself both to the sceptics at home and to observers abroad.

As a close friend of Grove, Mackenzie was, in effect, an 'insider'. A supporter of the German 'moderns' – of Liszt in particular – Mackenzie had been educated both in Germany and at the RAM. His reputation as a composer rested on operas and choral works which, although 'progressive' in many respects, were characterised dismissively by Ernest Walker (1907: 298) as 'highly modernized Mendelssohnianism'. Like Stanford, Mackenzie was committed to the use of folk-music, and championed opera. As the RAM's principal, he reformed both syllabus and staff, men like Prout yielding gradually to more dynamic figures, such as Frederick Corder, appointed professor of composition in 1888. Corder was an enthusiastic Wagnerian, and directed his students – including Bantock, Bax and Holbrooke – towards the 'expressive' milieu of Bayreuth. This, over time, was to make an interesting, but volatile, contrast with the essentially 'Brahmin' orientation of the RCM (Corder 1922: 82ff.).

Frederic Cowen (1852–1935) never quite assumed the same importance within the *kutchka*. Yet he was one of Grove's first choices for an RCM chair, and had made a reputation as a composer in the 1870s. His ('Scandinavian') *Symphony No. 3* (1880) gave him a 'European and an American reputation' (Edwards *MT* 1898). Above all, Cowen was the first distinguished native conductor produced by the revival. He occupied the podium at the Philharmonic Society (1888–92), commanding the level of remuneration previously monopolised by foreigners. The reputation of Goring Thomas (1850–92) rested on two operas, *Esmeralda* (1883) and *Nadeshda* (1885). Thomas came into contact with Grove through William Barclay Squire – a Cambridge friend of Stanford, who was given the task of writing him up for the *Dictionary* (FWLC BS 1881). *Esmeralda*, for which Barclay Squire wrote the libretto, was premiered by the Carl Rosa Company. Moreover, Thomas impressed Stanford to the extent that, after the young composer's suicide in 1892, he provided the orchestration for the unfinished cantata *The Sea and the Skylark* (Fuller Maitland 1904–10: V, 86).

From the beginning Grove grasped that the existence of a favourable musical press was a precondition of success. By 1889, the formation of such support was evident in the frequent identification, by a number of influential newspapers and magazines, of the RCM as the spearhead of English Music. But the task of recruiting journalists to the cause was problematic as well as urgent. The figure who had dominated the music columns of the mid-century was Henry Chorley of the *Athenaeum* magazine, epitome of the Mendelssohn-worship which the younger men loathed. Moreover, Chorley's position on English Music was very simple – there wasn't any! It had never had a 'distinctive face', even in Tudor times, and the national music of Wales, Ireland and Scotland was of far greater importance (Chorley 1880: 174ff.). Equally influential was Davison of *The Times*, who for over thirty years (1846–78) hectored readers with his opinions: Mendelssohn was 'an intellectual giant', Schubert 'morbid', while Wagner and Liszt were 'enemies of music' and 'hateful fungi' (Reid 1984: 225, 228). Davison was a friend of Sterndale Bennett and Macfarren, and in his case the 'generation gap' between the men of the Renaissance and the older mandarins was a yawning chasm.

One critic, however, proved himself a prophet of the Renaissance. As early as 1854, Henry C. Lunn (1817–94) set out the ideas which he was later to develop as editor of the *Musical Times* (1863–77). He believed in the humanising and unifying potential of music, and advocated that England should have its own 'definite school of music', best achieved through the creation of a 'grand National Opera' (Lunn 1854: 5). Music should be for all classes, and 'gentlemanly ignorance' should be swept away, along with the commercial tie between 'the opera-house and the music-shop, fatal to the genius of the composer' (p. 81). Lunn argued that state funding was essential to overcome the difficulties, greatest of which was 'musical conservatism', the mortal enemy of 'musical reform'. The *Musical Times* was bound to reflect its editor's sympathy with many of the objectives of Grove's Renaissance. However, as a house-journal of the Novello publishing firm, it remained if anything on the conservative wing of musical politics, influenced by the firm's commercial priorities; the sale of choral and vocal music – for which there was a constant and high-volume demand.

Lunn apart, the first of the 'new' men to inscribe the significance of the Renaissance was Francis Hueffer (1843–89), Davison's replacement at *The Times*. A committed Wagnerian, Hueffer was an

advocate of the so-called 'Music of the Future' and a champion of
the composer as 'a longed-for Messiah, who would deliver future
generations from the fetters of custom and prejudice' (Hueffer
1874: 13). For over ten years, readers of *The Times* were assured
that Beethoven and Wagner represented the authentic spirit of
Romanticism – 'spiritual and poetical liberation' – of which *Tristan
und Isolde* was the ultimate expression (Hueffer 1874: 255). Hueffer was an early ally of the Renaissance. Soon after his appointment,
he gave support to the Royal College scheme (complete with state
funding) which he saw as the only hope for the creation of 'a
national school of composers' (Hueffer 1880: 69). In Grove's own
Macmillan's Magazine, Hueffer argued that as national music went
ahead in other countries, in England 'the demand for a national
opera ... becomes irresistible' (Hueffer 1880: 235). Though he further forwarded this campaign by writing libretti for Mackenzie and
Cowen, Hueffer never became a confidant of the South Kensington
team, probably because of Grove's personal dislike for him (Young
1980: 156, 252).

The most persuasive advocacy came from younger men encouraged by Grove, the most influential being J. A. Fuller Maitland
(1856–1936). Another Cambridge associate of Stanford, Fuller
Maitland was designated as Grove's successor as editor of the *Dictionary* when he edited a major 'Appendix' for Macmillan in 1889.
The same year, he took over at *The Times*, following Hueffer's unexpected death. From these prestigious positions, Fuller Maitland
became an outright propagandist for South Kensington – attacking
both the oratorio conservatives and the advocates of 'Music of the
Future' with equal zeal. A typical piece of his early journalism was a
review of Parry's oratorio *Job*. 'Recent years have not seen a composition more free from flaw or weak point of any kind, or one
which more conclusively proves that the oratorio form can still
inspire works of the highest genius' (*The Times* 090992). As prolific
author, music editor of the *Encyclopaedia Britannica*, and contributor to the first edition of *The Oxford History of Music*, Fuller Maitland's was a dynamic voice within and on behalf of the Renaissance.
He lined up with the RCM men in the Schumann–Brahms camp,
and his interest in folksong, Purcell and the Tudor composers sealed
this affinity.

Others appeared who would promote the interests of the Renaissance well into the new century. For example, Robin Legge (another

Cambridge product) became Fuller Maitland's understudy at *The Times* in 1891, and proved a useful protégé. W. Barclay Squire – Fuller Maitland's brother-in-law – was a major contributor to the *Dictionary* and critic for several London periodicals. His primary service to the Renaissance, however, was as a librarian and archivist at the British Museum from 1885 onwards, for which post Grove and Stanford were his referees. Barclay Squire proceeded to transform the status of the Music Room, and compiled the 'Catalogue of Printed Music' (Barclay Squire 1912). He also secured many stunning benefactions, including the entire royal collection of Handel's music manuscripts (ninety-two volumes), as well as the bequest of the last ten string quartets of Mozart from a private collector (Hyatt King 1957: 4).

Golden Grove unleaving

> Mr Parry's Symphony in G ... is capital proof that English music has arrived at a renaissance period. (Joseph Bennett, *Daily Telegraph* 040982)

With these words the English Musical Renaissance received its christening. It was, in many ways, fitting that it should have been Joseph Bennett who hit upon what was to become the ideal presentational gambit of the musical revival. Bennett had long been one of the most powerful music critics in the land, using his position vigorously to promote the cause of a national music along conservative lines. Yet another biographer of Mendelssohn, Bennett became chief critic of the *Daily Telegraph* (in 1870) and was a prolific contributor to musical journals. Bennett was keen to promote himself as the people's critic, as a journalist who rejected notions of elitism and snobbery in music and who had his finger firmly on the pulse of the musical public. Although Bennett had promoted Sullivan as the standard-bearer of England's Music, in the early 1880s he began to look around for more convincing champions. He made it abundantly clear in his columns that his support was available only to those English composers who were prepared to reject modernism (especially Wagnerism) and place their talents at the disposal of the 'national music' project. Accordingly, when Parry presented his *Symphony No. 1* at the 1882 Birmingham Festival, Bennett was delighted to welcome him as a new champion of musical England. Bennett's conservative agenda for native composers, and indeed for the Musical Renaissance, is found in his concluding remarks on Parry's symphony which he described as 'modern in spirit, it belongs to our own time, but has, all the same, intimate relations with the past' (*Daily Telegraph* 040982). Within two years, as we have seen, Bennett had nominated a Parry-led school of native composers which he felt could lead England to musical greatness.

The word 'renaissance' means variously 'rebirth' and 'resurrection', and was given its first modern usage (as we have seen) by the Swiss historian Burckhardt in *The Civilization of the Renaissance in Italy* (1860). Although this was translated only in 1878, its influence in England had been established by Pater some years before. It had taken English Music a decade to appropriate the word and the idea as the lead inscription on its banner. But Bennett's usage was remarkable because he gave the new Renaissance credence by linking it with the notion, which had now gained acceptance, of an earlier period of revival, located in the sixteenth century. This created a direct comparison between the new men of the 1880s and a recognised 'Golden Age', establishing a line of spiritual descent. It conferred an aura of legitimacy on the Grove movement, which was seen to kiss hands with the Elizabethans – whose epoch the late Victorians fervently admired. Of at least equal importance is that Bennett's procedure by implication derogates, and in some respects seeks to suppress, the purportedly less dazzling generations which lay somewhere between Purcell and his own day. In order to establish its credentials as a 'resurrection', the Renaissance needed to condemn everything from Arne to Sterndale Bennett as useless, decayed – even dead; by extension 'fallen', and therefore a world in need of 'redemption'.

Bennett was thus tapping into some potent tropes of his culture and society. To the contemporary English mind, 'renaissance' conjured up the 'age of Shakespeare' – as it does even today on English literature syllabuses. The literary and political achievements of the Elizabethans were a source of pride. The age of Shakespeare was also that of another poet – Raleigh – and of navigation, exploration, colonisation, heroic defence of England's Protestant freedom against overwhelming odds, and the defeat of the Spanish Armada.

Celebrating as it did the third centenary of 1588, this generation descried in its ambit the origins of all that it held most dear – nationhood, religion, maritime–commercial traditions, civilisation and

empire. Little wonder that the statue of Prince Albert, 'erected by
public subscription' and placed above Prince Consort Road in 1871,
seems to express South Kensington's Renaissance precisely in these
terms. Clad in Tudor doublet, hose and boots, looking for all the
world like a mixture of Shakespeare and Drake, Albert surveys, with
an expression of earnest contemplation, the broad façade of the
Royal College of Music (Plate 3). The Victorians' identification with
the Elizabethans was such that Queen Victoria – the 'Widow of
Windsor', by metempsychosis become a Virgin Queen, married to
her people – was regarded as a latter-day Gloriana, long-lived and
wise, symbol of the nation's pride and self-confidence.

Joseph Bennett's ideal expression for the South Kensington project was soon taken up by others. Among the first was Morton
Latham, a student at Stanford's Cambridge faculty and a contributor to Grove's *Dictionary*, whose book *The Renaissance of
Music* (1890) cleverly elaborated on Bennett's formulation. Though

3 Prince Albert as 'Sir Francis Shakespeare': the statue of Prince Albert in
the precincts of the Albert Hall (*c.* 1870)

mainly concerned with the place of English Music in the European Renaissance of the sixteenth and seventeenth centuries, Latham made a connection between that 'Golden Age' and the topical present. He argued that as England had pioneered the first musical renaissance, so 'composers like Mackenzie, Parry and Stanford, give promise that musical England will hold her place among the nations in the century which we are rapidly approaching' (p. 175). A few years later, the English Musical Renaissance was formally recuperated into the mainstream of musical discourse by Fuller Maitland in his *English Music in the Nineteenth Century* (1902b).

Not surprisingly, within the RCM itself the notion 'renaissance' was warmly embraced. Stanford, in his essay 'Some Aspects of Musical Criticism', cautioned music journalists against over-hasty reviews, lest they harm 'the great renaissance of music in England which is every day becoming more marked' (1908: 75). Henceforward, Parry and Stanford spent almost as much time inscribing the Renaissance in prose as they did in writing music for it. Their publications – analysis, criticism and history – reflected a distinctive 'Grove' line, which developed into an ideology. For the time being, at least, the German tradition remained unassailable in terms of the study curriculum and performance repertoire – primarily the 'Three Bs', with Schubert, Mendelssohn and Schumann added according to taste. Yet, alongside this, students, practising musicians, lay-readers and listening audiences were steadily inculcated with the thesis that English Music was the earliest 'achieved' school of Western Christianity, enjoying a 'Golden Age' which ended only with the death of Purcell. A 'Dark Age' of foreign domination followed, initiated by Handel and the hegemony of Italian opera. For a century-and-a-half stagnation and ignorance prevailed, when neglect of, and even contempt for, music was the norm. Only in the provincial choral tradition was the flame kept alight. These basic hermeneutic formulations characterise not only Grove's *Dictionary* but a stream of writings from Parry, Stanford and many others which dominated the teaching curriculum until the First World War.

As professor of music history at the RCM, Parry had the key role in the writing and the teaching of the authorised version. It was one he accomplished brilliantly. In *The Art of Music* (1893), which went to ten editions by 1931, he elaborated the main lines of a historiographical interpretation shaped by the demands of a modern English Musical Renaissance. Dunstable and his contemporaries take the lead in medieval Europe, but this is ended by the Wars of the Roses. Then the greatness of Byrd and Gibbons is dissipated by Stuart corruption. The tragedy of Purcell's early death is followed by Handel and the 'foreign occupation'. According to Parry, around 1700 the crucial difference between England and Germany was J. S. Bach, who ensured the survival of German music until the salvation delivered by Beethoven and Brahms. (In this reading of the German tradition, we can detect a mistrust of Haydn and Mozart, whose work was thought to be tainted with the despised influences of Italy and Roman Catholicism.) For Parry, all great music was the product of evolutionary forces, and modern English Music had to 'evolve' in the German mainstream. Only thus could the English people be put in touch 'with the highest moments ... in music in which noble aspirations and noble sentiments were successfully embodied ... [so that] the humanising influences which democracy may hereafter have at its disposal may be infinitely enlarged' (Parry 1893: 369).

The Renaissance not only wrote its own history but had a consistent line in self-justification. The argument set out in Grove's 'Royal Addresses' was taken up by Stanford, Parry and Fuller Maitland. Much of this was to do with the social 'utility' of music – after all, the Renaissance could prosper only by persuading the captains of industry and trade to part with their money. As Latham remarked: 'Art in England suffers from an unpractical utilitarianism of the many, who see no incongruity in ventilating shafts on top of Marble Arch' (Latham 1890: 170). The movement directed from South Kensington presented itself as a force for drawing the nation together around a common musical culture. As Grove had pointed out, this effect might be extended to the Empire; where language and literature had gone before, then music could surely follow. The Renaissance needed to stress also its moral mission to improve the condition of the toiling classes – not least in assisting the Temperance Movement in providing a wholesome alternative to the tavern and the gin-palace. However, the greatest field for *utility* was that of education, since it was there that the future of society would be decided. Stanford put things succinctly in his 1889 lecture 'Music in Elementary Schools':

> The first effect of education upon the uneducated masses is the development of socialistic and even of revolutionary ideas amongst them ...
> the systematic development of art is a lever in the hands of education
> ... [which] will act more powerfully than any means of socialistic

repression; by raising the standard of refinement it will in time coun-
teract by fair means the dangers born of knowledge. (Stanford 1908:
44–5)

The South Kensington Renaissance did not, of course, encompass
the whole of music in England, and was not able to dictate every
aspect of its development. All the same, the conservative targets –
the provincial festivals, the Philharmonic Society, the Italian opera
season in London (Drury Lane and Covent Garden) – were often
brought under concerted pressure to change their ways. There were
other progressive institutions, too, which were formally independent of Grove's control. The best example was perhaps the innovative Carl Rosa Company, which began life in 1875 and proved an
important contributor to the Renaissance with its pioneering work
in English opera.

The foundation of the RCM encouraged a succession of other
educational, scholarly and professional institutions. Trinity College
of Music was founded to encourage church music in 1872. Intended
for the training of choirmasters, it maintained an Anglican character
while building up a relationship with the University of London. Trinity endowed the university's first chair of music – the King Edward
VII Professorship – with Frederick Bridge as its first incumbent. The
London College of Music, established in 1887 for the musical
tuition of amateurs, can be regarded as yet another (albeit minor)
aspect of the revivalist spirit of this era (Sadie 1981: VII, 211ff.).

Outside the RCM, however, the most significant institutional
development in the capital was the Royal College of Organists (Plate
4). This powerful institution was an early and close ally of the
Renaissance. Founded in 1864, it underwent a phase of expansion
alongside the NTS/RCM in 1876–86 and received a royal charter in
1893. Following 1890 its presidents were, successively, Grove,
Mackenzie and Parry, while its intimate association with the RCM
was expressed in the fact that it moved into the former NTS building in 1904. The Musical Association was initiated in 1874 'for the
investigation and discussion of subjects connected with the Science
and Art of music', with Stainer (soon to be recruited to the NTS) as
a co-founder. Parry became its president in 1901 (Fuller Maitland
1904–10: III, 335).

Meanwhile, the Guildhall School of Music was founded in 1880
by the City of London Corporation. Its original intention also was

4 The Goodly House (Mark I) – for sale in 1992: the National Training School for Music (1876), subsequently the Royal College of Music (1883–94) and thereafter the Royal College of Organists

to provide training for amateurs – though with hefty fees – and it also offered evening classes 'to suit City daytime workers' (Barty-King 1980: 22). Under its first principal Henry Weist Hill it became a major centre for music education, with its business-like and cost-effective approach. By the mid-1880s, it had 2,500 students and was taking £19,000 a year in fees. It was largely self-financing, though receiving modest assistance from the City of London. Its teaching staff were all part-time and included many teachers employed at the RAM. So successful was the Guildhall School that it was able to move into new buildings in 1886, at a cost of £20,000. However, in 1896 the School was firmly brought within the South Kensington ambit by the appointment of W. H. Cummings as principal. Cummings, 'a trusty genial friend' of both Mackenzie and Parry, was on the RAM staff and was the main scholarly progenitor of the Purcell revival. The links between these establishments were strong enough for there to be serious talk in the 1890s of their formal merger into a Faculty of Music for a new 'University of Westminster' (Barty-King 1980: 52–3). Although this never came to fruition, we can see in it the awesome scale of thinking behind the construction of the Goodly House.

Yet outside London a musical world continued to exist, and even evolve, independent of its direct influence. The most important institution to echo Grove's endeavours was the Royal Manchester College of Music, established in 1893. This was the brain-child of Sir Charles Hallé, who, as conductor of the orchestra which bore his name, had been at the centre of concert life in the north since 1858. Like Grove, Hallé canvassed subscriptions mainly from the northern business and civic communities. By 1893, with pledges for £11,000 (albeit only one-tenth of Grove's haul) and a 'Royal' appellation, the College opened with 135 students, Hallé as principal and several members of his orchestra on the staff. By 1904, with a royal patron – Queen Alexandra – it had sufficient funds to make Sir Edward Elgar an (abortive) offer of a professorship at the attractive salary of £400 (Kennedy 1971: 1–29).

Apart from Hallé, the outstanding individual who was able to pre-serve his career and influence more or less independently of South Kensington was Sir Arthur Sullivan. Sullivan's ambiguous relation-ship with the Renaissance is a fascinating indicator of its cultural politics. The paradox is that he remained the most popular musician in England until his death in 1900. As director of the Leeds Festival – not to mention his manifold personal connections – Sullivan had little practical need to shelter under the wing of South Kensington. While he and Grove preserved their friendship, mistrust slipped in with regard to the younger RCM men. Stanford's 1886 review of the premiere at Leeds of *The Golden Legend* encapsulates the dilemma. Having greeted the work as 'a masterly composition … [which] restores him to his legitimate position as one of the leaders of the English school', Stanford went on to criticise Sullivan for spending too long on 'a class of composition which … was below the level of his abilities' (Stanford 1908: 161–2). The Renaissance, it seemed, was prepared to embrace Sullivan – but only on its own terms. Sullivan's standing among Grove's men was further compro-mised in 1887, when *The Mikado* was given in Berlin (in German!), to be followed shortly afterwards by *The Golden Legend*. Both works met with scorn, a failure which was held to disgrace the name of English Music in the most sensitive area of its reception. Failure

rankled, and Sir Arthur's most ambitious attempt to rebuild his reputation, partly on South Kensington's terms, came some years later
with the 'Grand Opera' *Ivanhoe*. The initiative was rejected. In
1898, Sullivan was ousted from his Leeds post by Stanford's supporters on the committee. His death two years later was mourned by
millions as a national tragedy. Yet by the moulders of opinion he had
already come to be seen as a symbol of many profound and disabling
weaknesses in the English way of music.

Sir George Grove's leadership of the Musical Renaissance had
been inspired and determined. Its institutional trajectory and ideological dynamic were largely, if not exclusively, of his ordination.
However, his career came to a somewhat premature end. The RCM
relied heavily on public support, and its good name depended on
unimpeachable ethical standards. Sir George's private life, however,
had never quite conformed to the professed Victorian norm. In the
1840s, he fathered an illegitimate child, born in the Union Work-
house at Stratford-upon-Avon (Young 1980: 35). But, later, a potentially more serious threat to his reputation developed. From 1883,
he maintained an intimate friendship with Edith Oldham – one of
the RCM's first students – which continued until his death in 1900.
Whether or not this had a sexual dimension cannot now be determined, but from the surviving correspondence Grove regarded the
young lady as his emotional anchorage, and he 'confided to her
many of the College's secrets'. In any event, the relationship was not
made public in his lifetime.

It was not Grove's own indiscretions that hastened the end of his
career but the conduct of one of his staff, Henry Holmes. A scandal
threatened to break in the autumn of 1890, as information reached
Grove (in an anonymous letter) of the professorial seduction of a
female student. Possibly influenced by his own vulnerability, Grove
at first chose to ignore the matter. To his own student confidante, he
judged Holmes's behaviour to be merely 'foolish'. In 1893, however, details emerged of how his colleague had 'ruined' no fewer
than four students, and publicity was unavoidable (Young 1980:
211, 238). Holmes was sacked at this point, but Grove's position
had been fatally weakened, and he too had to go. Given the need for
music – above all in the inner sanctum of its new establishment – to
bury its low-life reputation, the scandal cast a shadow over the
whole Grove inheritance. It also gave heightened importance to the
question of a successor. In fact, as early as 1891 Grove had settled

on Hubert Parry, and it was into his hands that the succession was duly delivered.

Grove had launched the RCM as the engine of a Renaissance movement; and a team had been created which could take the institution forward into the new century. Begun without a penny of the anticipated state funding, the 1892 grant of £500 per annum probably acknowledged the RCM's initiative in finding the costs of building new premises and expanding its activities to match. Meanwhile the Renaissance had begun to extend its influence far beyond South Kensington: at court, through Bridge and Parratt; and in Oxford and Cambridge, via the professorships held by Stanford and Parry. Just as importantly, the RAM under Mackenzie offered its powerful networks – including links with Novello and the *Musical Times*. There were other connections, too: Barclay Squire at the British Museum; Stanford and the Bach Choir; Cowen at the Philharmonic Society; and a host of supporters abroad – not least Hans Richter and von Bulow. Perhaps the greatest of all the weapons forged by the Renaissance, however, was the power to inscribe itself, and to refashion English music history in its own image. All in all, it was a marvellous piece of late-Victorian engineering, an astonishing cultural construction – subtle, resourceful and, like the projects of Grove's first career, built to last.

2

A troubled inheritance
(1895–1914)

The apostolic succession

> Parry and Stanford are rapidly getting absolute control of all the music, sacred or secular, in England; and also over our provincial Festivals and Concert societies, and other performing bodies!!!; a nice prospect … they should compose more and talk less. (Sir John Stainer to Frederick G. Edwards, BLMC E3092/92: 211099)

Parry inherited the leadership of the English Musical Renaissance in January 1895. Later that year a scandal broke beside which the peccadilloes of Holmes and Grove paled into insignificance. After a long and sensational trial, Oscar Wilde was found guilty of homosexual offences and imprisoned. Yet these incidents were equally redolent of the atmosphere in which Parry had the responsibility of carrying forward Grove's inheritance, and it placed a heavy emphasis on the character of the new director. The Renaissance clearly had some of the character of a revolution – but, like other revolutions, it had strong conservative components, and, like all, it had to confront a number of fundamental questions. Should consolidation have priority over change? How should it renew its personnel and ideology to meet changing circumstances? The 'Art for art's sake' movement, with its high spiritual purpose, had turned rapidly towards a decadence which, by the time of the Wilde case, was generally perceived as corrupt and dangerous. The waters were turbulent, and the problem Parry inherited was how to trim his sails to the wind of artistic ferment while steering the Renaissance clear of the rocks. As one commentator remarked of the 1890s: 'Side by side with the poseur worked the reformer, urged on by the revolutionist. There were demands for culture and social redemption' (Jackson 1913: 25–6).

In the cultural flux of the *fin-de-siècle*, the academic leadership of
the RCM and the RAM felt distinctly uncomfortable. They had challenged Victorian philistinism by attempting the modernisation of
English Music, and although Brahms was still a contemporary composer in the 1890s, it was Wagner who had long since been recognised as the leader of 'progressivism' in continental music. In this
context, the Renaissance was seen by many as already wedded to an
outmoded musical style; it was a serious deficiency and it threatened
to undo much of Grove's hard work.

Another headache for Parry was the continuing low status of
music within the spectrum of English *culture*. Despite the efforts of
the Renaissance, it had shown itself incapable of mounting a challenge to the hegemony of literature and painting in intellectual life.
Music, and especially English Music, had still not achieved the elevated artistic profile and social respect it sought. This can be illustrated from the earliest retrospective writing about the 1890s. For
example, H. Jackson's *The Eighteen-Nineties* (1913) simply makes
no reference to music; and Blaike Murdoch's *The Renaissance of the
Nineties* (1911) contains only the bizarre observation that: 'the
nineties witnessed the rise of one widely considered the greatest
English composer. This is Mr Cyril Scott ... also MacDowell and the
greater Nevin' (Murdoch 1911: 81). In fact, the latter two were not
English, but citizens of the United States! Evidently, the ghosts of the
past were proving highly resistant to exorcism.

In his first directorial address to the students of the RCM (1895),
Parry paid fulsome tribute to Grove:

> His high ideals never yielded to the shallow solipsisms of a vulgar,
> greedy, vain and money-grubbing world ... [with Grove's example]
> this college will be an honour to our country, a very beacon set on a
> hill ... a centre from which light and enlightenment may radiate
> through all the country. (Parry 1920: 43)

In this invocation, Parry seems to draw on an imagery which sub-
liminally links him to his mentor – *he* was now the Captain (he was
indeed an enthusiastic yachtsman), relying on the guidance of the
Builder of Lighthouses. But there can be no doubt that, by the time
Parry assumed Grove's mantle, its fabric had begun to appear somewhat frayed. And as more power, influence and patronage accrued
to the Renaissance, the more it appeared captive to its own past and
ideological beginnings.

The leaders of the Renaissance were finding it impossible to meet both academic and artistic commitments. Mackenzie was regarded as the senior man when Grove retired, but by the time he became the first of the post-Grove generation to receive a knighthood (1895) his output had all but dried up. For his part, Parry, prone to bouts of illness and depression, and harbouring corrosive doubts about his talent as a composer, was under particular pressure as the 'figurehead' of English Music. His output also began to suffer, subsiding to an average of one major work a year; and when Parry took up the Oxford chair of music in 1899 – the year after his own knighthood – the pressures became well-nigh unbearable and his health worsened considerably (Graves 1926: II, 12).

Though Stanford continued to compose at his customary prolific rate, his music seemed to sum up the Renaissance's problem of stylistic self-consciousness. At the same time, he and Parry were by no means entirely in accord about this and other matters germane to the future. Stanford was much more given to 'programme music' than was Parry and his dedication to the cause of opera led to quarrels about priorities and resources. Also, in sharp contrast to his director, Stanford was deeply conservative – politically, socially and intellectually – a tendency revealed in his dedications. The *Requiem* (1897) was inscribed to Lord Leighton – celebrated artist and pillar of the establishment; and the *Symphony No. 6* (1905) to G. F. Watts, another 'eminent Victorian' painter, who enjoyed the soubriquet 'the English Michaelangelo' (Foreman 1988: Chandos 8627).

For Frederic Cowen – another figure in what was called by some contemporaries the 'Parry Group' – this was a paradoxical time. Cowen, one of the pioneers in the 1880s, thrived as a conductor rather than in the field of academe. He also composed the opera *Harold* (1895), which failed despite the presence of the Prince of Wales at its premiere, and his *Symphony No. 6* ('The Idyllic', 1897). He retained sufficient reputation to attract a commission to provide a coronation march for Edward VII in 1902. Despite his acknowledged eminence, Cowen gradually retreated further from composition into conducting, and zealously took up the cause of Elgar (Cowen 1913).

Whatever the morale of its leading individuals, support in the press for the cause remained secure to the end of the decade. Shaw's constant carpings were in most respects untypical, and in any case he retired from music-reviewing in 1894. Meanwhile, Fuller Maitland led the way in proclaiming the greatness of English Music in the making. In an extraordinary review of Parry's *Magnificat* (Hereford Festival, 1897), he declared:

> The interest of the whole festival culminated in the new *Magnificat*. [And, commenting on a motto similar to one of Mendelssohn's, he went on:] The English master works it into the innermost texture of his fabric, treating it moreover with a grandeur of conception, a certainty and power, which were entirely beyond Mendelssohn's reach. (Fuller Maitland, *The Times* 170997)

A loathing of Mendelssohn and his domination of English Music was characteristic of many younger men of the Renaissance. It was an influence seen as so pernicious – especially in choral music – that it had to be eliminated. It was hoped that the serious instructive works of Parry and others would fill the gap left by Mendelssohn's gradual relegation in the repertoire. The first leg of this particular campaign was alarmingly successful – to the extent, for example, that a massively popular work like *Elijah* was not given its Promenade Concert premiere until 1991!

Fuller Maitland wrote in a similar vein of the next Three Choirs Festival at Gloucester. *Elijah* and *The Creation* were dismissed as 'works of so hackneyed a kind' (*The Times* 140998). He declared bitingly that Sullivan's *Golden Legend* 'still retains its old power to conjure money from the pockets of the great country public' (*The Times* 150998). Once again a Parry work – *Song of Darkness and Light* – was deemed to be the 'culminating point'. *The Times* (160998) told its readers that 'it seems almost to exhaust the powers of music ... a work which we must not hesitate to pronounce sublime, in spite of the reluctance which all Englishmen seem to feel in acknowledging the presence of the highest qualities in a musical composition by a countryman'.

Renaissance journalism was waging war on the enemies of musical progress in England; festival conservatism, the Victorian passion for Sullivan, the philistinism and ignorance of a public more interested in county sociability than in the vitality of the music being performed. Fuller Maitland expressed (as no other) the zeal of the Renaissance crusade – in the name of music itself and for the sake of national prestige.

But the greatest challenge was not the traditional domestic enemy but the new foreign one – which had now arrived at, or already was

within, the gates. Enthusiasm for Wagner had been sweeping
through musical circles since his Albert Hall concerts of 1877. The
message was promulgated by Hans Richter, who included substantial Wagner extracts in his St James's Hall Concerts (1879–97).
Covent Garden performed '*Lohengrin*' (in Italian) in 1875; and the
Carl Rosa Company gave *The Flying Dutchman* and *Rienzi* (in English) later in the decade. The leading opera critic Hermann Klein
described 1882 as 'London's great Wagner year', when Richter
brought over the Hamburg Opera for the first *Ring* cycle in England
(Klein 1903: 124). In addition, Wagner's cause was advocated by a
handful of music critics, including, notably, such a committed
'Renaissance man' as Hueffer of *The Times*.

Sir George Grove found Wagner and his work essentially repug-
nant. Although Grove entertained the composer to lunch at the
Athenaeum during his 1877 visit, he regarded him as a fraud and
viewed his anti-semitism and overt German nationalism with distaste.
As for Parry, an early enthusiasm for Wagner – encouraged by his
mentor Edward Dannreuther – gradually turned to suspicion of
almost everything Bayreuth represented. Parry disliked opera, con-
sidering it (with an indirect reference to Wagner's patrons) 'the
lingering descendant of the paltry amusements of the courtly classes'
(Graves 1926: II, 213). But it was more than that: Wagner had 'unin-
tentionally led public taste away from the purity of abstract Art and
created a craving which could only be satisfied with draughts of ever-
increasing strengths' (Parry 1905: 119–20).

Parry considered that the ineluctable laws of musical evolution
had produced Brahms as their legitimate modern heir: Wagner was
thus an aberrant distraction. Parry was a convinced Brahmin in the
Wagner–Brahms controversy that was splitting German music; yet
he knew that to open up this debate in England was potentially disastrous for the future of the Renaissance, in which unity and team
spirit were perceived as essential.

For Stanford, Wagner presented both a dilemma and a challenge.
Although at one with Parry in veneration of Brahms, his commitment to opera led him to study Wagnerian music–drama, for which
he developed considerable admiration. Yet he remained wary of
Bayreuth as the 'head-centre of modernity' (Stanford 1914: 167).
Like Grove, he was repelled by Wagner's personality, remarking
that, 'the music is that of Jekyll, but the face was the face of Hyde'
(p. 171). The occasion for this was *The Ring*'s premiere in 1876,

when Stanford also found the works too long and the seats too hard. His position did not get much more comfortable, for he felt obliged to sit on the fence: as a conservative he valued Brahmsian traditionalism, and as a nationalist, he saw in opera – and Wagner's example – the potential source for extending music to a larger public. Stanford's contradictions in the eyes of his contemporaries were patent – a Brahmsian who wrote mostly 'programme music'; an Irish Anglican who became a pillar of the English Musical Renaissance, while passionately celebrating Irish national music in so much that he wrote.

By the mid-1890s, Wagner's influence was stalking the Renaissance: even within the corridors of academic power in South Kensington, it was being made secure. Frederick Corder's teaching of composition at the RAM was beginning to bear fruit, and a group of English Wagnerites – spearheaded by Granville Bantock – began to make its presence felt. Yet in both the main conservatoires the wind of change and innovation blew rarely and randomly. Many of the teaching personnel appointed by Grove and Mackenzie stayed in post until the end of (and beyond) the Great War. Parry remained in charge at the RCM until his death in 1918; Stanford retired in 1923, less than a year before his final illness; the indefatigable Frederick Bridge soldiered on until retirement in 1918; and likewise Mackenzie, at the Royal Academy, until 1924. In the unprecedented flux of the post-Wagnerian musical climate – the Pandora's Box of experimentation opened by *Tristan* – this seemed designed to ensure the fossilisation of English Music.

Among the critics, too, voices critical of the 'conservatism' and 'academicism' of the South Kensington Renaissance began to gain a hearing. One of the earliest Wagnerian supporters was G. B. Shaw, whose opinions as music-critic of the *Star* (1888–89) and the *World* (1890–94) stemmed entirely from the belief that Wagner's was, indeed, 'the Music of the Future'. This conviction led him to excoriate all he heard of the modern English variety. The flavour of Shaw's invective may be briefly tasted: 'I have been at the Royal Academy all day … my mind is unhinged by the contemplation of so much emptiness and so much bungling' (Laurence 1989: II, 57–8). Shaw's political and aesthetic prejudices dictated a marked hostility to the Renaissance 'establishment' which, as he saw it, had rejected Wagnerian progressivism in favour of Brahmsian conservatism. Shaw fulminated frequently, and in a personal tone: 'Dr Parry occupies a

position in the history of English art not unlike that occupied by
Charles I in English politics' (p. 168).

As Shaw moved away from music journalism, his sharp pen was
taken up by another Wagnerite who wished to goad the Renaissance
– Arthur Johnstone, at the *Manchester Guardian* (1896–1904).
Johnstone inaugurated a tradition of radical incumbents of the main
music desk in Manchester. An admirer of Nietzsche and Tolstoy, of
Franck and Richard Strauss, Johnstone prized 'articulation' and
'expression' above all else. He had little time for South Kensington's
examples, arguing that its output was superficial and lacking in 'psychological' depth. Of Parry, he wrote in 1902: 'Outside the circle of
his pupils and personal friends no-one now seems to care for his
music ... The impression that there is something wrong with his
music is undoubtedly a general one ... The quality is gritty, the
flavour somewhat acrid and inky, the bouquet artificial' (Reece and
Elton 1905: 184–6). As a product of Radley and Keble College
Oxford, Johnstone came from the same class and background as the
Renaissance academics. However, he was also a Catholic and an
early supporter of Elgar (1905: 78ff.). In any case, his views and the
quality of his writing were not easily ignored.

In the field of performance, it was Henry Wood who epitomised
the younger generation's disaffection with the Renaissance establishment. Wood arrived on the London scene in 1895 as conductor
of the Queen's Hall Promenade Concerts. Within three years, he
had established himself as one of the most dynamic personalities in
English Music. The Queen's Hall was a new – 1893 – commercial
venture, under the management of Robert Newman. It aimed to
become a venue for orchestral concerts for a new public interested
in classical and modern music. The key to the Proms was quality of
performance and value for money: during the first season seats
were priced 1–5 shillings, 'in the reach of everyone', as Wood put
it (1938: 70).

From Proms' programming it was clear that Wood and Newman
considered the music of the composers of the Renaissance neither
'classical' nor 'modern'. Once again it was Bayreuth which provided
the lever against South Kensington. Many Proms were given over to
Wagner 'selections'; and so rapidly did Wood's reputation as a Wagnerian grow that the Queen's Hall's forces gave a Royal Command
Performance at Windsor (1898), largely made up at the Queen's
request of excerpts from Wagner (Wood 1938: 121). Another

important aspect of Wood's career was his championing of Tchaikovsky and, more generally, of composers of the Russian Nationalist School – Glazunov and Rimsky-Korsakov having important premieres. Contemporary French music, too, fared well at the Queen's Hall, with Franck and Saint-Saëns featuring, and Debussy following early in the new century.

The academic composers were signally dismayed by all this. Although English music was played, almost all of it was that of the younger generation – Bantock, Coleridge-Taylor, Holbrooke, Cyril Scott, Percy Pitt and others. It was particularly galling since the Queen's Hall Orchestra was one of only three in the country – the others being at the Crystal Palace and Manchester – and it is hardly surprising that Wood was generally disliked in the common-rooms of South Kensington. Parry loathed Wood's Slav orientation – branding it as 'primitive emotional expression' which appealed to the masses through 'orgiastic frenzy' and 'unrestrained abandonment to physical excitement which is natural to underdeveloped races'. For him, the 'Russian musical invasion' began with Tchaikovsky and the *Symphonie Pathétique*, and Wood took the ensuing craze for Russian Music to new heights – or depths (Parry 1905: 118–19). As always, *The Times* was obedient to its masters' interests: 'This persistent boycotting of everything British at the Queen's Hall would be almost laughable did it not imply a severe indictment of our musical capacity … It is high time a most emphatic protest be entered' (Fuller Maitland, *The Times* 271002).

Wagner's British baby

> I raise my glass to the welfare and success of the first English progressivist, Meister Edward Elgar, and of the young progressivist school of English composers. (Richard Strauss in 1902, quoted by Jaeger, *MT* 1902: 402–3)

Elgar's 'arrival' on the musical scene represented at once the greatest opportunity and the most serious challenge that the Musical Renaissance had faced. The *Enigma Variations* and *The Dream of Gerontius* came at the turn of the new century, at a moment when its dynamic was at a low ebb. They revealed that Elgar was the most exciting talent in English music; yet his rise to become the outstanding English composer was accomplished without his ever being part of the London-led revival. Elgar's whole experience – and his musical vocation – made him an 'outsider', a provincial stranger to the precincts of South Kensington.

Elgar's background militated against a smooth relationship with Grove's academics. His sense of alienation stemmed in part from his Roman Catholicism and his awareness of the long-standing suspicions which English society harboured towards this confession, and in part from his provincial isolation. A lower-middle-class background compounded these disadvantages – his father was a shop-keeper and piano-tuner. Although the family was never poor, Elgar left school at 15 with no prospect of continuing his musical education. He was essentially self-taught and his only training came from playing, composing and studying the scores in the family shop. Until he was well into his 30s, he eked out a living in the Worcester area as a freelance teacher and part-time orchestral player.

Prior to his marriage in 1889, Elgar composed nothing of importance. That event changed his life, because his upper-class wife Caroline Alice Roberts resolutely set herself to overcome his social handicaps. With her husband's full co-operation, she designed a new man, one whose accent, appearance and interests were more in keeping with a gentlemanly image (Hughes 1989). All this was encompassed in order to improve his artistic opportunities, for just as the Renaissance was conscious of the need to improve the social standing of its rank-and-file, so Edward and Alice realised well enough that under Sir Charles Hubert Hastings Parry it placed gentility at a premium. In a sense, Elgar was a one-man Renaissance, whose career represents in random microcosm all the careful effort and planning of the larger phenomenon. His greatest patron, who played the primary roles in every area of support and management, was Caroline Alice (Hughes BBC R3: 260790). Elgar drew inexorably away from his background, and began to feel that his father's trade cast a shadow over his life. In a letter to the editor of the *Musical Times*, he wrote bitterly: 'as to the whole "shop" episode – I don't care a d–mn! I know it has ruined me and made life impossible until I what you call made a name – I only know I was kept out of everything decent "'cos his father kept a shop"' (BLMC E3090/39: 190900).

It took Elgar ten years to establish a national reputation, by composing for the provincial choral–festival circuit. These were difficult years, and his eventual success owed nothing to the patronage of the Renaissance. Elgar had to rely on his own skill and persistence – and on his wife's unflinching support. What patrons he had in these years were his own friends in the festival milieu; the men who counted were the like of Hugh Blair, Ivor Atkins and George Sinclair – now remembered only for their connection with Elgar. Perhaps the most important among them was Charles Swinnerton Heap – dedicatee of the *Organ Sonata* and of the oratorio *The Light of Life* – who commissioned Elgar to write *King Olaf*. Of this breakthrough in his career, Elgar wrote that, but for Heap, he would 'have remained in outer darkness' (Moore 1984: 218). At any rate, by 1900 he had made a solid reputation throughout the extra-metropolitan musical world, without South Kensington having evinced anything more than the slightest of interest. Indeed, the point may be made more strongly in another way: in 1896, if they had heard of Elgar at all, Parry and Stanford perceived him to be a representative of a tradition which they distrusted and wished to reform.

The first Renaissance 'scout' to spot the glowing new star was Sir Walter Parratt, Master of the Queen's Musick and one of Grove's professors – but Stanford was not far behind. Within months of meeting these two (in 1896) the composer was seeking Parratt's help in securing the Queen's permission for a dedication. Two years later this arrived – for *Caractacus*. Meanwhile, Parratt promoted Elgar's music with the Royal Family and encouraged him to write music for royal occasions. His colleague, Stanford, was deeply impressed by *The Light of Life* and drew it to the attention of both Parry and Mackenzie. Significantly, however, this friendship was immediately under strain because of Stanford's criticism of the patriotic block-buster *The Banner of St George*, written for the Royal Jubilee of 1897. Already, perhaps, Elgar felt that his need for London recognition was not so desperate that he was obliged to dance to the professorial fiddle.

Shortly afterwards, Elgar's royal connections were strengthened by a wealthy new supporter: Frank Schuster. A member of an Anglo-German banking family, who met Elgar in 1899, Schuster's value was in his access to prominent politicians and members of the aristocracy, as well as the Royal Family. He had excellent connections also in the highest circles of the Jewish financial community. There were patrons in the press, and here, too, Elgar made his own luck. As early as 1889, he courted the *Daily Telegraph*'s powerful critic Joseph Bennett, and his efforts duly secured an excellent review for

the premiere of *Froissart* (Moore 1984: 154). Bennett was an important ally who gave Elgar space in his notices throughout the decade.
With Arthur Johnstone of the *Manchester Guardian* also backing
him, Elgar had his own publicity team, existing independently of the
Renaissance centre (Hughes BBC R3: 030792).

The Leeds Festival premiere of *Caractacus* (1898) was the crucial
turning-point. It is interesting to reflect on the non-London, non-
academic origins of the work. The idea originated with Henry
Embleton, a wealthy Leeds businessman and secretary of its Choral
Union, who secured the commission. *Caractacus* owed something
also to Sir Arthur Sullivan – chief conductor at Leeds since 1880 –
who supported Embleton's initiative. Elgar thanked Sullivan for his
chance, and pointedly remarked that 'it contrasts very much with
what some people do to a person unconnected with the schools –
friendless and alone' (Jacobs 1984: 385).

Though it accurately conveyed the composer's feelings, in 1898
'friendless and alone' was perhaps a little strong. In fact, the list of
Elgar's admirers was quickly expanding. Among them was August
Jaeger – the German-born music-reader at Novello. Elgar's attitude
to the musical establishment can be gauged from his letters to
Jaeger. In February 1898, referring to the early sketches of *The
Dream of Gerontius*, his resentment blazed out: '"Hora Novissima"
contains more "music" than any of your other englishmen [sic] have
yet managed to knock out including Parry Stanford Mackenzie –
these great men seem to be busily employed in performing one
another's works: nobody else will?' He added in a later letter: 'Anything "genuine" and natural pleases me – the stuff I hate and which
I know is ruining any chance for good music in England is stuff like
Stanford's which is neither fish, flesh, fowl nor good red herring!'
(Young 1965: 9, 31).

In response, Jaeger offered an observation on Parry's *Te Deum* on
which he was working for Novello: 'Parry!, Oh, Parry!! very much
Parry!!! Toujours Parry!!!! Fiddles sawing all the time!!!!! Dear old
Parry!!!!!!' (HWRO 705 445/8472: 120700). It may not be unim-
portant to the case that Jaeger was married to Isabel Donkersley, one
of the students who had been compromised by Parry's colleague
Professor Holmes, the amorous violinist, in the 1890s (Young 1980:
255). In any case, Jaeger shared Elgar's dislike of the South Kensington academics, and of their supporters in the press, because of a
common Wagnerian commitment.

Elgar had for long been an enthusiastic Wagnerian and an admirer of the 'expressive' and the 'progressive' in European Music. In the 1890s, the Elgars made several trips (which they could ill-afford) to Bayreuth to drink deep at the well-head of Wagnerism. On his thirty-sixth birthday, Elgar bought an expensive piano–vocal score of *Tristan*, inscribing the flyleaf with a comment which – eloquently, yet portentously – attests to his love of Wagner: 'This Book contains the Height, – the Depth, – the Breadth, – the Sweetness, – the Sorrow, – the Best and the whole of the Best of this world and the Next' (EBCB). In 1893 such sentiments were in advance of opinion on this subject, even in general terms, leave alone that of the London professors. Elgar admired other aspects of continental 'progressivism'. He was steeped in the teachings of Berlioz on orchestration, and adhered to the fundamental principle that the orchestra was an 'instrument' in its own right. His contemporary musical hero was Richard Strauss, whom the academics regarded as an 'unhealthy' influence. Although he shared the common admiration for the Schumann–Brahms tradition, Elgar was convinced that this should be integrated with a more 'expressive' compositional style.

For all this, when the Renaissance made a serious approach to Elgar, he did not reject its embrace. The extraordinary reception accorded the *Enigma Variations* (1899) placed him in a category, at least in terms of performance, unique in the modern history of English Music. For once, public, press and professors were in harmony, and the Renaissance set out anew to recruit Elgar to its ranks. For five years it patronised and lionised him in an attempt to make him one of its own, reaching first for academic accolades. Stanford took the lead with the offer of an honorary degree of D. Mus. from Cambridge. At first Elgar was inclined to refuse on the grounds that it would forfeit 'some of his natural freedom' (Maine 1933: I, 118). Despite his distrust of the academic world, Elgar was also genuinely delighted, and that part of his personality which craved social status and public honours responded. As he told his sister: 'You must not think that this is a 2d. thing … but it is a great thing: it has of late only been given to Joachim, Tchaikowsky, Max Bruch and a few others' (HWRO 705 445/4597: 171000). In the event, Parry and Cowen (among others) went so far as to club together to purchase the academic robes for Elgar's installation. No fewer than three further university honours were awarded in 1904: from Durham – where Stanford had influence – a doctorate; an LL.D from Leeds,

again at Stanford's prompting; and an honorary fellowship from the
RAM. In 1905, during Parry's tenure as professor, an honorary doctorate was awarded by Oxford University.

Alongside these academic plaudits, social honours tumbled into
Elgar's lap, in particular an entrée into London's clubland. This was
a milieu which was to become an important part of his life, giving
vital sustenance to his 'gentlemanly' pretensions. Stanford once
again took the lead: 'May I put you down for the "Athenaeum"? I
know you are not much in town, but it is a place which is very welcome to persons of your tastes ... It is important to have music of
the best represented there as painting is and the supply is small'
(HWRO 705 445/7414: 200403).

Despite the insensitivity of the approach, Elgar simply couldn't
resist joining the Athenaeum in the spring of 1904 – under Rule 2,
which provided for a special invitation for 'persons of distinguished
eminence in science, literature or the arts' (Moore 1984: 438). He
had Parry as his proposer and Stanford as seconder.

However, Elgar found the patronage of South Kensington a trial.
Apart from a growing distaste for Stanford, and his deep misgivings
about their music, he was irritated by the demands which the academics sought to make on his time. Requests to stand examination
duty at the RCM and at Cambridge he consistently turned down.
The responsibilities of being a member of the establishment
extended also to his being pressed to support various musical causes:
in 1902, Stanford urged him to support a better deal from the music
publishers for English composers, declaring: 'if you and the other
prominent men won't move ... the younger generation must fight
the business and they won't be grateful if they are left to do it alone'
(HWRO 705 445/7416: 081102). Elgar simply ignored this request.
In his dim appreciation of the duties which recognition enjoined,
Elgar betrayed his lack of any sense of belonging to a team, a sensibility so vital to the 'official' Renaissance.

Moreover, although recognition by the establishment brought
some further success, the main element in Elgar's efflorescent career
was due not to this, but to his own circle of patrons and critics, and
his connections with the court. Elgar's music now became genuinely
popular. He was the first English composer to become a 'household
name', and was truly elevated to the position of 'the Rudyard
Kipling of the musicians', as the *Court Journal* had prophesied
(Moore 1984: 244). This role of 'musical Kipling' was closely linked

with Elgar's royal connections, a relationship sealed by the *Coronation Ode* for King Edward VII in 1902. This was followed by the unprecedented three-day Elgar Festival at the Royal Opera House, in March 1904. Not only were Richter and the Hallé Orchestra booked for the event, but so (as it turned out) were the King and Queen. As the *Sunday Times* reported: 'in its locale and patronage [the Festival] is an indication that our upper-classes are no longer disdainful of any movement in native music' (Moore 1984: 434). In turn, this led to Elgar's knighthood, announced only a few weeks later. As a result, Elgar began to enjoy the personal attention of the King, joining the sizeable group of leading professional and artistic figures who had periodic invitations to royal levées, garden parties and other similar events. The moving spirit behind all this was Schuster, who was, second only to Caroline Alice, the composer's most important patron, and no associate of South Kensington – who, for his efforts, was given the dedication of *In the South* which received its first performance at the Festival.

It seems certain that his triumph in Germany gave a finish to Elgar's reputation which totally eclipsed that achieved by Stanford a decade or so earlier. As early as 1898, he had personally secured the patronage of Hans Richter. But it was Jaeger who did much of the work on the 'German connection', by inviting two influential Germans to the premiere of *Gerontius*: Julius Buths and Otto Lessman. Buths was musical director at Düsseldorf and conductor of the Lower Rhine Festival, while Lessman was the editor of the influential *Allgemeine Musik-Zeitung*. The result was a celebrated review:

> The coming man has already arisen in the English musical world, an artist who has instinctively freed himself from the scholasticism which, until now, has bound English art firmly in its fetters, an artist who has thrown open mind and heart to the great achievements which the mighty tone masters of the century now departed have left us as a heritage for one to come – Edward Elgar, the composer of *The Dream of Gerontius*. (Lessman *MT* 1901: 2)

The words were a self-fulfilling prophecy which, at a stroke, put Elgar clear of the scholasticism of South Kensington. Buths shared Lessman's enthusiasm, and his advocacy of Elgar's music launched what can only be described as an 'Elgar boom' in Germany. Both the *Enigma Variations* and *Gerontius* were soon premiered in Dusseldorf, the latter in a German translation by Buths himself. The reputations of the

Renaissance academics implicitly suffered by comparison, though paradoxically they benefited from the Elgar boom, which improved the image of English music on the Continent. Where Buths had led, others now followed. Fritz Steinbach, conductor of the Meiningen Orchestra, in 1902 welcomed Elgar as 'an unexpected genius and a pathbreaker ... a real pioneer in the field of orchestration' (Speyer 1937: 174). Steinbach later gave *The Apostles* a sensational German premiere. But it was at the reception following the Dusseldorf *Gerontius* that Richard Strauss made his famous remarks, referring to Elgar as 'Meister' and the epitome of English progressivism.

Sir Edward enters the lists

The breach between Elgar and the Renaissance, when it came, was bitter and complete. Its precipitant agency was Elgar's personal relationship with Stanford. The two men had never developed a solid relationship and, by 1903–4, serious disagreements became obtrusive. The crisis developed from the confusion surrounding Elgar's commission – a projected symphony – for the 1904 Leeds Festival which Stanford had been instrumental in securing. In the autumn of 1903, Elgar wrote to the Festival committee withdrawing the 'Leeds Symphony' on a pretext – the *real* reason for his late decision was the promised dedication of the work to Richter, who had stated an interest in giving the first performance. Despite Elgar's awkward prioritising of his German connections over the domestic, Stanford smoothed the ruffled feathers of the Leeds committee, to the extent that another (extant) Elgar work was programmed instead (Moore 1984: 420, 445).

At the same time, Elgar had begun to consider more seriously the advantages attached to a permanent academic position. A number of offers accordingly came his way. The first approaches came from Manchester: both the University and the Royal Manchester College of Music (RMCM) offered him chairs, each of which he eventually declined. In October 1904, the new University of Leeds offered him its professorship; once again, Stanford's hand was at work in this proposal. But this, too, was rejected – a further rebuff to Stanford, the effect of which was exacerbated when, only a few weeks later, Elgar accepted the Richard Peyton Chair of Music at the University of Birmingham. Stanford was deeply hurt by Elgar's decision. His wounded feelings produced 'an odious letter' – as Lady Elgar described it – which marked the complete breakdown of Stanford's relationship with Elgar (Kennedy 1968/82: 152–4).

The Peyton professorship was tailor-made for Elgar. Richard Peyton was a wealthy businessman whose connection with the Birmingham Festival stretched back to 1846 and Mendelssohn's *Elijah*. Peyton was persuaded by Elgar's supporters in Birmingham that he would be amenable to an approach from the city's university. Writing to one of the sponsors of the idea, Peyton remarked: 'I understood you to say that the appointment in question was of Dr Elgar's own seeking … [T]hat he should desire the appointment is, of course, favourable' (HWRO 705 445/3356: 071104).

Why did Elgar seek the Birmingham professorship? To begin with, the terms were good and the prestige considerable: an endowment of £10,000; a salary of £400; and minimal teaching duties – six public lectures a year. There was no requirement that Elgar should even live in Birmingham. The reaction in local musical circles was ecstatic. One member wrote to Lady Elgar: 'I hasten to express our happiness in the prospect of our city and the Midlands of England, being in touch with one, whose influence on music will be so ennobling and so uplifting' (HWRO 705 445/3370: 281104). Elgar was under pressure from supporters to use his new-won prestige for the benefit of music in the Birmingham area. For his part, Elgar felt a loyalty to the region where his music had found early encouragement and in which his own Worcester was located. Above all – and contrary to many accounts – Elgar's vanity, as well as his innate competitiveness, drew him to the kudos of academe. His quarrel with Stanford served merely to reinforce his need to take on the professors and to beat them at their own game.

Elgar's acceptance of the Birmingham chair therefore had consequences more far-reaching than those which concerned his relationship with Stanford and his own personal circumstances. Stanford was merely the representative of an interest which Elgar increasingly wished to challenge, and the salary, though important, was far from being decisive. The whole affair has profound significance in terms of the politics of English Music. It marks Elgar's conscious decision to confront Grove's Renaissance directly – the first time a powerful dissenting voice had been publicly heard, and from the most potentially damaging source. The Peyton Lectures – delivered in 1905–6 – constitute a critique of almost everything that had been achieved in English Music in the previous thirty years. Furthermore, they set out a vision which amounted to an Elgarian 'manifesto'. In them, Elgar revealed his ambition to bring together his own artistic followers in Birmingham, in effect, founding a 'Midlands School'. As one such disciple, Havergal Brian, expressed it many years later, Birmingham was to become 'an English Leipzig', with Elgar as its presiding genius (Young 1968: 284).

The very first lecture posited the basic aesthetic issues which the composer had been formulating for so long. He proudly accepted Strauss's encomium as the 'English progressivist', carefully placed in the context of the Wagnerian title of his address – 'A Future for English Music'. On this premiss he exposed, on the one hand, the shortcomings of the Grove–Parry Renaissance; and, on the other, his own hopes for 'the Midlands School'. Elgar first turned his attention to the alleged achievements of the musical revival. He asserted that the works of the South Kensington Renaissance were backward-looking, 'dead and forgotten and ... [they] only exist as warnings to the student of the twentieth century'. He accused the London academics of a betrayal of the nation's hopes in music: 'It is saddening to those who hoped so much from the early days ... to find that we had inherited an art which has no hold on the affections of our own people, and is held in no respect abroad' (Young 1968: 35). Parry was singled out as the one composer who stood above the general mediocrity, acknowledged as 'the head of our art in this country' who would continue to exert a 'broad influence' on English Music (p. 49). Given the general thrust of the lecture, however, it would have been difficult to take these remarks at face value.

Elgar proceeded to isolate the fundamental aesthetic problem. This he saw to be 'the commonplace', so characteristic of English Music, which had no power to 'impress musicians or to captivate amateurs'. Elgar poured his own bitterness and social insecurity into his diatribe: 'The commonplace mind can never be anything but commonplace, and no amount of education, no polish of a University, can eradicate the stain from the low type of mind which is the English commonplace ... English Music is white, and *evades everything*' (p. 47). Elgar, so often hurt by the jibe that his origins were tainted with 'trade' and that his music was 'vulgar' and compromised by its populism, then asserted: 'Vulgarity may in the course of time be refined. Vulgarity often goes with inventiveness, and it can take the initiative' (p. 49).

Though never mentioned by name, it was Stanford at whom Sir Edward pointed his lance. English Music aped the foreigner, and especially in the fashionable cult of the 'Rhapsody': 'Could anything be more inconceivably inept? ... To rhapsodise is the one thing English men cannot do ... it points a moral showing how the Englishman always prefers to imitate'. It was surely no coincidence that Stanford had recently scored a great success with his *Irish Rhapsody No.1*. Elgar also dismissed the Purcell revival, in which Stanford was a leading figure: 'It is easy to go back to the days of Purcell and revel in the glories of those days and earlier ... but such thoughts have no practical value on the music of the present day' (pp. 51ff.).

Implicitly, at least, Elgar posed the claims of progressivism against those of the dead Renaissance, wrapping himself in the mantle of champion of the future, 'in the name of all that is healthy and sincere in the younger school of English musicians'. In Birmingham there would gather the 'best minds connected with our art ... I hold it to be a happy Providence which places this new movement in English music in that district of England which was parent of all that is bright, beautiful and good in the works of ... Shakespeare' (p. 29). Elgar's vision for the 'new movement', indeed, drew heavily on a connection with Shakespearean Englishness. Creative 'Englishness' – the salvation of the musical nation – was deeply provincial, non-urban and (like Shakespeare himself) non-academic in character and orientation. His affinity with and recognition of Shakespeare, the untutored 'wood-warbling' genius of Ben Jonson's epitaph, are surely significant.

Elgar set out several practical objectives for making Birmingham into the intended 'Leipzig'. The university should develop the facilities for establishing a music curriculum. The city itself should nurture a permanent orchestra, and even, one day, an opera-house. The lecture ended on a note of urgent optimism, affirming that Elgarian 'Englishness' which would represent all that the Renaissance had failed to encourage. The native would replace the foreign; the noble and the healthy, the imitative and the feeble; and where before the stifling interiors of academe had held sway, the English outdoors would inspire.

> There are many possible futures. But the one that I want to see coming into being is something that shall grow out of our own soil, something broad, noble, chivalrous, healthy and above all, an out-of-door sort of spirit. To arrive at this it will be necessary to throw over all imitation. It will be necessary to begin and look at things in a different spirit. (Young 1968: 57)

The first reaction came from the monthly *Musical Opinion*, which (perhaps surprisingly) concurred with Elgar on most of the issues. Its editorial agreed that the London Renaissance was old fashioned, and had inflated claims of its own importance, while its reading of English music history was deeply suspect. However, the piece was by no means exactly what Elgar wanted to read – for it was academia itself that was identified as the enemy. This conclusion turned the point of the lance back upon its wielder: 'I verily believe that the Royal College and the Royal Academy of Music have been the death of the creative life of Parry, Stanford and Mackenzie ... it is in the nature of irony that Sir Edward Elgar himself is doing his best to dig his own grave at Birmingham' (p. 65).

In more specific and therefore diluted ways the remaining lectures all reflected Elgar's unifying theme of 'A Future for English Music'. The second ('English Composers') though less rebarbative in tone – it even made a positive reference to the contribution of the Renaissance academies – repeated Elgar's basic criticisms of their achievements and the 'well-established coteries'. He identified the publication and copyright problems besetting English composers, and generally deplored the lack of state and municipal investment in music. The future, Elgar suggested, lay in democratising music by attracting 'a sixpenny audience' and a 'larger public' drawn from the 'working classes'. South Kensington had been too elitist, too concerned to write music for itself, too little regarding of the broader public. Elgar then identified the younger men to whom he had alluded in his first lecture – Walford Davies, Granville Bantock and Josef Holbrooke – as examples of those who would bring a new expressiveness to English Music: 'cannot we have simplicity, manhood, clearness and melody in our new school, I believe and hope so' (pp. 78–93).

These taunts at last brought Stanford out of his tent. In a letter to *The Times* (031105) he took particular exception to the comment that the 'serious compositions thus far produced had no hold on the affections of the people and were held in no respect abroad'. The counter-blast concentrated on Elgar's undeserved aspersion' and 'unjust disparagement'; his comments called in question 'the reputation for accuracy' enjoyed by English universities. Stanford went on to suggest that he should realise his error, 'even within the radius of his own experience'. Public battle was now irretrievably joined. Fifty years of careful work to immunise the English musical world against the divisive cultural politics of Germany and other countries were now at a discount. *Musical Opinion* again tended to the Midlands part, and dismissed Stanford's comments as 'exaggerated championship [that] always does harm ... The protests made against Sir Edward Elgar's lectures are proofs that the admirers of British music have already gone too far in their enthusiasm' (Young 1968: 95).

For his third lecture, on Brahms's *Symphony No. 3*, Elgar seemed to have chosen less controversial ground. The work was a favourite of his, and it was planned to concentrate on delivering an analysis from the keyboard. All went well until, with one injudicious remark, Elgar placed his whole credibility – both as professor and musician – at stake. The moment occurred when he mused on the relative merits of 'absolute', as opposed to 'programme', music: 'The height of music is when a piece calls up a certain set of emotions in each individual hearer ... and when it is simply a description of something else, it is carrying a large art somewhat further than I care for ... Music is a simple art being at its best when it is simple and without description' (p. 105).

In an innocuous attempt to praise Brahms, Elgar had casually pronounced on one of the most complex controversies in music, and in such a way as to call in question a large portion of the entire repertoire, to say nothing of his own output: the *Enigma Variations*, *Cockaigne* and *The Dream of Gerontius* all stood condemned. The critics – including allies like Ernest Newman – were quick to seize on such comments as at best muddleheaded, at worst embarrassingly stupid. There is no doubt that all this damaged Elgar and his professorship, to such an extent that the 'Elgar Challenge' to the Renaissance never recovered from the debacle.

The remaining lectures did little to pour oil on the waters that Elgar had disturbed. One of them ('English Executants') suggested that Britain had produced few great performing musicians, claiming for example, that conductors were as rare as snakes in Ireland (p. 129). His last lecture ('Retrospect') defiantly reiterated both the critique of 30 years of Renaissance and his own 'manifesto' for the Midland School. The press reaction was distinctly chilly, and even the initial support of *Musical Opinion* had faded. Its editor summed up the situation with accuracy and aplomb: 'Sir Edward Elgar has managed to set the musical world by the ears. It must be admitted that his speeches at Birmingham have not been characterised by the kind of discretion one expects from a professor of music' (pp. 147–8).

With his Peyton Lectures, Elgar had made an unmistakable bid for leadership in English Music – not just as its main creative figure, but also as its aesthetic model and intellectual guide. He wanted nothing less than his own 'renaissance' in the Midlands – an ambition suggestive of a Wagnerian cast of mind. The attempt, however, was a disastrous and ultimately humiliating failure, and placed its author under appalling strain. Lady Elgar's diaries record the build-up of tension which ate into her husband's psyche. Eventually, Elgar was obliged to leave the lists. Pleading health reasons, he delegated his remaining lectures and took only a fitful interest in university duties thereafter. His sense of failure was so acute that he chose to break the news of his resignation to his benefactor through Mrs Peyton rather than directly address his patron (HWRO 705 445/3282: 280808). Elgar's dreams had turned to nightmare and he withdrew from academe, this time for good.

Henceforward, Elgar would fight his battles only through his music. The years following the Peyton fiasco are seen by many as his greatest creative period. The two symphonies and the *Violin Concerto*, all strictly non-programmatic in design, were evidently conceived in some part as an answer to his critics. When asked by Walford Davies, one of his 'younger men', whether *Symphony No. 1* (1908) had a programme, he pointedly replied: 'There is no programme beyond a wide experience of human life with a great love and a massive hope in the future' (Young 1956: 187). Richter introduced the work to the Hallé Orchestra with the celebrated words: '[L]et us now rehearse the greatest symphony of modern times, written by the greatest modern composer – and not only in this country!' (Kennedy 1968/82: 227). Significantly enough, the symphony was premiered outside London, and *The Times* chose to ignore the Manchester event entirely. When it was given in London a few days later, Fuller Maitland's notice (*The Times* 211208) occupied only one-third of a column, and referred to 'rather wearisome working out' in the first movement and 'monotony in the finale', ending with the paradoxical comment that the work was 'definitely launched on a prosperous career'. Behind these words lay a reference to the barrage of advance publicity that Elgar's backers had laid down in front of the symphony's progress. After all, the work had not only been published – unlike the vast majority of earlier British symphonies – but had actually appeared in miniature score before it had received its first performance! (Moore 1987: II, 713). After a decent lapse, the point was drawn out explicitly, and not without malice, by Fuller Maitland's assistant H. C. Colles (1945: 76):

> We might find that to some extent the demand had been created by the supply, for to announce frequent performances is a sure way of arousing public interest ... Having got the idea that Sir Edward Elgar is a great composer, the British public thinks it 'greatly to his credit that he remains an Englishman' and is quite convinced that his music is all the better for its native origin ... It may be conceded that the symphony has had every advantage in its favour which a well-organised production and a well-prepared public could give it.

Elgar had entered the lists of a kind of tournament which, like the real thing, was a hazardous game (Plate 5). He challenged the Renaissance in a move which came as his first major enterprise following his actual knighthood in 1904 – when he sent Jaeger a little sketch of how he felt to be 'Sir Edward' (Moore 1987: II, 572). His adversary proved more resilient than he imagined, despite undoubted weaknesses, and was able to resist and strike back. The result of the tournament was a stand-off or stalemate – but in essence, South Kensington held on to its prize. Neither the extended

5 Sir Edward enters the lists: Edgar's sketch of 'a knight', from a letter to A. J. Jaeger, 26 July 1904

* *spur.*

a knight.

metaphor we use here, nor our reference to personality clashes which characterised the affair, are meant to trivialise these contests, since grave issues of artistic belief and commitment lay behind them. Elgar saw the progressive Wagner–Strauss school as the signpost to the future, and passionately believed that he could give a lead towards a native version. Connected to this was his feeling that the English Renaissance was creatively moribund and dominated by the London conservatoires and their satellite institutions, to an extent that excluded and asphyxiated other potentialities.

Elgar never was reconciled with his metropolitan rivals. As his national fame grew, the accusation of 'vulgarity' again began to appear in the London press. For example, under the byline 'Velgarity', *Vanity Fair* – the most fashionable society magazine – published an attack by Francis Toye, a graduate of Stanford's Cambridge. The writer taunted the composer with his 'rags to riches' success: 'he is likely to be overwhelmed by the torrents of snobbery, advertisement and flattery . . . "master and hero" though he may be, the time is not yet come for his deification' (Moore 1984: 594). As late as 1931, long after Elgar had ceased to compose music of any importance, E. J. Dent, who held Stanford's chair at Cambridge, reiterated the charges of populism and tastelessness against him: 'He was a violin-player by profession ... [and] moreover, a Catholic and a self-taught man ... For English ears Elgar's music is too emotional and not quite free from vulgarity' (Maine 1933: I, 256).

Historical–pastoral

> One reason why we have in England no national school of music is because we have so unaccountably neglected our folk-music ... Little or no effort to repair this deficiency is made ... at the music colleges.
> (Cecil Sharp 1906 in Karpeles 1967: 61)

When Sir Edward Elgar declared that there were 'many possible futures for English Music', he did not include in his mental panorama the version of the future which was already at his shoulder. On the other side, the 'official' Renaissance had been seriously damaged by Elgar's onslaught. The battle had further drained its reserves of energy, and focused the attention of Parry, Stanford and Mackenzie even more intensely on the need to produce a successor school which, while being (as it were) recognisably of its own body, was at the same time modern and reformist. In fact, salvation was near at hand: two composers were coming to think of themselves as 'heirs and rebels' – a dynamic tension of ideas which we later examine more critically. Vaughan Williams and Holst were products of the RCM, and profoundly marked by its traditions and preconceptions. However, the former was to be so much the more important in the process of succession that the latter almost fades into insignificance. It was Vaughan Williams, above all, who offered the ideal yet paradoxical solution to the central dilemma: that the future for English Music was to be found in its past, in the 'historical–pastoral' – as Shakespeare put it in *Hamlet* – the folksong, the Tudor inheritance, the eternal verities of history and landscape.

Vaughan Williams was a musician cast in a mould similar to Parry's. Born into a wealthy upper-middle-class family with gentry connections, he was educated at Charterhouse and entered the RCM in 1890 to study composition, with Sir Hubert himself. During this period, as well as being inculcated with the RCM's German bias, he was much influenced by its involvement in the Purcell revival. It was a formative time, when the Grove–Parry values decisively entered his soul. After two years in South Kensington, he broke off his studies to read for one of Stanford's reformed B.Mus. degrees (with some history) at Trinity College, Cambridge – that other epicentre of the Grove Renaissance. After taking his degree, he was back at the RCM to study with Stanford, and during this period (1895–97) he met Gustav Holst.

By the time that he embarked on his career, at the age of 25, Vaughan Williams was a true 'insider', steeped in the tastes and ethics of South Kensington. Like most of Grove's products – and contrary to the image often conveyed by his biographers – Vaughan Williams was an academic who thrived in musical scholarship and was keenly aware of its value. He felt at ease with intellectuals, and was soon admired by scholars such as Fuller Maitland and Barclay Squire. Indeed, he first made his mark through scholarship rather than as a composer; as editor of *The English Hymnal* (1906) and two volumes of Purcell's *Welcome Odes* (1905, 1910). He completed his Cambridge D.Mus. in 1899, after which he was ever proud of his academic title and refused to relinquish it for any other. Years later, when being offered various honours, his revealing response was that he preferred to remain 'plain Mr – Dr if you prefer it' (Vaughan Williams 1964: 207).

By the late 1890s, Vaughan Williams was engaged by two relatively new areas of musical interest, neither of which occupied a prominent place in the RCM curriculum – the revival of Tudor music and the 'rediscovery' of English folksong. These can be said to combine into an 'historical–pastoral' obsession, which was to characterise English Music for the best part of half a century. Despite his destiny as its creative figurehead, Vaughan Williams was not alone in his commitment. Around the turn of the new century, many musicians began to regard the twin legacies of Tudor polyphony and folksong as vital, and potentially renewing, areas of the English musical past.

The revival of Tudor music had started with George Grove and the first edition of his *Dictionary* (1879–89). This seminal text launched a profound reassessment of early and Tudor music which cannot be overestimated. For the first time it presented, in concentrated and accessible form, previously rarefied and fragmented scholarship on this period of English music history. There were several key contributions, including Barclay Squire on 'Collections of Virginal Music' and the venerable Rockstro on the madrigal, the motet and many more. The effect was to revolutionise perceptions about English Music and its history. In the wake of the *Dictionary* there had been a clutch of major scholarly developments. Fuller Maitland's *English Carols of the Fifteenth Century* appeared in 1893; and *The Fitzwilliam Virginal Book* (1894–99), edited by Barclay Squire and Fuller Maitland, was dedicated to Queen Victoria. Vaughan Williams was very close to all this. He knew several of the younger men personally and took great interest in developments. He was very familiar, too, with the work of Richard Terry, both at Downside School and (after 1901) at Westminster Cathedral.

Terry was a scholar in whom the Tudor revival had a true intellectual pioneer. He was, in fact, another product of the Renaissance and its intellectual hinterland: and he met Stanford at Cambridge in the 1880s. Vaughan Williams was probably familiar with Stanford's exhortation to his students to enjoy 'Palestrina for twopence', that being the bus fare from South Kensington to Westminster Cathedral, where Terry was establishing a performance tradition (Kennedy 1964/71: 159). Terry stressed the importance of the Tudor composers for English Music, and Fayrfax, Taverner, Tallis and Byrd, were all revived by his efforts. However, the last two of these were (of course) recusant Catholics, and Terry himself was a convert to Catholicism. Yet, despite the potentially anomalous elements in all this, he never lost the patronage of the Renaissance (Andrews 1948).

At Westminster Cathedral there was a demonstrable case of the new Renaissance discovering the old. Vaughan Williams, for his part, first encountered modal counterpoint at the RCM in 1894 and, as Wilfred Mellers remarks, his 'technical awakening was centred on Tudor polyphony' (Mellers 1989: 30).

The mainstream Anglican Tudor Revival rested largely (and appropriately) on a distinct source of scholarship – that of E. H. Fellowes, whose magisterial *English Madrigal School* was published in thirty-six volumes during 1913–24. Fellowes, a product of Winchester and Oxford, expressed in his life and work that almost affectedly modest, traditionalist Anglican side of the Musical Renaissance which seems to sanctify the enduring kinship between the organ-loft and South Kensington. Fellowes was a contributor to Colles's third edition of *The Grove Dictionary of Music and Musicians* (Colles 1927–28), and, as a serving clergyman, mainly at St George's Windsor, was much more of an establishment figure than even Terry could ever aspire to be. Canon Fellowes's work had a particularly fecund effect on Holst, after the latter 'discovered' Tudor music in 1914: 'Ever since Fellowes's edition of Morley's madrigals was published I think I can say that I have never been the same man' (Holst 1938/1969: 44).

In contrast to this clamantly indigenous strain, the English Folk-Music Revival derived to a significant degree from German musical scholarship of the mid-nineteenth century. In particular, Carl Engel, a German exile, wrote the key text *An Introduction to the Study of National Music*, first published in English and in London (1866). Engel was a Darwin of the folksong – although few of its later advocates cared to acknowledge him as such. A pupil of Hummel, he came to England in the 1840s, and established himself as an authority on musical instruments. In that capacity he formed a connection with the South Kensington Museum, and, until his death in 1882, he dedicated himself to 'archaeological studies' of the national musics of the world (Fuller Maitland 1904–10: I, 779). During this time, Engel actually lived at a South Kensington address – so that the folksong movement, too, had its origins in the shadow of Prince Albert's Memorial.

Engel specifically employed the German definition of 'National Music' (*Volksmusik*): 'music, which appertains to a nation or a tribe, whose individual emotions and passions it expresses, exhibiting certain peculiarities more or less characteristic' (Engel 1866: 1). His relatively broad concept took in 'national tunes' as well as 'folk-song', and compared National Music with the language of the country. In a metaphor later adopted (without acknowledgement) by Cecil Sharp, Engel likened national songs to the 'wild flowers indigenous to a country, which thrive unaided by art' (p. 23). He included folk-dancing and national poetry in his researches, and argued that they were inseparable from National Music.

Here was another challenge to the English Musical Renaissance – even as it came into existence – but never to be recognised as such by its inscribers. In the 1870s, Engel's *The Literature of National Music* first appeared in the *Musical Times*. This nine-part series – quickly republished by Novello (1879) – explained how the Germans had led the way in 'national music' research, with the Russians and the French not far behind. In Britain, the Scots and Welsh had documented their own traditions. Nevertheless:

> It seems rather singular that England should not possess any printed collection of its national songs with the airs as they are sung at the present day; while almost every other European nation possesses several comprehensive works of this kind
> [...]
> It certainly appears singular that English musicians should have neglected to investigate the national songs of the different provinces of their own country ... surely there are English musicians ... who might achieve good results if they would spend their autumnal holidays in some rural district of the country, associate with the villagers, and listen to their songs. (Engel 1879: 32, 99–100)

The putative Renaissance was galvanised by this German prompt. Michael Kennedy dates the beginning of 'the methodical collection of folksongs' to 1889, when *Sussex Songs*, an enlarged edition of John Broadwood's *Old English Songs* (1843) appeared (Kennedy 1964/71: 23). A spate of similar publications ensued: Baring-Gould's *Songs and Ballads of the West* (1889); Kidson's *Traditional Tunes* (1891); and the *English Country Songs* of Fuller Maitland and Lucy Broadwood (1893). Then, in 1898, the Folk-Song Society was founded, with Parry, Stanford and Mackenzie among its first vice-presidents. Within a year, the *Journal of the Folk-Song Society* was initiated.

In subsequent years the literature and history of the folk-music revival were anxious to diminish and distort the role played by Engel in its origin. Sharp's own basic text referred to him only in passing

– as someone 'of German extraction' – and in order to reject and marginalise his definitions (Sharp 1907/65: 2, 132). The order of events we find in the work of committed supporters of the Pastoral School – like Kennedy and Howes – strongly implies that the German scholar came into the picture at a time when native scholarship was already florescent (Kennedy 1964: 23–7; Howes 1966: 77). Maud Karpeles, in a widely read introduction to the subject (1973/87), does not even mention him. Yet in this context we are reminded of the legendary apothegm of Pope Gregory the Great – familiar to those schooled in a past tradition of British history. To paraphrase 'Non Anglorem sed Angelorum', the folksong revival was brought about 'not by Angles but an Angel' – Carl Engel was its truest begetter, a St Augustine who came bearing his fertile message from Germany (Marshall c. 1955: 61).

It was Cecil Sharp's egoism and proselytising skills, combined with the adulation of his supporters, which made him the spokes-man of the whole movement. He had a prosperous middle-class background, and was a Cambridge graduate. He turned late to com-posing and teaching, and around the same time was a convert to Fabian Socialism. Sharp's biographer and assistant explains that his 'conversion' to folksong occurred with two epiphanies. The first happened at Christmas 1899, when Sharp encountered the Head-ington Morris-Men on a dark and snowy day: 'a strange procession appeared: eight men in white decorated with ribbons'. However, 'the seed that was sown at Headington took time to germinate' (Karpeles 1967: 25). Four years later, another pastoral 'ghost' mate-rialised – the gardener John England and his song *The Seeds of Love*. This occurred in the grounds of Hambridge vicarage in Hampshire, an appropriately close homophone to the 'Ambridge' of the BBC Radio national soap-opera which centres our rural nostalgia.

In 1903, Vaughan Williams felt very much at the crossroads of his career. The critics were, in the main, friendly but frank. Barclay Squire, while singling out Vaughan Williams's potential for leadership, added: 'His work, so far as one can judge, is at present undecided in its tendencies … One may hope that something really original may arise, and that the birth of a really individual school of English com-posers may be looked for' (Kennedy 1964/71: 54–5).Vaughan Williams confided his anxieties to Holst, who was himself going through a stylistic crisis. Holst suggested that they should consult Elgar. His words betray apprehensions, in general about the ageing

Renaissance – even among its own progeny – and in particular about their reception at Malvern: 'Don't you think we ought to victimize Elgar? Write to him first and then bicycle to Worcester to see him a lot ... I think we are "all right" in a mild sort of way ... Something must happen and we must make it happen' (p. 57).

What actually 'happened' to Vaughan Williams – subsequent to his rejection by Elgar – was folksong. As with Sharp, the discovery occurred in an English vicarage garden – Ingrave's, in Essex – when he heard 'a labourer' sing 'Bushes and Briars', which evoked a 'deep sense of recognition' in him (R. Palmer 1983: ix). Meanwhile, Sharp had launched 'a folk-song crusade', with the dual objectives of encouraging collection and 'bringing the songs back into the daily lives of the English people' (Karpeles 1967: 46). He had no compunction about taking on the RCM and the Board of Education in the national press – crossing swords with both Stanford and Somervell – to make his case. The tone of these exchanges was uncompromising, as Sharp questioned the Renaissance's achievements and its complacency with regard to the new movement – and Vaughan Williams weighed in to support him (p. 60). Sharp set out his whole approach in his book *English Folk Song: Some Conclusions* (1907), by which time the pastoral movement was well under way. As early as October 1904, a *Musical Times* article was entitled 'Hints to Collectors of Folk Music' (Broadwood, *MT* 1904); and later the same journal commented that 'the cult of folk-songs is interesting ever-widening circles, and it even bids to become a social fashion' (Anon., *MT* 1906).

In this way, Vaughan Williams became Sharp's disciple. For each of the next ten years, he spent on average thirty days 'in the field' collecting folksongs. Eventually he was responsible for over 800 findings, though after the peak year of 1904 the annual total was in decline. He saw the essence of folksong as 'fine tunes' and tended to take less interest in the words than did Sharp. Vaughan Williams can be seen as a highly selective purist, whose idea of 'rescue archaeology' was hardly exhaustive. His main motive was an idea of transmitting these tunes as quickly and effectively as possible to the nation at large (Palmer 1983: i–x).

His first opportunity of doing just that came with his appointment as music editor of the new *English Hymnal* (1906). Vaughan Williams was recommended for this post by Cecil Sharp, and was accepted despite his (later-acknowledged) agnosticism. This

enterprise was the first creative contact between the Anglican
Church and the English Musical Renaissance. Vaughan Williams's
academic outlook, coupled with his love of Tudor music and his new
dedication to folksong, forged the *Hymnal* as an entirely new
weapon for national music, to be wielded through the Church on the
life of the nation. His inspiration was explicitly ideological, stem-
ming from the convictions that the established Church was a vital
pillar of 'Englishness' and that its music should be purged of Victorian sentimentalism and 'bad taste'. Holst and John Ireland were
recruited to help select and arrange the tunes, and about twenty new
ones were included. The incorporation of Tudor tunes was, however, more significant, with, for example, Gibbons and Tallis being
firmly brought back into Anglican worship. Even more significant
was the inclusion of folksong – with thirty-five tunes from a variety
of sources. By 1956 – its silver jubilee – the *Hymnal* had sold 5
million copies. Vaughan Williams's choice, as he explained in his
Preface, 'seeks to ensure purity of musical taste, perhaps even lean-
ing to the side of severity ... [and yet] a tune has no more right to be
dull than demoralising ... Hymns are essentially for the congregation' (Kennedy 1964/71: 65–74). We cannot help but reflect that
Vaughan Williams had more of a mind to put Anglicans in touch
with the English Musical Renaissance than with the Almighty.

After he had finished his work on *The English Hymnal*, Vaughan
Williams was ready to resume his compositional output with a new
conviction and sense of purpose. The first substantial work to reflect
this was his setting of Whitman's *Toward the Unknown Region*
(1907), which excited expectations that he would prove to be the
modernising spirit, the saviour of the Musical Renaissance from age
and decay. First performed at the Leeds Festival – still a province of
Stanford – it was acknowledged by Fuller Maitland in *The Times* as
a pocket masterpiece: 'Here we see the perfect maturity of his
genius, the art that conceals art most effectually, and a nobility and
earnestness of invention which mark the composer as the foremost
of the younger generation' (12 October 1907; our emphasis). The
Renaissance had nominated its 'coming man': the successor to Parry
had been found, and found triumphantly, among its own.

Vaughan Williams himself was not so sure. The doubts he harboured, indeed, were still of such a heretical nature that he contacted
Delius – that pariah of South Kensington – as a possible tutor (Carley and Threlfall 1977: 61). Ultimately, however, it was to Ravel that

Vaughan Williams went in 1908 for extended tuition. It is surely significant that of the orchestral works written before the Ravel period, only the *Norfolk Rhapsody No.1* survived in its original form (Kennedy 1964/71: 91). During 1909–10 the turning-point came, with the Housman settings *On Wenlock Edge* and the completion of *A Sea Symphony*. This provided conclusive proof – to the many who demanded it – that Vaughan Williams could compose in the largest forms. In comparison, only a few weeks before, at the Three Choirs Festival, the *Tallis Fantasia* had been premiered to general indifference, excepting the enthusiasm of the Renaissance faithful. 'Throughout its course one is never quite sure whether one is listening to something very old or very new ... One is living in two centuries at once ... It cannot be assigned to a time or a school but it is full of the visions which have haunted the seers of all times' (Colles, *The Times* 071010)

From now on, Vaughan Williams's output was characterised by his twin obsessions. He spent much of his time on his folk-opera *Hugh the Drover*; and, as a leading Tudor revivalist, he accepted the musical directorship of the Shakespeare Company for the 1913 Stratford Festival. As the peace crumbled in 1914, Vaughan Williams stood second only to Elgar in the public estimation. Although the older musician's appeal had never been greater, his reputation had nevertheless suffered from the double failure of his *Symphony No. 2* (1911) and *Falstaff* (1913), and some critics were already concluding that his best days were behind him. The 'official' Renaissance had no doubt that the future belonged to the 'historical–pastoral'.

3

War, post-war, pre-war, more war (1914–40)

Special services to the nation

> The Royal College of Music has always been a place with big aims of doing special services to the nation, and it was organised from the start with a view to their attainment. (Parry to RCM students, 1915, in Parry 1920: 257)

Just after the outbreak of war in 1914, a book entitled *Das Land ohne Musik* was published in Germany by a certain Oscar Schmitz. This was the first attributable use of the celebrated phrase, which in this version, as previously in less concrete ones, acted as both shadow and spur to so much English musical effort (Schmitz 1914/26). Although the book was essentially a dissection of the English national character, Herr Schmitz broadcast a widely held, if hitherto muted, maxim from the perspective of the most powerful musical nation in the world. That it was published soon after the two nations became locked in conflict is surely significant. It was immediately seen as a scurrilous German attack on the achievements of the English Musical Renaissance.

The Great War brought bitter disillusionment for some of the fundamental ideals pursued by Grove and Parry. The inspiration of Germany's profound and vibrant artistic civilisation, the product – so it had seemed – of a people steeped in the Protestant Reformation and given over to peace and hard work, was now definitively sullied. From the start of the hostilities residual pro-German sentiment was rudely swept aside. The invasion of neutral Belgium, the atrocities committed against civilians, the shelling of cities and the burning of libraries; the bitter fighting on the Marne; and the first air raid on Britain (Christmas Eve 1914) – all caused a profound reaction against 'the Hun'. In 1915, things got immeasurably worse. Germany used poison gas on the western front and a submarine to sink the liner *Lusitania*, with heavy loss of civilian life. Anti-German feeling, whipped up by propaganda, became public and violent. August Jaeger's widow changed her name to 'Hunter'; but perhaps the defining moment in the new perception of things German came when, in July 1917, the Royal House itself – that of 'Saxe–Coburg–Gotha' – changed its name to the 'House of Windsor'.

Voices warned against similarly symbolic change in the nation's musical culture. Perhaps the most influential was that of the critic Ernest Newman, whose article 'The War and the Future of Music' argued that should war cause a retreat into a 'Little England', music itself would suffer, since it was, of all the arts, the 'most cosmopolitan'. He pleaded that a 'small music', based on a narrow nationalism, would be a disaster and that only the 'emotional solidarity of mankind' could provide the 'real music of the future'. For Newman, the future remained with Elgar, and he dismissed the pastoralists as 'the crowd of younger men [among whom] it is impossible to distinguish one who has the least chance of making history' (Newman *MT* 1914b). In the previous number of the *Musical Times*, Newman had informed 'folk-song friends' that nationalism did not help a composer to be 'national': 'we are asked to believe that the "English national character" is fully expressed in the folk-songs of a few humble country singers of several generations ago!' (Newman *MT* 1914a). Newman's fears proved to be amply justified, for it was the war which delivered to the Pastoral School its inheritance.

Yet not even Elgar stayed loyal to the spirit of Newman's appeal. Too old for the colours, he enlisted instead in the Hampstead Special Constabulary. Elgar, ever the nation's 'bard', responded outwardly with bluff determination, though inwardly he felt disorientated: 'It's a pity I am too old to be a soldier. I am so active. Everything is at a standstill and we have nothing left in the world ... But we are cheerful and I will die a man if not a musician' (Kennedy 1968/82: 265).

Even Vaughan Williams, despite his deep reservations about the war, volunteered for the Royal Army Medical Corps. The odd voice of dissent went unheard – like that of Philip Heseltine, who commented to Delius: 'I have never been able to understand the sentiment of patriotism, the love of Empire; it has always seemed to me so empty and intangible an idea' (Foreman 1987: 62).

At first it was thought that all music would cease for the duration of the war, and the provincial festivals were cancelled (although some reappeared in 1915). At the same time, the Government imposed a ban on performances of German music, and 'enemy' musicians were interned as 'enemy aliens'. The main beneficiaries were to be a cluster of new talents (*pace* Newman) for whom exigencies of this kind provided opportunity. By the end of 1914, musicians still in civilian life were turning their talents to serving the nation through their profession. For example, as British works began to take over concert programming in 1915, one Mrs Lucy Clifford wrote to Percy Pitt of the British National Opera, reminding him about a children's opera of her composition he had previously been unwilling to perform. 'There is such a boom in everything British now that I have been wondering if you would care to see it again, or if not, whether you would put me on to anyone who would?' (BLMC E3304/103).

Yet when it did become apparent that music would have a role to play, it was Elgar, and not Mrs Clifford, who gave the lead. The composer, who had seemed exhausted to many in the immediate pre-war years, suddenly uncovered a rich vein – and in many ways a new one (Crump 1986). In November 1914 he produced *Carillon*, which celebrated the resistance of 'Gallant Little Belgium' to the German invasion. It was very much a work of the first autumn of the war, stressing the importance of music in the unfolding tragedy:

Sing Belgians, sing!
Although our wounds may bleed,
Although our voices break,
Louder than the storm, louder than the guns ...

After some tumultuous London performances, *Carillon* toured the provinces with Sir Edward himself, and was recorded for phonograph in early 1915. It proved the first of a series of populist warworks with which Elgar boosted his career and bolstered his finances. The symphonic prelude *Polonia* (1915, dedicated to Paderewski) was a work written at the request of his old friend Charles Stuart-Wortley, the Conservative MP who was involved in the Polish Relief Fund. Like *Carillon*, two further war-works used recitation with orchestra, but neither emulated the huge success of the original.

As well as writing serious propaganda, Elgar tried to help morale with several 'lighter' works. The incidental music to *The Starlight*

Express (1915) and the ballet *The Sanguine Fan* (1917) proved as popular as anything he had written for years. By far the most successful of his later war-works was *Fringes of the Fleet* (1917). These settings of Kipling and others were dedicated to his friend Admiral Lord Beresford. They illustrate how the 'official' Elgar could move from expressing the nation's grief to uninhibited and belligerent defiance of the foe. Although he claimed to dislike Kipling's 'vulgar' ethos and rejected all suggestions of affinity with the arch-jingoist, Elgar seized upon these with relish. The manager of London's Coliseum must have expressed the thoughts of many when, in a newspaper interview, he asserted: 'the great hope ... [will be] of Edward Elgar standing out as a master-mind in musical composition after the War' (Moore 1984: 709–10).

Elgar's offerings to the nation culminated with *The Spirit of England*. Binyon himself was enthusiastic about Elgar's setting of his war-poems, perceiving the prospect of a work of national importance. He urged the composer to 'think of England, of the English-speaking peoples, in whom the blood stirs as never before ... I think of the thousands who will be craving to have their grief glorified and lifted up and transformed by an art like yours' (HWRO 705 445/6350: 270315). *To Women* and *For the Fallen* were premiered in May 1916. Newman was in no doubt that: 'Here in truth is the very voice of England ... moved to the very centre of her being in this War as she has never been moved before in all her history' (Newman *MT* 1916). The King, the Queen and the Queen Mother attended; in a week of performances in aid of the Red Cross, £2,700 was eventually donated. But Elgar did not complete the work for over a year. The carnage of the Somme, the campaign of unrestricted submarine warfare and the March Revolution in Russia – all conspired to suppress his will to compose. His final setting, *The Fourth of August*, reflects a deep disappointment with and anger over German civilisation – especially bitter since, like Parry and Stanford, he had felt so close to it. In June 1917, he confided his sense of betrayal to Newman: 'the Hun is branded as less than a beast for many generations ... great intellects gibber and snarl knowing they have fallen: this is exactly the case with the Germans now ... The horror of the fallen intellect -knowing that they have fallen' (Moore 1984: 705). The completed score of *The Spirit of England* was premiered in November 1917. Elgar inscribed it: 'To the memory of our glorious men, with a special thought for the Worcesters'.

None of these pieces, however, was actually commissioned by the Government. At no time during the Great War did the Government have a 'policy' to use music in the cause of victory. Consequently, there is hardly an example of the Ministry of Information's commissioning an important piece of native music. It was only in the last year of the struggle that the Ministry evinced any interest in promoting music as a national asset – when the critic Edwin Evans was asked to write articles for the Danish and Spanish press on 'Modern British Composers' (Evans *MT* 1919). In general, there was little official consideration of how music might serve the nation. It seems likely that familiar and long-standing attitudes towards music had much to do with this – an interesting reflection on the status of the Musical Renaissance even in wartime. Major projects therefore originated from individuals, interest groups or war charities. Even in Elgar's case, only one minor piece was commissioned – the song *Big Steamers* (1918), a setting of Kipling, for the Ministry of Food, celebrating the convoy lifeline to the United States.

Alongside Elgar's performance, the work of the London professors was distinctly low-key. Parry hated the war, although he thought it to be 'righteous and inevitable'. As a musician who had extolled the moral value of the great German tradition, Parry found himself in a dilemma which he attempted to resolve by making a distinction between 'good' and 'bad' Germans. In 1914, he declared: 'I have been for a quarter of a century and more a pro-Teuton'; but he was obliged to bite the bullet of 'the butchers and brigands of Berlin':

> Throwing all honour and truth and decency to the winds … what can have perverted them? … The hideous militarism of the Prussians that has poisoned the wells of the spirit throughout Germany … If Prussia should succeed, then the people would prefer extermination to submission. (Parry 1920: 221–6)

Parry added that music should reflect 'heroism', but not 'the fussy, aggressive blatant heroism of the Prussian *Heldenleben*'. Even so, he was against his students' enlisting on two counts: that they would serve the nation better as musicians; and that they should be sheltered from danger because they were musicians. Nothing could shake Sir Hubert's conviction that musicians were special, elevated beings.

Parry worked as hard as his health would allow during the war years. Although the list of his compositions is relatively meagre, his broader involvement was considerable. His most substantial musical comment on the tragedy was the symphonic poem *From Death to Life* (1914) – written as a response to the outbreak of hostilities. Two shorter works followed: *A Hymn for Aviators* (1915) and the choral song *Jerusalem*, to William Blake's words, premiered at a 'Fight For Right' meeting in March 1916. For the rest, only the *Naval Ode: The Chivalry of the Sea* is significant: dedicated to the Royal and Merchant Navies, it was written in the year of Jutland (1916). Throughout the war, Parry worked in musical charities, like the 'Music in Wartime' movement, dedicated to supporting needy musicians. In the first six months of 1915, he helped to raise over £2,000 to provide work for unemployed musicians by organising concerts in hospitals, camps and schools (Anon., *MT* 1915).

For Stanford, too, the war posed fundamental problems over the status of German civilisation; while, in addition, his dual identity as an Irishman and an Englishman came under pressure, as the Irish problem came to a head in the Easter Rebellion of 1916. In some ways a response to this challenge was the *Irish Rhapsody No. 5* (1917) – dedicated to the Irish Guards – which reasserted his conservative vision of his native island. Perhaps his major work was the five *Organ Sonatas* (1917–18), the second of which – subtitled 'Eroica' – was intended as a tribute to the allied armies on the Western Front (Colles 1927–8: V, 121–2). More importantly, in 1916 he published *A History of Music* – the last major prose utterance by the Grove–Parry Renaissance on the state of Western music and, in particular, on future prospects and directions in England. The central idea of the book confronted Newman head-on: only through nationalism could music progress. Perhaps under the influence of his collaborator Cecil Forsyth, Stanford at last was brought to reject the Germanic tradition and its influence on the future of English Music:

> [T]here are two classes of men ... the nationalists and the denationalists. And the artistic health and productivity of any community increases exactly with its proportion of nationalists ... It is a quarrel of the creative mind with the receptive ... of the man who loves his country and the man who loves someone else's. (Stanford and Forsyth 1916: 305)

The broad national spirit of Forsyth's part of the *History* recuperates both Elgar and Sullivan into the mainstream of the Renaissance, naming them among the founding elect. The war's emergency had healed internal wounds, and the two 'outsiders' were restored to the bosom of their nation, and perhaps to 'country membership' of the South Kensington Club.

In practice, only the pastoralists could benefit from Stanford's analysis. He had earned the right, in some respects, to regard the new generation as his own. He now went so far as to spell out that only when English composers had learned the lesson that folk-music was the bedrock of all music could they become 'free-born citizens of their own country' (Stanford and Forsyth 1916: 209). Meanwhile, in Flanders, George Butterworth and Ernest Farrar were providing the Pastoral School with its first martyrs, and Vaughan Williams was near to the first sketches of his *Pastoral Symphony*. Folksong was to be the salvation of the Renaissance. The Grove–Parry generation met the rising 'historical pastoralists' in the pages of Stanford's *History*. And yet – for all that – Stanford declined to foreswear his honour as the only English member of the Royal Academy of Arts in Berlin.

By 1918, the Grove–Parry phase had long since run its course. A signal of its passing was the rejection of Parry's treatise 'Instinct and Character' (BLMC KTC 28 b. 26) by Macmillan – a publishing house which had always worked hand-in-glove with the men of South Kensington. The decision disappointed Parry greatly, since the work offered his thoughts on the moral condition of England and (as he put it to the publisher) 'the spiritual and material influences in life which in these times has become so urgent' (BLMC A55239/2/129: 300518). The Victorian vision of the Renaissance – ethical, evolutionary and essentially internationalist in its nationalism – was deemed out-of-touch, even by its most loyal supporters. In his last music, the *Songs of Farewell* (1916–18), Parry expressed a yearning to escape from a world that was destroying itself through nationalistic obsessions. The first of the set expressed the thoughts of many in 1918, that real peace could only be found 'elsewhere':

> My soul there is a country
> Far beyond the stars,
> There, above noise and danger,
> Sweet Peace sits crowned with smiles.

In the *Songs of Farewell*, Parry evokes the spirit of Brahms and the *Vier Ernste Gesänge*, possibly expressing a final faith in the spiritual 'purity' of German music, uncorrupted by militarism and hatred.

They are a pained and complex epitaph on Grove's Renaissance and the society for which it was constructed.

As it happened, the effective end of Elgar's creative career coincided in time with Parry's farewell and death. In 1918, depressed by the course of the war, Elgar retreated to the rural seclusion of Sussex to write the *Cello Concerto* and the last chamber works. When they were premiered, public and critics alike were cool, even hostile. Predictably, *The Times*, unmoved by Elgar in Fuller Maitland's day, remained so under H. C. Colles: 'An immediate effect of listening to Sir Edward Elgar's Opp. 82, 83 and 84 in succession is to give one a new sympathy with the modern revolt against beauty of line and colour ... One craves an antidote to the Elgarian type of beauty' (Moore 1984: 740).

Colles was just one of the many supporters of the 'Pastoral School' who occupied (or were about to occupy) important positions in musical and cultural life. These younger men had no intention of accommodating Elgar in the post-war Goodly House. For them, his brand of 'English progressivism' was neither English nor progressive: rather, it was seen as sub-Teutonic and reactionary. The emphasis was now upon national music. Partly as a result, Colles speculated as to the effect of the war on England's musical development: 'As the poets of today have come from the trenches, may we not expect that the British musical future is being born in the fields of France?' (1984: 710). In many ways this question was to be answered in the affirmative.

Even before 1914, the Boer War, together with the deepening of the Irish crisis, had impelled the transition from a 'British' notion of the national culture to a more exclusively 'English' one. The Victorian ideology of 'Britishness' had concentrated on aspects of the national project that were inclusive: the British Empire, British engineering, the British Army, the British Monarchy, and so on. In all of these, the national orientations within the British Isles could be safely accommodated. However, the arena of culture and customs had always been more fraught. After all, the English language and its literature had never been 'British', and this was so with a multitude of other institutions that had resisted the incursion of 'Britishness'. By the closing decades of the Victorian age, the essentially eighteenth-century ideal of Britain – as encapsulated in the Acts of Union of 1707 and 1801 with Scotland and Ireland – was breaking down. The Boer War, the interminable Home Rule crisis in Ireland and the growth of socialism at home, all threatened to tear apart the fabric of British politics and society. The Great War, like all wars in all ages, presented the country with challenges from within, as well as dangers from without.

The influence of the Irish crisis on the development of English Music was considerable. Long before the First World War, interest in the Celtic Renaissance, as pioneered by Yeats and Synge, had had an impact on music. Granville Bantock, friend and ally of Elgar, stressed its value, and several young English composers – most notably Bax, with Ireland, and Joseph Holbrooke, with Wales – identified this alternative source of inspiration. The Easter Rebellion finally shattered the notion of the inviolable unity of Britain. The Pastoral School was reactively strengthened in the post-war era by Irish independence and the break-up of the Union.

The idea of the so-called 'Lost Generation' had its influence on music as well as on literature. Butterworth and Farrar were by no means the only victims. Two other aspiring youngsters of the pastoralist persuasion, W. D. Browne and Frederick Kelly, were killed in France. Among the casualties of the trenches were Ivor Gurney and Ernest Moeran. Gurney was regarded by Stanford as his most brilliant pupil. A friend of Vaughan Williams and Herbert Howells, he was a passionate supporter of the Pastoral School, the influence of which suffused his large output of songs. He was invalided out of the Gloucester Regiment, and ended his days in an asylum. Moeran, who suffered a severe head wound, was also a Stanford product, and much involved in post-war pastoralism and folksong-collecting.

It was not only folksong which fascinated the pastoralists. Just before the war (1911), the English Folk Dance Society had been founded, in which Vaughan Williams, Butterworth and Sharp were key figures. It was a new area for the extension of pastoralism, and by August 1914 Sharp and Butterworth alone had collected 200 dances. Sharp grasped the potential of folk-dance to win young people to his cause and contribute to 'the quickening of the national spirit' (Sharp *MT* 1915). At the first post-war 'Peace Day' celebrations in Hyde Park (1919), the centrepiece of the festivities was 1,000 folk dancers performing to the accompaniment of the Band of the Fourth Fusiliers (Karpeles 1967: 173–4). The opportunities and contradictions of peace were about to pose a new challenge.

Back to Hucbald

> Directorship of the RCM is an excellent example of the sort of big job
> that kills an artist. Parry sacrificed himself to save an awkward situa-
> tion ... I don't mind Allen taking it on but I dread RVW being offered
> something of that sort. I suppose he would decline. But he would
> accept if the question of self-sacrifice and duty came in as it did with
> Parry. (Holst (1919) in Short 1991: 173)

The first post-war task for the musical establishment was to choose
a new leader. However, the man on whom the succession had been
settled was not available in a formal capacity. Vaughan Williams
made it clear that he preferred composition to teaching, and confessed to no talent or desire for administration. A surrogate had to
be found, preferably an 'insider', who knew the ways of the RCM
but would guide the institution, and the greater Renaissance movement, towards an uncertain future. Fortunately, the right man was
on hand – Hugh Allen, whom the *Dictionary of National Biography*
(*DNB*) candidly refers to as a 'musician and musical statesman'
(*DNB* 1941–50). Allen proved an inspired choice. The son of a
wealthy industrialist, he trained at Oxford as a cathedral organist. At
Cambridge in the 1890s he became friends not only with Vaughan
Williams but with Edward J. Dent – who eventually succeeded to the
professorship. Allen later became, *inter alia*, director of music at
Reading University (1908–18, succeeding Parratt) and director of
the Leeds Festival (1913–28, succeeding Stanford).

Allen was a trained Renaissance man, whose orientation, like that
of Parry, was dominated by a love of German music. His academic
specialism was Schutz and the early German school, but his greatest
loves were J. S. Bach and Brahms. On the face of things, such loyalties were, in 1919, politically unpromising as well as outworn. Yet,
like Parry, Allen had strong liberal–humanist convictions which
favoured progress. To him, Parry was a 'sheet-anchor ... in musical
taste and in the wider principles of life' (Bailey 1948: 138). His deep
sympathies with the Pastoral School stemmed from a close friendship with Vaughan Williams, and guaranteed harmony at the highest
level. He was knighted in 1920, perhaps in anticipation of 'special
services to the nation' at South Kensington.

One of the reasons why Allen accepted the RCM appointment –
despite recently succeeding to the Oxford chair – was a conviction
that the RCM was the premier institution of English musical life. He

appreciated its intimate connection with the Royal Family, and was impressed by its leading role in the Musical Renaissance (1948: 94). He set out to shape the RCM on the lines of a university. More state investment was promised for the universities in the post-war period, and Allen wanted the RCM to be at the forefront of this develop-ment. He was aware also of the opportunities of the mechanisation of music, and took a keen interest in the advances in gramophone technology and in the discussions over a radio service (Colles 1933: 46). Allen was determined that the RCM should move with the times. With this in mind, he resolved that 'uninstructed popular enthusiasm' for music should be guided into 'profitable channels' for the College.

The first step was to expand the staff, and in 1919–20 alone twenty-six new teaching appointments were made. Alongside this, he nearly doubled the student intake; ballet and conducting classes were initiated; the College's orchestra was supplemented by another two; and a teacher training course was put into the curriculum. The leading figure in the new RCM team was Vaughan Williams himself, who agreed to become part-time professor of composition – a post which he held throughout the interwar years. Holst too was brought in, as part-time professor of composition (1919–24).

The Allen–Vaughan Williams axis was the backbone of the Renais-sance in the inter-war period. In its genteel anti-establishment instincts, it was, ironically, the *new* establishment. Allen's enthusi-asm for opera was one aspect of his championing of Vaughan Williams and Holst. It is not surprising, therefore, that opera was given an unprecedented importance within the Renaissance, and its popular and populist aspects stressed. The RCM was still receiving only £500 per annum from the State and Allen's ambitious plans had to be financed from student fees and the generosity of patrons. The outcome was an extension of the long-standing Patrons' Fund towards the inauguration of a new opera theatre. Opened in 1921, it was named for Parry – a strange decision, which surely placed the demand for political harmony above historical reality. In the realm of sheer protocol, it was made feasible by the convenient fact that Stanford was still alive and in post. In fact, Allen's uncompromising style had already led to 'hot collisions' with the ageing Stanford (Bai-ley 1948: 73).

Allen's speeches reveal his dynamic yet sympathetic approach to his task. His sense of responsibility to the generation whose lives had been devastated by war was patent. As he asserted to the students in 1921: 'You went to war in order that you might enjoy Peace. The higher virtues of life and the aim for nobler things must be the supreme end' (Allen 1922). Allen's talent was as an energiser and 'fixer': within weeks of his arrival he had secured the Prince of Wales's agreement to be president of the RCM; and when Stanford became too infirm to continue as conductor of the orchestra, Allen persuaded Adrian Boult to assist (Kennedy 1987/89: 91). This connection was soon to prove enormously influential in the development of the BBC as a vehicle for the post-war Musical Renaissance.

It is hardly surprising that other music institutions remained in the RCM's shade. At the RAM, Mackenzie's long and successful tenure as principal ended in 1924, when he retired. The Academy had experienced a transformation under Mackenzie's stewardship: the 1900s had been 'an exceptionally brilliant period', and it moved into sumptuous new buildings on Marylebone Road in 1912 (Corder 1922: 89). Its finances were sound, but the 1920s were not reckoned as years of innovation or distinction, and its staff lacked the overall excellence of the RCM's personnel. When Mackenzie left, the principalship passed to another Scot, John McEwen, with whom it remained for twelve rather uneventful years. McEwen's was an 'in-house' appointment, he having been a member of the RAM's professorial staff since 1898. Although described as a 'progressive', McEwen had only a limited reputation as a composer. One of the first appointments he made was of Sir Henry Wood to train the RAM orchestra, on a part-time basis.

Meanwhile, under the prompting of the State, the universities began to regard music as a serious academic subject. Until the First World War, the universities had shown little systematic response to the musical revival. As far as even Oxford was concerned, Grove, Stanford and Parry (its own Heatherian professor) had more or less laboured in vain: 'The position of musical degrees at Oxford is at present one of curiously anomalous character. Holders of musical degrees may in a purely technical sense be members of the University ... but the ordinary custom is undoubtedly to consider them as ... outside the academical pale' (Fuller Maitland 1904–10: 1, 608).

The prospect of increased funding altered this situation rapidly. Among the first to benefit was the University of Wales. The University had only one dedicated music department (at Cardiff) in its three constituent colleges, together with a number of senior music posts; for example, a director at Bangor and a professor at Aberystwyth. It was felt by the Haldane Commission – which reported on university education in Wales – that the music provision was inadequate 'in a country so musically gifted as Wales' (Haldane 1918: 157). It was decided that that each constituent college was to have a fully staffed music department and that the university would appoint a music director, who would act also as chairman of a council to advise on musical education generally in the Principality.

In this affair the musical renaissance can be seen to be reaching for its first major provincial – and, in a sense, colonial – expansion. The Haldane recommendations concerning music were written by Sir W. H. Hadow, friend of Parry and editor of *The Oxford History of Music* (Hadow 1901–5). Furthermore, the appointment of Walford Davies to the post of music director had already been decided upon in South Kensington – by Sir Hubert himself, in one of his last acts as leader. Like Parry, Davies had been born on the Welsh Borders and boasted Welsh ancestry. He was yet another Renaissance man. A pupil of Parratt at Windsor, he went on to Parry and Stanford at the RCM. After a brief flirtation with the abortive Elgarian Counter-Renaissance – to be excused, perhaps, by his Midlands' origins – he returned to the London fold. As early as September 1917, even before the Haldane report was published, he was corresponding with Parry on the subject of the new post. In mid-1918 Parry wrote to congratulate him: 'So it's to be Aberystwyth when the war ceases its roarings! No doubt you will inspire the Welsh with great ardour; and I hope induce them to look beyond the borders for some things they can't provide inside them!' (Colles 1942: 116).

Significantly, Colles gave his biographical chapter covering Davies's period in Wales the title 'The Welsh Mission'. Walford Davies held his missionary post until 1926, during which time he was knighted. He was a strong supporter of the Liberal Party and Lloyd George, and the Haldane recommendations (and their funding) were approved during Lloyd George's last ministry. Davies left Wales in 1926 for St George's Chapel, Windsor, and later succeeded Elgar as Master of the King's Musick.

During this decade Elgar apparently remained aloof as a 'Grand Old Man' but behind the scenes he doggedly pursued the official honours he coveted so much (Hughes 1989). Significantly, it was only his lobbying that ensured the retention of the office of Master of the King's Musick after Parratt's death in 1924. King George V himself had no interest, and in 'radical' post-war South Kensington the post of musical courtier was regarded as a moribund relic from a demeaning age. Consequently, Elgar's own appointment to the vacancy elicited indifference, but no opposition. Of course, Sir Edward had a loyal following almost everywhere outside the London academies and their press allies. His seventieth and seventy-fifth birthdays were fulsomely celebrated, not least by the BBC, and such was the Elgarian influence within the Corporation that in 1932 it was persuaded to commission a third symphony – for a fee of £1,000. This was by far the most substantial reward yet received by an English composer for any work.

Nevertheless, the greater influence in terms of performance and publicity now belonged to the Pastoral School, the official chorus of the academies and the Renaissance. Vaughan Williams's *Pastoral Symphony* was ready for performance in 1922, and its London success was followed by a strong reception in the USA. With Boult's advocacy, it gained an immediate place in the repertoire (Vaughan Williams 1964: 159). An important arena for Vaughan Williams's music was the International Society for Contemporary Music (ISCM), founded in 1923 by E. J. Dent. The ISCM and its British branch reflected the internationalist mood and the League of Nations' spirit of a generation devastated by war. Dent enjoyed enormous influence: not only was he the driving force behind the ISCM, but he was appointed to the Cambridge Chair in 1926. It was through him that the *Pastoral Symphony* was given at an ISCM gathering in Prague, in 1925.

One of Vaughan Williams's most cherished ideals had always been of a style which could bridge the divide between composer and public. In the 1920s, he pursued this attempt to achieve a synthesis of the public and the personal since, for him, the modernism of Schoenberg, Bartók and Stravinsky was largely unacceptable. Although he admired many of Stravinsky's qualities, he rejected atonality as 'ugly', and because 'it meant fetters' for English Music. By the same token, the native followers of the moderns – like Walton – he distrusted as purveyors of 'superficial flippancy' (Kennedy 1964: 186–92). Vaughan Williams adhered to the supreme value of folksong – he was elected vice-president of the Folk Song Society in 1921. As in pre-war days, his summers were characterised by periodic teaching commitments on the Society's vacation courses.

In the relevant historical works, Vaughan Williams's music is still associated with that of Holst. Having made little impact outside RCM circles before the war, Holst became a major figure with the success of *The Planets* (1919). When this work was given at the Leeds Festival in 1922, Holst found himself mobbed by well-wishers and autograph-hunters, and had to take shelter in a police station (Short 1991: 205). Vaughan Williams and Holst did not always admire each other's work, and in musical terms the routine linkage of the two – as Kennedy (1964: 186) points out – is in some respects misleading. All the same, the two shared both a vaguely Left-inclined politics and the Pastoral Muse, and often their careers seemed to move in parallel (Harrington 1989).

At this stage, however, neither enjoyed the support of a major publisher. This disturbed Vaughan Williams especially, given several unfortunate experiences; for example, an early draft of *A London Symphony* was sent to a German publisher before the outbreak of the Great War – never to return. In 1925, he was taken up by the Oxford University Press – an arrangement which came about through Hubert Foss, who placed OUP's new music department at his disposal. For the rest of his life, Vaughan Williams's music appeared in this prestigious livery; Foss proved as committed a supporter as, in a similar capacity, Jaeger had been for Elgar – and an indefatigable publicist into the bargain (Foss 1950; Vaughan Williams 1964: 157).

Another such was H. C. Colles, an influential friend and professional contact of both Hugh Allen and Vaughan Williams. Colles made sure that the heirs of the Renaissance had coverage, via *The Times*, on the breakfast tables of the great and the good. Like Fuller Maitland before him, he was a thoroughbred collegiate, and was duly appointed professor of music history at the RCM in 1919. For Colles, the Pastoral School was the only English Music. It was all the more unfortunate, therefore, that in his review of Vaughan Williams's *Mass in G Minor*, he inadvertently offered comfort to the enemy:

> All the beautiful interest of the work is far too much of a tale to be told at this moment ... The spire, not losing itself in the clouds, allowed for its fine and serviceable proportions to be perceived! The texture is intensely personal, however the personal expressiveness is subjugated. Have there since Hucbald been so many consecutive fifths in a Mass? (Colles, *MT* 1923: 36–7)

Hucbald was a Walloon monk of the ninth century, to whom was attributed the earliest extant musical treatise. Colles's pedantic slip contained implications of a hopelessly atavistic technique – and, for a time, it stuck to the whole Pastoral movement. It was widely repeated, to the general consternation of Vaughan Williams and his supporters. Its author must have agonised over this casual indiscretion, and he certainly dedicated himself to atoning for it in full measure.

Colles followed Fuller Maitland as editor of the *Grove Dictionary*, the third edition of which appeared in 1929. As with its predecessors, therefore, this new edition was concerned to immortalise English composers and intimately to reflect the ideas and priorities of the Renaissance movement. Colles exploited the opportunity to document and extol the achievements of its 'second wave' – the Folklorist–Pastoral School – since the previous edition of 1904–10. His entries included essays on, among others, Sharp, Butterworth, Allen and Vaughan Williams. The last-named was given eulogistic treatment: he was portrayed as a democrat who 'lived among the people' on his folksong-collecting expeditions; as the leader of the young men, of whom so many had been lost in the war; and as a musician who 'refused to be bound by material restrictions'. In a carefully chosen image – appropriate to the composer of *A Sea Symphony*, and now the skipper of the good ship Renaissance – Colles claimed that Vaughan Williams's music 'holds the attention in a distracted age as the work of one who has admitted no distraction from his course, and who steers "for the deep waters only"'(Colles 1927–8: V, 463).

The 1920s thus saw Vaughan Williams becoming more and more revered as the 'national' composer. *Songs of Praise* was published by Oxford University Press in 1925. It was intended to provide a 'national collection' which drew on English poets and musicians, regardless of their faith. As with the earlier *Hymnal*, it was a stunning success. It went into an enlarged edition in 1931, was adopted widely in schools, and the BBC drew on it regularly for religious broadcasting. Folksongs and tunes from contemporary composers were skilfully blended (Kennedy 1964/71: 187–8).

Hardly less important was the *Oxford Book of Carols* (1928), edited like the *Songs* by Vaughan Williams, in collaboration with Martin Shaw. No effort was spared in the preparation. The texts were worked on by G. K. Chesterton, A. A. Milne and Walter de la

Mare; carols collected by Sharp, Vaughan Williams and others were included; and new tunes were commissioned from Holst, Warlock and Rutland Boughton. It was here that Vaughan Williams introduced the tune 'Greensleeves', which he had first encountered in an obscure publication of 1584. In the popular mind, there is no more potent musical expression of English pastoralism than this simple and pure melody. Thus the Tudor revival and its overtones of a rural utopia reached out to the masses. To the book as a whole 'the modern revival of carols is in great measure due' (1964/71: 197). Together, these collections provided a source of propaganda for a new generation of radio listeners, as the *Hymnal* had done for an earlier generation of churchgoers.

Like Parry, Vaughan Williams, though a firm agnostic, was prepared to write works reflecting the credo of the state religion. His *Te Deum*, for example, was written for the enthronement of Dr Cosmo Gordon Lang as Archbishop of Canterbury in 1928. Many other works illustrate his conviction that English Christianity was part of the historic fibre of the nation, and that its traditions and liturgy provided both fundamental emotional centre and unifying ethical and social cement. Although Vaughan Williams was generally hostile to the notion of accepting honours, he did consent to the award of the Order of Merit in 1935 – thereby joining an elite group of twenty-four individuals honoured for their achievements in art, literature, science or war. It was fitting, given Vaughan Williams's role as unofficial musical laureate, that the vacancy within the ranks of this most exclusive of honours was created by the death of Elgar.

By the end of the 1920s, the Folksong School seemed all powerful, its dominance guaranteed for many years to come. It was making new converts all the time – for example Gerald Finzi, who met Vaughan Williams in 1928. Among musical opinion-formers, too, the pastoralists gained adherents. Perhaps the most important of the latter was Frank Howes, Colles's assistant at *The Times*. Howes as editor of the *Folk-Song Journal* was a committed supporter of the Pastoral School. On Colles's death, he duly succeeded to the senior post in Printing House Square. Howes was recruited to the staff of the RCM in 1938, and subsequently produced several standard works on English music history, including studies of Byrd (1928), Vaughan Williams (1954), and – towards the end of his life – a retrospective survey entitled *The English Musical Renaissance* (1966).

Yet there were those who found the Pastoral Muse insular and stifling. While prepared to affirm the importance of a native creative element, composers like Walton and Berners dissented from its 'nationalist' content. Not for them the security of the 'historical–pastoral', with its 'folky-wolky modal melodies on the cor anglais' – as one young radical, Elizabeth Lutyens, put it (Harries and Harries 1989: 53). Theirs was an internationalist outlook, an overtly challenging temper – much more in keeping with the experimental mood of the 1920s – which sought inspiration in the contemporary and 'modern', and which consistently distanced itself from the failed politics, the failed values and (therefore) the failed music of the pre-war establishment.

Nothing that Vaughan Williams and his supporters might stand for prevented Stravinsky from having a sensational impact on the London musical scene. He was the epitome of the rebelliousness which was so important to the 'Lost Generation'. Walton's friend Siegfried Sassoon captured the hedonistic violence which Stravinsky represented in his *Concert-Interpretation: Le Sacre du Printemps*:

> Lynch the conductor! Jugulate the drums!
> Butcher the brass! Ensanguinate the strings!
> Throttle the flutes
> [...]
> Stravinsky's April comes
> With pitiless pomp and pain of sacred springs.
>
> (Reeves 1962: 102–3)

Alongside Stravinsky there were other important influences: the new language of jazz, and the fertile musical life of France – especially Ravel, Satie and *Les Six*. It was a new and promiscuous mixture of the tendencies so excoriated by the Renaissance in the pre-war years – the neurotic Russians, the decadent French and the frivolous, degenerate – and, above all, Black – music of the Americans. Improved transport and communications had opened the floodgates. The moral high-ground which Grove and Parry had gained, and which Vaughan Williams now so benignly occupied, seemed in danger of being inundated by a rising tide of alien culture. For many, the appeal of the 'made-in-England' Pastoral School was enhanced by this siege mentality. Sir Alexander Mackenzie spoke out in an interview in the *Musical Times*: 'I can't help thinking that since the musical free trade we are supposed to enjoy at present is almost entirely on one side, we might do worse than put the protection screw on for a while' (Anon., *MT*:1924). As early as 1929, Robin Hull, though a supporter of the movement, tolled a passing-bell for folksong in the same journal: 'It appears that the more extravagant phases of the folk-song revival in England are now at an end ... It has been exalted to a position it was never intended to occupy ... and it may be only a matter of time before the present exponents recover their sense of proportion' (Hull, *MT* 1929).

Consequently, by 1930, even the main champion of the Pastoral was being tempted to explore new pastures. Vaughan Williams's *Job* was a partial concession to the foreign genre of ballet – although it was subtitled 'A Masque for Dancing', set in the English landscape and incorporated old English dance forms. Its harmonic language anticipated the obsessively harsh *Symphony No. 4*, premiered in 1934, which for many musicians and music-lovers revealed a frightening metamorphosis of 'Uncle Ralph' into an 'Igor Hyde' who had throttled his flutes and might even ensanguinate his whole orchestra.

Radio to make us musical

> This is the most hopeful moment for British Music since the death of Purcell. My reasons for this assertion are partly based on the special promise of the present and partly on the general promise of the past ... Our past history shows us to be at heart a musical nation. (Percy Scholes in *Tristram RT*: 070324)

The British Broadcasting Corporation first went on the air in November 1922. The early years were a time of experimentation for technology and programming alike, but it was clear from the outset that music would have an important position. For the musical world, the advent of broadcasting presented a challenge greater even than that of the gramophone. At first, the establishment looked on it as a competitive rather than a complementary aspect, or even a potential ally, of its concerns. Indeed, for most of the interwar period, there was apprehension that radio would effectively destroy 'live' music; throw musicians out of work; create a nation of 40 million passive listeners rather than music-makers; and, in its wide use of recorded material, reinforce the deleterious effects of the gramophone. The result was that, at first, no concert promoter would co-operate with the BBC. The powerful publishing houses also felt themselves threatened. The music business, in short, saw the BBC as an alternative centre of power and influence, which enjoyed the unfair advantage of government subsidy through a national radio licence fee. The BBC was not a profit-making venture, and its only commercial responsibility was a return on initial capital invested by wireless manufacturers in setting up its technology base. It was nothing less than a state monopoly in culture, and especially in music, seen by some as a 'ministry for music'.

These fears were intensified by the fact that the BBC's ambition was on a grand scale. By 1925, it appeared an unstoppable force, with its projected revenue of £500,000 and a network of twenty-one stations which would have 80 per cent of the population within 'crystal range of some station' (Anon., RT: 130325). While acknowledging some of the reservations of the musical world, BBC staff were eager to grasp opportunities. Their programme was potentially the answer to the prayers of all those who had battled long and hard for an Art Music worthy of the nation. Therefore, the heirs to the founding fathers of the Musical Renaissance had no choice but to bid for influence with the founding fathers of this new era of publicity and patronage.

For its first sixteen years the BBC was managed by John Reith, who had no connections with music. In 1923, Reith appointed Percy Pitt – a successful composer and conductor – as music adviser. The Leipzig-trained Pitt also stood somewhat outside the central Renaissance networks. His career had developed in the areas of commercial performance and theatrical administration, as opposed to those of teaching and scholarship, mainly at the Queen's Hall (in the Wood–Newman era) and generally in the London opera milieu. At the time of his BBC appointment, he was artistic director of the British National Opera Company (BNOC). Consequently, BNOC performances at Covent Garden were among the first live relays carried by the BBC – a perverse (if entirely characteristic) decision to prioritise a visual genre on an aural medium. Yet anti-operatic prejudices were still entrenched in certain quarters. Compounding these difficulties, Pitt had a strong commitment to modern music, particularly of continental origin. Contrariwise, the music establishment was coming to identify itself with a crusade for a very different national music. Accordingly, there were mixed feelings when Pitt was appointed music director in 1924.

During his six years in post, with the full co-operation of Reith, Pitt placed music on a firm footing. In terms of personnel, he sought to appoint like-minded assistants, such as Schoenberg's pupil Edward Clark. He took the decision to promote the BBC's public concerts, featuring well-known musicians, and he consistently expanded performance resources. Pitt's long connection with Henry Wood enabled him to negotiate for the Promenade Concerts from the Queen's Hall to be broadcast, starting in 1927 (Kennedy 1987/89: 137–8). One of Pitt's closest allies was Percy Scholes, who became the *Radio Times*'s music critic in 1923.

The late-1920s was a time of intense debate about music within the BBC – a debate reflected in the pages of the *Radio Times*. The crucial issues centred on whether broadcasting would enhance or destroy the nation's music. To win over the critics, and to reassure listeners, the BBC claimed to be 'the largest concert organisation in the world'; underlining the point, the *Radio Times* announced that it would be publishing concert notes as a feature in every edition (Anon., *RT*: 241126). It managed to attract a number of well-known musicians into the propaganda battle. The pianist Benno Moiseiwitsch contributed a piece entitled 'Radio to Make Us Musical'. He emphasised the BBC's educational function and the benefits it held for music. He also stressed the inspiration of studio playing, and backed the idea of 'more cooperation between concert agencies, promoters and the broadcasting authorities' (Moiseiwitsch, *RT*: 061125). Though this hardly met the case as far as South Kensington was concerned, W. H. Hadow, a Renaissance grandee (and member of the Crawford Committee, which had recommended the setting up of the BBC – see Linsay 1926), wrote two articles which set out the advantages of music broadcasting (Hadow, *RT*: 040227, 110227). It can be sensed in Hadow's pieces that the establishment was already moving in on its prey.

Pitt wished to combat the innate conservatism of the audience, by mixing in some contemporary music with the repertoire of well-known 'classics'. To that end, Bartók and Stravinsky were given an exposure hitherto denied them in this country. Scholes supported this approach both in his broadcast talks and in the *Radio Times*. There was, however, much opposition to the broadcasting of contemporary music. The issue came to a head in 1927, when Scholes took on his critics with a (seemingly) light-hearted piece entitled 'Is Bartók Mad – or Are We?' He chided listeners for their inability to give 'ultra-modern music' a fair hearing: 'Surely our musical sympathies are pathetically limited ... I believe that Bartók is a great composer ... *the human ear is a very conservative member*' (Scholes, *RT*: 091227, our emphasis). This article, in turn, had to be defended. 'On no issue is public opinion more sharply divided than on that of Modern Music ... [and it] drew to the Editor thousands of letters from listeners in every part of the country' (Scholes, *RT*: 180528). Radio was to make us musical – that had been already decided; but with what kind of music? The music-loving public and the establishment – including the BBC establishment – was divided.

The Renaissance, since its origins, had sought to arbitrate the direction and tastes of music in England, and it could not remain outside the struggle for long. Its view was that modern music was in an anarchic and highly disruptive phase. Scriabin, Bartók and Schoenberg were variously regarded as morbid and neurotic, and certainly as 'cosmopolitan'. For the BBC to promote them in the teeth of public rejection was a development which threatened to discredit music as a whole. Apart from any specific stylistic issue, since music was to move away from the concert rooms and into the living-rooms of the nation, South Kensington wanted to be much more closely involved in the BBC and its policy-making.

Accordingly, the Renaissance intensified its attempts to secure influence in the BBC. Apart from Hadow's involvement in the Crawford Committee, the first advance came when Walford Davies joined the dozen or so members of the Music Advisory Committee in 1924. Allen was soon drafted on to the same body (1927), and, in 1928, he was joined by Adrian Boult. When, in the following year, Pitt reached the mandatory retirement age of 60, he read about his 'forthcoming resignation' in a newspaper. A few months earlier, Scholes had resigned from the *Radio Times*. South Kensington, in its own inimitable way, had already smoothed the path for their man to replace Pitt as music director (Kennedy 1987/89: 139). Musical opinion was swift to point up the significance of Boult's appointment:

> The BBC is in a parlous condition. All its best people are leaving it ... Influence is as powerful at the BBC as elsewhere. Music is mostly run in England ... by the academies, the head of whom is Sir Hugh Allen ... He seems to think that no musical good can come out of England except through the academies and the universities. He likes pleasant young men with Oxford voices ... The rise of Mr Boult is typical. (Kennedy 1987/89: 140)

Boult took up his duties in May 1930. He was a dynamic presence from the start, creating the BBC Symphony Orchestra in his first year and combining the posts of conductor and music director. His policy – remarkably consistent on the whole – was to perform music that was held to be important, regardless of his own preferences (1987/89: 157). Boult's relations with Sir Thomas Beecham – then Britain's most celebrated conductor – were poor, understandably, in view of Beecham's contempt for Boult as a representative of the Renaissance establishment. This schism had artistic implications throughout the 1930s, as, for example, when Beecham made sure that Boult was never to conduct at the Covent Garden Opera. Of Beecham, Boult later wrote (1987/89: 154): 'Somehow I used to find him absolutely repulsive both as a man and as a musician, and his treatment of people I knew … so absolutely beastly that his complete neglect of me didn't seem to matter a bit'.

Partisanship did not end there. Frank Bridge had been widely canvassed for the BBC conductorship, having recognised credentials as composer, conductor and performer. Bridge's attitude to the Renaissance and the RCM was not dissimilar to that of Elgar thirty years earlier, holding it to be both parochial and overly academic. In return, he was 'persona non grata as far as the RCM and BBC hierarchies were concerned' (1987/89: 156). Bridge and his many supporters – not least the young Benjamin Britten – were intensely disappointed at his being passed over.

Despite the voices of critics, under Allen's leadership the Goodly House established a vitally important annexe in Portland Place. But it was Boult who brought English Music firmly into the mainstream of broadcasting. Not least important was the part that he played in bringing Elgar somewhat closer to the Renaissance after his years of alienation. Boult was the instigator of the important 1920 revival of Elgar's *Symphony No. 2*. Relations between them were such that Elgar successfully proposed Boult for membership of The Athenaeum in that same year – with Hugh Allen seconding (1987/89: 102). The connection tended to underscore Boult's mediating presence between Elgar and South Kensington – despite the fact that Allen was known to refer to *The Dream of Gerontius* as 'the Nightmare' (Kennedy 1964/71: 240).

Boult's influence lay behind the important seventy-fifth birthday celebrations for Elgar of 1932 in which the BBC took the lead, which in turn led to the commissioning of a third symphony,

at a time when the BBC had not properly thought-through its
policy in this area. The Elgar commission, however, was not quite
unique in the BBC's early years. The first recorded commissioning
approaches were made to Bantock and Holst, in 1927. This was a
typical attempt to be even-handed, since one was an 'insider' and
the other an 'outsider' in Renaissance terms (BBCC R27/55/L:
190330). In 1930, an idea was canvassed for 'something in the
nature of a Nobel prize for music' – an annual award of £100 for
the best British composition of the year. Boult was 'thoroughly in
favour', but nothing came of the idea (BBCC R27/55/L: 270330).
Later that year, concerted plans were made to commission works,
and negotiations began with Walton, Lambert and Victor Hely-
Hutchinson. This project was to take into account the limited
audio technology (no more than fifteen musicians) and should
'appeal to the masses irrespective of the actual music' (BBCC
R27/55/L: 111130). After protracted exchanges, all three composers turned the proposal down. Not until 1937 and the Coronation of George VI, did the BBC finally manage to commission
music which was incontrovertibly its own. During Boult's first
years, therefore, the Corporation was an uncertain, though potentially lavish, patron.

During 1933, the BBC's music policies came in for sustained criticism from various quarters – including *The Times*, the *Daily Telegraph* and the *Observer*. The most serious assault was delivered by
Harvey Grace, editor of the *Musical Times*. In a hard-hitting article,
Grace complained of a dearth of live performances of 'serious'
music, and a corresponding excess of record recitals and relays from
'cinemas, dancehalls, restaurants and hotels'. He went on to attack
the prevalence of repetition and the deficiencies imposed by the
alleged technical shortcomings of radio as a medium for Art Music
– as, for instance, when the *Ride of the Valkyries* was given by 'six
fiddlers and a pianist'. This was indefensible at a time of 'economic
collapse' and rising unemployment among musicians. Turning to
musical education, Grace asserted that the BBC had 'never really
tackled this question. Its policy throughout has been half-hearted.'
What was surely one of the most expressive grace-notes ever penned
ended with a plea for more consensus:

> Musicians feel cold-shouldered by the BBC ... Too little use seems to
> have been made in an advisory capacity of the heads of the profession

... Under the existing regime the musical future of the country is in the hands of an unrepresentative body, to which additions may be made on grounds of influence rather than merit. (Grace, *MT* 1933)

The BBC defended itself vigorously, publishing a series of well-argued articles and figures which demonstrated that its support of British Music was (in relative terms) far greater than that of any other domestic music-making organisation (Anon., *RT*: 140733, 210733, 280733). Nevertheless, the attacks had struck home, for in the mid-1930s, the BBC intensified its coverage and analysis of British music, more generally conceived, in the *Radio Times*.

On top of everything, by 1934 Boult's policies were coming under attack from his own erstwhile power-base, the Music Advisory Committee. Chaired by Reith himself, this body included Allen and McEwen, the heads of the two London academies; Sir Landon Ronald, conductor and principal of the Guildhall School of Music; the director of programmes (and Beecham supporter) Roger Eckersley; Sir Walford Davies, who that year succeeded Elgar as Master of the King's Musick; and Boult himself. The general feeling was that Boult was too inclined towards contemporary continentals. A complicating factor was that the BBC's charter was due for renewal in 1936, and the Ullswater Committee was charged by the Government to review the Corporation's performance over its first decade. When Boult gave evidence to the Ullswater Committee in 1935, he defended his record. Not sparing the blushes of his senior colleagues on the committee, he asserted that his aim was

> to guide musical opinion [and] give the public the great classics together with such novelties as we consider of prime importance ... [We place] a high value on the disinterested advice of the senior members of the music profession, but I seldom get that advice from the Music Advisory Committee, of which Sir Hugh Allen, Sir John McEwen and Sir Landon Ronald are all members. (Kennedy 1987/89: 175–6)

However, this did not prevent the actual succession of Allen to the chair of the Advisory Committee in 1936 – an appointment which considerably strengthened South Kensington's influence on music broadcasting. But the central debate of the 1880s over contemporaneity and popularity remained, if now projected to involve public attention on a far wider scale: how 'modern' should British music be? – how 'modern' could it be?

By the 1930s, the film industry and popular music were powerful forces with the 'common man' – a concept which held a new and enhanced influence. The notion that culture could be handed down to the ignorant but grateful masses was under pressure: the Great War; the diversification of the mass media; the ferment in the arts; the spread of socialism and the general dislocation of the times – all made for uncertainty about the nature and the value of 'High Culture'. Many feared that the Musical Renaissance might see its gains wiped out by the explosion in popular music – as easily as the world's wealth had been by the Depression. Jazz, 'swing', 'variety' and 'the musical' were all making huge advances with a public that turned avidly to inexpensive entertainment to help cope with difficult lives. Furthermore, those institutions which in Victorian times had sustained 'improving' music and provided a foundation on which the Renaissance could build – the choral festivals, the oratorio tradition and the competition festival movement – were in terminal decline.

Edwin Evans of the *Daily Mail*, defender of contemporary music, bewailed what he referred to as the 'Great Schism' between 'classical' and 'popular' music: 'I regard that estrangement between these two worlds, which are really one, as the greatest calamity that has ever befallen the art of music' (Evans, *RT*: 260735). In fact, the BBC had taken the lead in the work of divisive taxonomy which both mass demand and competitive supply seemed to make necessary. Between them, Pitt and Scholes foisted upon the music schedules of the BBC different (subordinate) categories of 'light' or 'light classical' music, which had previously been unknown. Scholes set himself to make appropriate definitions in the *Radio Times* with a series of *obiter dicta*. This procedure was of multiple convenience. It made programming easier, allowed the BBC to claim a proselytising role for 'serious' music, and also provided a suitably reduced role for certain composers (Ketèlby, Coates) who were genuinely popular but could not be allowed to appear alongside Holst and Vaughan Williams. During the earliest programmes it had not been unusual to find a Mozart quartet sharing concert space with a Kreisler hit or even a 'sentimental ballad'. In the late 1920s such miscegenation ceased, almost abruptly.

Consequently there were increasingly bitter exchanges between the champions of 'high-brow' and 'low-brow', accompanied by disputes inside the ranks of the former. For many, Elgar remained the incomparable champion of British greatness, with all its myriad nostalgic connotations. One of his most illustrious devots was T. E. Lawrence ('Lawrence of Arabia') who had met the composer through G. B. Shaw. In a letter of his last years, Lawrence wrote to the composer and confessed: 'I have liked most of your music – or most that I have heard – for many years; and your 2nd. Symphony hits me between wind and water' (HWRO 705 445/1053: 121032). Elgar, for Lawrence and many others, still represented beauty and 'expressiveness' in music, and was to be all the more valued in a decade in which only the Schoenbergian future beckoned.

The Pastoral School on the other hand, stood for the continuities of the Renaissance. It saw itself as occupying a middle-ground in the cultural politics of British music, offering a nationalist prospectus which could also lay claim to certain modernist credentials. Aware of the extent of the problem, Vaughan Williams himself (with *Job* and *Symphony No. 4*) attempted to demonstrate that national and contemporary styles were not incompatible. In E. J. Dent South Kensington had an important ally in the world of contemporary music. Dent was a close friend of both Allen and Vaughan Williams, but also had widespread connections on the continent, and as president of the ISCM did much to advance the cause of modernism in European music. At the same time, he ensured that English Music was fully represented in the annual festivals of the Society, held all over Europe. In 1931, Oxford provided the venue of the Ninth Festival: the BBC Orchestra was heavily involved, and *Job* was given among the selection of contemporary works. Dent's contribution to the Renaissance was to continually coax native music closer to the continental mainstream.

On the whole, Vaughan Williams's *Symphony No. 4* was welcomed by the modernists, although some (rightly, as it proved) were not altogether convinced of his conversion. Edwin Evans greeted it without reserve: 'It is a vigorous, uncompromising work … He has definitely bid adieu to the folk-song influence. His material includes no corduroy tunes.' But Neville Cardus in the *Manchester Guardian* was less sure of the work's credentials: 'I could not … believe that it is likely to be listened to twenty years from today or that it will take its place in the works that enter the mind as an utterance of conviction' (Kennedy 1964/71: 244–5).

Not long afterwards, the administrative stewardship of the Renaissance changed hands, when in 1937 Sir Hugh Allen decided to retire. George Dyson, who inherited the RCM in January 1938, was a challenging choice, made partly in order to justify the radical pretensions of the musical establishment – and one in which Vaughan Williams's hand can surely be detected. Dyson was a man of northern, authentically working-class origins, who had arrived at the RCM as a scholarship student in 1900. Early gifts in composition, coupled with a subsequent career in the upper echelons of the public-school system, were the basis of a solid curriculum vitae. He explained his appointment in his first address to the RCM students as one where 'the first Old Boy has been chosen to be Director' (Dyson 1938: 12). Certainly Dyson, like his predecessor, was appointed more for his RCM pedigree and administrative competence than for any perceived distinction as a composer. The fact that he was a veteran of the Great War and the author of the War Office's manual *Grenade Warfare* (1915) could only have counted in his favour. Of Dyson's musical style, his biographer writes: 'What language does he speak? English, no mistake.' Palmer also argues that:

> There is some kind of received notion of Dyson as an 'academic' composer ... Certainly ... [his work] is very English–traditional, and perhaps best described as a kind of enriched Parry ... Not an original idiom, as Dyson himself was first to admit; but you don't have to be original to compose worthwhile or interesting music. (Palmer 1986: Unicorn/Kanchana UKCD 2013)

In 1940, with the Hun again at the gates, there were obvious parallels with 1914 – and even with 1871 and George Grove's beginnings. But now the island home never had so much of its own music, the better to protect itself in the testing times to come. One way or another, radio had certainly played its part in making us musical, and 'Music While You Work' was just around the corner. Meanwhile, who better than another George – George Dyson – to captain the First XI of the Musical Renaissance? With an expert in grenade throwing in charge, South Kensington and the nation's music would never succumb. Not 'original', but a soldier–director for a time when further 'special services to the nation' were expected.

Parry had been right about those 'special services'. In many ways, the Renaissance had never ceased waging cultural war against enemies within as well as foes without. The Goodly House, like all great fortifications, was designed to have an attacking as well as a defensive function. As a movement, the Musical Renaissance has always had deep within itself an assertive and competitive – even conflict-ual – streak. Yet its main function was to express and confirm what was at once the most profound and most dangerous of all political realities – the nationalism which determined the history of its time, as also of our own. To that extent, the English Musical Renaissance is still with us.

Part II

Aspects of cultural formation

4

Being beastly to the Hun

The chains of colonisation

By the 1970s, it seemed that Britain had completed the fashioning of an independent musical culture. Many claimed the final attainment of that leadership in world music to which the nation had long aspired. To Sir Robert Mayer, a veteran of the campaign, the achievement was 'a miracle' (Mayer 1979: 61(f.). Like many others who believed implicitly in the ethical power of music, Mayer saw it as the consummation of a crusade to capture the commanding heights of international morality. Like some earlier writers he identified a 'cultural shift' away from material preoccupations and towards artistic endeavour. It was a comforting notion – seemingly custom-designed to counter the hypothesis of Britain's twentieth-century decline currently being aired in academic and media circles.

> The decline in Britain's political and economic power may coincide with her emergence as musically the most prominent nation. Such counterbalancing phenomena have often happened in past history. I am convinced that Britain's position in the world generally can become unassailable. (Mayer 1979: 48)

Mayer's premiss can be illustrated quantitatively. In the period 1880–1914, Britain fell behind her competitors – above all, Germany – in the race for the modernisation of industrial infrastructures. During the same generation the domestic profile of Art Music and the numbers involved in it, areas long dominated by Germans and other foreigners, improved dramatically (Ehrlich 1989: 235–7). Though Germany strode ahead in what has been called the 'Second Industrial Revolution', British composers began to compete successfully for the attention of British audiences (Nettel 1948: 258). In later years, many of its producers and consumers were satisfied at the exchange; it was felt that outstanding achievement in Art Music helped significantly to enable the process of psychological adjustment to imperial decline. Great Britain had at last shuffled off the grubby coils of political empire, replacing them with an escutcheon of moral grandeur and spiritual authority.

Yet Mayer was himself an immigrant from Germany. He actually hailed from Mannheim, one of the key centres of Germany's musical heritage. In the late eighteenth century Mozart and his contemporaries had been astonished at the technical proficiency of the Mannheim Orchestra, with its dynamic acoustic, the so-called 'Mannheim Rocket'. Britain had Stephenson's *Rocket* – an equally kinetic symbol of its lead in the Industrial Revolution. But, in time, Germany forged ahead on the ringing rails of economic change; and, moreover, left Britain lagging far behind in the increasingly resonant zone of musical development. Even in mid-twentieth century, Mayer could be seen as a missionary, a colonial representative, bringing music from its fountainhead to *Das Land ohne Musik* – 'The Land Without Music' – as his adopted country was often characterised in that from which he had fled. Indeed, Mayer's use of the word 'miracle' has an ambiguity which hardly flatters the native element in the English Musical Renaissance. It suggests a certain surprise on Mayer's part that such primitives should have successfully adopted the discourse of German culture – in the same way as Britons once marvelled at productions of Shakespeare in India, or at English-language novelists from the African ex-colonies winning a Nobel prize.

At the close of the Victorian age, two British journalists, experiencing a 'patriotic desire to record the achievements of British workers in the field of musical art', published the first *British Musical Biography*. They announced that 'a country is musical only by the music it produces for itself, not by what it takes from others' (Brown and Stratton 1897/1977: i–ii). Subjected to this acid test, Mayer's memoirs expose the limits of his belief in 'the miracle' – for in practice he regarded the creative aspect of English music as second-rate. No English composer rated a mention in his catalogue of 'greats' (Mayer 1979: 61–2). The publisher and patron, Victor Gollancz – also derived from recent German origins – made little effort to disguise a similar lack of conviction (Gollancz 1964). In 1963, another 'missionary', William Glock, defended his policy as music director of the BBC. He claimed that all periods and styles received an airing; and – 'to begin with the great masters' – reeled off statistics on Mozart, Schubert, Beethoven, Bach, Brahms and Haydn. Meanwhile, Glock set about ensuring that the Schoenbergian revolution (meant by its author to ensure the supremacy of German music for another century) would provide the very foundation of the new specialist Art Music channel Radio 3 (Glock 1963: 4–6; Reich 1971: 130).

The assumptions illustrated here hint at complex contradictions within the project of the English Musical Renaissance, which remain deeply ingrained in its collective psyche. Even today, only a minority of British musicians–musicologists and (for that matter) of the broader 'music-loving' public would consider the composers produced by the Renaissance – say, Elgar, Delius, Holst or Vaughan Williams – as the equals of the German masters. These disabling attitudes illustrate a factor of profound and wide-ranging significance. Despite its acknowledged triumphs, and the hard-edged determination with which it was advanced, the 'Goodly House' was built on sand. Its architects had failed to resolve the structural dilemma imposed by the historical hegemony of German music. This hegemony was enshrined, above all, in an aesthetic discourse, inscribed by German philosophers from Goethe to Adorno, by German musicologists from Hoffman to Schenker, which had achieved the parataxic stature of scripture. It was a grand narrative, constructed solidly around the reputations of the great German Masters, who constituted an apostolic succession from J. S. Bach to Richard Strauss. Indeed, since the English Musical Renaissance had attempted to challenge this discourse on its own terms – linguistically, as it were, from within – its failure is hardly surprising.

The reality of this cultural process should be understood in the historical context in which it began – the era of European nationalism. During this formative period of nation–state assertiveness in every field of human endeavour, English musical culture assessed its own image by reference to the received images of other nations. The tendency towards comparison was elemental and ubiquitous: constant self-audit was necessary to self-definition. The standard of comparison had always been Germany; after 1870 it became the new united Reich. Germany and its musical *Kultur* formed the stone upon which the blade of English Music, that great Excalibur, could be honed – and, ultimately, the enemy against whom it was to be wielded. Indeed, an alternative Wagnerian metaphor might readily replace the Arthurian – for, after all, the first target of Siegfried's *Notung* was the very anvil upon which it had been re-forged.

The increasing tempo of international exchange served to sharpen national competitiveness. In the 1860s, when the founding fathers of English Music were beginning to apply themselves to their task, there was great interest in Italy's struggle for political freedom, which took place (as it happened) mainly against Austro-German domination. Britain was swept by admiration for the heroes of the *Risorgimento*, including the hymnodist of independence, Giuseppe Verdi. The child-prodigy Frederic Cowen wrote an operetta titled *Garibaldi* in 1860, when he was only 8 years old (Cowen 1913: 5). The widespread belief in Grand Opera as a potent agency of national communion and political communication was not a result simply of the Wagnerian episode in the grand narrative. Music in other countries that were (broadly speaking) culturally satellite to Germany now displayed what were widely regarded as *national* characteristics. New genres of Art Music – even in small nations which had barely achieved political independence, like Bohemia and Norway – were apparently founded on 'traditional' song and dance. Dvořák and Grieg excited both public enthusiasm and private envy in Britain. Such figures were portrayed as products of the natural magma of their 'native soil', and as patriots who used this privileged medium to emancipate their art from German hegemony. Like Verdi, they were at once prophets and bards of independence. The use of melodic and rhythmic elements derived from the music of peasant communities carried a revolutionary message about 'national self-determination'. It initiated a centrifugal movement in what had been a centripetal musical universe. Much of the music produced by the emergent national consciousnesses of Europe fed back into the process itself, decorating political aspiration and forti- fying its competitive function. Several nations therefore experienced their own 'musical renaissance' – indeed, with the exception of Spain's, they decisively antedated the English version in chronolog- ical terms.

Nevertheless, commentators rarely saw schools of 'nationalist' composition as worthy of measurement against the established Ger- man canon. When the historian A. J. P. Taylor published his study *The Habsburg Monarchy* (1948) he was admonished by his former Viennese tutor for suggesting that Smetana and Dvořák were the equals of Brahms and Wagner. Impressed by the fact that Professor

Pribram was by then in Britain, a refugee from Nazism, Taylor saw this as 'curious evidence of the German claim to superiority of culture' (Taylor 1948/64: 169). However, most of Taylor's English readers would have agreed with Pribram; and, in private, Taylor himself was a worshipper at the shrine of German music (Taylor 1976). Even Sibelius, a 'nationalist' figure regarded as more substantial than (say) Smetana and Dvořák, is seen by musicologists as operating within the framework of Germanic forms and traditions; the Beethovenian symphony and the Lisztian symphonic poem. Given such attitudes, the egalitarian claims of Elgar and Delius could hardly expect confident promotion. In any case, during the early years of the new century – the epoch leading to the First World War – if any musical leadership alternative to Germany's was emerging, it was offered by *other* world powers, such as Russia or France, rather than by the smaller nations, independent or otherwise (Banfield in Morgan 1993).

Perceptions of German hegemony

A major onslaught against German domination of English musical life appeared in 1911, *Music and Nationalism*, the work of the critic and composer Cecil Forsyth. It came at a time of increasing public suspicion of imperial Germany, during a phase of heightening warfever. The Foreign Office had identified Germany as Britain's most dangerous potential enemy, and the great naval race was in full swing. The ostensible purpose of Forsyth's book was to demand a national opera which would be ruthlessly ethnocentric, banning foreigners from every department, from composing to scene-shifting. He demanded patriotic support from the music-loving public for state endowment, as the only way by which a native opera could achieve permanent establishment. He attacked the compromises made by the commercial opera companies, the apathy of the London bourgeoisie and the indifference of government. But Forsyth's greatest spleen was reserved for the foreign foe – Germany.

Forsyth argued, by means of a language derived directly from that of politics, that musical England was a German colony. It had all the features of an underdeveloped and dependent – even an oppressed – nation: German composers and performers, German standards and tastes, were in occupation of the English musical terrain. The native establishment willingly collaborated with the conqueror.

Sooner or later, asserted Forsyth, John Bull 'will view the idea of German Opera in possession of Covent Garden in much the same light as he now views the idea of the "Nassau" or the "Westphalen" in dry dock at Portsmouth' (Forsyth 1911: 285). Meanwhile, however, the native composer

> is beaten, and beaten not in foreign battle nor in downright civil war, but by his own people in secret and murderous league with their own enemies. How long will it be before we realise the fact that where the foreign musician is there is the enemy? He may come to this island in shoals, but he comes for one purpose only – the money he can take back across the water, and he well knows that the surest way to make his position firm here is to denationalise our music. Whether the foreign composer has been merely the idol of a generation or the repressing force of two centuries, the Englishman has always imitated him ... Bach, Haydn, Mozart, gave themselves with a simple and perfect sincerity to the service of German art, and in doing so made Germany august. But what have they done for us? (Forsyth 1911: 260–8)

Forsyth maintained that all Art Music – even that of Bach – was national music, a conviction evocative of the paranoid atmosphere of his time. What was needed (he proposed) was a resistance movement, a kind of English Music Liberation Front, for 'a nation struggling towards its destiny'. He employed a striking inversion of what most of his readers regarded as the natural order of political things. He identified in England a Romantic yearning for unity and freedom: feelings which his readers would rather have associated with the immemorial sufferings of Germans and Italians. While England was depicted, in the musical context, as a 'have-not' nation, Germany was presented as dominant in power and central in culture, able and willing to block the aspirations of other peoples. This ingenious dialectic had its influence on some of the rising stars of the native firmament – like the ex-Cambridge history student Vaughan Williams. But in forwarding his thesis Forsyth was less subtle. He belted crudely upon a jingoist tocsin, in terms which drew on a new-minted store of English nationalist myth:

> The history which we have is ... the history of a continual struggle between a foreign culture imposed upon us by our own upper classes and a national popular culture ... In this struggle it is noteworthy that, though the foreign composer always won, the Englishman was beaten but never killed; he rose to his feet again, and with a certain doggedness of purpose, renewed the contest, fighting in his old way and with

his old weapons ... Always defeated, he refused, with a curiously sure instinct, to get himself the rapier and light suit of foreign armour with which alone, it might have been supposed, he could fight successfully. Homespun and leather with a good English broadsword were, he knew, the only implements with which he could ultimately win; but what amazes us is his stupidity in not seeing that the condition of his success was that his leather and homespun should be made good and sound and his rusty blade resharpened. (pp. 124–5)

Such imagery recalls legends of King Alfred and Hereward the Wake, the leaders of resistance to earlier invasions. It enlists the language of battle, a deadly confrontation between the Unknown English Composer and his better-equipped Prussian Adversary. And in his demand for state assistance for the struggle, Forsyth crossed the frontier between metaphor and reality. He demanded government intervention in language almost identical to that which any industrial manufacturer and supporter of Joseph Chamberlain would have used in arguing one of the central issues of contemporary politics:

No countries are more completely insular and protectionist in art – and rightly so – than France and Germany ... while here the public seems to glory in maintaining a long string of foreigners who, with their parasites and go-betweens, are all bound together by their mutual desire for English gold and their ill-concealed contempt for the people who supply it. (p. 139)

Forsyth went on to align his thinking closely with that of the Tariff Reform Movement, which – some historians believe – wished to effect a revolutionary alteration in the structure and trajectory of British political culture (Newton and Porter 1988: 15–22). The fundamental explanation for Britain's failure in music was its historical mission of overseas expansion, which siphoned off the nation's energy and diverted attention from the finer things. To Forsyth, it was no accident that the first imperial longings coincided with the passing of Purcell, and that no sooner was the Empire established than Handel inaugurated the age of alien domination. In a bizarre refinement of this idea, Britain's failure was attributed to the national obsession with the sea. The landlocked countries (Germany, Austria, Bohemia), never tempted to waste their spiritual substance in empire building, had produced great musical cultures. Therefore, 'national musical productivity is in inverse ratio to sea-power' (Forsyth 1911: 32–45, 87). The basic desideratum was a 'little England' – a sated imperial power. But other tactics were available in the meantime: the citizen who wished for Britain's greatness in High Art as well as world power had to adopt patriotic priorities. At the psychological roots, this must include a consistently applied determination to 'recognise' the English composer's work as worthwhile, even (it was implied) where it was not. The atmosphere of 'recognition' would produce the necessary structures of material encouragement; in turn, the catalyst of success would eventually produce genuine gold from baser metals (pp. 257–8). The final exhortation was consistent and characteristic:

> We have, unfortunately, always had the imitator with us, and he has produced for us endless imitations of Handel, Haydn, Beethoven ... now he is beginning to turn his attention to Richard Strauss ... But however clever his imitations may be – and they are often diabolically clever – there is in them the seed of death. It is dishonest music; or worse, it is traitorous. (pp. 270–1)

We devote attention to Forsyth's book because of its textual significance in the ideology of the Renaissance. However extreme its vocabulary and bizarre its hypotheses, it expressed what many English musicians inwardly believed or suspected. Forsyth voiced anti-German feelings which were present long before his day, and which flourished for decades thereafter. Yet his advocacy of 'recognition' – as defined above – ultimately vitiates the whole manifesto, since the 'recognition' it inscribes, the 'structured absence' of its whole dialectic, is that English Music is ineluctably inferior to the ruling Austro-Germanic canon. If inadvertently, Forsyth advocated a kind of marxian intervention in history (in order to change it). But he was unable to identify (as modern critics do) the role of genre in issues of hegemony, and he assumed that opera was generically neutral and thus available as a vehicle of counter-cultural expression – a Boudicea's chariot for his time.

A further incongruity in Forsyth's work was that, although he used economic metaphors (particularly those of protectionism), sometimes using the actual slogans employed by industrial barons, what he was selling was a belief in the replacement of material goals by others of allegedly superior value. The march of industry and empire had led England away from its true destiny. To paraphrase a scriptural apothegm often present – if inarticulately – in the minds of writers on English Music, the English people had gained the whole world but suffered the loss of their collective soul. It was this soul which music offered to restore: renaissance equalled salvation. But this too – the teleology of 'music's redemptive power' – was a copyright element of German aesthetic discourse (Dahlhaus 1989). Thus, painful ambiguities of relationship with the Teutonic tradition is a thread which runs through the whole era of the Musical Renaissance, permeating its institutions, its successive schools and coteries, and the attitudes of its foremost personalities. They were constantly renewed, as the twentieth century unfolded, by the flinty history of Germany's political relations with Britain and the rest of the world.

In 1945, during his trial at Nuremberg for complicity in the Nazi conspiracy to wage war for world domination, no less a materialist icon than Hjalmar Schacht, the German arch-mammon – 'financial wizard' and economic enabler of Hitler's rearmament programme – stated his personal beliefs about political power:

> I have always been proud to belong to a nation which for more than a thousand years has been one of the leading civilised nations of the world ... which has given the world men like Luther, Kant, Goethe, Beethoven, to mention only these. I have always interpreted nationalism as the desire of a nation to be an example to other nations, and to maintain a leading position in the field of spiritual and cultural achievement through high moral standards and intellectual attainment. (Schacht 1947: 378)

Schacht's words, based on the irenic philosophy of Friedrich Herder, succeeded in wringing the withers of his judges, and he was acquitted. Schacht was typical of influential Germans who envied and resented Great Britain's maritime tradition and the global political influence that came with it. Conversely, many influential Britons envied and resented German music and the ethical–spiritual influence it mediated.

During the epoch of Germany's challenge for world power such feelings flourished. Versions of it appear in the films made by Powell and Pressburger in the 1940s – explorations of the nature of 'Englishness' arising from a struggle for national survival. *The Life and Death of Colonel Blimp* (1943), a fictional account of Anglo-German relations from the Boer War to the Blitz, gives a prominent role to music as the obvious medium of comparison. In the earliest encounter of the English character (General Candy) with Germany, his young Teutonic contemporaries are portrayed as beer-swilling and quarrelsome – but also as enjoying music – in the students' club. In contrast, the Englishman's life is devoted mainly to hunting, the atavistic passion of a philistine ruling class. Our hero is familiar with only one 'classical' melody (the waltz from *Mignon*), and this because it was the only music available during his regiment's defence of Ladysmith. As the narrative unfolds, and the walls of the Englishman's den fill up with the heads of every animal it is possible to shoot, the German character who fulfils the role of his 'opposite' is captured during the First World War. Visiting the latter in a PoW camp at the end of hostilities, Candy discovers him among a crowd of German officers listening intently to a performance of Schubert's 'Unfinished' symphony. But his orderly refuses to disturb him. Someone is heard to comment: 'These are strange people. They spend centuries writing beautiful music and poetry, and suddenly they start a war. They commit hundreds of appalling atrocities, are defeated, and then they settle down to listen to Schubert and Mendelssohn again.' The point of this remark seems clear. The Germans would have done better to stick to their authentic vocation, music, leaving world politics to the people most experienced in running them – that is, the British.

Thus music was intimately assumed, inside and outside the frontiers of the Reich, to be the *echt*-German medium. Equally certainly – and here Forsyth was astute enough – many prominent musical sons of the Fatherland regarded their vocation not as distinct from their nationality but as an indissoluble part of it. In 1870, explicit celebration of Bismarck's unification of Germany, in the music of composers otherwise as different (indeed, in common perception, opposed) as Wagner and Brahms, caused unease among British musicians. Those who attended Bayreuth for the premiere of *The Ring* cycle in 1876, and heard Wagner's speech in which he donated to the new Germany a new art worthy of its unsurpassed greatness, must have felt that something even more portentous than the *Gesamtkunstwerk* was being inaugurated. Years later, Mayer was hardly alone in pointing out that Germany had always used music as propaganda (Mayer 1979: 31). Yet this could cut both ways, for by that very fact Germany was approachable, and even susceptible to influence. Throughout the course of the English Renaissance, we encounter the argument that music, as an international medium, was the best vehicle of communication, more capable than any other of gaining respect and of promoting Anglo-German fellowship.

By 1900, however, vague notions of escaping from Germanic influence in their creative work began to take hold of composers. Where were the Moses and the Aaron destined to lead the chosen people forth from captivity? It was a trope which, along with other biblical images, was beginning to be formulated in musical circles. What we hereinafter refer to as the 'mainstream' texts (those of Howes, Pirie and Trend) usually define this development as a pulling away from the German centre of gravity. Indeed, it would be feasible to present our whole subject in similarly monothematic terms. In what came to be a favourite metaphor of Ralph Vaughan Williams, the development of national music was the pilgrimage of Bunyan's Christian, whose purer impulses would put the march of Mammon into reverse. To recall Forsyth's preconceptions, we might characterise it as a 'great trek' of a musical people away from German hegemony, on the analogy of the Boers' escape from the increasingly anglophone Cape Province toward the distant *veldt* where their culture could be preserved and developed. But the motives for the exodus are easier to establish than is its essential character. What constituted the wagon train? Which emigrants were welcome on board, and which not? What conception did its leaders have of the promised land? Finally, did they ever reach this utopia?

The Babylonian captivity

If, before 1861, anyone had mused on the fact that the head of the British Royal Family, the Prince Consort, was a German composer, they were tactful enough not to advertise any chauvinistic conclusions. In point of fact, no one could doubt that Prince Albert had stoutly advanced the cause of music in his adopted land. A decade after Albert's death, the astounding military achievements of Bismarck's Prussia had a salutary effect on English Music, as on many other areas of public life. The first agglutinations of the Renaissance's elements – personal and philosophical – took place in the 1860s, and were followed by the forging of links with the government of the day. Ideologues, like other people, sink their personal differences and unite in response to external threat. By the early 1880s, the revivalists, headed by Grove, had generated South Kensington, a designated zone of National Music's productivity, dedicated to the memory of Prince Albert, and modelled after similar concentrations at Berlin and Munich. Grove and his colleagues were well aware how the events of 1870 had changed the parameters of artistic relations with Germany. The superb administrative–military machine which had overwhelmed the French Empire in a few short weeks was organised by men whose main intellectual pastime was the avocation of music. It followed that a strong musical presence was necessary in the new elementary schools set up by Forster's Education Act (1870). In the meantime, John Hullah, an experienced teacher and campaigner for musical education, was sent to investigate the grass roots of German endeavour. His report was so highly regarded that it earned him a resting place in St Paul's, alongside other warriors who have come to the rescue of a nation in crisis (Hullah 1886).

Others were able to observe things in Germany at first hand. Since Mozart's day, English musicians had gravitated towards the Teutonic stars and returned home to bask in their reflected brilliance. Domestic distinction depended on association with a major German figure and/or graduation in one of the main German conservatoires. As Forsyth complained, recognition in Germany was almost the only 'recognition' which mattered. Grove and Sullivan contributed to the further glorification of German music by their rediscovery of Schubert. The earliest speech of the Renaissance 'baby' – in G. B. Shaw's retrospective image – bore an unmistakably Teutonic accent (Laurence 1989: III, 416). This was literally the case, since the Prince of Wales and his brothers publicly uttered the words written for them by Grove in the slight German accent they had acquired from their father and a succession of German tutors. Whatever else may be said of the music of Cowen, Mackenzie, Parry and Stanford, its fundamental structure and morphology was unmistakably that of the Germanic axes: Beethoven–Brahms and/or Liszt–Wagner. Cowen et al. achieved 'recognition' by Germans long before their acclaim of Elgar catapulted an English composer to unique fame. Cowen pioneered the trend when his Scandinavian Symphony was published in Vienna and performed there by Richter in 1882. Subsequently, no fewer than four of Stanford's operas were launched in the Reich. Mackenzie also wrote orchestral works for German performance (Blom 1942: 170). Ethel Smyth actually set her operas in the German language, and gained the reward of three major premieres (Wimbush 1968: Columbia ASD 2400). For his part, Parry seems to have contented himself with submitting everything he wrote for the approval of his

German guru Dannreuther. All these composers spent an important period of their education in Germany.

Stanford's relationship with Germany is also instructive. His 'Irish' symphony (*Symphony No. 3*) achieved popularity there, and a fourth symphony was commissioned by the Berlin Philharmonic. It was first heard at an all-Stanford concert in 1889, along with a *Suite for Violin*, played by Joachim. The event moved Lewis Foreman to ask: '[E]ven 100 years later, what 35-year-old British composer could attract a large audience in Berlin with a one-man programme, and including a major commission and the leading violinist of his day as soloist?' This posits that because Stanford was seen in contemporary Germany as a major creative figure he should be worthy of consideration in that category today (Foreman 1990: Chandos 8884). But use of this argument demonstrates more surely that, when it comes to the confidence of British critics in British music, little has changed since 1884. In any case, in what sense was British Music on offer on that Berlin occasion? Stanford's symphony was, in everything except the explicit sense, an act of homage to Brahms, whose style, harmony and instrumentation is palpable in almost every bar. At several points in the score, the music trembles on the brink of actual metamorphosis into one or other of Brahms's symphonies. Even those Berliners who attended mainly in order to hear Joachim would have been gratified by the progamme's content. They heard nothing that was not familiar from their own environment. The British composer was no threat – on the contrary, his presence was a welcome demonstration that Britain's finest composers were well-trained practitioners of *Kultur*. Meanwhile, German newspapers continued to patronise the British musical scene in another sense: a few months before Stanford's concert, the *Berliner Tageblatt* had carried an article which described Balfe and Sullivan as 'worthy of interest' but everything else as 'depressed and miserable' (Spiegl BBC R3: 010188).

Stanford was aware of being susceptible to the charge of dishonest imitation – a treasonable one in the sense patented by Forsyth (with whom, however, he was later to write a book). Throughout his career he cultivated the popular melody of his native Ireland – or a pale (as it were) Anglo-Irish version thereof – as a conscious counterweight to the heavy Germanic mould in which his music was cast. His six Irish Rhapsodies, incorporating 'folk-tunes', were intended to exploit the market Brahms had discovered for his *Hungarian Dances*, but also attested to his 'national' independence in the British context.

However, his fellow-Protestant Dubliner G. B. Shaw attacked the validity of this technique, which he mischievously reviled as 'Going Fantee' (Laurence 1989: II, 876–83). Stanford never escaped from the Brahmsian stranglehold on his aesthetic. Not long before his death in 1924, he wrote two works which illustrate his dilemma: a *Concert Piece for Organ and Orchestra*, in his 'Brahmin' style, and the last of his Irish Rhapsodies. The former was rejected by no fewer than eight British publishing houses – a fairly comprehensive indication of the opinions of Stanford's peers, who (presumably) acted as publishers' consultants (Anon., BBC R3: 200491). The critic Robin Legge told Percy Pitt, the director of Covent Garden, that 'CVS ought to be ashamed of himself ... If he ... has at 65 to go to a "Charity" to get his stuff printed it seems that he is a bit fly-blown' (BLMC E3305/56v: 280417). Stanford was now regarded, through long association with Germany, as the satrap of an enemy culture. In the aftermath of 'Germany's Grab for World Power', the iconoclastic youth of England's musical life openly despised everything he stood for (Heseltine and Gray 1920–2: II, 47).

Even thirty years earlier, as the Renaissance gathered strength in both its institutions and the press, the dangers of being drawn into the German ambit were brought home to composers. A mutually hostile atmosphere was engendered in the 1890s, when Bismarck's departure removed a rein on the expression of German anti-British feeling, and English journalists responded in kind. An article in *The Strand* attacked German street musicians – the 'German Bands' of cockney rhyming-slang fame. It noted that 'our German friends are happily getting less numerous every year', but warned that they were nevertheless determined to 'fleece the English if they could' (Guerdon 1892). The anticipated reduction in numbers apparently never happened, since the magazine soon took up the cudgels again, surmising that 'the average citizen, asked to define his pet aversion, might conceivably indicate a brass band manipulated by German fingers ... the number with us is probably considerable' (Salmon 1894; 542). In 1914, the young Robert Graves, in charge of rounding up German citizens in the Manchester area, was impressed by the number of bandsmen among his haul (Graves 1929/73: 15, 63–4). Middle-class prejudice was stoked up in the theatre as well as by the press. Gilbert and Sullivan used the Savoy Theatre to poke gentle fun at German humourlessness. This became somewhat less gentle after the humiliating failure of the Berlin production of *The Mikado*.

In 1896, Sullivan's final operetta *The Grand Duke* was advertised by a poster in which the eponymous hero was presented as a caricature of Frederick the Great (Plate 6). Such a move was bound to give offence. The Kaiser's ancestor was venerated in the Reich both as soldier and composer – facts which underline the identity of music and *Machtpolitik*.

In 1908, Ethel Smyth was angling for a production of *The Wreckers* in London. She told Percy Pitt that 'this opera and the songs are in my "later manner" – i.e. absolutely out of the German wood', adding disingenuously: 'I think that I who have fought the good fight for English art abroad as no one else has ... should have first chance here' (BLMC E3096/75: 190308). The latter remark was a swipe at Elgar and Delius, whose recent successes had been precipitated by German approval. Such symptoms of an inferiority complex in English society were mordantly criticised by *The Times*. J. A. Fuller Maitland coldly observed of the first London performance of *The Dream of Gerontius* (1903):

> The important thing in its history was not so much the performances in Germany, but the lavish praise that was bestowed upon it by Herr Richard Strauss, who, no doubt, speaking with an authority based on an exhaustive knowledge of the whole of British music, declared it to be the most original composition that had proceeded from England. It may have been the case that it was under consideration for the Worcester and Sheffield festivals of last year, before this remarkable tribute was paid to it by the German composer; but, whether that were so or not, the public flocked to hear it at both these performances, and it is now a prime favourite, since many who would not venture to express a favourable opinion of anything English on their own account have the satisfaction of feeling that they have the right to admire what has been so warmly praised in Germany. (Nettel 1945/76: 25)

If not exactly *donner und blitzen* by Forsyth's standards, the roar of 'The Thunderer' was still loud enough to be heard in the Reich. Indeed, *The Times* and its proprietor Lord Northcliffe were soon to be identified by the Kaiser as sources of consistently unhelpful comment upon things German (Morris 1984: 13ff.).

A year later, Richard Strauss came to London for his first English festival. It was hugely successful, but the strain of the occasion obliged Strauss to spend the rest of the summer convalescing on the Isle of Wight. In this vulnerable underbelly of England he produced the bellicose cantata *Taillefer*, written for forces enormous even by Straussian

6 Frederick the Great cut down to size: poster advertising Gilbert and Sullivan's *The Grand Duke* (1896)*

standards (Krause 1964: 175, 274; Marek 1967: 143). Uhland's ballad relates how, during the voyage of the Norman invaders to England,
William the Conqueror's troubadour, the eponymous hero of the
work, pleases the duke with his song, and asks for the honour of
setting the first foot on enemy soil. The warrior–composer meets a
glorious death in the van of the triumphant army. The work blares out
the military march 'Ich hat' ein Kamerad' (words also by Uhland).
Given Strauss's proclivities, it seems that he was primarily celebrating
his personal 'conquest' of the English public; but it was also a mission
achieved for the Fatherland. Moreover, it would be surprising, at the
height of the naval race between Germany and Great Britain, if the
massive chorus and audience at performances of *Taillefer* were not put
in mind of challenges more immediate than those of 1066. Indeed, a
British newspaper cartoon of this period portrayed Kaiser Wilhelm as
William the Conqueror, sword upraised, in the prow of a Norman
longship about to land on the Sussex coast: the ominous implication
was that he aspired to the same title as his famous namesake and for a
similar reason (Plate 7).

7 Wilhelm the Conqueror – the English await their fate: Kaiser Wilhelm as
William the Conqueror (from a cartoon by Will David *c.* 1900)*

Around the same time Delius was rehearsing a performance of his *Appalachia* in Hanley, Staffordshire. Upset by the absence of key orchestral players, he reacted in typical – and surely topical – terms: "'Call yourselves an orchestra ... you're no better than a bloody village band." Then, in a voice rising to a scream, he added, "My God, if this country ever goes to war with Germany, what a hiding you will get! You don't know the first thing about organisation'" (Nettel 1945/76: 50).

As far as the practical business of music-making was concerned, any invasion of these islands would have been superfluous to the requirements of *Kultur*. Down to 1914, German music and artists continued in great demand. The Austro-German canon comprised most of the teaching curriculum in London's conservatoires. Faculties were stiffened by first- and second-generation German immigrants who advocated the music and the performing techniques of the *Vaterland*. The content of concert programmes indicated little decline in the appeal of the Austro-German repertoire, despite the efforts of Henry Wood (a 'German Wood' at least in the sense that he modelled his beard on that of the great conductor Artur Nikisch) to encourage home talent. The first all-British Promenade Concert at the Queen's Hall did not take place until the Victorian age had – at least chronologically – passed; and even then (October 1901) its most substantial work was Parry's Brahmsian *Symphonic Variations* (Cox 1980: 48–9).

The programmes of the Philharmonic Society's annual concerts reveal that although the relative proportion of native to German works (i.e. first performances) began to alter in Britain's favour as early as the 1830s, the process was slow. In the 1860s, the two were still evenly balanced, but thirty years later British premieres outnumbered German by four to one. The atmosphere which produced Strauss's vicarious sabre-rattling and Forsyth's jingoism is reflected in the Society's record for the Edwardian period, when thirty-one new British works were put on compared to only two by Germans (Nettel 1948: 258). Despite this, a German pedigree continued to be an advantage for any working musician. Artists with Teutonic names were prioritised by concert promoters, and natives often disguised themselves accordingly (Mackerness 1964: 207–8). Edward Jones dropped his uninspiring surname in favour of a providential secondary baptismal name – 'German'. Imogen Holst recalled her father's memories of this situation from the days when he pumped his trombone in various south-coast resorts, when his name was still 'von Holst' (Holst 1938/69: 15). The most unfortunate case of per-sonification was surely that of the conductor Basil Cameron, who early in his career elected to be known as 'Hindenburg' – an authen-tic *nom-de-guerre* if ever there was one. He was later to be wounded helping to push the *real* Hindenburg back across the Rhine! (Palmer 1946: 52; Mackerness 1964: 220).

These tendencies were more strongly entrenched in the provinces than in the capital. In Lancashire, for example, the German yoke remained firmly in place. Beecham recalled that English musicians contributed nothing worthwhile to the advancement of the Renais-sance cause in the north-west. For Sir Thomas, its whole history can be summed up

> in a single word – Germany. For there was scarcely a town of any size with the slightest musical culture (outside choral singing) that did not owe every ounce of it to some enterprising son of the Fatherland, ama-teur or professional, who had settled there ... Spiritually we were a conquered, or at least an occupied, territory, and over it all reigned [Sir Charles] Hallé. (Beecham 1944:20)

Indeed, Hallé's Manchester heritage ensured that his orchestra remained tenaciously attached to the German canon. This was the case not only in the Free Trade Hall – whose very name proclaimed it a sanctuary of the principles under attack from Forsyth – but in the teaching of the RMCM. Adolph Brodsky, long-serving leader of the orchestra, and Hallé's successor as principal of the College, continued his traditions, under the eye of a new taskmaster, none less than Hans Richter (Nettel 1945/76: 48). Accordingly, forty years after Hallé's death, the orchestra was still far more comfortable in Strauss than in Elgar, while the local educational curriculum for theory and practice was monopolised by the German canon (Burgess 1982: 21–2).

As in composing, teaching and performing, so also in publishing. Before 1914, few London houses were prepared to run the finan-cial risk of issuing British compositions. Unable to gain the neces-sary subsidy, like that afforded the privileged few by private means or patronage, most composers were obliged to look elsewhere, and in practice this meant Germany. Among others, Delius, Holst, Smyth and Scott were taken up by German publishers. Even where London publication was available, the terms were unattractive. Shortly before the outbreak of war, Holst informed the Society of Authors that 'an unknown admirer of an orchestral work of mine called *Beni Mora* has given me £50 to have it published. Orchestral music must be published through a big continental firm – English publishers cannot command sufficient market. So it reduces itself to a choice between Schott's and Breitkopf' (BLMC A56726113: 090614).

The notable exception to these rules was Elgar, who attracted a lucrative contract from Novello, a firm which had long pursued a policy of native patronage. Yet the celebrated art-nouveaux design which adorned Novello scores represents the context within which Elgar's greatness was encased in order to be best understood by purchaser and reader. Until 1914, inscribed on the cover, acting as a sort of framework for Novello scores, were the names of eight German composers (Plate 8). Even Spohr was regarded as more worthy of a place than any non-German master. They were the unchallenged guardians of the art. (Later, to be sure, Spohr and Weber were to be

8 English Music hemmed in by its foes: cover to Novello's *Choral Scores* (1912)*

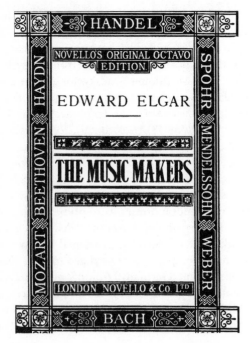

9 The Teutonic gods, guardians of English music's Valhalla: the façade of the National Training School for Music, subsequently the Royal College of Organists (detail), incorporating medallions of Handel, Mozart, Beethoven and Mendelssohn

replaced – by Purcell, and by Elgar himself.) Meanwhile another German sentinel patrolled inside Novello's offices – A. J. Jaeger, who vetted all major compositions submitted to them. Novello's German elite reflects a similar pantheon to be descried on the façade of the first building occupied by Grove's men as staff of the National Training School in 1876 (Plate 9). Even today, J. S. Bach is the only

composer permitted to stand guard in the foyer of the RCM building in Prince Consort Road. His marble bust occupies this unique
representative position just as 'naturally' as does the statue of Shakespeare in the new British Library.

Searching for the true path

As every authoritative source assured them, the Germans of the Wil-
helmine Reich had found their *Sonderweg*, the 'special path' to
national greatness whose essential characteristic was precisely its
immunity to outside influences. Exactly as Wagner preached in *Die
Meistersinger*, the musical world had been an enthusiastic part of this
process (Deathridge 1991). What was to be the 'special path' of English Music? Or, to employ Ethel Smyth's phrase, who could reveal
the way 'positively out of the German wood'?

The leaders of the Musical Renaissance, who concurred in a
hatred of Handel and a wish to marginalise Mendelssohn, were in
a quandary over what to offer worshippers in place of these alien
cults. By definition, their project precluded the option of elevating
any recent Briton to exemplary status – on the contrary, potential
candidates had to be rejected as a premiss of the argument on which
renaissance itself was predicated. For, if 'Great English Composer(s)'
had flourished in the generations before 1860, what need for
a renaissance? Purcell, whose revival was well under way, offered a
safe and distant option as a model from the historical past. But this
promotion was at once inspired and overshadowed by the rediscovery of J. S. Bach, a movement now reaching epic proportions in England (Thomas 1998). Meanwhile, the need for a native *Messiah* – or,
at least, an *Elijah* – became ever-more urgent. Grove's generation
was obsessed by the new German masters, Wagner and Brahms, who
were creating the new musical universe, and whose influence threatened, unless prophylactic measures were taken, to suppress indigenous development just as rigorously as had those of Handel or
Mendelssohn before them. By the 1880s, the decade when the creative aspect of the English Renaissance is held to have begun,
Germany exercised a control of the present and the past of European music which seemed almost absolute.

The gravamen of the charge that even the most eminent English
composers were (at best) expert mimics of the Germans is familiar
from much existing music history. In allocating 'originality' the

nuclear role in the products of genius, British teachers and critics were behaving according to German rules (Dahlhaus 1989). But, even were this not the case, how else were they to behave? British composers' lack of originality, precisely in the German comparative sphere, was documented at the time by G. B. Shaw in a sequence of caustic reviews and essays. Unlike critics such as Joseph Bennett and Francis Hueffer, Shaw took no positive role in the Renaissance. A part of GBS – perhaps the Irish part – seems to have relished the 'land without music' slur, convinced as he was of his own island's superior musicality. His distaste for Schumann and Brahms led him to excoriate their minions (his compatriot, Stanford, with less vehemence than Parry). On the other hand, his passion for Bayreuth failed to inspire sympathy for the Scottish Wagnerites, Mackenzie and Wallace. Yet no one reading his musical criticism today could accuse Shaw of being indifferent to English aspirations, which he clearly regarded as legitimate and ultimately achievable (Laurence 1989).

Seeking a way 'out of the German wood' implied in advance an admission about 'colonial' subordination. All the same, by Ethel Smyth's day it had become a *basso ostinato* of public reflections on the English Musical Renaissance. The first explicit call for a 'national music', inspired by the example of Germany, but free of its language and aesthetic, was made in 1905 by Elgar in his inaugural lecture as professor of music at Birmingham (Young 1968: 22ff.). Elgar's case was strengthened by his innocence of a German education, coupled with the fact that (nonetheless) he was 'recognised' in Germany. But his trumpet sounded an uncertain note. In his lecture, foreign imitation was identified as the root of evil, but only in vague terms. Like Shaw, Elgar was hampered by personal considerations, though in this case the effect was reversed. He implied a disapproval of Stanford, but was careful to praise his other patron (and friend), Parry. With such a flawed weapon, the quarry could only be wounded to anger and retaliation. The political unity of the Renaissance was suddenly under threat, with the potential creation of an alternative ('Midlands') centre of activity. Worse still, Elgar offered no hint of what elements might constitute a national style; nor was any other formal guidance offered, except for the strong recommendation of 'the symphony without a programme' – hardly a decisive pointer away from the genus of Beethoven and Brahms. Their stranglehold was, if anything, confirmed by much of what Elgar said: and one lecture, from a total of only six, was given over entirely to Brahms's *Symphony No. 3*.

Such was the buffetting he received from the press that Elgar quickly surrendered the baton. His successor Granville Bantock never enjoyed sufficient stature to pursue the struggle. All the same, the composers associated with the University and the Midlands Institute in Birmingham felt the burden of this Elgarian legacy. The new generation, represented in this context by Holbrooke, Boughton and Brian, had not been educated in Germany. They attempted to eradicate Germanic elements from their work. In the years before the Great War, Bantock's pupils attracted attention as a 'modernist' group, and aspired towards recognition as a 'national' school. But Bantock himself shortly succumbed to the influence of the new German hero, Strauss (Foreman 1987: 13). Holbrooke's chamber music, for all its striving, remained anchored to the Brahms style. Boughton launched a campaign for an English version of music–drama which – though his music did not sound Wagnerian – remained basically dependent on its Bayreuth exemplar.

Havergal Brian is perhaps the most dramatic case. Born and brought up in a peculiar industrial colony of Germany – Dresden, Staffordshire – he was in many ways a product of *Kultur*. German art demonstrated its power not only in capturing the ruling class – who imbibed the gospel in Germany itself and again at the feet of their teachers in London – but in subordinating this son of a pottery-worker in the provinces. Living as he did through the whole period of British musical revival (1876–1972), Brian remained a fervent admirer of German philosophy and literature. He taught himself to read German, as a natural accessory to the language of music itself; his 'mind-forged manacles' were palpable. Many of Brian's works were inspired by his vicarious experience of Germany (MacDonald 1974). Yet he began as a disciple of Elgar and a patriot. His early orchestral music reveals a personality able to resist – at least more stoutly than did Bantock – the Straussian seduction. It was saturated, too, with the atmosphere of military readiness, in the wake of the Boer War and the approaching confrontation with Germany. In 1910, Brian wrote a large-scale funeral march, *In Memoriam*: 'at the peroration', a phrase from *Deutschland Über Alles*, is used three times, with an emphasis which now seems deliberately prophetic. Though arguably more independent of German models than any English contemporary, Brian was never to lead a column forward on the 'great trek': his father's Black Country pots, among other factors, lacked the cultural connotations of RVW's Wedgwood antecedents. Brian enjoyed a brief spell of success, and thereafter was gradually pushed into obscurity. Yet, in some ways, Brian was much more the 'unknown warrior' of English Music than its official martyr, Butterworth.

Brian may be set at one end of the spectrum, Stanford at the other. But they were not the only composers to suffer the backlash which came after the Armistice of 1918. Elgar entered a difficult period, in which he too was characterised, *inter alia*, as an exponent of Germanic principles – a charge rather confirmed than otherwise by the style of the chamber-music works he composed around this time. Even Sir Edward's most redoubtable champion failed to banish such sentiments from his mind. Elgar's fame dated from a period after Shaw had given up music criticism; and, for many years, the latter published no opinion on the former. Perhaps stimulated by public indifference towards his *Symphony No. 2*, perhaps by reading Forsyth, in 1911 Shaw suddenly stepped forward to accord Elgar his personal 'recognition'. 'I consider', he imperiously informed the editor of the *Morning Post*, 'that the history of original music [in England], broken off by the death of Purcell, begins again with Sir Edward Elgar' (Laurence 1989: I, 19–20). After the war, during which Elgar had worked hard for the national cause, Shaw again hailed the composer of *Fringes of the Fleet* as 'the figurehead of music in England' (Laurence 1989: III, 721). Yet even in his song of praise a counter-text poked awkwardly through. Shaw frequently compared Elgar with the German masters, and recorded the Englishman's indebtedness to them as an assay-mark of quality.

> Music wrote itself on the skies for him and wrote itself in the language of Beethoven.
>
> [...]
>
> When Elgar startled us by suddenly reasserting the British character in music, he did it in an idiom which was no more distinctively English than the idiom of Schumann.
>
> [...]
>
> Elgar followed Beethoven and Schumann, and [thus] secured his niche in the temple. (Laurence 1989: III, 533, 717, 723)

The inescapable cultural bind of the Renaissance project thus produced an insecure discourse, which arose – according to the precepts of Arnoldian criticism – from the perceived character of the musical artefacts themselves. Basil Maine, one of Elgar's staunchest champions during the debate sparked off by E. J. Dent's later attack, was, it seems, congenitally predisposed against ranking the English composer alongside the Germans. In 1937, Maine praised the Promenade Concerts for bringing music to the masses: that is, 'the great masterpieces, all Wagner, all Mozart, all Beethoven ... all Brahms, all Bach, all Haydn ... all Schubert' (Maine 1945: 102). Elgar evidently did not belong in such company, any more than did the most obscure of his compatriots. From this perspective it seemed that the English musical establishment of the inter-war years – Henry Wood, the BBC, opera and ballet companies, orchestras and teaching institutions, the Goodly House of Renaissance, filled with multifarious talent and energy – (all this) existed, as far as Maine and many others were concerned, primarily in order to advance the transcendental claims of German art.

Yet from the slough of despond had already emerged a new group of prophets proclaiming an 'authentic' English style. This 'national music' was founded on folk-music. At first, this solution was not acclaimed by everyone. 'Silly as these people are', commented Shaw, in 1910, on his old stalking-horse, the English musical public, 'they only need plenty of opportunities of hearing good music, especially real English music like Elgar's (not sham English music produced by simply writing in the old dance forms)' (Laurence 1989: III, 630–1). The allegedly traditional forms being adopted by scholars and younger composers were, to Shaw, just as 'fantee' as anything of Stanford. Elgar himself rejected claims that folksong was indispensable to a national language, with the notoriously Bourbon remark: 'I am folk music' (Trend 1985: 31). In contrast to Shaw, later chroniclers of the English Musical Renaissance accepted the folk-music movement, on its own terms, as the authentic and unique answer to the great riddle. Here (they say) is the path which leads forth from captivity; it may be narrow and difficult, but it is straight and true. Premiss led to conclusion: 'the actual emancipation of our national music from bondage to the continent, the potential foundation of an English national school of composition, was the work of two composers, RVW and Gustav Holst' (Howes 1966: 230).

Howes's heroes were acutely conscious of the need to purge their work of Teutonic elements. Identification of new music with the material essence of England – the local habitations and the names – seemed an essential first step. Holst's *Cotswold Symphony* was produced as early as 1900, while RVW planned a series of 'Norfolk rhapsodies'. However, although using 'traditional' tunes, this music represented no advance on the techniques of Liszt and Dvořák, any more than had that of Stanford, their teacher at the RCM. Then came the encounter of the two composers with Sharp, and their 'field trips' to collect folksongs in East Anglia. Yet such 'low' folk material stubbornly resisted transmutation into a national High Art. A frustrated Holst sought instead the non-European experience favoured by other artists, and – vicariously at least – pursued the fad of Orientalism as far as India and the Sanskrit sagas. Equally desperate, RVW headed for Paris, seeking the tutorship of Ravel, and what he was later to characterise as 'a little French polish':

> I came home [he added] with a bad attack of French fever and wrote a string quartet which caused a friend to say that I must have been having tea with Debussy ... But I was quite incapable of inventing Ravel's *nouvelle harmonies* ... I usually feel content to provide good plain cooking ... My French fever soon subsided. (Vaughan Williams 1912/50: 34–6)

RVW was already in his mid-30s, three years older than his tutor. His decision reflected the *entente cordiale* by which France and Great Britain began to draw together on the plane of international politics in the face of a common danger from Germany. Other radical students of his generation had made contact with French culture, partly as a sympathetic response to the underdog following the calamity of 1870. Shortly after returning from Paris, RVW began to produce works which sounded fresh and, above all, English, to many ears. With *On Wenlock Edge* and the *Fantasia on a Theme of Thomas Tallis* (both 1909) he gave the signal for the 'great trek' to get under way. Nevertheless the English Pastoral style was not due to a single source of generation. Deryck Cooke (1982: 116–22) suggested that Delius (with *Brigg Fair*, in 1908, and *On Hearing the First Cuckoo in Spring*, 1912) was its chief begetter; though Delius was arguably more German than English (Stradling 1989). Several of the composers known as 'the Frankfurt Gang' were strongly attracted to English folksong. As this categorisation suggests, they were German-trained (Lloyd 1984: 34f.). One of them, the Australian-born Percy Grainger, experimented intensively with the use of folk materials, with results markedly different from those of the mainstream. Much of his output was free of German influence to an extent arguably never attained by any English contemporary. At the same time, Arnold Bax, saturated with German precepts by his professors at the RAM, was producing music inspired by Irish folk-song, which took the techniques of textural assimilation further than any other composer.

Little of this is of great importance for the prevailing narrative conventions. Apart from those placed by RVW and Holst, the only foundation-stone acknowledged by music historians is that of George Butterworth – his Housman song settings, and two orchestral poems, *A Shropshire Lad* and *The Banks of Green Willow*. The second of these was premiered by the famous German conductor Nikisch, just before the war that sundered the links between English and German musicians. Most critics accept that Butterworth achieved an idealisation of idiom never surpassed by later exponents of the English Pastoral style. But equally important in the reification of this style was Butterworth's symbolic significance as hero and martyr. The handsome young genius was the musical equivalent of Rupert Brooke for a music-conscious generation. Cecil Sharp's 'favourite son', with the brave new world of High Art at his feet, sacrificed himself in the struggle against Germany, leading his men forward into the crucible where the Anglo-German *Kulturkrieg* was reaching its awful culmination – the battlefield of the Somme.

Culture wars

For much of the twentieth century, the British people's existence was dominated by the experience of war with Germany. The sacrifice and the suffering touched every citizen, and helped to structure our collective mentality. Narration of its modes has assumed that universal binary form which sustains cultures – good versus evil, David versus Goliath, freedom versus tyranny, democracy versus totalitarianism. The meaning invested in the Anglo-German wars, and subscribed to by Britons, was that of a deadly struggle between two incompatible cultures. By this we mean human systems which understand themselves as mutually exclusive, irreconcilable, and autarkic. They achieve diachronic self-definition in contrast to a concrete opposite, and synchronic stability by purging all elements (real or imagined) of this predatory 'other'. The latter process resembles the communal cleansing of a group of animals, whose members intuitively and obsessively examine themselves in the interests of health and security. The world of music fits uncomfortably with this 'official' picture. Britons literate in 'classical' music were (and are) simply unable to feel unambiguous hostility to things German. True, even before 1914, German Music was seen by the more radical and patriotic English musicians as comprehensively stultifying. For the majority, however, it represented an object of profound reverence and eternal veracity. The oscillations of these extreme feelings – which successive phases of international crisis exacerbated, and which sometimes existed in the same person – permeated the period 1914–45.

The outbreak of war in August 1914 caused a reaction within the music profession. Renunciation of past friendships, recommended earlier by Forsyth as a voluntary sacrifice for the cause, was now imposed arbitrarily by events. Things were made easier by the attitudes of figures like Hans Richter, the most eminent German to have worked regularly in Britain, who in a widely publicised move renounced all his British honours (Foreman 1987: 61). At first, some of Richter's closest associates – Elgar, Parry and Stanford among them – were content to scapegoat Prussian militarism, carefully setting German culture aside from blame. There was no immediate anti-German campaign in concert- and lecture-halls, but other consequences were noticed. 'War has tremendously changed the outlook of the English public regarding British artists', wrote the conductor Landon Ronald. 'Yesterday at the Albert Hall, for Kirkby Lunn, Katherine Goodson and myself the place was packed out, and you know as well as I do that 6 months ago it would have been comparatively speaking empty' (BLMC L48–13–38/217: 051014). From a different standpoint, Alexander Mackenzie bewailed to Percy Pitt the loss of many German students, and their fees, from the enrolment lists of the Royal Academy (BLMC E3305/93v: 200914).

Pressure built up from the younger musicians to exclude more than the 'parasite' personnel. Arnold Bax wrote to the *Sunday Times* in favour of a complete ban on German music, 'and was surprised how badly the proposal was received' (Foreman 1988: 182–3). Havergal Brian, advancing a similar policy, pointed out in the *Daily Mail* that 'there are few quarters of British musical life which do not live in state of complete servility' to Germany (Eastaugh 1976: 51–2). Holbrooke, who wisely abandoned usage of the Germanic form ('Josef') of his first name, contributed to the magazine *The New Age* a series of chauvinistic articles about the relative merits of German and British music (Tomlinson 1976: 19). The prevailing mood swept the provinces. In Bristol, a performance of Stanford's

Songs of the Fleet coincided with the defeat of a German task-force
near the Falkland Islands, the announcement of which was 'received
with such a burst of enthusiasm as had not before been heard in the
hall at the concert. The stirring songs were … taken up with readiness by the choir and must have deepened the patriotic fervour of
the assembly' (BRBC DM433: 101214).

The correspondent of the *Western Daily Press* noted the special
excitement evoked by Stanford's setting of lines by the local poet,
Henry Newbolt:

> Some day we're bound to sight the enemy,
> He's come, and at last we know his name,
> Keel to keel, and gun to gun he'll challenge us,
> To meet him at the Great Armada game.

As war dragged on, programmes organised by the Bristol Musical
Society reflected national commitment. One of several all-British
concerts in the Victoria Hall (March 1918) wound up with a rendition of Parry's *Jerusalem*. This anticipated what was soon to become
a national ritual. Meanwhile, a now-notorious incident occurred in
one of the remotest regions, when the rendering of Schubert *lieder*
at night led to accusations of spying against D. H. Lawrence and
Frieda (née Richtofen), and to their virtual ejection from Cornwall
(Dakers 1987: 66). Back in the capital, the Promenade Concerts
gradually squeezed out German items. For almost a decade
(1913–22) no new works by German or Austrian composers gained
a hearing at the Proms (Cox 1980: 70–1, 266–71). (A similar policy
has been identified (Tischler 1986: 68ff.) in programmes of the
Boston and New York orchestras, once the USA entered the war in
1917.) It also allowed Henry Wood to indulge his proclivity for the
music of Britain's Russian ally alongside the home-grown produce.
Some English critics did not appreciate this offering:

> In our desire to be rid of the music of the heavy German type of Bruck-
> ner, the megalomania of Mahler and the risky sanity of Schoenberg, we
> have thrown ourselves somewhat thoughtlessly into the arms of the
> lachrymose Russians, and at the present moment we seem inclined to
> swallow anything under a Slav patronymic … Our British composers
> are at the least the equal of those of any other country and should be
> so recognised. (Hull *c*. 1918: 180)

Susan Hill's fictional picture (1971: 127) of young British officers on
the Western Front listening to phonographs of Elgar and Schubert

has a basis in fact. Private Ivor Gurney was inspired by *The Dream of Gerontius*, which brought home to him 'the flood of German beastliness'. 'The Hun is at the gate', the young composer added, 'and Civilisation is a dream merely' (Thornton 1984: 76–9). The message reached the YMCA London Club for men on leave from active service which 'gradually introduced into their repertory works by British composers such as Frank Bridge, Sir Edward Elgar, Percival Fletcher, Edward German, Percy Grainger, Roger Quilter [and] Coleridge-Taylor' (Ashwell 1922: 213). Musical chauvinism during the Great War achieved a strange echo seventy years later when Colin MacLaren used it as the context of his whimsical radio series 'Broomhouse Reach'. The story incorporates variations – only slightly distorted – on incidents surrounding (*inter alia*) Delius, Holst and Holbrooke. A British composer is forced because of his surname (Mendel) to take refuge in the country house of his patroness, Lady Hester, and together they set up a 'British Musical Heritage Society … to drive the Hun from the Halls' (MacLaren BBC R3: 200885).

In the post-war period concert promoters returned to the employ-ment of German music (and musicians) sooner than many regarded as decent. There were complaints, for example, in the correspon-dence columns of the *South Wales Daily News* that German music was being played in public on Armistice Day (12 November 1919). However, the struggle of national music against German influence was renewed on less unequal terms than before. The hottest fire was concentrated in a new and vitally important area of competition. The BBC was strongly committed to a non-insular music policy. Music was the primary business of the wireless programme; through it, John Reith intended to discharge the burden of the motto 'Nation shall speak peace unto nation'. Thanks to guidance from critics like Donald Tovey and Walford Davies, the traditional German canon formed the staple content of 'serious' music on the airwaves. The BBC thus became the battlefield, the 'site of struggle', of opposed ideologues of Britain's musical future.

The BBC's first music director Percy Pitt 'was regarded askance in some circles because of his interest in what was happening in Euro-pean contemporary music' (Kennedy 1987/89: 137). After Pitt's retirement, the 'modernist' corner was fought by Edward Clark. This dynamic and radical musicologist had spent most of his early years in Austria, and was a close associate of Schoenberg. In 1914 he was apprehended at the Bayreuth Festival and interned, along with dozens of other British musicians, in the beautifully named camp at Ruhleben. There the Anglo-Viennese conductor Charles Adler conducted concerts of German music, while British composers wrote Strauss-sounding songs, including one based on Swinburne's *Ode to England*'! (Foreman, BBC Radio 3: 241295). Later, in the 1920s, Clark used his BBC post to influence Pitt's successor Adrian Boult in favour of the continental avant-garde. Indeed, the BBC's orchestra was a veteran of some ambitious modernist premieres even before Boult took over in 1930 (Foreman 1987: xiv, 140ff.). Other sections of the Corporation were less keen. C. C. Dalmaine was conductor of the Wireless Singers, and apparently was being groomed as Boult's understudy. But his affections were towards Elgar, and he also featured his old RCM tutors – RVW, Armstrong Gibbs and others – in the broadcast repertoire. He exhibited little sympathy for the indigestible contemporary monoliths of German-dom. Before being abruptly dismissed, ostensibly for an illicit liaison with one of his choristers, Dalmaine was a member of the policy-making group (Barrington *c.* 1948: 66ff.). Meanwhile, the BBC's Music Advisory Committee, including eminent extra-mural figures, was lobbying for a leading domestic edge in its programmes. 'It seemed to believe', as Boult's biographer puts it with an almost visible sneer, 'that British music and musicians should be the primary, if not sole, concern of the BBC' (Kennedy 1987/89: 169). In 1934, the BBC broadcast a series devoted to native music, yet pointedly followed it a few weeks later with the British premiere of Berg's *Wozzek*.

Clark's problem was that the usual terms of engagement had been reversed. Because of the war, the music he advocated was now dis-advantaged rather than privileged by its Austro-German origin. It had the further impediment of being identified with 'left-wing' ten-dencies. Indeed, this was part of its attraction for Clark, whose socialist commitment was intensified by the frustrating BBC ban on all overtly 'political' programme content. Moreover, whereas the German classics had traditionally been regarded as more approach-able than any native product, the latter had now, for the first time, achieved a respectable popular following. Its mellifluous Pastoral style conveyed sentiments which many music lovers loved to indulge. In contrast, among the new German generation, Hindemith alone utilised a language which any but a tiny minority of the

cognoscenti could understand. In this way, German music, previously a source of Apollonian order and beauty, became one of anarchy and subversion. The worsening international situation and the
increasing unpopularity of things German wore down the resolution
of Clark, who resigned in 1937 (Harries and Harries 1989: 72–86).

When nationalistic feelings surfaced again in 1939, they were
notably diluted, and complicated by fresh ideological gradations.
Early in the war, RVW informed Reith that 'high art' was the only
way to inspire 'ordinary men' for the challenge of war. He deplored
the BBC's alleged pandering to the people's desire for 'the loath-
some noises of the so-called cinema organ ... second-rate material
which nobody wants ... In times like these when so many are looking for comfort we ought to give them something which will grip ...
Discriminating listeners are tuning in to Germany for their spiritual
sustenance' (Johnson, BBC R3: 171090).

To help counter propaganda that evidently was seen as more dangerous than that of 'Lord Haw-Haw', the BBC asked RVW himself
to compose a patriotic song. He obliged with a setting of Henley's
England, My England. But then he threatened to withdraw the song,
because the BBC had banned the works of his friend Alan Bush
(Foreman 1987: 239–40). In a separate incident, Sir Hamilton
Harty was discouraged by officialdom from his intention to conduct
Tchaikovsky at an Anglo-Soviet Friendship Concert sponsored by
the Communist Party. (BLMC A52256/151: 030440). Bush was a
communist, at a time when the USSR was effectively an ally of the
Third Reich. In obedience to the dictates of Moscow, communists
were actively campaigning against the war. Given Stalin's attack on
Finland, some justification existed for the feelings involved; but
motives within governmental circles – which now included the BBC
– were by no means straightforward.

Such vigilance was relaxed even before Hitler's invasion of
the Soviet Union in June 1941. John Ireland informed his fel-
low-traveller Edward Clark that the BBC had commissioned 'an
anti-Fascist piece, if there is such a thing' (BLMC A52256/199:
050341). In addition to this *Epic March* (1942), Ireland contributed
Sarnia, a tribute to Guernsey, part of the only region of British ter-
ritory 'now overrun by the unspeakable Hun' (BLMC A52256/200:
021142). But it was again RVW to whom the BBC turned in 1943,
to celebrate the victory descried on the horizon. Though not a piece
of blatant triumphalism at the expense of an 'unspeakable' enemy,

A Song of Thanksgiving, heard at last in 1945, certainly did not fudge the basic issues of the culture war.

'Our Bach': the Johann Sebastian effect

Above all other foreign geniuses the Germans admire Shakespeare. During the nineteenth century this gave rise to an indigenous industry of Shakespeare criticism and performance, which – as in the parallel cases of industrial output in general, and of Dreadnoughts in particular – soon came to rival English achievements. In the university towns of the Reich, there were dozens of musicians who, like Thomas Mann's fictional Adrian Leverkuhn in *Doktor Faustus*, aspired to set Shakespeare, and as many literary men, like Mann's Rudiger Schildknap, able to provide the necessary libretto (Mann 1947/68: 157). The fashion has not faded: one of modern Germany's leading younger composers has achieved a great success with an opera of *King Lear*. But it culminated, during the tricentennial celebrations held in the besieged Germany of 1916, in a perfectly serious claim that the Bard was not the property of the besiegers – he was '*unser* Shakespeare' (Engler 1992).

It was perhaps in the knowledge that the German scholar Schlegel had adumbrated this claim that E. M. Forster gave this very name to the central characters of his best-known novel. In *Howard's End*, set in Edwardian London, the Anglo-German Schlegels are entertaining their *echt*-German cousins at a Queen's Hall concert. During a discussion, one of the latter is told: 'Frieda, you despise English music. You know you do. And English art. And English literature, except Shakespeare, and he's a German' (Forster 1910/83: 49). When it came to war, like God and Holy Writ, the sanction of Shakespeare was invoked by both sides. On the Somme, therefore, the two nations' armies came to fight for ultimate possession of England's most elemental attribute. 'Our young men must write on a diet largely composed of Folk Song and Shakespeare', announced Ivor Gurney from his frontline dug-out (Thornton 1984: 34). But a generation after this issue was apparently resolved, the Germans were at it again – at least in the propaganda imagination of the film studios. In *Pimpernel Smith* (1940) a Cambridge don rescues intellectual (i.e. 'good') Germans from the Gestapo. A Goering-type character (Francis Sullivan) informs the Pimpernel (Leslie Howard): 'Shakespeare is a German, Professor Schussbacher has proved it once and for all.'

The screenwriter cannot resist other swipes at the enemy: a character named 'Wagner' describes the Pimpernel's whistled signature as 'quite nice – for an English tune'.

If Shakespeare was a major site of Anglo-German struggle, so too was J. S. Bach. In the years following his revival by Mendelssohn, Bach came to occupy the highest niche on the High Altar of Music's Temple. Among most English musicians, his fame reduced that of Handel to a shadow. Bach scholarship and performances proliferated, and JSB claimed pole-position in almost any history of music written between 1880 and 1960. English musicians expressed special reverence for the music and affection for the man. 'I need music, which means Bach, very badly', Ivor Gurney complained after his baptism of fire on the Somme (Thornton 1984: 76). For all his 'Gloster' sentiments and solid patriotism, Gurney spent far more time thinking about Bach than about Elgar and RVW combined, and constantly ached to play from 'the 48'. The attitude of Gurney, who fought on the Western Front, and the polemics of another kind of front, by an 'engaged' writer like Frank Howes, are examples of the prevailing ambiguity. Howes notes that the great figures of national music paid allegiance to Bach, writing in terms which imply the latter was a necessary qualification for enrolment among the former; yet these (we are told) were precisely the composers who emancipated English Music from German domination (Howes 1966: 246ff.). Both cases illustrate how essential it was for Bach to be assimilated into English culture. His music was believed to possess such potency that it could not be allowed to remain the preserve of a hostile culture. Thus he was admired for virtues perceived as English, and his art was 'recognised' as an expression of these virtues. In effect, the English counterattack on the artistic front laid a claim to 'our Bach'.

In the 1870s, middle-class enthusiasts founded the London Bach Choir. Originally they met to sing in the spacious drawing-rooms of Kensington, not far away from the organisational hub of the Renaissance movement. Stanford soon took charge; and their activities dominated a Bach industry in the capital. For such 'English amateurs', Bach was the repository of Anglo-Saxon genius – sober, industrious, respectable, domestic, Protestant, peace-loving – an ordinary man who expressed the divine. Hubert Parry's writings frequently emphasised Bach's humility and spirituality (Parry 1887/1950; 1902). Frederick Crowest (1902: 34) added that 'his character was amiable in the extreme ... while no family was ever more united'. Bach's genius was (thus) the complete opposite of Liszt's, the Romantic archetype who in one version was wickedly secular and in another, even more dangerous, subversively Catholic. Before 1860, English music lovers had been able to sample Romanticism through Mendelssohn's melodiously classical version. The rebirth of Bach – via Mendelssohn's midwifery – was timely. His role as sanctified symbol of musical essences was thrown into relief by the social–artistic context of late Victorian London. The decadent excesses of the likes of Swinburne, Wilde and Beardsley confirmed all English prejudices against 'Art'. During the backlash which followed the Wilde–Queensberry case, persecuted bohemia found in Bach a perfect antidote to the philistines. For the ten years prior to 1914, the English composer most noted for his flamboyant 'bohemian' lifestyle and exotic interests was Cyril Scott, who had trained in Germany. The young genius's appearance and persona was in perfect Romantic accord with his music. But his biographer was careful to stress that Scott sought to emulate one exemplar above all others – J. S. Bach. Consequently, potential admirers were assured that Scott had developed 'that calm and reserve, that poise and quiet confidence, which I can only liken to the chief characteristics of the music of the grandest of all musical geniuses' (Hull *c.* 1918: 31–2, 176).

Although in the last analysis it was impossible to disguise Bach's national affiliations, he could at least be presented as a 'good' German. Thus he was made to stand for an earlier Germany, small-town, divided, unambitious, which had been no threat to the British Empire. In an argument later directly contradicted by Forsyth, Crowest emphasised that Bach had 'worked for art – and art alone' (Crowest 1902: 34). Other commentators demonstrated how the greatest composer was above mere nationality. He was not in the same category as Wagner and Brahms, who had diminished their art by association with German militarism. Bach, like Shakespeare, was universal: a profound spiritual vessel, in whom music and religion were synonymous, yet who was appreciated also for the scientific and mathematical qualities of his work. By the 1920s it was a brave or mischievous critic who dared to challenge prevailing opinion (Turner 1928: 24–36). 'The ideal, in my mind, would be to start with the greatest of all the classics, J. S. Bach', advised M. D. Calvocoressi, close associate of RVW, in his

Musical Taste and How to Form It (1925: 11). A book introducing children to the 'colossal genius' encapsulated in a few pages of fictionalised domestic narrative all the qualities we have referred to above, as evidence of 'the old German temper in its best form' (Byron *c*. 1925).

Under the auspices of writers like Grove and Tovey, Beethoven came to represent a similar relationship – though never quite in the ideal way of Bach. In Germany itself, Beethoven's reputation had become a subject of political contest even before his death (Dennis 1993). In England, he was regarded as untainted by the malign spirit of modern Germany. Of course, he was a true patriot, but a 'good German', too (in other words, an honorary Englishman); above all, he was a heroic proponent of the liberal and proto-democratic forces which lost their way in 1848. Beethoven's perceived opposition to tyranny appealed to the deepest instincts of Englishmen. His pro-English sentiments, enshrined in several works, and his connections with the Philharmonic Society, were a source of pride. In 1926, Lord Balfour, retired Tory leader and one-time prime minister, was invited to deliver the address at the Royal Philharmonic Society's planned memorial concert to mark the centenary of Beethoven's death (BLMC L48–13–38/37: 290126). In the way of official formations, and precisely because he spoke the political language of Englishmen, Beethoven was removed from the arena of controversy. His political significance was neutralised; so that, when the time came, a German symphony could be used as the motto theme of universal resistance to Germany.

What might be called the 'J. S. Bach effect' underlines the ambivalence in the Anglo-German cultural relationship. Many Englishmen, whether living in 1840, 1900 or 1940, were deeply impressed by their historical connections with the Teutonic lands. Aspects of English nationalism derived from the common ethnic origins of Englishman and German: religious fraternity was forged in the long struggle against Rome, and rested firmly on the vernacular Bible; their alliance against the tyranny of Napoleon was symbolised in nineteenth-century imagery by the meeting of Wellington and Blücher at Waterloo. Many believed that the Englishman's self-reliance and love of freedom derived from German ethnic origins. Prominent English historians and other writers of the nineteenth century developed such arguments (MacDougall 1982). The year 1714 was seen as a crucial moment, when renewal of the royal dynasty from a German source permitted the development of a constitution freed from the Catholic absolutism of the Stuarts. This conceit formed a key element of the mainstream Whig interpretation of English history, which dominated the curriculum into the second half of the twentieth century.

There was no greater apostle of Bach than RVW, who apostrophised him as 'the Great Bourgeois', and in terms of performance, defiantly recuperated the *St Matthew Passion* into the English choral tradition (Vaughan Williams 1934/87: 170–6; Thomas 1998). In 1937, RVW went to Hamburg to receive a prestigious prize. He pointed out to his hosts that the visit 'implies no political propaganda and that I shall feel free as an honourable man … to hold and express any views on the general state of Germany which are allowable to any British citizen'. More privately, he cited membership 'of more than one English society whose object is to combat all that the present German regime stands for'. But he was conscious of the importance of making English music better known in Germany (Vaughan Williams 1964: 217). On the very eve of war, the BBC hoped that extracts from RVW's *Dona Nobis Pacem*, scheduled for broadcast to Germany, might somehow influence Germany's leaders to draw back from the brink (Foreman 1987: 220). Perhaps someone recognised that the *Volkisch* aspects of RVW's music appealed to Nazi musical prejudices. For example his *Five Tudor Portraits* (1935) was oddly similar in spirit and style to the work of a composer favoured by the Nazis – *Carmina Burana* by Carl Orff. In fact, no possibility existed of Germany's accepting the broadcast, since Vaughan Williams's music had been banned in the Reich the previous February (1939).

This represented an honour which the English composer shared with Mendelssohn. One night in 1936, a few days before Sir Thomas Beecham arrived in Leipzig on tour with the London Philharmonic Orchestra, the Nazis removed the statue of Mendelssohn from its plinth in front of the Gewandhaus. A citizen wrote anonymously to Beecham, asking him to protest to the authorities (Geissmar 1944: 238–9). Beecham had little taste for Bach, but Mendelssohn was a different matter. On this occasion he was helpless, having personally sanctioned an analogical act of suppression. At the prior demand of the Nazis, he removed Mendelssohn's *'Scottish' Symphony* – designed both for its programmatic content and its dedication to Queen Victoria as an appropriate reference to the history of

German–British friendship – from his proposed tour programme (Reid 1962: 216). In the event, music by Berners, Delius, Elgar and RVW (the two latter representing acts of endurance on Sir Thomas's part) was played by the LPO to German audiences (Geissmar 1944: 232ff.). Beecham's influence in Germany was seen as of great political importance, and not only by the man himself. He was the first English conductor to achieve a reputation as the equal of Mengelberg, Furtwängler and Strauss, and to perform the repertoire works of the Austro-German tradition with German orchestras. Beecham had been the first non-German to conduct *Rosenkavalier* in Germany and his current projects included a complete *Ring* cycle (Jefferson 1979: 207ff.). He was certainly not ignorant of the fate suffered by many musicians at Nazi hands. Indeed, he had engaged Furtwängler''s Jewish assistant Bertha Geissmar as his own concert secretary when she was forced into exile. Geissmar was among those who believed that neither Nazi policies in general, nor even her own particular fate, should stand in the way of music – the transcendental force that was ultimately capable of abolishing all evils. Beecham insisted on her presence throughout the 1936 tour, and in the cause of music and peace she endured the ordeal of facing not only her persecutors but – even worse – the ex-colleagues who had displayed such indifference to her persecution.

For all this, Beecham's willingness to make compromises rather than sever relations was noted in the inner circles of the Nazi hierarchy, just as were the attitudes of British politicians, expressed in the developing policy of appeasement. In the interval of his Berlin concert, Sir Thomas was invited to Hitler's box, where he chatted with the Führer, Goebbels – minister of art as well as of propaganda – and the virulent anti-semite Julius Streicher. Upon his return to England (in an affectation he doubtless learned from Delius) Beecham was heard to compare many things at home unfavourably with their German counterparts (Reid 1962: 217). In 1937, Hitler's ambassador, Ribbentrop, included Sir Thomas among the prominent people he cultivated in London, in the hope of 'explaining' Nazi policies and enlisting a support which might be spread around the best dinner-tables and clubs (D. Irving 1978: 56). For his part, Beecham returned to Germany several times before 1939 in pursuit of a major recording project (*Die Zauberflöte* with all-German forces) (Jefferson 1979: 211–16). During the war, in writing his memoirs, he shamelessly boasted about his past connections with the Nazi hierarchy (Beecham 1944: 151–2). Sir Thomas's ex-mistress Lady Cunard was a frequent companion of Ribbentrop on the London social round (Reid 1962: 216. Channon 1970: 45ff.). Another member of this circle was the Marchioness of Londonderry, who with her husband, the senior Mitfords, and other luminaries were stalwarts of the Anglo-German Fellowship Society. Lady Londonderry was also patron of Rutland Boughton, a composer who was an active member of the Communist Party. As her disaffected son later wrote to Boughton, 'being a domestic dictator herself she was impressed with Nazism. She found a regime which was violently anti-Jewish, anti-Russian & which openly scoffed at democracy. This was just what the doctor ordered' (BLMC A52366: 250144).

At an even more significant level of 'high politics' than London society, music was called on to exert its emollient spell. In 1939, following Germany's occupation of Czechoslovakia, Arthur Bryant, the popular writer and historian, was used by Neville Chamberlain as an unofficial go-between with certain German academics who, it was felt, might have influence with Hitler. Two months before the attack on Poland, Bryant wrote to his Nazi contact Dr Blohm, assuring him that if the Führer were to abjure the use of violence, he would achieve not only most of his mundane objectives but even eternal fame as the greatest German of all time. England and Germany, he pointed out, were brother-nations before the bar of history. He ended with what he hoped would be a plangent appeal:

> I have been listening for the last hour to the music of your countrymen relayed over our wireless – Handel, Mozart, Bach and Wagner following each other in almost continuous succession from different stations, and I suddenly felt how impossible it was that our two races who have give n the world so much should destroy each other. (PROK PREM 1/333: 030739)

During the war of mutual destruction that followed, Thomas Mann wrote his novel *Doktor Faustus*, a set of cultural reflections which saw the positive Anglo-German relationship enshrined in Bach, Beethoven and Shakespeare as vital to the future of 'European civilisation', and to the peace of the world. He created a kind of 'Johann van Shakespeare' in the person of Adrian Leverkühn, an anglophile noted for his 'dislike of his very own Germanness' (Mann 1947/68: 160). Leverkühn worships Shakespeare and aspires to make an opera of *Love's Labours Lost*. His work espouses the 'Anglicised'

oratorio genre rather than the more properly Germanic abstract–
symphonic one. His early symphonic poem, roughly contemporary
with Vaughan Williams's *A Sea Symphony*, is called *Ocean Lights*.
He sets a particular Blake poem to music, in Leipzig – at exactly the
same time that Havergal Brian does so in Dresden, Staffordshire.
Such correspondence of the imagination and the empirical can
hardly be dismissed as mere coincidence.

The fruits of independence

A survey of its literature of criticism and historiography hardly
leaves room for doubt that the English Musical Renaissance considered itself to have achieved its primary aim of creating an independent and self-sufficient 'national style'. Indeed, it has been
claimed even that by the 1950s composers like Hugh Wood had
to swim against the tide if they wished to learn from continental
practice.

> Ironically, it was the opposite of the dilemma which had faced Vaughan
> Williams and Holst half a century earlier. They, in order to achieve
> individuality, felt they must escape from the influence of the Teutonic
> accent with which the British music of their youth spoke. For Hugh
> Wood and his contemporaries the result of the revolution wrought by
> the nationalists was that they felt stifled by 'parochialism' and cut off
> from the developments pioneered before 1914 by Schoenberg, Berg
> and Webern. (Kennedy 1991)

We would argue, however, that the earlier generation did not (were
powerless to) 'escape from the influence of the Teutonic accent'. By
the time the problem was identified it was too late. For one thing,
music is too permeable a medium to permit 'protection'. British
writers of the English language – at least down to 1900 – could control its development in conditions of cultural autarky, because they
were communicating to an audience all but isolated from other literary traditions. In contrast, English musicians and their audiences
had been exposed to continental styles since the early sixteenth century. For another, the very discourse of 'classical' music had become
inherently Germanic –to a degree which (in Bakhtinian terms) might
be defined as almost 'monological'. Or, as a British Marxist critic put
it, Germany had 'built around music an entire mythology' (Darnton
1940: 93). Before Germany began its 'grab for world power',

arguably even before it gained political unity, its culture had already encompassed what was to prove its sole universal dimension – but had achieved it for all time.

By the time of Beethoven's death, in 1827, German musicians had either invented or perfected every genre, and every technique, subsequently acknowledged to be of lasting significance. The most fertile procedures of harmony and counterpoint: fugue, sonata and variation forms, rondo, aria, and every variety of refined dance form; concerto, symphony, 'programmatic' overture (or symphonic poem); large-scale choral music (whether secular or religious); and, finally, opera and ballet. Works of complexity and scale for keyboard and other solo instruments, all major instrumental combinations of chamber music, the art-song and song-cycle, were all likewise patented in the Germanic lands. The 'symphony' orchestra itself was given fundamental shape in Germany. Above all, the self-conscious concept of 'national music', and its historical projects, especially centred in a 'National Opera', were products of German Romanticism (Hughes in Stradling *et al.* 1997). These 'facts' have not been selected to support our hypothesis. They are verified by the writings of numerous non-German musicologists. The extent of the unanimity on this subject in every country and culture represents a unique epistemological phenomenon. Thus we are confronted by one of the most resilient hegemonic *blocs* of modern times – resembling, in broad anthropological terms, one of the great world religions.

Thus, no substantial corpus of English music written in the century 1860–1960 is entirely free of Germanic (or 'Germanised') modes. Of course, there are individual exceptions to this rule, such as RVW's *Tallis* fantasia or (more arguably) Walton's *Façade*. RVW's work itself belonged to a fad for the 'fantasy', which various experts held up at the time as an authentic 'English' form; but in the present context, *Tallis* is an isolated case. Of course, resort to any number of German precepts does not necessarily mean that a piece of music thereby becomes German. The quantitative toll does, however, reduce commensurately a claim to cultural independence on the part of any given work, composer or school – a claim, that is, to be in any meaningful way 'English'. Even after 'the revolution wrought by the nationalists', the overwhelming majority of native compositions continued to occupy this grey area. Even had it been possible to bifurcate, separating the biological cell, exploring a distinctively fresh palette of techniques and forms, an even more subtle element of dependence would still have remained. We refer again to the German musical aesthetic, the spiritual burden allegedly carried – *ipso facto* and *sui generis* – by all 'higher' forms of composition, which was the supreme heritage of the Austro-German school. It was acknowledged as the German-speaking people's most stupendous contribution to civilisation, which Thomas Mann studied in all its explosive ethical complexity in *Doktor Faustus*, and which even a Marxist critic like Theodor Adorno found imperative. Beyond good and evil, Germany had made the agenda for what Stanford handed down to his students at the RCM as 'The Eternal Verities' (Guyatt 1979: Unicorn KP 8000).

The English Musical Renaissance was never able to evolve indigenous genres. To tread at once upon the main battleground of argument, most of its prominent composers were tempted to prove themselves in the 'symphony without a programme', which Elgar identified as the *ne plus ultra*. Parry and Stanford clearly subscribed to Elgar's opinion (though both wrote faintly 'programmatic' as well as 'abstract' symphonies). Even during a period when fashionable opinion saw the symphony as extinct, rebels like Bax and *enfants terribles* like Walton could not resist the challenge to contribute at the level still exalted by Tovey at home and by Einstein abroad. The success of Walton's *Symphony* (1934) – with its 'Germanic' fugal finale – increased incentives for others to conform. Many whose aesthetic was demonstrably unsuited to the symphony found it impossible to avoid. To take an extreme example: Delius's music is – paradoxically – less involved with Germany than is most. Yet when he composed a work evocative of his English origins, it proved to be a quasi-symphonic structure – *North Country Sketches*. Constant Lambert stuck largely to his *métier*, the ballet, when composing, but in his critical study *Music Ho!* he hailed the non-programmatic Sibelius symphonies as the most fertile repository of modern music (Lambert 1934/85: 276–90). Even the avant-garde Bridge was drawn, via a series of movement-based chamber works, towards the symphonic form, as evidenced by the symphony (unfinished) on which he was working at the time of his death.

At the outset of the 'great trek', Butterworth composed his earliest essay in orchestralising folksong, the first of the two *English Idylls*. The folk-tune subject rolls confidently along the rolling English road, until suddenly it is waylaid by a footpad in the shape of *Tristan*, and collapses into the famous Wagnerian chord. Not surprisingly, Butterworth had in fact been absorbed in the study of Wagner's music–drama (LB 361/43: 090613). The rougher treatment that *Tristan* received at the hands of Debussy in the *Children's Corner Suite* is perhaps an illustration of the greater maturity of the French Renaissance than was achieved by its English counterpart. Near the end of the 'trek', to be precise, between the Munich Crisis of 1938 and the outbreak of war a year later, Eugene Goossens worked on his first symphony in London and Sussex. He insisted that his symphony had no 'message' and no 'programme'. Such a disavowal was usual practice among composers in this period; but Goossens felt it incumbent upon him to go further, declaring in advance that the symphony was quite specifically not about the threat which hung over Europe and the world from Germany. Goossens added: 'I wrote it in the mood of a man who having for some length of time refrained from taking part in a debate, feels that he is justified in saying his say and saying it at length. But the topic of the debate in this case is neither personal nor topical' (Guyatt 1979: Unicorn KP 8000). But whether Goossens liked it or not, his symphony – an 'abstract' work of conventional design – was inevitably a contribution to a debate about German power.

During the period in which all these English composers flourished, Ralph Vaughan Williams achieved 'recognition' as the greatest. When Richard Strauss came to London in 1947, for a festival which Beecham arranged in his honour, he met RVW, apparently for the first time. An anecdote relates that Strauss asked his English contemporary 'Und vot keint ov musik do you reit, Misster Villjams?' (or words to that effect). Strauss's gauche attempt to be ingratiating – inspired perhaps by the overwhelming defeat of his nation, though more probably by the fact that the festival was designed to lift him out of financial difficulty – reveals how superior the Germans must inevitably be about the discourse which they have invented. But the crucial question remains: what kind of music *did* RVW write?

His life's work included nine symphonies, a series which played at least as important a role as that of Beethoven in the original case. From the 1922 *Pastoral Symphony* onwards, RVW's symphonism. came to be widely accepted as an 'essentially English' expression – and thus as overcoming–escaping its Germanic genre. At the time of their meeting, RVW had just completed his sixth symphony, and Strauss his *Metamorphosen*. Both works are threnodies of wartime destruction. Both proceed largely by means of an intense Bachian counterpoint. Three of RVW's four movements are dominated by formal variants of this technique – canon, imitation, fugato and fugue. Yet the sleeve-note for an early recording of *Symphony No. 6* celebrated the fact that

> [t]hroughout his career Vaughan Williams has remained undisturbed by influences from Central Europe and other alien parts of the continent and has steadily pursued his own path. This has resulted in the revival and establishment of the style and idiom which is unique to this country. Whereas other composers have taken their impulse from the virtuosic ideas of Richard Strauss, the grey classicism of Brahms ... Vaughan Williams has relied on his own thoughts ... and posterity may well place him in a niche to himself next to the other great composers of all time ... The Sixth widens what has been called the insularity of the English style to a manner universally acceptable ... It has indeed put the English symphony on the musical map and has awakened continental awareness to the fact that English music is not a derived quantity. (Demuth *c.* 1954: HMV BLP 10001)

The author of these lines, Norman Demuth, was a teacher of composition at the RAM – but also a veteran of the Great War and author of the army training manual *Harrying the Hun* (Palmer 1947: 76–7). His use of a metaphorical 'musical map' indicates an exasperated sub-text. We British (it complains) have defeated Germany outright, and twice over, on the politico-military plane – but still we have not acquired our *Musikalische Lebensraum*.

In fact, all of RVW's symphonies adopt the basic German scheme of four movements. The series alternates – if not quite perfectly – between the lyrical and the dramatic modes, not unlike its Beethovenian precedent. Several examples employ sonata form in the internal construction of movements. Others pay specific and formal obeisance to Beethoven (*No. 4*), Brahms (*No. 5*) or Haydn (*No. 9*). Despite the constant presence of modal harmonic inflexions and Tudor polyphony, textbook diatonicism and Bachian stretto are also often utilised. RVW's fervour for Bach had few equals, emerging in creative terms in the 1920s in several works with 'neo-classical' characteristics. An example is the *Concerto Accademico*, an obvious experiment in the fusing of German and English modes, and contemporary with Holst's *Fugal Concerto*.

Our contention is that a truly autonomous English style was not possible. Between them, Bach and Beethoven barred and obscured any way out of the woods. British culture's worship of the principles of form, order and development yields little to that of the German. To utilise Nietzschean categories, the Apollonian schema of classically proportioned beauty is by definition antipathetic to the Dionysiac, disordered, potentially anarchic. Again, the music of the avowedly Nietzschean composer Delius provides a striking case. Superficially, at first hearing, it has many resemblances to that of the English pastoralists, and often deals with similar subject matter. Yet Delius's music remains anathema to many English music lovers – who lovingly embrace that of RVW – because of the former's perceived disdain for organic form, order and development (Cooke 1982: 123–42; Stradling 1989: 86–71). In short, if often for the wrong reasons, the pro-German element in English life had a plangent point. Britain's past, and much of its history, had conditioned English society in a multitude of ways to resemble, more closely than any other, that of Germany. For those in the world of music who perceived this reality, and even for those who did not, continued German domination was for many years preferable to the risks of chaos attendant on abandoning it.

During the whole period of the struggle for a 'national music', the burden of demonstration fell largely upon 'folk-music'. This was the element which, when admixed with Tudor polyphonic procedures, held out the hope of providing a purgative of the Teutonic. It was this, we are told, which made RVW's symphonies 'sound English'. However, resorting to folksong and dance for aesthetic inspiration and musical material was thoroughly Germanic in theory and practice. As we have seen, even its scholarly origin in this country was the work of a German immigrant, Carl Engel. In the 1890s, RVW decided to learn the craft of composition in Germany. As with his tutelage by Ravel, studies of RVW pass lightly over this episode, though the composer was single-minded enough to spend his honeymoon in its pursuit (Vaughan Williams 1964: 52). He attended the Berlin Hochschule für Musik for a year under the tutelage of Max Bruch – who had taught in Liverpool in the 1880s, and had composed a *Scottish Fantasia* on the basis of appropriate 'national' tunes. Bruch reinforced RVW's incipient feeling that he should exploit the folk materials of his own people (M. Norris 1989). But the English folk-music movement was an archaism. It came a half-century later than similar phenomena in the lands of central Europe. Only the renewed efforts of Kodály and Bartók, who gave the technique a modernist edge, saved it from being an outright anachronism in twentieth-century terms. After all, the melody of rural communities had been utilised ubiquitously by composers of the milieu of Haydn and Mozart. Indeed, the glories of German music were believed to have risen to an important degree out of 'folk' genres. This was a tradition in which Mahler – whose songs (at least) did not remain unknown in England – was still creatively engaged. In sum, there is a historically ineradicable German presence in this bulwark area of the Renaissance and its alleged 'independence'.

In the 1930s, Michael Tippett was searching for an individual voice. His music from this period is suffused with 'English' elements of the kind nurtured in the folk-infused Pastoral style. But it is also fixed within a wider German context. Tippett's profound admiration of Beethoven can be traced in the early string quartets. When he came to make his first protest against oppression, in *A Child of Our Time*, the subject matter was Nazi racial persecution. Tippett enlisted 'the blues', the discourse of the racially oppressed African-American. But he turned to the Bach 'passion' for both formal structure and fertilising analogy; and to the *Lehrstück*, a didactic medium patented by the communist artists of the Weimar Republic to arouse political commitment and action (Kemp 1991). Much of Tippett's later music – and prose writing – centres around painful philosophical questions posed by German culture and its contemporary history (Tippett 1959/74). Even as late as the *Symphony No. 3* (1973), a subliminal awareness of the imprisonment of English music within the bars of a German medium screams out in a distorted version of Beethoven's *Choral Symphony*. 'O Freunde, nicht diese Töne': the overt intention is doubtless to protest together with Beethoven; the sub-text reveals a protest against him. In MacLaren's 'Broomhouse Reach', the composer Mendel's attempt to set up an anti-German lobby in 1914 is vitiated by the fact that – like Delius, Holst and Scott – his pre-war music had been published in Germany. But as late as 1939, Tippett could not find a publisher for what became his best-known (because most 'English') work, the *Concerto for Double String Orchestra* – so he sent it to Germany. A letter of acceptance from Wilhelm Strecker reached Tippett almost simultaneously with Britain's declaration of war (Grosvenor and McMillan 1973: 500). His experience closely replicated that of RVW, who sent *A London Symphony* to a German publisher in 1914. Vaughan Williams had recently published an intemperate outburst ('Who Wants the English

Composer?') in The *RCM Magazine*, stimulated by a report that 'the head of a famous publishing firm once said "Why do you young Englishmen go on composing? Nobody wants you"' (Foss 1950: 197).

As these examples illustrate, the 'German wood' surrounded the English 'babes' in a multi-layered complex of conditionings. Ethel Smyth's metaphor betrayed a profound reality. Everywhere the German forest murmured: think of *Freischütz*, *Walküre*, *Parsifal* and *Hansel und Gretel*. Bax was entranced by the mythic and sexual potency of the woodlands, and many of his works were forest-oriented. Smyth's own first opera was actually called *Der Wald*, while Boughton's *Immortal Hour* is plunged in a celticised forest. Delius's *Arabesque* inhabits a cold Scandinavian version. Perhaps the first line of RVW's Housman song-cycle was a political pronouncement: 'On Wenlock Edge, the wood's in trouble'. Having made the statement, the composer demonstrated its meaning by launching himself proudly and deliberately into the open air, and onto the waves ruled by Britannia (in *A Sea Symphony*). But even by 1985 – the year by which RVW expected his countrymen to have achieved a 'national music' – a composer of a younger generation than Hugh Wood's not only had failed to escape from but positively rejoiced in the German heritage. The first success of Robin Holloway – born during the Second World War – was *Scenes from Schumann*, and he has consciously associated much of his music with the aesthetic of the German Romantics. The year 1985 was also 'European Music Year', and the Royal Mail marked the occasion by issuing a set of stamps dedicated to 'British' composers. Of the four chosen – Handel, Elgar, Delius and Holst – two were entirely of German ethnic origin (Gibbons 1991: 71–2).

In the 1960s, British companies were at the forefront of new developments in audio reproduction. A further testament to the ambiguity of British 'independence' came when, amid huge publicity, Decca completed its epoch-making stereo recording, not of Holbrooke or Boughton but of Wagner's *Ring* cycle – well ahead of its German rival Deutsche Grammophon. However, a decade later, labour and production problems in the relevant British industries led to serious decline in the quality of LP pressings, and firms began to look to Germany for assistance. For some years, a sticker bearing the legend 'Disc manufactured in Western Germany' had to be prominently displayed on the sleeves of LP discs in order to inspire purchasers' confidence. The coming of the CD confirmed this trend. For at least the first decade of this new medium, the overwhelming majority of discs retailing in the UK were manufactured in Germany, even when the recording and marketing companies were home-based firms, such as Chandos and Hyperion, dedicated to premieres of British music,. In 1988, HMV issued the first recording of Havergal Brian's *Symphony No. 7*, written forty years earlier (EL 7 49558 1). Not only the LP itself, but even the sleeve was manufactured in Germany. The symphony is cast in the 'classical' German form, with four movements including a scherzo. It was inspired by a reading of Goethe's autobiography, and bears a bizarre dedication to the anonymous medieval architect of Strasburg Cathedral, the emotional centre of Goethe's book, which Brian had never seen (MacDonald 1974: 130–1). The cathedral bells – German music heard before that of even the first Bach – ring out in the symphony's closing bars.

Many resonances of the themes developed in this chapter are to be traced in *Howard's End*, written and set in the England of the pre-1914 decade. Forster's protagonists, the Schlegels, are an artistic, liberal family. Their father fought patriotically in Bismarck's wars, but underwent a spiritual trauma upon witnessing 'the smashed windows of the Tuileries' in 1870. He fled in disgust from the perverted nationalism of the new Germany, and married a rich English lady. Their children are dual 'nationals', yet also intellectuals who distrust both British imperialism and the German 'political' character. They are carefully defined by Forster via their relationship to Beethoven and his *Symphony No. 5*, 'the most sublime noise in existence'.

> 'The Beethoven's fine,' said Margaret, 'I don't like the Brahms, though, nor the Mendelssohn that came first – and ugh! I don't like this Elgar that's coming.'
>
> 'What, what?' called Herr Liesecke, overhearing. 'The "Pomp and Circumstance" will not be fine?'
>
> 'Oh Margaret, you tiresome girl!' cried the aunt. 'Here have I been persuading Herr Liesecke to stop for "Pomp and Circumstance", and you are undoing all my work. I am so anxious for him to hear what we are doing in music. Oh, you mustn't run down our English composers, Margaret.' (Forster 1910/83: 49)

5

Crusading for a national music

> England, after two centuries of imitative negligibility, has suddenly
> flung into the field a cohort of composers whose methods have made
> a technical revolution in musical composition ... Messrs Bax, Ireland,
> Cyril Scott, Holst, Goossens, Vaughan Williams, Frank Bridge,
> Boughton, Holbrooke, Howells and the rest. (G. B. Shaw in Laurence
> 1989: III, 415)

Shaw's selection of an elite cadre of English composers was made in
1922. It exhibits a patriotic pride in the warrior generation which
had followed up, pouring into the gap made by Elgar's breakthrough.
Shaw takes the salute at a triumphal march-past of musicians in full
military metaphor. *Corno di Bassetto* (retd) still had his finger on the
pulse of 'Music in London'; though perhaps (as the remark about
technique betrays) he had lost touch with what was happening on the
Continent. If, in effect, discriminating against 'the rest' – and by
1922, despite the cull of the trenches, contenders were legion rather
than cohort – the selection process seems internally indiscriminate.
No apparent differences of background, education, aesthetics or
alphabetical order divide these composers one from another: they are
united in a national *Musikverein*. It may be nervously observed that
Shaw's canoneers are all specifically English, at least in origin. Yet, to
Shaw, what may separate them is not important. They are coupon
conscripts in the khaki cause of national music.

Shaw's words reflect the assertive self-confidence of English
music in the immediate post-war years (cf. Bliss 1991: 29–30).
However, at deeper levels, unanimity was already breaking down.
Differences over the nature and meaning of composition and the
role of music in society divided the team, setting group against
group. The internecine wars of the 1920s and 1930s were fought

out in characteristically discreet ways. On the public surface of journalism and criticism, bitter personal and political quarrels were conducted by means of a cosmetic discourse of euphemism and innuendo. The protocols of 'dirty linen' and (more appropriately) 'closed ranks' were maintained by the gentlemen of the musical press, as well as by the BBC. Though not always easy to discern beneath the *parole de politesse*, lines of battle were nonetheless drawn and occupied. The historian can decrypt the signifiers, not only via the actual canons of repertoire and performance which evolved, but by the supplementary use of literary material from the archives, above all private papers and correspondence.

Pastoral oat and stop: the image of English Music

The BBC began its work in the same year as Shaw's canon was forged: 1922. This was also the year in which two seminal works by Ralph Vaughan Williams, *The Lark Ascending* and *A Pastoral Symphony* were first performed. Nearly seventy years later, on 23 April 1990, BBC Radio 3 devoted its entire evening schedule to a 'Vaughan Williams Evening', an unprecedented tribute to an individual British composer. The programme was a mixture of live discussion, taped interviews and recordings of the composer conducting his own works. The treatment was comprehensive and often scholarly. Apprentice conductors must have felt suitably instructed, since fully 15 minutes were dedicated to a discussion of the proper metrical rendition of a certain passage in *Symphony No. 5*. At no time during the three uninterrupted hours of broadcasting was the question put: 'Why should we spotlight the career of RVW on St George's Day?' The need to explain seems never to have occurred to the programme makers. The absolute identification of composer with nation – 'my own country, England', as RVW himself put it (R. Vaughan Williams 1934/87: 5) – is taken for granted. It may be deduced that RVW was not, after all, being celebrated as an individual, but rather as a representative institution. The monument has been in place for at least sixty years. As Frank Howes informs us:

> When in 1935 the British Council invited the leading European music critics to sample a week of English music-making they used the name of Richard Strauss by which to convey to their readers the kind of music that Elgar's was; of Vaughan Williams they simply said 'Here is the authentic voice of England'. (Howes 1966: 240)

Most people, including many to whose lives 'serious' music is not central, have a mental portfolio of the English variety as comprising images of the countryside. The Australian personality Barry Humphries, who might be regarded as Everage, recalls a time in youth when he 'mostly listened to English music: Vaughan Williams and Delius in particular, romantic "pastoral" music' (Lahr 1992: 69). English National Music is wedded indissolubly and publicly to a 'pastoral' mood (Howkins 1986). Over forty years after the death of RVW, founder of the 'Pastoral School' of composition, these images have lost little of their power. The BBC's 'Fairest Isle', a year-long Radio 3 celebration of British music, ostensibly marking the 400th anniversary of the death of Henry Purcell, massively reinforced them (Fraser 1995). A Spanish musician working in London confirms the net effect: for him, British Music consists of 'a poetic description of the green serenity of the country's landscape' (Lluna 1998: 12–13). In a series which formed part of 'Fairest Isle', several other continental executants made a similar point ('As Others See Us', R3 1995). For most of us, however, the images derive not directly from the music but rather from its packaging: presentation and representation. Discourse mediates meaning. Indeed, 'discourse' seems an apt word for the illustrations which accompany hundreds of LPs and CDs of English Music; seductive landscape photographs or reproductions of Palmer, Turner or Constable. Sleeve-notes and insert booklets often complement the desired impression by utilising an upholstered vocabulary of rural warmth, beauty and tranquillity.

If subject to time's normative edicts, these hardy perennials would appear as little more than pale and wilted descendants of a florescent imagery produced by the early critical advocates of the Pastoral style and the folksong movement. Theirs was a political campaign, intended to fuse 'national' with 'natural', and to place the end-product at the centre of ideas of 'Englishness'. Jack Westrup collected and concentrated the essences in a compendium – *The Character of England* – issued at the end of the Second World War, and intent on celebrating ethnic endurance and victory. His tribute to the nation was a bouquet culled from hillside and hedgerow; here, the literal Latin-based double meaning of *floreat*.

We recognize a quality in English music that makes us appear different. English music is inclined to be romantic yet reserved. Much of it avoids expansive gestures not from a lack of feeling but from a habit of restraint ... What is particularly noticeable in English music is a nostalgic quality that defies precise analysis. It is present in folk-song ... There is in our music something that recalls the English countryside, where there is often no challenge to the eye but a pervading tenderness of harmony and outline. (Westrup 1947: 406)

In 1994 Sir Thomas Armstrong, long-time director of the RAM, used similar constructions when asked about the Englishness of English music. 'There is a certain reticence about it. It's always influenced by the English countryside, though this may not be apparent on the surface' (BBC R3: 131194). The 'pastoral' discourse has been freshly privileged in the present generation by a ubiquitous propaganda of conservation, whether from the 'ecological awareness' lobby or, from the opposite political direction, 'the countryside campaign'. In any case, the vocabulary of English music history and music criticism is so green that the innocent reader might be forgiven for thinking that its subject matter was horticulture rather than High Culture.

A special relationship between English Music and the land was first proclaimed around 1900, and thereafter assumed an important role in the presentation of cultural hegemony. The broad intellectual background from which the proposition emerged centred upon the work of William Morris, and thence was distributed to middle-class household, London club and college common-room via the influence of George Meredith, Richard Jefferies and Thomas Hardy. In his address to the inaugural meeting of the Folk Song Society (1898), Hubert Parry sounded the keynote of 'return to nature', positing the vitality of the countryside as the antidote to the decadence of the city. It was a binary mode of definition and opposition adapted from England's 'literary renaissance' (Parry, *MT* 1899). After 1902, the process was intensified by the exploratory ventures into the countryside itself of folksong collectors such as Cecil Sharp, RVW and Grainger. From the first it had a double message, since not only the inimitable aesthetic beauty and emotional appeal of 'nature', but even its physical matter, its soil and thus its working denizens, were apostrophised. Sharp's subject, in his *English Folk Song: Some Conclusions* (1907/72), was not primarily music, but rather the evolutionary destiny of the race, deriving from the eternal abstraction of the land and the traditions of its living communities. Such beliefs became prevalent among musicians. In 1915, the influential choral conductor C. K. Scott wrote to encourage Rutland Boughton's project to make a new beginning for English choral music in rural Somerset.

> How very little we produce in our country places nowadays that future generations will come to reverence! [You will] put this wrong to rights & see that the countryside produces as fair or fairer things than the town. And indeed it should, for nature herself is for the most part unspoiled there & can continuously guide and inspire ... that national and local touch without which art is a fungus & not a firmly rooted growth. (BLMC A52364/177–8v: 250715)

Between the Boer War and the outbreak of the Great War there was an increasing introversion in Britain's sense of musical identity and destiny, which contrasts oddly with the ending of political isolation. Cecil Forsyth (1911) employed an extended vocabulary of pastoral imagery – a lexicon of the 'natural' – 'soil', 'seed', 'roots', 'garden', 'harvest'. Fifty years later, Howes's synthesis deploys the same lexicon, on an amplified scale and more conscious level. Howes claims, for example, that in the works of Gerald Finzi 'one can hear the English pastoral note, which is to say the gentle, undramatic but strong and persistent musical equivalent of the English countryside' (1966: 26). Even in later surveys, the tendency remains strong. Pirie's book – by no means a work of homage to the 'national music' ideal – opens with a poetic description of 'The Soil', from which all great music somehow emanates (Pirie 1979: 11–13).

The 'pastoral' message was much disseminated in the pages of *The Times*. H. C. Colles, who took over its music desk in 1911 (to be succeeded in 1943 by Howes), was a fervent advocate. In Colles's ecstatic prose the music of some English composers not only reproduces the land in a sensory way – as Strauss represents a flock of sheep in *Don Quixote* – but actually achieves identity with it. An example is this review of RVW's *Pastoral Symphony*, in 1922:

> One has climbed the hill, and can look away to a horizon which seems infinitely distant as the eye is led to it through infinite gradations of blue ... To me this symphony speaks like that wide Down country in which, because there is no incident, every blade of grass and tuft of moss is an incident ... One may appeal to these twenty fragments of tune which are put forward in its thematic material. Every one of them is based on the simplest diatonic intervals of music. They are of the stuff of plainsong and folk-song, the blades of grass and tufts of moss, the primitive growth of musical nature ... The interlacing growth of

these intervals brings a polyphony on which the ear rests, as one's foot does in the turf of the hillside. (Colles 1945: 92–4)

Despite its central place in *The Times* and other London-based organs, this discourse was capable of appeal across the political (and geographical) divide. Ernest Newman of the *Manchester Guardian* – no uncritical supporter of 'national music' – made it a testament to our collective genetic relationship to Green Man and Earth Mother:

> For my part I find much of Vaughan Williams's music absolutely English. These things appeal to me profoundly as they do because the English fields and streams and the English poetry that have gone into the making of them have also gone into the making of part of myself. When I muse in the lovely green and quiet English fields in summertime I do so with a host of greatly loved English poets from Chaucer onwards; and when Vaughan Williams joins the company with certain compositions of his I find that this music is English to its very marrow. (Quoted in Palmer 1979: Lyrita SRCS 68)

Just as the given language unites otherwise divergent minds over space and time – operating exactly like the nation itself – so its range of reference was not restricted to the 'school' of composers who followed the precepts of English Pastoral and/or folk-music. Elgar, despite his robust dismissal of folk-music, was too important not to be given the embrace of this heritage. For the sake of the extrinsic unity and uniformity of the national cause, his music had to be recuperated. Few writings on Elgar from the middle decades of the last century failed to include reference to some atavistic relationship between his music and the English landscape. Indeed, in deliberately fostering the 'Malvern Hills' perspective on his output, Elgar himself had arguably initiated the discourse of pastoralism, exploiting journalists' interest in order to put an attractive 'spin' on his works (Hughes 1998: 239–40, 247, 254–6). In the process the composer contributed mightily to the formation of cultural hegemony. It is not surprising, in this context, that later opinion formers were prepared to take Elgar on his own terms, accepting his notorious claim: 'I am folk music.'

Similarly, the maverick figures of 'royster-doysterers' like Heseltine/Warlock were allocated – willy-nilly, or rather hey-nonny-nonny – a place in the Pastoral utopia. Heseltine was genuinely interested in the folk revival, though his own music made little use of it. His magazine *The Sackbut* attacked artistic shibboleths, refusing to privilege those of the Pastoral School. Heseltine himself once described RVW's *Pastoral Symphony*, in a visionary moment somewhat more mundane than that experienced by H. C. Colles, as 'a cow looking over a gate' (Trend 1985: 102). Yet his own lifestyle valued the rural idyll, and his alcoholic excesses usually took place against a country village backdrop. Cognate habits, related to the interests of the charlatan necromancer Aleister Crowley ('the wickedest man in Europe'), were consigned to silence, even by fellow inconoclast and biographer Cecil Gray (Gray 1934). Thus, over time and typewriter, Heseltine's legacy was surreptitiously incorporated into the mythology of haystack, hillside and village green (Trend 1985: 184–92).

The most striking testament to the centripetal power of mainstream representation is the case of Delius. A composer of German parentage, who often expressed a distaste for things English – especially for 'English Music' – Delius realised late in life that his music had failed to gain a foothold anywhere outside the country of his birth. Much against the grain, he collaborated with a group of admirers in order to procure artistic immortality. The conspirators were not supporters of the 'orthodox' idiom, nor part of its network. Its leaders, Heseltine, Beecham and Gardiner, were perfectly aware of what they were doing. They disguised Delius with appropriate features in order to forge an entry (as it were) past the doorkeepers of the Goodly House. Delius's personal and musical images were manipulated to fit the requirements laid down by the 'English Pastoral'. So intractable was the raw material that the process was protracted and expensive. In 1929, a Delius festival was held in London, which the blind and crippled composer (who lived in France) attended. It was accompanied by a gush of publicity linking Delius's music with every conceivable 'English' element, and especially – aided by carefully selected works like *Brigg Fair* and the new *Song of Summer* – with the English countryside. Some months after his death in 1934, the campaign culminated in an amazing charade: the disinterment and reburial – literally the 'repatriation' – of the decomposing composer in an English country churchyard. The fact that the BBC sent engineers to make a recording of this event registered its ultimate success. Delius duly became an icon of Englishness (Stradling 1989).

The purchase obtained on our thought patterns by the pastoralist overtones of English Music is regularly exploited by advertising copyists in the broadcasting media to sell products whose actual link with the countryside is tenuous. It is hardly possible to sit through a commercial break on TV without hearing some music of 'English Pastoral' derivation. Here, the confidence placed in its effect is actuarial: nothing could better demonstrate the political power of music, when linked to a seductive, descriptive and communicative message. English pastoralism has thus become a 'genealogy' (Foucault) or a 'metanarrative' (Lyotard) in the senses suggested by modern cultural theorists. Its message, conservative to the core, was voiced by composers who often proclaimed themselves socialist, or at least radically anti-establishment, in sympathy. Its effect is all the more powerful because subliminal. Some of English Music's greatest devotees fail to recognise the cultural processes that are here at work. For example, in 1988 the film director Ken Russell produced a TV programme in which he delivered a personal view of English Music's essences. His presentation was typically unconventional, not just through its advocacy of some 'undeservedly neglected' composers. At times it seemed that the topographical interest of his subject centred on women's bodies rather than the English landscape. But the script foregrounded the importance of the countryside to English composers, and their matchless talent in responding to this source of inspiration. Russell concluded: 'This country has produced pastoral music like no other. Its unique quality is inspired by and instilled with the spirit of the British countryside – which is the best thing about Britain anyway' (ITV: 020488).

Russell made a bitter attack on the two leading English composers of his own time, Tippett and Britten, both of whom happened to be gay. Tippett's operas were condemned for their radical musical language and political content. However, Russell's programme included the slow movement of Tippett's *Concerto for Double String Orchestra*, one of its composer's early 'English Pastoral' inspirations. 'Now that's better', exclaimed Russell's voice-over, 'no message!' What is national, he was unconsciously telling us, cannot be political. Similarly, he expressed a preference for the mainstream heterosexual lyricism of Walton (in *Troilus and Cressida*) over Britten's queer version of Shakespeare (in *A Midsummer Night's Dream*). Like the Bard, with whom it is often linked – Colles's review of RVW, quoted above, confessed to receiving a strong impression of *Sonnet 18* and 'the darling buds of May' – the English Pastoral style is presented as having no political meaning. It is above and beyond the corrupting influence of politics, precisely because it is part of the national heritage – eternal, ineluctable, 'natural'.

From Scruton to *Scrutiny*: Englishness and the folk ethic

Not long after Russell's programme, a quite different personality appeared on our domestic screens, under the rubric 'Think of England'. Indeed we refer to the busiest thinker of the so-called 'New Right', Roger Scruton, who returned to the tireless trope of country versus town ('England's Green and Pleasant Land', BBC 2: 221091), the obsession of conservative thinkers since Virgil. Scruton's hypothesis was that the English countryside tangibly represents its people's alleged genius for political compromise. The argument was underlined by a verdant musical carpet, including RVW's *The Lark Ascending*, and Tippett's *Concerto for Double String Orchestra*. Scruton's script was ideologically more sensitive than Russell's, and, for example, the significance of brass bands playing Parry's *Jerusalem* was neatly expounded. All the same, it was liberally sprinkled with the instinctual – or perhaps in this case blatant – vocabulary of the pastoral: 'green', 'organic', 'spiritual' and 'peace'.

Scruton's world-picture included many cognate images referring to 'eternal verities' of our existence, located not far away from the 'natural' landscape itself. Such images were already anachronistic in the heyday of *Volkisch* fascism. In 1931, reviewing W. H. Hadow's *English Music*, in the Longman series 'The English Heritage', H. C. Colles emphasised the book's historical significance and portentously denominated these icons.

> English musicians must be glad to see their art enshrined in company with 'Shakespeare', 'The English Public School', 'Cricket', and other matters which are part and parcel of our national inheritance … [It is] in itself an acknowledgement that music holds, and has always held, a place among the lively interests of the people, and that their interest in and practice of music has produced types different from the music of other nations. It means that in music we have something that we take for granted as our own, that just as our speech is coloured by familiar quotations from Shakespeare, our manners, even to the trivialities of dress, by those of the Public School, and our views on sportsmanship by the very word 'cricket', so there is something in English music which informs and limits our outlook on art as a whole. (1945: 107–9)

By such tokens, the heritage of English music is not located in the urban environment, and emphatically not among the industrial proletariat. It is the eternal encapsulation of village, green, and salad days. *Pace* Colles, it was far above and beyond 'the lively interests of the people'. Even as *The Times*'s critic pronounced, despite all that the writers, and even the power of the State itself, could do, it was becoming irretrievably lost to (or rather, lost on) the vast majority, because of the inundation of the Western industrialised world by transatlantic culture.

Yet on the surface the campaign for a 'national music' seemed to be tasting success. Not long after Hadow's book, Odhams published a school textbook of general information based on the catechistical method popular in the interwar years. Its references to English Music illustrated the monopoly of attention then enjoyed by the folk-music movement.(Wheeler *c.* 1936: 253). The question 'Who founded the English Folk-Dance Society?' (cf. the Roman Catholic Catechism's 'Who made you?') elicited the answer 'Cecil Sharp' – godfather of the folk revival. Sharp had indelibly associated the origins of folk-music with the 'historical' beginnings of race and nation. In his day, it was confidently believed that to identify origin was synonymous with the exposition of scientific truth. Other heirs of the Victorians went in search of primary moments along the rocky seashore, in Sussex gravel-pits, or among the manuscripts of the British Museum – variously discovering obscure fossils, 'Piltdown Man', and 'Sumer Is Icomen In'. Likewise, Sharp pursued the incontrovertible 'scientific' evidence of England's musical evolution. He was himself a schoolteacher, and his work was directly addressed with a political–didactic purpose to the Board of Education.

Behind the English Musical Renaissance lay profound misgivings over whether England possessed the raw materials with which to make a 'musical nation' in the only sense that ultimately counted – creative composition. In 1884, an article for *Cassell's Magazine* implied a need to close the semantic ground between the terms 'musical nation' and 'national music':

> The term 'national music' has been misunderstood by some. Carl Engel defines it as 'that music which, appertaining to a nation or tribe, whose individual emotions and passions it expresses, exhibits certain peculiarities more or less characteristic, which distinguish it from the music of any other nation or tribe'. The Germans very appropriately call it *Volksmusik*, a term which we might translate into 'folk music' were

such a word permissible. National music, then, may be tersely defined
as that music which the people themselves have made ... Hence it is
that composers who have attempted to write national airs have nearly
always failed, for [they] have not embodied the essential elements of
really national music. (Hadden 1884)

A decade later the issue of 'national music' was receiving a national
airing. *The Strand Magazine* – aimed at a wide middle-class readership – asked a number of composers whether England was 'a musical
nation'. Most respondents prevaricated. Gounod, a pioneer of the
entente cordiale, praised the Lord and kicked for touch in declaring
that 'every nation is a musical nation' (Jones 1894). The manifold
stirrings of 'Englishness', and even of English nationalism, took place
in a period when Britain's long political isolation was entering its
final and most insecure phase (Rich 1989). Likewise, it is notable that
the foundation of the Folk Song Society and the intensive fieldwork
of its acolytes coincided exactly with the crisis in South Africa. Like
other British socialists, Cecil Sharp believed in the justice and humanity of his people's colonial role, especially when contrasted with the
Boer–German alternative. It was right to fight for the preservation,
and even the geographical extension, of the uniquely free and fulfilling way of life which had evolved under English leadership.

At the time of his inaugural lecture to the Folk Song Society in
1898, Sir Hubert Parry was the acknowledged leader of the musical
establishment. He saw folk-music as an answer not only to musical
evil but even to social and political vice. Parry identified the *ethnic*
with the *ethical* in its value and power for improvement. Coming to
us direct from the arcadian past of the race, an English Eden free
from original sin, folk-music was a talisman, a grail of purification in
the here and now. He excoriated the popular song of the urban
masses in a *tour de force* of invective. It was 'repulsive and insidious',
'shoddy', 'sham', 'stale', 'false', 'unhealthy'; in contrast, 'wholesome' folk-melody would drive out these evils. 'In these days of high
pressure and commercialism there is nothing in it common or
unclean.' Parry referred, elliptically but unmistakably, to the profound national significance of the task which faced the Society: 'all
the things which mark the folk-music of the race, also betoken the
qualities of the race' (*MT* 1899).

It was a perfect political conjunction, therefore, that in the year of
victory over the Boers (1902) Cecil Sharp collected his first folksong, while staying in a Somerset vicarage; that it was called 'The

Seeds of Love'; and that it was sung by a gardener whose name was John England.

> I sowed my seeds of love
> It was all in the spring ...
> The gardener was standing by,
> I asked him to choose for me.

Sharp, indeed, saw himself as a gardener, and his songs as 'simple ditties which have sprung like wild flowers from the very hearts of our countrymen'. The 'original' country song, 'purified' of its generational accretions, was a seed which, if planted in the soil of the nation, would release a spring, a renaissance in all its affairs. 'Folk song', he proclaimed, 'is essentially a communal as well as a racial product ... as redolent of the English race as its language' (Sharp 1907/72: 165).

> Our system of education is, at present, too cosmopolitan: it is calculated to produce citizens of the world rather than Englishmen. And it is Englishmen, English citizens, that we want. How can this be remedied? By taking care ... that every child born of English parents is, in its earliest years, placed in possession of all those things which are the distinctive product of its race ... [Thus] he will know and understand his country and his countrymen, and ... will love them the more, realize that he is united to them by the subtle bond of blood and of kinship, and become, in the highest sense of the word, a better citizen and a truer patriot. (Sharpe 1907: 173–4)

Sharp aimed to build up from the grass roots. His twin tasks were to persuade the Board of Education to introduce his formula in schools, looking forward to a School of Native English Genius:

> If the Board of Education take any action in this matter it must, to be effective, be based upon the theory propounded in the foregoing pages.
> [...]
> There exists at the present day no National School of English Music ... The discoveries of English Folk Song ... will eventually lead to the foundation of an English National School of composition. (163–4, 177)

The Parry–Sharp prescription was indeed taken up by the State: folk-music became a staple of the education system, and passed into the nation's bloodstream. Even after the war against Nazi Germany, essays could appear which – while avoiding the discredited word 'race' – emphasised the sound 'stock' of English composers (God-dard 1946: 11–29). The lead role in maintaining the philosophy of an English ethnic ethic was assumed by the academics. *Music and Letters*, a journal founded by A. H. Fox-Strangways, provided constant propaganda for the Pastoral School (Revill 1991). The Cambridge review *Scrutiny* was the most influential voice in critical circles for a generation after 1933. Its founder, F. R. Leavis, was dedicated to the proposition that English culture was derived from an organic tradition, a communitarian, populist past which was the only refuge from the subversive alienation of modernism (Mulhern 1979: 46ff.). In addition, Leavis was concerned at the rejection of High Art by many who associated it with the narcissism of 'art for art's sake', which denied it a social purpose: and, above all, with the alleged perversions of the Wilde–Beardsley generation. The enemy was not far away. In the same common-rooms as the Scrutineers were other groups which the former saw as a direct threat to nation and society – above all, communist homosexuals like the 'Apostles'. Against such influence they posed an art of bourgeois values – responsible, respectable, worthy of the trust of society and the burden of power it carried. This produced a discourse of 'biological hygiene', so obviously imbricated in the political context of the 1930s that its political meaning quite escaped its prophets; an atavistic, governing reality of culture, with normative references based on health, vigour and virility.

Scrutiny's first music writer was Bruce Pattinson, who looked to what many intellectuals (influenced by historians like Bryant and Rowse) saw as the most perfect manifestation of the English nation, the Tudor age, to provide inspiration for English Music. England's greatest artist was a country lad equally familiar with the folksongs of his local farms, the popular catches of the taverns and the madrigals and motets of the court.

> The organic community had traditional ways of filling its leisure, in which music played a large part. The rustics Cecil Sharp found were very far from being bores; on the contrary he was impressed with their natural courtesy and poise. Folk Song was the heritage of all classes … and thus there was no cleavage between the musical background of the educated and that of the illiterate. (Pattinson 1935)

So specifically did Pattinson – in 1935 – see national music in terms of the Tudor period that he seems almost to have conjured up a major composition of that year: RVW's *Five Tudor Portraits*. Pattinson was convinced that the revival of English Music from its moribund past had been achieved by the composer and his associates. The use of English polyphonic modes, 'together with our folk music, are enriching the idiom of a by no means negligible group of modern composers'. In the interests of the crusade, he applauded the folk-based principles of music education, which had been reasserted by a report commissioned by Cambridgeshire county authorities (Dent 1933; Pattinson 1934).

Pattinson's successor was less enthusiastic about folk-music. Wilfrid Mellers was an undergraduate at the time, and perhaps more aware of folklore's fascist undercurrents. Yet his hostility towards Benjamin Britten obediently reflected the suspicion with which his patrons, like Leavis himself, treated the composer's associate W.H. Auden. Homosexuality was an area of undesirable 'otherness' for *Scrutiny*, and in combination with the quasi-communism professed by the Auden circle, it represented an anathema.

> Britten is yet another twentieth-century artist destroyed by the chief evil of our cultural life today – the formation, in default of solidarity, of clique and coterie. Rubbra has austerely avoided contact with any such clique, either of the Britten–Berkeley–Auden–Isherwood type ... or of the Van Dieren–Heseltine–Grey [*sic*] type ... [He] depends ultimately and unanswerably on the artist's toughness and virility. Rubbra's toughness and virility are not in doubt but his is indeed a heavy responsibility. (Mellers 1939: 70)

Thus Mellers elected to select Edmund Rubbra as the composer who would carry onwards the torch of Parry, RVW and national music into the lives of future generations: 'Essentially this is masculine music ... strong, civilised, inherently sane and healthy ... Rubbra is the son of a worker in a Northampton boot factory and has himself been errand boy and railway clerk. His music suggests that here is a man ... to write music for the people' (Mellers 1937: 76).

From the year 2000, looking back on Rubbra's career and the nature of his output, it is not difficult to see that this prophecy was wide of the mark. But in 1937, such a man, with boots, errands and the railways in his blood, seemed the ideal messenger to send ahead along the King's Highway.

The King's Highway

The poet–composer Ivor Gurney was a post-dated victim of the Western Front. Although signs of mental illness were present before his enlistment, the appalling experience of war exacerbated the condition. After many years in a London asylum, he died in 1937. An appreciation written by his one-time teacher, Vaughan Williams, reads like the report of a commanding officer, informing next of kin of a loss in action.

> In the history of our art there has always been the good way, 'the King's highway', cast up by Patriarchs or Prophets, as straight as a rule can make it, the way we must go. Those who tread this way are not merely blind followers of the blind – not slaves but free; each one makes his own footsteps on the road and leaves his own impress. Here lies the true originality of inevitableness. There are others who say 'we will not walk therein', but they seldom find that rest to their souls, that simplicity and serenity which is surely the final aim of all art. Too often they merely avoid the Hill Difficulty and wander into 'a wide field full of dark mountains where they stumble and fall to rise no more'.
> (Vaughan Williams 1934/87: 256)

By this time, exponents of RVW's version of 'national music' were in command of the elite regiments. Most of the key posts in the musical establishment were filled by men who strode the narrow path of folk-music with a doctrinal surety, and who strove for the cause of a 'serious' music based thereon. Teaching faculties in London and elsewhere were dominated by folklorists. Influential critics – Legge, Colles, and Fox-Strangways among them – were enthusiastic. In performance terms things were perhaps less satisfactory. Beecham, for example, was sceptical. A positively blasphemous anecdote has him loudly exclaiming 'Thank God' – not meant in Haydn's sense – when the double bar was reached during a rehearsal of RVW's *Pastoral Symphony*, sacrosanct work of the orthodox idiom (Cardus 1961: 31). On the other hand, Henry Wood consistently made space for the pastoralists in Proms programmes, and their main practical advocate, Adrian Boult, was in control at the BBC. In the provincial centres, national music assumed a strong position. Arthur Barter gave loyal support in Bristol, programming works by RVW and his associates for the Concerts Society (BRBC DM 433). In Birmingham, Leslie Heward firmly established a 'national' repertoire (King-Smith 1970: 14–19). At Bournemouth,

Dan Godfrey continued a mission which benefited many composers
of the 'Folk Music School' (Le Fleming 1982: 27–38). But the most
powerful reply to Beecham came from the rising star of John Barbirolli – Toscanini's sensational successor – which inclined itself
towards the Pastoral Bethlehem. In 1943, 'Glorious John' introduced RVW's *Pastoral* to the Carnegie Hall (Rigby 1948: 114). All
in all, the first historian of the orchestra in England felt justified in
characterising these decades as 'the Nationalist Period'(Nettel
1946).

The new establishment was underpinned by Sharp's programme,
incorporated into the curriculum by the Education Act of 1919. The
architect of this legislation was RVW's brother-in-law H. A. L.
Fisher. It gave state 'recognition' to the unique national status of
folk-music, and committed its resources accordingly. Editions of
English folk-music were placed on the piano of every primary-
school classroom in the land. The poet D. J. Enright, brought up in
working-class London of the 1920s, recalled that one of the 'two
good things' about infants' school was

> Dancing Sellinger's Round, and dancing and
> Dancing it, and getting it perfect forever.
> (Enright, And Two Good Things [1990: 74])

The process went through under the benign supervision of Chief
Government Inspector of School Music Arthur Somervell, inspired
by the example of his master, Stanford. Somervell's activity on
behalf of the folk message did not cease with his retirement (and
knighthood) in 1929 (Howes 1966: 158–60).

Supplementing the activities of the Folk Song and Folk Dance
Societies, the Rural Music Schools' Association (founded 1929) re-
planted the seeds of folk music in the villages, where the folk lived
but where their musical traditions had apparently died (Le Fleming
1982: 62–3). Back on the other side of the five-bar gate, Walter Carroll was appointed as the first-ever municipal director of music, in
Manchester (1921), and began to cultivate 'Bushes and Briars' in the
back streets of Salford. Carroll also produced children's piano exer-
cises based on cosy rural tableaux – *Scenes at a Farm* and *Tunes from
Nature* – with appropriate cover scenes by Arthur Rackham, famous
illustrator of Wagner's *Ring* (Walker 1989). Carroll's career culminated in 1929 when he persuaded Columbia to record one of the
least likely hits in the history of commercial recording: hundreds of

kids from the Manchester slums took the roles of Purcell's 'Nymphs and Shepherds' – but with their back-street accents carefully trained away! (Anon. BBC R4: 301289).

The Great War of 1914–18 gave a huge fillip to the task of identifying folk-music with national music. Before the war, RVW, Holst and Butterworth had failed to register a definitive breakthrough. Of course, Gurney, Howells and other pilgrims had experienced the revelatory moment of 'recognition' upon hearing RVW's *Fantasia on a Theme of Thomas Tallis*. This precise experience was later to be described in similar terms by many musicians and music-lovers. But only with the war did folk-referenced English 'nature-music' begin to obtain a place in programmes. At the same time, the army was introduced to folksong and folk-dancing by Lena Ashwell's concert-party organisation. As Ashwell later recalled:

> At one time there was quite a big vogue in France for the country dances, folk dances, morris and sword dances. All this work was started by Miss Dakin, and there were a number of teachers in different bases who undertook to teach these dances to the men. Some of them were wildly enthusiastic ... some 'bored to tears'. The dancing was especially used in convalescent camps ... I heard delightful stories of the band playing on the sands at Trouville whilst the convalescents danced themselves back to health. There were in all about fifteen teachers. (Ashwell 1922: 178–9)

Indeed, folk-dancing – as one heartrending piece of documentary film records – was prescribed as official therapy for the injured (and often limbless) multitude. The spiritual essence of the England for which these men had fought and suffered was thus instilled in order to restore them to health. Thaumaturgy had its place alongside surgery in the shambles of the Somme – evocative enough of what folk-music had come to stand for, and of the power with which it was invested.

Meanwhile the sheer quantity of native works performed in 'serious' concerts is reflected in the prolific output of their composers. In 1912, William Wallace, secretary of the Philharmonic Society, complained that attempts to encourage British Music during the Society's centenary year had been financially disastrous (BLMC L48–33–13/34: 170212). But shortly after the Great War, Balfour Gardiner, a committed benefactor of British Music, expressed a diametrically opposite concern to Wallace's successor.

> If Nielka chooses something English & Muriel Foster sings *Four Mystical Songs* by Vaughan Williams the result will be that our singers will sing nothing but English works: there will not be a foreign aria or song of any description. This is too great a disproportion, and I think the programmes are becoming overloaded with English names.

He recommended dropping the Vaughan Williams work, so as to avoid 'excessive Anglicisation' of the RPS repertoire (BLMC L48–33–38/129: 231019). Gardiner himself was a one-time folk-song collector (in Hampshire), and his *Shepherd Fennel's Dance* remained a popular folksy favourite for many years (Lloyd 1984: 34ff.). Perhaps he sensed, and was wary of, the change by which what, prior to 1914, had been a generalised crusade for British Music was focused by the intensity of war on to a more specifically English culture (Foreman 1987: 119). For the music of RVW was about to become – in the sense used by Bakhtin about literary genres – a 'monological discourse'. The critic Edwin Evans accepted national music as providing the currency of England's claims to *international* artistic worthiness.

> Paradoxically, the nationalists in music are the real internationalists ... and when they claim that art has no frontiers they often mean that the frontiers of that nation, and the ideas it represents, should be extended ... The English musical idiom is no longer submerged. We hear it everywhere [in] the music of Vaughan Williams, Holst, Whittaker, Butterworth, and others. (Evans 1924: 45–6)

This observation was becoming a major dialectical point of debate, used against those who feared the ethnocentric effects of 'national music'. By now, established musical voices sang in pastoral accents. After Sharp's death in 1926, RVW edged modestly into the limelight, and took up the conductor's (or field marshal's) baton. As Howes rightly comments, the subscribers to (and, we may add, the inscribers of) the Pastoral style had become 'sufficiently homogeneous as a group in spirit as well as time to constitute the nationalist succession ... to the actual rebirth of English music' (Howes 1966: 263). RVW's personal qualifications were matchless. He was a member of the English aristocracy by birth and connection, yet was impeccably social-democratic in his convictions. He was an agnostic, yet treasured the heritage of English religion. His descent was from the finest scholarly lineage (he was a nephew of Charles Darwin), yet likewise was from the hardy 'stock' of English business enterprise (the Wedgwoods). He reached the solid age of 50 in 1922; he had helped to pioneer folksong research; he was a convincing exponent of the complementary academic revival of 'Tudor polyphony'. To such a man no door in the land was closed.

Vaughan Williams thus seemed the culmination of a line of biological and intellectual evolution. In an age when racially based genetics was accepted science, and many less respectable versions of its hypotheses were widely disseminated, he appeared a worthy successor of his distinguished ancestors – and of his mentor Hubert Parry, who had brilliantly applied the principle of evolution to the history of music. Of equal significance, however, was that RVW was a war-veteran. He had served first in ambulance units, and latterly as a gunner. His advocate, Colles, also an artillery officer, once wrote home amid the hideous cacophony – Wilfred Owen's 'monstrous anger of the guns' – that 'somewhere in the middle of me I know that it is not the cause of humanity, or of the allies, or of the British Empire or the British Isles that I'm here to help in my small trifling way, but just ENGLAND' (Colles 1945: 205).

Members of the Pastoral School, like Butterworth and Farrar, made the ultimate blood sacrifice so crucial to the reification of style and cause. Many other composers who paid homage to the 'pastoral' ideal and received place and reward in return, were survivors of the war. Holst, RVW's closest confidant, had served as a non-combatant. Patrick Hadley and E. J. Moeran had been seriously wounded in the trenches. Another man in step with the company along the King's highway was George Dyson, director of the RCM from 1937. He had been a serving officer, and was also the author of official textbooks on aspects of military tactics. Arthur Bliss was a slightly different case. Intensely chauvinistic as a result of his wartime experiences – a brother was killed not far away from him on the Western Front – Bliss at first composed in a 'modernist' idiom redolent of the French 'Six'. But his rejection of Germanic influences led him towards the orthodox 'English' style. He was taken under the supervision of RVW and his brother-in-law R.O. Morris, composing much of the *Colour Symphony* – the first of his works to adopt a 'national' profile – in the house which the two families shared in Chelsea (Bliss 1970: 74–5). By the late 1920s Bliss's works even resorted to a 'folkish' character, as his *Pastoral* and *Clarinet Quintet* indicate (Fox-Strangways 1936/68: 129).

Of true pastoralists close to the founders, only Howells and Finzi were not war-veterans. The former was, however, a promising composer. He had demonstrated a rigorous application of folk-music principles to extended (chamber) works. His *Piano Quartet* and *Phantasy Quintet* (both 1917) were of a striking idiomatic fluency and contained original elements which influenced the master, RVW, himself – this, moreover, at a time when the latter's definitive statements (*The Lark Ascending* and *A Pastoral Symphony*) were still on the drawing-board. By the mid-1920s, however, Howells was becoming dissatisfied with the expressive and rhythmic limitations of the idiom, particularly as regards orchestral music. In *Piano Concerto No. 2* (1925) he turned to continental models for guidance. Howells's heresy was a minor one. His solution was to invoke the aid of Bartók, the most innovative contemporary exponent of folk-music. But his attempt to branch out – on a different but parallel highway, hardly 'a wide field full of dark mountains' – did not succeed. He was pulled back by the centripetal forces of orthodoxy, then at their strongest. The concerto's premiere at the Proms was a disaster, the work being savaged by a unanimous critical corps. Howells was shell-shocked by the barrage received from Colles and company. He withdrew from secular instrumental music, gave up the quest for wide public 'recognition', and sought thereafter only the consolations of the classroom and the sanctuary of the chapel (Spicer BBC R3: 230489). This case was a salutary one for others who flirted with the temptation of experiment. Howells may have escaped the trenches, but he ended by suffering a fate metaphorically akin to those who deserted in the face of the enemy.

Whatever their backgrounds – and Dyson started at the other end of the social scale from the rest – the composers mentioned above were bonded together by 'national' attitudes crystallised by the war. It was no coincidence that 'serious' composers now started to write for a medium they had previously ignored and/or despised: the brass band. Such activity was inspired in part by sentiments similar to the guilty desire of the ruling class to build 'homes fit for heroes'. In the lead were Holst and RVW, whose most successful pieces were military marches. During the years of conscription the brass bands of industrial England had changed their uniforms. Music for wind groups became not only an area where army and workers fused, but one where the 'two nations' of Dyson's north and Allen's south united their efforts in the common cause. What more ideal a vehicle

for national music? Shortly before the war, Holst made folk-tunes
the basis of two *Suites for Military Band*. In 1922 (again) RVW wrote
Three English Folk Songs. Ostensibly intended to improve the quality of marching tunes at Kneller Hall, the real motive was to replace
an existing repertoire in which a 'national' benchmark was lacking.
The right tunes would help the band, and thus the troops, to march
along the King's highway (Vaughan Williams 1964: 151–2. The official history of the Royal Military School of Music at Kneller Hall
eschews these issues: see Binns 1959). In 1930, even Elgar – a
special constable during the Great War – dutifully fell in step with
the cohorts by producing his *Severn Suite* for brass band.

In the post-1918 world, what the Germans called *Fronterlebnis*
(memories of the Front) imparted an *esprit de corps* of the Western
Front to many groups, including British musicians (Fussell 1990).
Such feelings were not shared by all. Among the sceptics were some
who had been in uniform, such as Havergal Brian and Rutland
Boughton. Nor was every composer whose creative life was influenced by the 'folk–pastoral' idiom therefore a fully paid-up member
of the ruling guild – Bridge and Ireland, for example, were exceptions. A corps mentality was present all the same; a set of discrete but
converging lines of consciousness, mostly to do with landscapes of
memory. In addition to the Western Front, similar common denomi-
nators linked the leaders of 'national music' with the RCM, and with
Cambridge. These communal loyalties again illustrate the centrality
of RVW, as an alumnus of both. His disciple, Hadley, was to succeed
his supporter, Dent, as professor at his old university, and many other
associates had a Cambridge background. RVW always preserved his
links with the Royal College, though his professorial commitments
involved many difficulties. He did not need the money the post
brought him, and was not a gifted teacher, yet he regarded it as
important to maintain contact with the *crème de la crème* of young
talent. In the 1920s, prizes in memory of the warrior dead, Farrar and
Butterworth, were instituted at the RCM. These awards were used to
encourage students such as Stanley Bate and Benjamin Britten to step
out along the King's highway (Barlow and Barnett 1991).

Teme, theme and team spirit

Another landscape in the world-picture of this generation was provided by one English county. Gloucestershire had been prominent

since the beginning of the Musical Renaissance: Hubert Parry was a
Gloucestershire man, often in residence at his ancestral towers,
Highnam Court. It seems there was something in the Severn's
waters. RVW's birth at Down Ampney was followed by those of
Holst and C. W. Orr in Cheltenham, Gurney and Herbert Sumsion
in Gloucester city, and Howells at Lydney (G. Norris 1981: 331–5).
In 1900, Holst composed his *Cotswold Symphony*, Howells his
string quartet *In Gloucestershire* in 1922. The wartime correspon-
dence between Gurney and Howells profusely illustrates the intense
feelings nurtured for the places of the county they loved (Thornton
1984). In the early 1920s, Vaughan Williams set his 'folk-opera'
Hugh the Drover – designed as an English equivalent of *The Bartered
Bride* – in a Cotswold village. In 1929, the Labour Prime Minister
Ramsay MacDonald, a Scotsman of urban origins, visited the
Cotswolds, and saw there the very heart of 'the England of long past
centuries' (Wiener 1985: 121). But, long before this, associations
evoked by Bredon Hill had linked together the composers who fell
under the spell of the Cambridge don and lyric poet A. E. Housman
(Stradling 1998).

When rehearsing *Symphony No. 1*, Elgar was apt to suggest that
his orchestra played the trio of the second movement 'like something
you hear down by the river' (Kennedy 1970: 55). He was recalling
youthful days spent along the River Teme, a tributary of the Severn
which joins its great partner a few miles south of the city of Worcester. The Teme Valley lies between Housman's two vantages of Bredon
Hill and Wenlock Edge. Its local 'capital' is the town of Ludlow.
Composers and poets focused on this region, following the discovery
of Housman's poetry by a whole generation. Housman's anthology *A
Shropshire Lad* (1896) was more thoroughly explored by English
musicians than any aspect of the actual region to which it is dedicated. The teenaged Ivor Gurney began the craze with songs later
incorporated into cycles with evocative titles – *Ludlow and Teme* and
The Western Playland – whilst Moeran called his Housman collection
Ludlow Town (1915). The craze for *A Shropshire Lad* coincided with
publication of Sharp's folksong research. The poet's backdrop of
village and farm; his diapason of work and play; his protagonists,
simple but sturdy yeomen; an emotional range of stoical irony and
gentle nostalgia; all these elements harmonised perfectly with the
turn towards folksong. Thus Housman's lyrics became a meeting-
place for the Pastoral School, an *agora* where disciples engaged with

the master in a Socratic dialogue about the essence of Englishness. At the same time, their expression of the tension between continuity and change, individual death set in an ageless landscape, evoked the forebodings of a pre-war epoch. Housman was a *locus classicus* of love and peace, not of struggle. But it is precisely the localised essences of love and peace that are worth fighting for: and the English husbandman (or 'house-man') came forth in arms to defend cottage and village in 1914. Thousands of letters from the Front were, consciously or otherwise, to echo Housman's sentiments and even the cadences of his lines (Tapert 1984). Likewise, from Gurney to Julius Harrison, via Somervell, Butterworth, Orr, Ireland, Moeran and RVW himself, settings of Housman became a passport for travel along the King's highway.

Housman explored a further topic of crucial importance to national music. In the poems, personal tragedy is set beside and balanced against the demands of the community. Despite the archaism of his style, Housman was aware of what characterised the local community in the late nineteenth century. He included references to Association Football, a game which had deep traditional roots among the lower classes of town and country alike. Apart from its broad socio-cultural significance, the national organisation of sport in this epoch was an insidious form of mobilisation (Mason 1980; Vamplew 1988). Housman's demotic use of 'lads' to describe his subjects also hints at the role of sport and war in the development of male-bonding, so important during the crisis of imperialism, and which reached fulfilment in the trenches. The title of the poem most often chosen by composers – *Is My Team Ploughing?* – carries a series of overtones. It refers to the team of horses which the ghostly speaker used in the fields, but also to his soccer team and the collective endeavour of its members. After his death, both his equine team and his human teammates go on ploughing, the former in the fertile earth, the latter with the girl he left behind. In the best-known version of *Is My Team Ploughing?*, in his song-cycle *On Wenlock Edge* (1909), RVW was not embarrassed by its sexual innuendo, but he omitted the poem's central stanzas about a soccer match, regarding them as inappropriate to the concert-room. This act of bowdlerisation appalled the poet, who did not stint in his complaints. For us it provides confirmation of the class origins and destiny of 'national music'.

Gloucestershire's cathedral city was an apt focus of a national heartland, not only because it is a classic rural apex, but in its modest industrial dimension. Here the matches called 'England's Glory' were manufactured by the firm of Samuel Moreland, and retailed in small cardboard boxes. In an age when tobacco smoking was universal, once the original contents were exhausted, the boxes were passed on to boys, who used them for storing collections of everything from spiders to sweets. The gender reference here is not exclusive: many women took up smoking during the Great War, and innumerable housewives used matches to light the living-room fire or the gas mantle. It was Gloucester's matches which (literally) kept the home fires burning. The matchbox cover was illustrated by a Union Jack, with a superimposed picture of an early type of Dreadnought battleship – 'England's Glory'. Thus the daily lives of millions were accompanied by a symbol of chauvinism and empire, nation and navy. The advertising emblemology of smoking was intimately bound up with the sea and the fleet. England's forests, once plundered for the building material of its wooden walls, were now dedicated to another cause – but one which maintained the link with the Senior Service. The old symbiosis was replaced by another, connecting British industry and native genius with the sea.

Hubert Parry, born between the Forest of Dean and the Severn estuary, became a keen yachtsman. He built his new home ('Knight's Croft') a few hundred yards from the slipway at Rustington in Sussex. Vaughan Williams moved out of Wenlock Wood to write *A Sea Symphony* (1911) at a time when hopes for the survival of empire, nation and culture were focused on the Royal Navy. Things maritime became a ubiquitous interest of composers. Smyth, Delius, Bantock, Holbrooke, Bridge and many others contributed relevant works of importance. Henry Wood premiered pieces like *Two Sea Pictures* by the highly appropriate Hubert Bath (1909) and *A Sea Poem* by the highly unlikely Hyam Greenbaum (1923) (Cox 1980: 264, 271). Next to Housman, Kipling, Newbolt and Masefield were popular with song-writers. Perhaps Cecil Forsyth's assertion that native genius was being diluted with brine was not as bizarre at it seemed at first dash. Yet we must not overstate the national significance of all this. The sea was a universal musical theme, by no means exclusive to composers with Gloucester connections (Proctor 1992: 113–27). Neither was it restricted to those who supported the campaign for national music, in the sense expounded above. Its most chauvinistic examples were Stanford's *Songs of the Fleet* and Elgar's *Fringes of the Fleet*, the latter written to highlight 'the Nelson touch'

during the Great War, by a composer who had been explicitly compared to Nelson (Hughes 1989).

Since ancient Greece, the warship has been the most fertile
metaphor for the nation. For generations of English public-school
boys, Greece was admired not only as the birthplace of democracy,
but as the greatest example of a successful *thalassocracy*, that is, a
nation which bases its power on the sea. In 1912, Arthur Somervell
gave his only symphony the title *Thalassa* ('The Sea'). Its programme
was a tribute to a national vocation and to the German symphonic
tradition. The German conductor Artur Nikisch gave its first performance in 1913, the same year as he premiered Butterworth's
Housman elegy *A Shropshire Lad* (Anon. BBC R3: 221191). The sea
offered a multi-dimensional medium for composers. Another of its
aspects presented the siren call of nature, with its ubiquitous bitonal
clash of promise and danger (Bridge's *The Sea*, Bax's *Tintagel*). In
Boughton – or rather, in the choreography of his partner Christina
Walshe – the chorus becomes the tumultuous sea, beating against the
rocky coast (the opera *The Queen of Cornwall*). In the ongoing ritual of the Last Night of the Proms, the maritime aspect of our
national identity remains the most prominent. It is encapsulated in
the name, and the presiding image, of the composer of the celebrated *Fantasia on Sea Songs*, written for the Trafalgar centenary in
1905, and culminating in *Rule Britannia*: Sir Henry Wood, 'Old
Timbers', with his nautical beard and laurel wreath.

'National music' in the Sharp–Vaughan Williams sense had a
definitive role in maritime mythology. In elemental ways, the themes
of the sea and democracy are connected in the cultural myths of
England (Behrman 1977). The sea's spiritual environment was
regarded as one of liberation. 'Immortal Sea – a world whereon to
triumph and be free' ran the dedication to Somervell's symphony.
However, the freedom it endows was not subjective, but was rather
achieved within the objectivised ambit of the crew. Extrinsically it
represented challenge, especially in an age of desperate naval competition with Germany: intrinsically it was a site of communality,
and thus of peace. A battleship was the most magniloquent example
of a 'team' in action, a microcosm of all that was finest and most progressive in the nation. Before the age of propeller and steam, all the
crew – as a metaphor still in common usage reminds us – had pulled
on the same rope. As they hauled on the sails or pushed the capstan
they improvised the shanties which helped to form the folksong

heritage. The fact that so many songs were linked to the world of the jolly jack tar added to their 'democratic' status. Dozens of sea-songs, rediscovered by Sharp and others, at some point in their evolution had come amphibiously ashore, and, after passing through other phases of organic transformation, finally leeched into the music of the National/Pastoral School.

English landscape and seascape fused musically as early as Vaughan Williams's *Norfolk Rhapsody No. 1* (1906), a work utilising three folk-shanties (Foss 1950: 111–12). As late as Alan Bush's *Variations, Nocturne and Finale on an Old English Sea Song* (1965) the melding of the communities of land and sea, farmer and fisherman, continued to register a political meaning. While the communist Bush related stylistically throughout his career to the Folksong School, the communist-inclined Britten distanced himself from it: but his *Peter Grimes* (1945) none the less paid tribute to the same meaningful complex of myth. Vaughan Williams's *A Sea Symphony* (1910) is where these fertilising waters meet and mingle. The massed choirs sing out Whitman's paean to a vision of freedom and democracy. 'Write choral music', Parry advised RVW, 'as befits an Englishman and a democrat' (Vaughan Williams 1950: 24). The younger man faithfully carried out this task during a long creative life.

The choir, like a warship's crew, was a disciplined, highly trained, large-scale 'team', drawn (in theory) from a wide class base in English society. However, this period saw a decline in the size and activities of such organisations compared to the previous century, and a parallel contraction in the importance of the choral festivals (both ecclesiastical and civic). Pressure came from both sides of the political divide to keep the tradition alive. Before 1900, the socialist thinker Robert Blatchford realised the potential importance of choral singing to the Labour movement and began to organise accordingly. This torch was passed on to Rutland Boughton, who in the 1920s – at the height of his fame – was engaged by Herbert Morrison to lead the London Labour Choirs. The initiative flourished only briefly, and by 1930 it was discontinued in the face of evidence that film shows and soccer aroused more interest (and subscriptions) from the workers (Hurd 1962: 90ff.; Donohue and Jones 1973: 71–2). *The Cambridgeshire Report* of 1933 again emphasised – from a different perspective of class politics – how important choral training was to the musical and social health of the nation (Dent 1933: 2, 12). Yet even in London's leafy dormitory suburbs, Vaughan

Williams had to struggle to maintain the vitality of the choral contribution. This struggle still retains symbolic meaning for middle England – as witness the BBC TV serial 'The Choir', broadcast in 1995, based on a novel with a contemporary setting by Joanna Trollope (1988). On the screen, the part of the fictional cathedral city of Aldminster is played by Gloucester; the battle is fought out between the philistine dean in alliance with a local councillor ('a cultural fascist'), who wish to abandon the cathedral choir, and the forces of light led by intellectual headmaster and young choirmaster, who see it as the essence of the nation. In such hegemonic discourse there can be only one winner.

Countryside and village, sea and ships, people and song, choir and church, were all part of the transfiguration of nature into art. For an English audience, 'nature' was a theme which provided the ideal filtre of Romantic feelings. Too direct a subjective 'expression' of emotion was frowned upon as un-British; self-indulgent and ultimately effeminate. This vocabulary was mobilised against successive waves of continental corrupters, noticeable in reaction to Liszt and Wagner, but reaching a significant level of invective in opposition to the championing of Tchaikovsky by Henry Wood and Rosa Newmarch in the late 1890s (Parry 1905: 118–19). The struggle was renewed in defence of national values against Strauss, then against Scriabin – whom Adrian Boult single-handedly kept off the airwaves between the wars – and, perhaps most infamously, in the protracted rearguard action against Mahler. English Pastoral was custom-designed as the best mode of abstraction of the affective subject into what was simultaneously immanent and commonplace – but above all corporative.

Of course, evocation of the 'natural world' was a ubiquitous phenomenon in the artistic world of 1900. All over Europe, the growth of urban society, factory industry and mechanised transport inspired anxiety about the vanishing rural environment. It was only in music that 'nature' was able to give voice to its own elegy. The instruments of the modern orchestra, that 'mighty engine' as Elgar called it, which reached its most mighty in Strauss, are manufactured from the flora and fauna, the animal, vegetable and mineral elements. Countless musical titles from the century 1850–1950 manifest an ideal payment of homage, from 'modernism' – industry, invention, urban civilisation itself – to the original elements from which it sprang, and whose corporeal plunder gave it life. English composers took up the song and brought it into harmony with their assertive need to apostrophise a specifically English landscape. If a single work of this genre has been projected as the leading exemplar, it is RVW's *The Lark Ascending*, also completed in 1922 and based on a poem by the 'pastoralist' writer George Meredith. It juxtaposes a free-ranging rhapsody, given to solo violin – the lark – with an orchestral section utilising modal music based on folk-dance – land and people (Revill 1991). In *The Lark Ascending*, the listener is meant to find a commingling of the spirits of liberty and community. As in the *Sea Symphony*, RVW achieves a dynamic synthesis – tension between freedom and responsibility, its resolution, and its fusion into a rhetorical discourse. Above the mundane textures, the lark/violin hovers incandescently, like the Holy Spirit. Its dove-like benediction falls upon eternal England and upon English art, evoking a chauvinistic mission similar to that of Hans Sachs's speech in *Die Meistersinger*. RVW's *Lark* was the progenitor of hundreds of works by British composers, celebrating the rural world and seeking to convey its spiritual sanction. A variety of reference points were utilised: actual places marked on Ordnance Survey maps; the landscape's physical appearance; the seasons of the year, the times of the day and their elemental atmospheres; folksong- and folk-dance-based pieces; and, last but not least, appropriate works of Shakespeare or Housman (Cox 1980: 256–76). In 1922, with Vaughan Williams's *A Pastoral Symphony*, this idiom reached its culminating destiny of fusion with large-scale symphonic utterance.

Already, however, distaste for the excesses of late Romanticism was entering a phase in which a premium was placed on abstract, or 'absolute', music. Beginning in the mid-1920s, apprehensions over 'nationalism in music', inspired by growing pacifist beliefs among the ruling class, went hand-in-hand with suspicion of 'programmes'. For many leaders of opinion, the national community – 'the team' – ought to be something with international, even supranational, resonances, centred on the League of Nations. 'Absolute' music was to be preferred, for it suited the gift of the individual Englishman for reticence and objectivity, and at the same time removed any overt and parochial 'Englishness' which might impede understanding abroad. It is noteworthy that both of the continental composers who attracted a following in interwar England – Sibelius and Stravinsky – were held to exemplify the superior claims of 'absolute music'. From the commanding heights of the critical press the message was transmitted that music with programmatic associations was somehow inferior. It was given added point by the invention of the category of 'light music', into which Ketèlby's Persian markets and Coates's sleepy lagoons so conveniently fitted. By the 1930s the fashionable reaction was in full swing. (It was no accident that in the most intensely political decade of the century, the hermeneutics of music took decisive steps towards the autonomous, self-referenced universe they still doggedly occupy today.) Although 'pastoral' works remained to some extent a privileged exception to the rise of neo-classicism, RVW himself responded to the altered atmosphere by composing his first large-scale 'abstract' work, the *Symphony No. 4*, in which no rustic character obtrudes on the dialectic. Senior members of the Pastoral School, and many fellow-travellers along the King's highway (among them Arnold Bax) fell under the influence of Sibelius; juniors (like Britten and Tippett) opted for Stravinsky. 'Programmatic' associations were often suppressed, removed like scaffolding, once a work was complete. Composers strenuously explained that their work had no 'extra-musical' character, or even denied allegations to the contrary (Foreman 1987: 146).

This regime was to hold sway until the 1960s. RVW and others of the Pastoral School conformed to its basic imperatives, since the eternal cause of national music was more important than the ephemeral need to reflect the nation's morphology to itself in works with suitably descriptive titles. However, the difficulties of coexistence are exposed in Vaughan Williams's comments about the genesis of his last major work, made in the year of his death, 1958. *Symphony No. 9* is an elegiac evocation of a past rural England, inspired by Thomas Hardy's Tess and Egdon Heath. The composer, in a heavily ironic apologia, confessed about its 'Andante Sostenuto' that 'it is quite true that this movement started off with a programme, but it got lost on the journey – so now, oh no, we never mention it' (Hall: WRC T144). The Captain had outlived most of his crew; the leader had gone farthest along the King's highway toward the Unknown Region; but the landscape in which he moved was becoming bleaker and emptier.

1934 – the crumbling cenotaph

If 1922 was a year of fulfilment, 1934 was a year of crisis. The crusade for a national music reached its culmination in the year which has ever since been the most resonant for historians of modern English Music. In the course of 1934, Elgar, Holst and Delius all died, as if in obedience to some decree of destiny. According to the mythology examined in this book, they left a collective legacy, the English Musical Renaissance, which, as their individual genius testified, was now a finished and perfect structure. Students and music-lovers are encouraged by music history and criticism to look back upon 1934 with a kind of ritual reverence. It has become a kind of monument, an intangible but all-pervasive cenotaph of English Music.

Despite fashionable reservations, between the wars national music was a mainstream idiom, demanding the affiliation of composers who were indifferent or even unsympathetic. In the music written with Eric Fenby's assistance, towards the end of his life (*A Song of Summer* and the *Violin Sonata No. 3*), Delius made obeisance to English folk-melody. He submitted a portfolio of 'national' music – premiered in London between 1929 and 1931 – as a belated application for membership of the team (Stradling 1989). Just as the movement consciously reached back to Elgar and Delius, so it reached forward to their younger successors. Much of Britten's early music at least recognised the dominant mode (*A Boy Was Born* – which the Welsh composer Grace Williams described as 'too typically English' – and the *Sinfonietta*) (Foreman 1987: 161). In early 1934, Britten completed his *Simple Symphony*, suffused with folksy sounds and paying tribute to the strings' writing of Elgar (who died during its composition) and RVW. Tippett also began his composing inside this ambit, as (doubtless) his suppressed juvenilia would illustrate as well as the early string quartets. One of RVW's most successful disciples was Stanley Bate, who achieved success in Australia and the USA with music that reminded many of his distinguished mentor (Barlow and Barnett 1991).

The arbiters of style and standards, whose interest was in a national music based on folksong, looked to Vaughan Williams for example and leadership. In 1930, the Folk Song Society and the Folk Dance Society merged to form a single lobby. RVW became its president, and a splendid new building sprang up in Regent's Park to serve as the headquarters of their activities, which had spread into every corner of the land, as well as to the dominions and the USA. Thus another 'Goodly House' came into existence – this particular branch being named after Cecil Sharp. The movement had reached the height of its power, with government patronage, a national festival held annually in the Albert Hall, its importance recognised throughout the education system, a battery of journals and other publications, and a satisfying list of acknowledged 'masterpieces' by the nation's leading composers.

But all was not as it seemed in the fruitful garden. The 1930s was the most politically turbulent decade of the century. British institutions were everywhere under strain: challenge, subversion and even outright revolution were apprehended on every side. The 'low, dishonest decade' which Auden surveyed in *1st September 1939*, was filled with suspicion, fear and brutality. Friendships and families foundered on ideological rocks which had previously been kept safely below the surface. Fissures suddenly opened up in British society – especially the 'polite' society with which 'serious' music was so thoroughly implicated; many tumbled into them and disappeared. The rise of fascism, and particularly the outbreak of the Spanish Civil War in 1936, profoundly disturbed intellectual lives, and radicalised composers from different generations, like Ireland and Britten (Foreman 1987: 153). Others, more determined not to squander energies or distort objectives by plunging into the imperative sociopolitical issues of the day, sublimated prevailing anxieties in the debate over national music. In March 1934, Bruce Pattinson touched off a chain-reaction of polemic, when *Scrutiny* published his article supporting the folklorists on the grounds that they had brought indigenous music back into the centre of English culture. Pattinson also applauded an education system that stressed the heritage of early English composers and organic local communities – ending with the hope that if this 'can succeed against the forces of modern "democracy", English life as a whole will be the better for it' (Pattinson 1934: 404).

Later that year, under the uncompromising title 'National Music', RVW published a set of lectures originally given in the USA. He stated his beliefs that folk music was the precious ore from which all good music was wrought; that it formed the foundation of any national music; and that national music was the only music which could be international in appeal. The composer advanced his arguments with a deterministic zeal, drawing on a sub-Hegelian dialectic nurtured by the political atmosphere of the period. Historical and musical evidence were provided from 'my own country, England', and he demanded rhetorically: 'why should not the musician be the servant of the state and build national monuments like the painter, the writer, or the architect?' (Vaughan Williams 1934/87: 5, 10). A pacifist himself, in an age of pacifism, addressing an audience in which similar feelings were strong, the composer consciously attempted to disavow chauvinistic motives (p. 71). He hoped for an eventual world government, but with the caveat that this could only be encompassed via the survival, not the suppression, of national features. Accordingly, he took as his starting-point Hubert Parry's dictum that 'style is ultimately national', and studded his text with quotations of Parry and Sharp. RVW adopted Sharp's emphasis on a racially organic community, along with its efflorescent discourse. He repeated a well-rehearsed image – originating in RVW's song composed, in 1925, on the theme – that 'it is the millstream forcing its way through narrow channels which gathers strength to turn the water wheel' (p. 9). He claimed that the folk-music movement had been largely responsible for creating the climate in which 'serious' composition could flourish in England. In some revealing passages he asserted that iconoclastic youngsters who currently derided its influence were, in effect, its products: 'we are inevitably the children of our fathers. We may curse our parents, but it is they who have made us and not we ourselves' (p. 60).

Early in his book, Vaughan Williams ventured a list of those he considered to be worthy English composers. He nominated two 'founding fathers'; two more who had survived from Shaw's cohort; and two of the new generation. His terms of reference were aggressively nationalist:

> We have in England today a certain number of composers who have achieved fame. In the older generation, Elgar and Parry, among those of middle age Holst and Bax, and of the quite young Walton and Lambert. All these served their apprenticeship at home. There are several others who thought that their own country was not good enough for them and went off in the early stages to become little Germans or little Frenchmen. Their names I will not give to you because they are unknown even to their fellow-countrymen. (p. 11)

Unfortunately, one putative member of this 'national front' indignantly rejected conscription. Despite 'Uncle Ralph's' accolade, Constant Lambert, *enfant terrible* of British music, strenuously resisted adoption. On the contrary, he proceeded to launch an attack on the concept of 'national music', in his blistering squib *Music Ho!* Lambert was the spoiled darling of elite musical society, and one of the so-called 'Fitzrovian' group of intellectual hedonists (Motion 1986: 193ff.). Influenced by the pacifist movement which in 1933 had brought off a sensational coup in the 'King and Country' resolution of the Oxford Union , Lambert gave eloquent voice to fears that nationalism in music, under any guise, was a potential danger. He hit directly on a sensitive nerve: 'It is doubtful whether the war would have lasted six months without the aid of that purest of the arts, music, whose latest gift to civilization is the notorious Horst Wessel song ... No political pamphlet or poster can get a hundredth of the recruits that are enrolled by a cornet and a bass-drum' (Lambert 1934/85: 133).

Lambert was convinced that Vaughan Williams's ethnocentric style of composition would isolate his music from any universal appeal; an opinion which has (so far) proven accurate enough. He challenged the rationale not only of national music but of the whole Renaissance Movement in its creative dimension. Lambert argued that the folksong was not a musical 'seed' but a finished flower, unsuitable as the basis for the development of 'serious' music – a point Shaw had registered forty years earlier (cf. Laurence 1989: II, 890). He asserted (with reference to RVW's opera *Hugh the Drover*) that 'the particular type of self-conscious Englishry practised by the folk-song composers is in itself curiously un-English' (Lambert 1934/85: 137, 153). Warming to his task, and in terms which amounted to a wholesale butchery of the sacred cows of national music, Lambert went on:

> There is about this music something both unbearably precious and unbearably hearty. Its preciosity recalls the admirably meant endeavours of William Morris and his followers to combat the products of those dark satanic mills with green and unpleasant handwoven materials while its heartiness conjures up the hideous *faux bonhommie* of the hiker, noisily wading his way through the petrol pumps of metroland, singing obsolete sea shanties. (p. 154)

In a final subversive exercise, where Vaughan Williams (lecturing to an audience of southern whites) had condemned the influence of 'Negroid emetics' (Vaughan Williams 1934/87: 47), Lambert devoted a whole section to the earnest appraisal of Jazz, and hailed Duke Ellington as 'a real composer, the first jazz composer of distinction' (Lambert 1934/85: 187).

Frank Bridge, the most committed pacifist among composers, agreed with his younger colleague. His scepticism about the folk-music movement was turning into outright suspicion (BLMC A52256/78). He commented trenchantly that 'so long as we have no consciously national music, I think all should be well with the future' (*RT* 220788). This attitude brought the reproof from *Scrutiny* that Bridge 'was without the moral backbone to bring his gifts to fruition' (Mellers 1947/76: 193). Meanwhile, John Foulds had joined the onslaught on the citadel of nationalism in his *Music Today* – a book which also appeared in 1934.

> There are a number of persons ... who would base a new national music upon old folk-songs. Frankly, I am not one of these ... For present-day composers and protagonists to concentrate upon such ... narrow nationalistic phenomena, goes clean against the main evolutionary trend of the art.
>
> [...]
>
> It is all very well for Vaughan Williams to scoff at those musicians who profess in their art what he calls a 'backboneless cosmopolitanism', and to instance Wagner's *Meistersinger* as his greatest work because it was his most German one in its philosophy ... No 'backboneless cosmopolitanism' for me, but also ... no 'little Englander' music either. English music in the main has been of little or no effect abroad because – as E.J. Dent says somewhere or other – 'it has been the wrong kind of English music because it was composed for purely English audiences'. (Foulds 1934: 17–18, 224)

As if Lambert, Bridge and Foulds were not sufficient in the ranks of the mutineers, 1934 had still not ended when there was a further notable desertion. Rutland Boughton's book *The Reality of Music* assailed the Goodly House from a different angle – the 'Marxist'. Boughton argued that use of folk-music was merely another form of capitalist exploitation – a cynical one, for it transformed the protest songs of the suffering workers into the frothy entertainment of the bourgeoisie, in a *reductio ad absurdum* of Proudhon's dictum that 'property is theft' (Boughton 1934: 49–50, 78ff., 91–4). The effect was to support Lambert's manifesto against a *volkisch* culture which distorted the pure voice of the community in the salon or mobilised it into the military band.

By the time another Communist Party stalwart, the composer Christian Darnton, had been commissioned (by Penguin Books) to offer his opinion, it was 1940. In the prevailing international circumstances, Darnton refrained from exploring the ideological minefield indicated by his co-religionist. But he was damning on the subject

of national music, which he saw as 'parochial' and (in a direct contra-
diction of Sharp) disastrous for 'the first nation whose people became
Citizens of the World'. He attacked the artificial, introverted world
where 'folk music is kept precariously alive in the hothouses of the
English Folk Dance Society'. In one area, Darnton went a step further
than Boughton. He sent a salvo in the direction of South Kensington
and Regent's Park with his *tout court* dismissal of the whole creative
achievement of the English Renaissance: 'Important though the effects
of this revival have been for this country, no composer of international
consequence has as yet been thrown up' (Darnton 1940: 126). A similar conclusion was later drawn by Cecil Gray, an observer more in
sympathy with fascism than communism. Gray was an Anglo-Scot
who studied with Bantock – though he subsequently rejected both
'Celtic' and 'Midlands' affiliations. Despite his personal links with
influential figures, Gray's music was ignored, and he was obliged to
seek secondary and (in his own eyes) parasitical fame as a critic. To a
gentleman of private means such servile work was intolerable, and his
writings are infused with misanthropic resentment.

> 'Englishness' as such I have always disliked ... As for the English musi-
> cal renaissance in modern times, of which one heard so much in my
> youth, the little I knew of it meant less than nothing to me ... The form
> of art to which I am least drawn temperamentally is English art, espe-
> cially as exemplified in such typical artists as Thomas Hardy and
> Vaughan Williams. (Gray 1948/85: 19–28)

During the years after 'national music', therefore, criticism of
the cause championed by RVW gathered force. In the attempt to
establish a convincing 'national front', he became more willing to
compromise. His admiration for Elgar had always fallen on the
proper side of idolatry. In 1930, when Professor Dent deprecated
Elgar in a major reference work published in Germany, and Heseltine
organised a round-robin protest letter to the press, RVW and Holst
did not appear among the signatories (Fox-Strangways 1936/68:
86–7; Foreman 1987: 147). But the building pressure of the 1930s
made a new *ralliement* necessary. After Elgar's death, RVW recruited
his spirit to the national cause. In a symposium volume of homage to
the great man, he announced that Elgar's music 'gives us, his fellow-
countrymen, a sense of something familiar – the intimate and personal beauty of our own fields and lanes', arguing that the wells of
Elgar's musical inspiration were exclusively English (Vaughan

Williams 1934/87: 251). Unlike the putative son, Lambert, the adoptive grandfather was in no position to protest.

There were some compromises which RVW was very reluctant to make. In contrast to his posthumous embracing of Worcestershire's great son, he was anxious to exclude from the national cohorts the – ethnically German – 'Yorkshireman' Delius. RVW's 'inveterate hostility' to both the man and his music was an open secret (Palmer 1976: 147). To RVW Delius was the epitome of the 'colourless cosmopolitanism ... which makes me occasionally despair of England as a musical nation' (Vaughan Williams 1931: xii). In the event, however, this battle was lost through the contrary influence of Beecham (no admirer of the Folksong School) and the pro-Delius lobby. Indeed, in May 1935, RVW himself felt obliged to attend the reburial of Delius, held in Limpsfield, Surrey. The occasion was designed to set the seal on Delius's 'repatriation' as one of the National School and part of England's musical heritage. It was a glorious day in early summer, and Vaughan Williams sought consolation in defeat by loading a picnic into the car and enjoying it on the way home (Vaughan Williams 1964: 206).

During the year 1934, when much of the critical–polemical work discussed above was published, an equally important struggle for control of British music was taking place in another part of the field. After fierce intra-institutional debate, the BBC responded to mounting demands for its patronage of native music with a series dedicated to living British composers (Anon., *RT*: 140733, 210733, 280733). The full resources of the BBC (and a team of outstanding domestic soloists) were mobilised. The 'Six Concerts of British Music', broadcast during the first two weeks of 1934, were varied in content. The only single-person programme was devoted to Ethel Smyth, whose cantata *The Prison*, an appropriate subject for both composer and period – Smyth had been briefly imprisoned during her suffragette days – was premiered by Beecham. Even older monuments, like Sir Alexander Mackenzie, were dusted off for the occasion. Token appearances were also made by Bantock, Holbrooke, Boughton and Scott. A high profile was obtained by the National Music School, which dominated the big orchestral and choral areas. RVW (*Flos Campi*) led the way, together with his brother-in-law R. O. Morris (a new symphony). Close behind marched Holst, Moeran, Hadley, McEwen and Bliss, all under the baton of bandmaster Boult (Anon., *RT*: 291233; 050134).

The series was greeted in the *Radio Times* as marking 'the jubilee of the Renaissance of British Music' – by dumb implication dating its beginning to the year 1884 – and as drawing a line under the age of foreign dependence (Klein, *RT*: 050134; Einstein *RT*: 050134). Its coincidence in time with the passing of Elgar and company lent it critical importance in the definitive canon-formation of British Music. National music had not, it is true, achieved the outright victory for which its advocates looked. Moeran, for example, complained that its younger tribunes (Finzi, Rubbra, Maconchy) had been ignored (Foreman 1987: 169). Holbrooke, on the other hand, roundly asserted that all the best British Music had been deliberately omitted (BUBM F2: 170134, 151135). Bax and Bridge – the latter now in a firmly avant-garde phase – along with Lambert, Walton and Goossens, had substantial pieces featured. The concert devoted to Dame Ethel turned out to have been an early and extravagant example of what feminists would later dismiss as 'tokenism'. Yet if, *pace* RVW, we include the contributions of Delius as well as those of Elgar, well over half the available schedule was occupied by music that had a national music profile.

All the tensions of the 1930s burst their banks at last in the crisis of 1939–40. Predictably enough, war revived the fortunes of 'national music'. As Britain stood alone against the German-dominated Continent, Julius Harrison's 'pastoral' rhapsody *Bredon Hill* was the most publicised new work commissioned by the BBC. (Foreman 1987: 240–1) It was transmitted, on successive nights in the autumn of 1941, to Africa, North America and the Pacific. Harrison's piece, based on the poetry of Housman, was redolent of folk-song, and written for violin and orchestra.

> Here of a Sunday morning
> My love and I would lie,
> And see the coloured counties
> And hear the larks so high …

But if the lark was once again ascendant, the air it hovered in was no longer clear. Recumbent lovers on the English Downs heard the dull drone of the bomber fleets and witnessed the dogfights of a struggle for national survival.

Tribal battles long ago

In the event, no alternative highway was ever discovered to set against RVW's royal road. Several composers turned aside from the latter, with varying degrees of success; but the problems of agglutination precluded the emergence of any competitive group. Nothing resembling the aesthetic complexity and political homogeneity of the Pastoral School was ever constructed. Almost by definition, proudly independent and bitterly disaffected individuals could find no lasting unity. The curious can glimpse them jostling outside London's Green Rooms, or holding out like lonely chieftains in remote fastnesses. However, one personality constantly threatened to set up an alternative focus of attention.

Joseph Holbrooke was 'recognised' by no less than Ernest Newman in 1902 as a phenomenon 'absolutely without parallel in English music'. Holbrooke was a tireless advocate of his own genius and had no rivals in the ring of pugilistic polemics (Newman 1902/37: 36–41; Scholes 1947: 482). Throughout a long and embattled artistic life Holbrooke enjoyed the dedicated support of a wealthy patron. This endowed him with the resources, lacked by most others, to contest decisions taken in the corridors of power. He had worthy claims to be regarded as an early exponent of the 'national' cause. Prior to 1914, like Balfour Gardiner and others, Holbrooke worked to create a space for British Music, and was a vocal member of the chauvinist lobby during the war. Then the shift – subtle, gradual, yet obvious – from a 'British' to an 'English' emphasis began to overtake Holbrooke: a problem exacerbated by the decline of the Romantic culture which had sustained his aesthetic.

In 1925, Holbrooke published a survey of contemporary British composers. 'I confess' – he announced – 'that I am a Nationalist in art, as in politics ... Yes, nationality does exist in art, intensely.' But soon after he had also to confess that 'it would be difficult to say what is a British style' (Holbrooke 1925: 1, 15, 18). Although Holbrooke placed Vaughan Williams in the first 'class' of British composers, RVW was obliged to share this space not only with Elgar, but with Boughton and Brian. Moreover, while the author 'recognised' members of the pastoralist team, like Holst, Howells, Harrison (and even Bliss), they too rubbed shoulders with a host of others whose names now constitute little more than an ossuary of the obscure. Holbrooke acknowledged that the folklore ideal was a

legitimate way of asserting British uniqueness in music. But his section on RVW concluded with the barbed observation: 'There is a
heavy suspicion to many when any artist meets favour from the academics in power. Vaughan Williams has had this huge misfortune.
His art pleases the dull ones of our profession ...both Vaughan
Williams and Holst, to me, are in the past, and not in the present'
(pp. 94, 165).

In a provocative gesture, Holbrooke published Havergal Brian's
desperate response to his request for biographical details: 'I have no
wish to be in any book. I am anxious to avoid disaster for my family. The "Hidden Hand" is too much for me, and any discussion of
my work is useless.' 'We all suffer from the "Hidden Hand"', Holbrooke himself darkly added (p. 132).

Despite his combative style, Holbrooke was reluctant to precipi-
tate a confrontation with the establishment. He vainly encouraged
Bantock – a lifetime ally – to pursue the still-born Elgarian heritage
of a 'Midlands School'. But ultimately he could offer no serious
alternative to RVW's version of 'national music', either in terms of
ideological policy or aesthetic programme. He grasped at a vaguely
'British' manifesto, seeking a 'Celtic' ethos. The composer he singled
out was Rutland Boughton – his political opposite, yet a 'giant [of]
divine work [who] may be termed as British, or as Celtic, as can be
imagined' (Holbrooke 1925: 109–19). Lord Howard de Walden,
Holbrooke's patron, was a scholar–philanthropist who dabbled in
'Celtic' history as well as writing the libretti, based on the *Mabinogion*, for his protégé's operatic cycle. Two years before Holbrooke's
book – and notwithstanding its fulminations against foreigners – one
of these epics (*The Children of Don*) was premiered at the Vienna
Volksoper under Weingartner (Foreman 1987: 125–7). Howard de
Walden, Holbrooke and Boughton were none of them remotely
Celtic in origin or nurture. Like Arnold Bax, the most remarkable
musical product of the Celtic revival, they all hailed from Greater
London. Yet the appeal of writers like William Sharp ('Fiona
Macleod') and the young W. B. Yeats was felt across ethnic and cul-
tural boundaries. Even Delius was prompted into posing as a Bard:
'What you say about the Celtic element in my music is perfectly
true', he wrote to Heseltine. 'I have a latent streak somewhere deep
down in my being which flames up every now and again – probably
atavistic from my Northern forbears' (BLMC A52548/70: 141021).
This typical piece of opportunism suggests that the Celtic twilight

still provided a focus of emotional (and political) allegiance as late as 1921. Indeed, years later, another Delius champion expressed a concern at the growth of its power which betrayed a quasi-racialist paranoia.

> The influence of the Celt has grown stage by stage in England so imperceptibly that the English themselves have failed to realize the meaning and consequence of it. Consider for a moment that great organ of opinion and communication the Press of London. How many of the leading journals are in English hands and reflect the temper and psychology of the English people itself? ... Even the greatest and most representative of British newspapers is only partly under English control. The voice of that part of Britain which is essentially and characteristically English is silent today in the capital of the Empire, and this strange revolution has taken place almost entirely in the past sixty years. Is it possible that there may be some connection between this phenomenon of the resurgence of the Celt and the steady decline visible in every part of the Empire? (Beecham 1944: 150–1)

Holbrooke repeatedly attempted to unite composers who felt passed over, behind his (or Bantock's) leadership, against the 'Hidden Hand' (BUBM: F1–4). One public arena of competition had assumed an overwhelming importance. As the *Observer*'s critic put it in 1930: 'It would be idle to deny that the Broadcasting Corporation has now taken a decisive part in musical politics' (Fox-Strangways 1936/68: 80). The BBC was keenly aware of the multicultural identity, and the political resonances, implicit in its title. The ethnic background of its first director, John Reith, ensured they were given a certain priority. In music, diversity was encouraged by Walford Davies, a figure with considerable influence at the BBC. An Englishman born in Oswestry of Welsh forbears, Davies was engaged in the task of building an infrastructure for 'serious' music in the Principality (Colles 1942: 116ff.). His influence meant that one of the first opera broadcasts from the regions (1925) featured Joseph Parry's *Blodwen* – with libretto in English translation (Scholes, *RT*: 080525). At Gregynog, in mid-Wales, Davies presided over a festival, patronised by two millionaire sisters, and regularly attended by Holst and RVW. The greatest practical exponent of 'national music', the BBC's Adrian Boult, was often guest conductor (Parrott *c*. 1969: 117ff.). Depending on your point of view, this was an outpost of colonial occupation or a meeting-place of Celtic and Anglo-Saxon ideas. Holst and RVW were anxious to build bridges across the Severn. They composed settings of 'Welsh' tunes, and in 1929 discussed with Boughton the possibility of reviving an Anglo-Celtic festival of choral drama in the Welsh valleys (Vaughan Williams 1964: 176–7).

Several of Holbrooke's associates liked to be seen as draped with 'Celtic' trappings, or even in full Druidic robes. Holbrooke spent his summers near Harlech; Bantock had a cottage nearby (and had his ashes scattered on Snowdonia); while Heseltine, born just inside the Welsh border, was a frequent visitor to the Principality. One of the contributions to a volume of essays on Holbrooke appeared in the Welsh language. The editor attributed neglect of this 'great composer' entirely to the jaundice of the BBC and Dr Boult (Banister 1937: 8, 42). Indeed, members of the Bantock–Holbrooke connection were not on Gregynog's guest-list. Yet Holbrooke, Bantock and Boughton gave a high profile to song and melody associated with the Celtic lands. Apart from Holbrooke's series of 'Cymric' operas, Boughton set his *Immortal Hour* in legendary Ireland, and out-did Holbrooke with his cycle of Arthurian 'choral dramas' (completed in 1945). In 1936, Boughton's *Oboe Concerto* – which left its impression on Vaughan Williams – utilised Irish jigs and reels. Bantock's sporadic encounters with this particular corner of his exotic imagination – a 'Gaelic afflatus' one sceptical observer called it (Le Fleming 1982: 45) – culminated in 1940 with his *Celtic Symphony*, which overwhelms the listener with ethnic authenticity by the deployment of six harps. During the 'Fairest Isle' celebrations of 1995, BBC Radio 3 adopted a transparently tokenist approach to non-English composers. For example, one week in February carried a daily spot about 'Wales since the War'. The double-CD set issued to exploit the occasion featured thirty-two *English* composers, including short works by Mackenzie and Stanford, English at least by residence (*BBC Music Magazine* 1995: BM1–2). Despite Beecham's worries, therefore, no 'Celtic' challenge ever assailed the borders of the Empire; but the Celtic card was one which in certain circumstances could be played to advantage by individuals.

In one case, at least, this last remark is both understatement and trivialisation. Arnold Bax was as independent a figure as private means and public success could make him, and had no important links with the Bantock–Holbrooke clique – indeed, he seems to have attracted only a typically jealous spleen from Holbrooke in the 1930s. Yet his 'Celtic' affiliation was much more than afflatus, being emotionally sincere and musically profound. Bax stood at an awkward angle to national music, though he never had sufficient confidence or interest to turn passive implications into active challenge. From its beginnings the English Folksong revival had been haunted by the suspicion that the popular music of the Celtic countries was older, richer, more original and less corrupted than that of the Anglo-Saxon homeland. Sharp himself (1907/72: 173) pointed out that, by their own lights, the Irish Fenians, enemies of everything English, behaved with good sense in seeking to anchor their politics in the solid historical reality of folk traditions. Occasionally thereafter, the heretical claim was heard that even the tunes discovered by Sharp were not English at all. On a notable occasion in 1913, a debate between English composers was stimulated when, on holiday together in Spain, they heard some local 'folk' music. Arnold Bax challenged his companions, Gardiner and Holst, in disturbing terms: 'Come now ... you can't honestly say that you think much of English folk songs. Why, they're all either bad or Irish' (Bax 1925: 211–44).

Forty years on, Vaughan Williams (1934/87: xii) devoted a memorial lecture for Bax, given at the University of Cork, to a belated riposte. In his widow's words, he proved 'that all the Irish folk-songs came from the English Pale. The audience did not lynch him, but some of them would have liked to. This he knew and wickedly enjoyed, describing the operation as "making them think".'

The 'operation' may well have gone to the lecturer's satisfaction, but it also betrayed a residual insecurity which seems of equal significance. As this incident suggests, and RVW's published 'tribute' to Bax amply confirms, the two men had an equivocal relationship (Vaughan Williams 1987: 243–4). In his younger days, Bax (who was RAM trained) evinced a jejune 'team' hostility towards the RCM, and was capable of sarcastic reference to 'a new rhapsody on Little Fluddleswick drinking songs by R. Vaughan Williams Mus. Doc.'. In 1925, an Australian student sought out Bax in order to be tutored by someone she regarded as free from the sway of 'the dressed-up folk song that was all the rage' (Foreman 1988: 109, 219). The two composers remained on good personal terms. In the late 1920s, each paid homage to the other's style (Bax in his *Symphony No. 3*, Vaughan Williams in his *Piano Concerto*). This period also saw RVW working on his opera *Riders to the Sea*, based on Synge and set in the Gaelic west of Ireland, terrain which was Bax's spiritual home. At the height of his fame in 1934, Bax was accepted in RVW's book as one of the worthies of 'national music', and received the dedication of the elder composer's *Symphony No. 4*. Shortly afterwards, Boult pressured the BBC to apologise formally to RVW after a *Radio Times*'s item had suggested he was inferior as a symphonist to Bax (Foreman 1987: 184–5). When Elgar died, RVW rejected the invitation to succeed him as Master of the King's Musick, allowing the palm to pass instead to Walford Davies. When the latter also died in 1941, RVW once more stood aside – this time, as it proved, in favour of Arnold Bax.

It was murmured abroad that Bax was a dubious choice for Churchill's Government to make in the hour of national emergency (Howes 1966: 205). In *Scrutiny*, Wilfrid Mellers hailed RVW as the true Master, characterising Bax's appointment as 'both surprising and perverse' (Mellers 1947/76: 179–86). These reservations were understandable. Much of Bax's life and work represented a challenge to 'Englishness' in many ways more subversive than that of Delius. As a young man he had surrendered to the lure of the mythic Ireland of Yeats and Synge. Beginning with the tone-poem on Yeats's *Cathaleen ni Hoolihan* (1903), Bax's music was permeated with Irish melody, infused into the content and diffused in the texture. Like Yeats, Bax was uncomfortable with the religious elements of the nationalist cause. On the other hand, unlike Yeats, he became fluent in Gaelic, publishing short stories and verse in a medium which had been appropriated as an instrument of Irish Catholic nationalism. Bax's allegiance to Republican ideals may have been rooted in adolescent need, but it developed with earnest gravity. On his marriage in 1911, he abandoned England in order to establish his household and rear his children among his nation's enemies. He formed links with several intellectuals – including Padraig Pearse – who were later to be heroes and martyrs of the Easter Rebellion.

During 1916, while many English friends and fellow-students were fighting and dying on the Somme, Bax wrote a poem called *A Dublin Ballad*:

> O write it up above your hearth
> And troll it out to sun and moon
> To all true Irishmen on earth
> Arrest and death come late or soon.

Simultaneously, he began a tone-poem, *In Memoriam Padraig Pearse*, which opened a series of elegiac works associated with the birthpangs of the new Republic (Foreman 1988: 139–40). Bax drew up short of actually running guns to the rebels – unlike some other sons of the English ruling class – but his attitudes exposed him to potential hatred and harassment. As things stood, his poems were banned by the censor in Dublin Castle. Though he refrained from publishing some of his most overtly treasonable ideas, the need to make a self-sacrificial gesture of identification remained strong. In 1920, at a time when the infant Irish Republic was formally at war with Great Britain, he wrote an extended work, *Rhapsody for Viola and Orchestra*, which incorporated Irish folk-tunes and culminated in a triumphal intonement of *The Soldier's Song*, the IRA hymn later to become the Irish national anthem. This music was exactly contemporaneous with *The Lark Ascending*, and may be taken as its political antithesis.

In the social dimension of life in post-war England, Bax kept his feelings to himself. He occupied himself with cricket – ideal therapy for an incipient traitor – and slowly the fire seeped out his belly and his work. A series of compositions reflect the transformation. Many were straightforwardly 'Irish', with considerable use of folksong. He was inspired by hearing a Byrd mass – not unlike composers of the 'national' style – to write two a capella carols based on Old English texts. However, these were addressed to the Catholic Virgin, patroness of the Irish cause, who was also celebrated (if less directly) in the choral and orchestral piece *Walsinghame*. It seems likely that both the symphonies completed in this period involve a traumatic purgation of his political soul. By the later 1920s – fortified by the diversions of a young mistress, growing fame, and the regular administration of alcohol – Bax had shuffled off the most painful memories (Foreman 1988: 162ff.)

Bax's subsequent career is another story of 'repatriation', if less bizarre than that of Delius. By 1937, when he accepted a knighthood, his 'Celtic' past had all but disappeared. In the 1940s, the reformed rebel incorporated themes composed for his unpublished tribute to Pearse into a score for the David Lean film of *Oliver Twist*, a much-published tribute to 'Englishness'. It was a suitable act of atonement. By the time of his appointment as Master of the King's Musick he had gone to live in the Home Counties, which he celebrated in the *aubade* dedicated to Princess Elizabeth – *Maytime in Sussex* (1947). Living a few miles away from RVW, Bax had found the King's highway, and his final recuperation represented a triumph for the dominant cultural centre of 'national music'.

After the *Pastoral Symphony* – mucking out

That well-known observer of the countryside Ludwig van Beethoven once described his own *Pastoral Symphony* as 'not so much painting as feeling (*empfindung*)' (Bacharach and Pearce 1934/77: 337). To proceed from the views of some of its critics – Heseltine, Lambert, Beecham and Elizabeth Lutyens among them – it might be said that the *Pastoral Symphony* of Vaughan Williams took the dung from the Beethovenian *empfindung* and turned it into authentically English manure. It was Lutyens, Britain's first serialist composer, who coined the phrase which reduced the English Pastoral School to its basics – 'cow-pat music' (Harries and Harries 1989: 53). An American conductor (Bernstein, we suppose) once described English music as 'too much organ voluntary in Lincoln Cathedral, too much Coronation in Westminster Abbey, too much lark ascending, too much clod-hopping on the fucking village green' (Burgess 1982: 23). Had she been inclined in print to utilise this less English but very Anglo-Saxon discourse, Lutyens might have said that 'national music' was 'bullshit'. In the interests of the ecological cycle, we may approach this metaphor from the fly's point of view. Upon investigation, 'the King's highway' – the long and winding road which the wagon-train of Renaissance had traversed since the 1840s – proves to be littered with the detritus of its various beasts of draught and sustenance. Likewise, the bones of crusaders and missionaries, who set out in hope, or were attracted to the caravan during its journey, bleached sometimes beyond chance of 'recognition', some too fragile even to emit a dirge of grievance when played upon by the passing music historian, lie in the surrounding wasteland.

Take the celebrated year of 1934. Two other English composers, well known at the time, died in the same year as Elgar, Holst and Delius. They rest in obscurity, uncommemorated by performance or history. The cenotaph of English Music does not record their names: no flame burns for them even in some hypothetical place set apart for the symbolic anonymity of 'The Unknown Crusader'. One of them does not rate a single mention in the mainstream texts. This was Edward Naylor, composer of the prize-winning opera *The Angelus*, which had been a success when premiered by the British National Opera Company in 1909 (BLMC E3305/173–7). Naylor was renowned as a liturgical composer, and had more music in print at his death than either Holst or Delius (Foreman 1987: 304). The 'aesthetic' reasons why Naylor does not figure in the Renaissance can only be guessed at, but the political reasons seem clear. In the view of the prevailing temperament, he lacked the qualifications for recognition as a 'national' composer. The second figure was Norman O'Neill, dismissed in one phrase by Howes, unnoticed by Pirie, but enjoying a whole page in Trend – by whom, nonetheless, his cause is regarded as lost. The diagnosis here is even more definitive. Although O'Neill was a stalwart of the Royal Philharmonic Society, and regarded highly in his lifetime, he is now seen as a composer not of 'serious', but of 'light' music (Hudson 1945). O'Neill was one of several victims of the careful process of categorisation which divided Art Music into 'light' and 'serious' (or 'classical') and can be located in the 1920s. His Irish origins and German training perhaps hindered his cause. But, most importantly, both Naylor and O'Neill had overlooked the message of 'Tudor polyphony' and the call of the folk. In return, they were overlooked by the nation.

The highest objectives were claimed, and the most profound matters were ordained in the name of a national music. But according to Cecil Gray, its decrees were as sounding cymbals and tinkling brass, vitiated by moral backsliding and habitual hypocrisy. Writing in 1936, Gray concluded:

> This spirit of smug, pharasaical gentlemanliness, complicated with social snobbery, permeates every aspect of English musical life at the present time, from top to bottom ... It is the absolute antithesis of everything we call art, and must be fought as one fights the devil ... There is no hope for English music until this fatal confusion of artistic with false social and ethical values has been broken down. (Gray 1936: 291–2)

For all the personal bitterness lying behind them, such utterances cannot be lightly dismissed. We might examine RVW's nomination of six worthy English composers (like Parry), and his implied condemnation of others (*sine nomine*, but like O'Neill) who sought forbidden sources of inspiration. The latter, the reader will remember, were those 'who thought that their own country was not good enough for them and went off ... to become little Germans or little Frenchmen'. In writing this, did Vaughan Williams conveniently forget, not only that Parry had in fact served an apprenticeship in Germany, but that he himself had considered his own country not good enough, and had gone off to be both a little German and a little Frenchman? The composer himself patronisingly dismissed the

Parisian episode of his apprenticeship as 'a little French polish'. Nearly all accounts of the composer deferentially take this cue, minimising a crucially important episode in his artistic formation (Foss 1950: 102; Vaughan Williams 1964: 79–81). It is almost as if the 'French fever' was something unspeakable, akin to that which Fritz Delius, degenerate offspring of a German businessman, as opposed to Ralph Vaughan Williams, upstanding son of a Gloucester clergyman, had contracted in Paris. To RVW's advocates – Howes, Foss, and even Mellers (1989: 34) – this episode was unseemly for a different reason. They were reluctant to draw attention to the fact (rightly acknowledged by Michael Kennedy) that it was a Frenchman who brought about RVW's belated access to a mature style, and thus to the leadership of an 'authentic' National School (Oliver BBC R3: 080392).

The ruling principles of 'national music' may be addressed as directly as its ruling personalities. Research by social historians and ethnomusicologists has revealed that folk-music never was the source of 'pure' creative energy that Sharp imagined (Middleton 1978: 37–41; Harker 1985). Even in the 1930s it was known that the Morris-Men and many of their tunes (such as 'Dos y Dos') originated in medieval Spain; indeed some dances possibly have even older roots, in Castile's Arab past (Winter 1973: 75). Holst's *Beni Mora* may have been an unconscious 'recognition' of the North African ancestry of English village festivals. Moreover, countryside tunes were recorded by Sharp and company only at the interventionist moment of their local, temporal evolution; at any given moment in the past, they may have been radically different. Sharp himself in effect acknowledged this fundamental flaw by his tours of the Appalachian mountains during the Great War in search of a 'Lost Valley' of emigrant English communities where the 'original' versions of folksongs might have been preserved, like Conan Doyle's prehistoric monsters (Karpeles 1973/87: 94–8).

As we have seen, the folksongs presented to society audiences were regularly bowdlerised. Many of Sharp's 'peasant songs' had 'anomalous' musical features – micro-tone intervals on the one hand, insistent diatonicism on the other – smoothed out to meet the modal preconceptions of their collectors. Arrangements of monodic lines for piano and voice by Holst and RVW were influenced by art-song styles, and above all – irremediably – by the style of Schubert. RVW's accompaniment to *The Seeds of Love*, for example, is a rustling arpeggio reminiscent of *Die Schöne Müllerin*. Little wonder that a guest at the primary rendition of Sharp's version of the same song remarked that 'it was the first time [it] had been put into evening dress' (Harker 1985: 178). Since, in most cases of the genre, the tune is simply repeated stanza by stanza, it is the added piano part which has to provide variety of rhythm, tone and dynamics. The 'original' harmonic inflection, and even the melodic line itself, are often submerged – for example (aptly enough), in Holst's almost orchestral setting of *Our Ship*. Another good illustration of the forces at work is RVW's version of *Lovely Joan*. It was used in the opera *Sir John in Love*; rearranged as the *Fantasia on Greensleeves*, it became a kind of signature-tune. The 'original' song is a ballad-narrative about a country lass approached by a squire who offers to make her his lady. Joan tricks the would-be trickster and makes off to her rustic lover with the squire's horse and gold. In the end, however, Joan fails to escape gentrification. The composer has the last trick – tricking Joan out in all the finery of High Art: and her knightly suitor rides a milk-white steed not unlike that featured in Schubert's *Erlkönig*. In folksong arrangements, lilies are gilded and horses gelded: not at all what the crusaders of national music affected to recognise as essential to their culture.

Other reservations about the 'authentic' claims of 'national music' have been expressed by musicologists in recent years. One of these concerns an area which we have had little chance to explore in these pages. The second of the twin pillars upon which the Goodly House rested was the heritage of Tudor music, relatively unknown and unperformed before 1900. The pioneer work of Edmund Fellowes in Tudor polyphony was almost as seminal to the evolution of the Pastoral style, and especially the exemplary RVW canon, as had been that of Cecil Sharp in folk-music. Despite the attempts of some commentators (like Pattinson) to discern a common ancestor for motet, madrigal and folksong, Tudor music remained an academic interest, gaining little practical relevance in mass education or popular perception. Nevertheless, following the *Tallis Fantasia* (1909) it remained a strong branch of 'English' development, and in the 1930s RVW gave voice to it once more in large-scale 'public' works written for both ecclesiastical and secular occasions (*Five Tudor Portraits* and *Te Deum*). In the 1950s, this trope came into its own with the succession of another young Queen Elizabeth, when a positive riot of neo-Tudor nonsense was written about the mellifluously blended and artistically effervescent society of Shakespeare's England. Subsequent scholarship found that the first English Musical Renaissance, and the 'indigenous' styles of the Tudor age – the church-music of Tallis, the secular madrigals of Morley – were as much indebted to Italy as was the Second Renaissance, and the music of Parry, Stanford and Elgar, to Germany (Kerman 1962: 70–2; and 1985: 47, 124–51). Furthermore, its main exponents, Tallis and Byrd, were crypto-Catholics, Counter-Reformation sympathisers who privately despised the ideology of the court in which they were obliged to subsist. Even a composer endowed with the name of John Bull – once thought to be the originator of the current British national anthem – could not be trusted to conform to the resplendent myth. He was a recusant who, when his cover was blown, deserted to the Catholic Habsburg court at Brussels.

This minor threat to the Anglo-Protestant ascendancy of national music was discerned in the 1920s. The composer Bernard Van Dieren, a Catholic Dutchman, settled in London around 1910. Some years later, he was 'recognised' by Heseltine and Gray, who began stridently to promote his music. Sick and bed-ridden, he became an alternative martyr–hero to Butterworth for *The Sackbut*'s fraternity and others who were suspicious of national music (Lambert 1934/85: 278–9; Foreman 1987: 308). Van Dieren worked in a recondite, atonally 'expressive' style, which made no concessions to English tastes. Despite the energy of his advocates, and his own dunning of Clark at the BBC, he got few performances (BLMC A52256/120–35v). Indeed a fellow-Catholic, Anthony Burgess, remarked that Van Dieren's *Chinese Symphony* was the most talked about and least heard work of his musical youth (Burgess 1982: 43). In 1935, the composer produced a book, aptly entitled *Down Among the Dead Men*, which (if not in so many words) prophesied that one day his artistic life, at least, would be reborn – a claim strenuously endorsed by Gray (Van Dieren 1935: 145ff.; Gray 1948/85: 179). Van Dieren asserted that the only achievement of modern English music was Sir Richard Terry's scholarly revival of the Counter-Reformation masterpieces – thus, Westminster's Cathedral, and not its Abbey, was the real musical centre of England (Van Dieren 1935: 224).

In 1937, the year following Van Dieren's death and the abdication of Edward VIII, Westminster Abbey remained the setting for the Coronation of George VI. The main musical commission was a *Te Deum* by RVW (Vaughan Williams 1964: 213–14). Howes asserts

(1966: 233–4) that the composer showed his disdain for the establishment and displayed his radical credentials by incorporating an
English folksong into the work. Pathetic fallacies of this sort are
germane to the propaganda – conscious or otherwise – of the English Musical Renaissance. They pretend that it was an essentially
revolutionary phenomenon, challenging the established order, and
above all popular in its origins and appeal. In this way they claim an
intimate relationship with the progressive traditions of English lib-
eralism, picturing a 'national music' nurtured by the same elements
which had nurtured popular democracy and social advancement.
There is no need to question the radical inclinations, or the human
qualities, of the leader of national music in order to deconstruct this
self-image. It is deeply self-contradictory: the cloth cap donned by
Howes falls around his face when he condemns all political affecta-
tions in music – the example chosen being those of Ethel Smyth in
The Prison (Howes 1966: 66). Blatant contradictions arise from the
ideological need of the 'radical' imposture to coexist with the pre-
tence that music is an autonomous entity which has no connection
with politics.

At the BBC's Coronation Concert of 1937, the main commissioned work was John Ireland's *These Things Shall Be*, composed to
a text by J. Addington Symonds. Howes indulged in an attack on this
piece which at first dash seems gratuitous: 'as hollow a work as the
aspirations of the poem are shallow ... the cantata lacks fundamental sincerity' (p. 224). Ireland complained to Edward Clark that even
if 'one wrote better than the Holy Ghost and the Blessed Virgin
Mary combined they would still piss on one's works as insignificant
rubbish' (BLMC A52256/189: 100837). A recording under Barbirolli was made in Manchester after the Second World War – to be
exact, on 1 May 1948. Significant date: for in the transition to the
last section of the work, the choir sings:

> And every life a song shall be
> When all the earth is paradise.

Immediately, a solo horn plays a *mezzo-forte* descant to the main
melody which is nothing other than *The Internationale*. In response
to the choir's whispered question 'Say, heart, what will the future
bring?', a syncopated version of the hymn crashes out on full
orchestra. Political conclusions are inescapable. The strangest thing
should be that the work was broadcast at the official Coronation

Concert. At this period, Ireland was (along with Bantock, Boughton and Britten) a supporter of the communist-led Workers' Musical Association (Hill and Hinrichsen 1944: 132–4). His piece was a propaganda product of the Soviet-inspired 'Popular Front' initiative during the crisis years of anti-fascist struggle. Yet it was Boult who recommended the work for performance, with the ambiguous words 'it has in it the germ of real popularity and importance at the present time' (Foreman 1987: 208). In a sleeve-note for the re-issue of Barbirolli's recording, Michael Kennedy fails to identify *The Internationale*, describing it as 'a broad, uplifting Parry-like melody'! (Kennedy 1984: HMV EX 29 0107 3). This is hardly surprising, since the composer's biographer, who (according to her publisher's blurb) 'could hardly have had a more intensely musical background', likewise missed the communist anthem in her subject's best-known choral work – though pointing out that the orchestration was done by Alan Bush, a prominent member of the CPGB! (Searle 1979: 87–8.)

One of the present writers taught an option on 'English Music and National Identity' to an outstanding group of MA students in 1997–98. The class agreed that pastoralism represented the central image of English Music, and also accepted that myths of the sea and chivalry had a strong cognate presence in the discourse. But they added some further ideas, not all of them mere variations on the theme. They gave more emphasis than will be found above to the role of the established Church, and of ceremonial music associated with the British Monarchy. Yet whatever priorities we give to these features, the overall picture will always support the remarks made by 'Bernstein'. But we could hardly expect a politically radical and demotic musician, Jewish by origin, New Yorker by adoption and bisexual by gender, to submit a reliable appreciation of a musical tradition which privileges land, Church and Monarchy directly, and which foregrounds state power and the national armed forces – at least by implication – in much of its cultural history and ambience.

6

Slaying the false prophets

See how the Fates their gifts allot
For A is happy, B is not.
Yet B is worthy I daresay
Of more prosperity than A.
Is B more worthy? I should say
He's worth a great deal more than A.

If I were Fortune, which I'm not
B should enjoy a happy lot,
And A should die in misery
That is, assuming I am B!

(Gilbert and Sullivan, *The Mikado*, Act II)

I would define genius as the right man in the right place at the right time. We know, of course, too many instances of the time being ripe and the place being vacant and no man to fill it. But we shall never know of the numbers of 'mute and inglorious Miltons' who failed because the place and time were not ready for them. Was not Purcell a genius born before his time? Was not Sullivan a jewel in the wrong setting? (Vaughan Williams 1934/87: 3)

Like most kinds of historiography, the extant history of English Music is an assemblage of events, often referred to as the 'building-blocks' of the craft. Events are placed in structurally key positions, serving as foundation stones, linchpins, buttresses and so on. Thus the historian–architect constructs Goodly Houses; in this case, a palace in which the English Musical Renaissance continues to reside in more-or-less lordly comfort.

Such building-blocks act as elements of what Gramsci called the 'Historical *Bloc*'. The culture of a given society – typically but not exclusively bourgeois society – becomes articulated via signifying monuments, icons of its representation and objects of its ritual. The present – the problems it poses, and the decisions it requires – is mediated by a dominant narrative mythology of the past. To alter our metaphor, historians (consciously or otherwise) select the events they wish to include as part of a 'history', weaving these threads into a convincing pattern, symmetrically and aesthetically attractive, creating a coverlet laid over the past so that it should be properly 'read' by the present. The strength and verisimilitude of interpretation permeates the sensibilities of the recipient, who is thereby individually 'interpellated' – as Althusser put it – into belief and commitment (Thompson 1986). In social terms, this equates with collective desire to identify with a positive tradition, a heritage all the more seductive because mediated through a logocentric discourse.

Constructions of the past become ideal when a series of 'facts' can be made to fuse together; diachronically, by arranging them into an apparently inevitable sequence which illustrates 'development' – or better still 'evolution'; and synchronically, by focusing their combined fertility on one idea, a highlight which lends the object colour, dimension and profile. When such facts are derived from a wide range of the physical and human sciences – 'biology', 'philosophy' or 'literature' as well as 'history' – the end-product is even more convincing and resilient. To utilise a particular technique of historical understanding, 'grouped' events are often seen as 'conjunctures' (Chaunu) or, in less francophone parlance, 'watersheds' or 'milestones'. Thus a given 'conjuncture' formed a major turning-point in history. Things fall apart, new and terrible beauties slouch towards Bethlehem to be born; or, in a less apocalyptic manifestation, a key stage is reached in the final consummation of the inner logic (or destiny) of the subject phenomenon.

The present chapter is itself based on a version of this sub-marxian dialectic, with the radical difference that it seeks to stand outside the structure, and to illuminate the events which shaped the dining- and drawing-rooms of the Goodly House, and the characters in occupation thereof, by juxtaposing them with others long forgotten, ghosts confined to the cellars, and even some which flit about in the dark cold, beyond the tradesman's entrance. This procedure is partly derived from the post-marxian technique of 'deconstruction' patented by scholars such as Paul de Man and Jacques Derrida.

The virtuous Parry

In 1988, one of the present writers attended the memorial service for Irene, Countess of Plymouth, in the church of St Augustine's in Penarth, south Wales. The parish owes its existence to the patronage of the countess's family of Other-Windsor-Clive. The church stands on a coastal promontory, a vantage-point from which places associated with the family can be descried – Penarth Docks, which the family built, to the north; the Vale of Glamorgan, where the family were major landowners, to the west; and Penarth town, to which it made many benefactions, to the south. The family history, typified by that of Countess Irene herself, is a testament to the vigorous and rewarding presence of an Anglo-Welsh capitalist aristocracy in south Wales.

In St Augustine's graveyard lies buried one who – in the days when the Plymouth interest was at its height, and the Welsh nation was being rediscovered – was regarded as Wales's greatest composer. Joseph Parry (1841–1903) was the author of many celebrated hymns and arias. He was born of working-class parents in Merthyr, became the bard of immigrant Welsh miners in the USA, and later, inaugural lecturer in music at the University College of South Wales and Monmouthshire. But the music of this Dr Parry went unheard on the occasion in question. Instead, the distinguished Welsh congregation gave an enthusiastic rendition of the hymn *Jerusalem*, sometimes called 'the English national anthem', composed by Sir Charles Hubert Hastings Parry, scion of an aristocratic Gloucestershire family, ex-Lloyd's broker and inaugurate of the chair of composition at the Royal College of Music, South Kensington, London. Mighty are the myths of Wales – extolled in the works of Joseph Parry among other places – but they have been mightily overlaid, even inside its borders, by a much greater force, a force in which Art Music has been profoundly implicated. Indeed, Joseph Parry himself was proud to confirm the proper degrees of colonial relationship: he gave his elder son the forenames 'Joseph Haydn' (Austro-German), while the younger became 'William Sterndale' (given names of the contemporary English composer Bennett).

To label Hubert Parry's hymn 'the English national anthem' advances a proposition which the text of William Blake's poem amply bears out.

> And did those feet in ancient time
> Walk upon England's mountain green?

And was the holy lamb of God
On England's pleasant pasture seen?

And did the Countenance Divine
Shine forth upon our clouded hills?
And was Jerusalem builded here
Among these dark Satanic Mills?

Bring me my Bow of burning gold:
Bring me my Arrows of desire:
Bring me my Spear: O clouds unfold!
Bring me my Chariot of fire.

I will not cease from Mental Fight,
Nor shall my Sword sleep in my hand
Till we have built Jerusalem
In England's green and pleasant Land.

Despite its nation-specific reference, the hymn has served various institutions: the patriotic lobby 'Fight for the Right' which commissioned it during the First World War; the Women's Institute; the Labour Party; and, of course, the Last Night of the Proms, where it is taken far more seriously than *Land of Hope and Glory*. Its appeal to Britons of different social origins and political persuasions is patent and lasting. It seems to represent an adaptable expression of diverse communal aspirations (Semper BBC R4: 180589).

Thus only at the end of his life, and in the most modest of musical forms, did Parry succeed in transmitting an uplifting message, a popular (or at least populist) song which carried a meaning of central importance to twentieth-century Britain. It involves commitment to the Christian–humanist tradition and to the values of democratic justice which – so the 'Whig interpretation' of our history assures us – have always been the purpose of Britain's evolution as a nation. Via Blake's images, Parry envisioned a crusade against oppression, corruption and deprivation; in his anthem, each singer is both armed prophet and crusading knight. Indeed, Parry was an earnest liberal thinker who spent much of his career as writer, teacher and composer in attempting to communicate 'improving' ideas. His ethical notions of personal liberty, collective responsibility and social progress were regarded by many as politically 'radical'. The list of his works, many of them encapsulating this strenuous philosophy, and often requiring considerable forces and duration, is truly enormous.

But despite his eminence in the musical community of his day, few of Parry's large-scale compositions ever achieved a second performance or survived in the memory of audiences. Were it not for *Jerusalem*, Parry would have been utterly forgotten as a composer, except among a small circle of pupils. Indeed, his reputation did not survive him long. Writing in the *Sunday Times* eight years after his death, Ernest Newman (1926a,b) concluded that Parry's music 'has any number of qualities, but it lacks quality'. In 1947, *Jerusalem* was the only piece by Parry which rated a mention in a popular dictionary of British Music (Palmer 1947: 280–1). By 1984, in a study of James Davison, music-critic of *The Times* – clearly addressed to a musically knowledgeable readership – one author felt it necessary to identify Parry as the composer of *Jerusalem*, 'regularly sung at the last London Promenade Concert of the Season' (Reid 1984: 111). Parry's choral and orchestral works only recently achieved commercial recordings, and none has yet made it into the standard repertoire of a professional British ensemble. In this fate, the English Parry, interred in St Paul's Cathedral, is at one with the Welsh namesake whose remains lie in the obscurity of a south Wales churchyard.

As it proved, Parry's single living artistic legacy was perfectly suited to the purposes of his legatee, the English Musical Renaissance. *Jerusalem* committed the latter to no special effort, relieving it of the need for tedious acts of homage, yet providing enough to memorialise Parry as a foundation composer. Yet in 1898, in terms apostolically intended to evoke Schumann's famous apostrophe to Brahms, Henry Hadow proclaimed: 'There has risen amongst us a composer who is capable of restoring our national music to its true place in the art of Europe' (Benoliel: Chandos 8896). He was referring not to Elgar – then writing his *Enigma Variations* – but to Parry. *The Times*'s music critic Fuller Maitland heartily concurred. Fuller Maitland was instrumental in selecting the premiere of Parry's cantata *Scenes from Shelley's 'Prometheus Unbound'*, which had taken place in 1880, as the sacred moment of 're-birth' (Fuller Maitland 1902b: 188, 197–201). This initiative hardened into a policy, maintained by successive music critics of this newspaper, which thus became, appropriately enough, the buttress of the nation's musical, as of its political, establishment. Fuller Maitland was supported by many other writers, who began to make frequent references to Parry as the first significant creative figure of modern English Music.

By 1907, this construction of the past had achieved a dogmatic status in Ernest Walker's *A History of Music in England*, destined to become the staple of music libraries on its subject (Walker 1907: 300). In subsequent accounts of the Renaissance, Parry's cantata becomes an entrance arch – almost overgrown with climbers, but, in the rhetorical gestures of memorialists, recognisably grand – through which the reader was led into the grounds of the Goodly House. In the 1920s, Newman reaffirmed it as 'true enough that the renaissance in modern English music dates from *Prometheus Unbound*' (Newman 1926a,b). Yet Newman, in common with his colleagues, had never heard nor read the score. Indeed, *Prometheus*, allegedly the seminal work of the English Musical Renaissance, was not even included in the spate of Parry recordings referred to above. But the fertile influence of this sterile shibboleth was illustrated in 1986, when a study of English music appeared in the famous series of undergraduate textbooks *Que Sais-Je?*, published by the Presses Universitaires de France. French music and history students were informed that of all English compositions in the generation before Elgar 'le plus célèbre est *Prometheus Unbound* d'Hubert Parry, généralement considerée comme le point de départ de la résurrection musicale brittanique' (Rouville 1986: 69).

An explanation for the success of this petty larceny was, in part, that although no one knew the music, the text alone sufficed. Parry had chosen the work of England's most radical poet, the heir of Blake, and a trenchant critic of both aristocratic and industrial society. It celebrates a potent myth, recreated not only by Shelley but by his contemporary Beethoven (Talmon 1967: 160–1). As we have seen, Beethoven was a model to many English musicians. His daring challenge to the social limitations of his calling set the pattern of a radical tradition, through music which hymned the glories of Liberty, Equality and Fraternity. The Philharmonic Society counted patronage of Beethoven – and in particular of his *Symphony No. 9*, with its 'Ode to Joy/Freedom' – as its greatest splendour. In his *Eroica Symphony* and a series of other works, Beethoven had endorsed humanity's aspiration towards liberty, specifically utilising the Greek myth of Prometheus, heroic challenger of the gods, caretaker of the flame symbolising artistic creation, and the spirits of innovation and freedom in general. His pupil, Herbert Howells, later claimed that Parry intended *Prometheus Unbound* as a consciously revolutionary statement. Parry was born in the *echt*-revolutionary year of 1848, and his German adviser Dannreuther (in whose home the Shelley cantata was conceived) encouraged him to think in terms of Wagnerian political gestures. Yet Parry's 'revolution' was traditional, even moribund, in its symbolism – a safe, heavily insured revolution of a kind uniquely attractive to a failed Lloyds underwriter.

In this privileging of an utterly anonymous work as its standard-bearer, the Renaissance appropriated a reformist ideology. The auto-presentation of English music characterised it as an instrument of freedom and progress, an enemy of servitude and conservatism. As Prometheus, selected as its earliest champion, sings: 'I would feign be what it is my destiny to be – the saviour and the strength of suffering man.' Parry himself, too, was an ideal figurehead – English gentleman, self-reformed representative of finance capital, liberal agnostic who hated privilege. By adopting him as its first 'Great Composer', the Renaissance affected to place itself on the side of the common man and his 'long march' to political fulfilment. Yet its main mouthpiece was the newspaper widely regarded as the official organ of the British Government, and it was physically established in its very own 'Whitehall' at South Kensington.

It is not difficult to deconstruct the pharisaical procedures which placed a spurious banner of revolution on the towers of the Goodly House. Though Fuller Maitland may have inscribed the nation's 'recognition' of Parry's genius, *The Times* had not always seen the point. His predecessor, Francis Hueffer, who actually reviewed the premiere of *Prometheus*, had been only mildly impressed. In the most important aspect, indeed, he flatly contradicted the later assessment, pointing out that Parry's music had 'a total absence of the demonstrative defiance which is so prominent a feature in Shelley's picture' (Howes 1966: 136–8). A century later the rigid decrees of myth – and its associated 'Historical *Bloc*' – was revealed by the BBC's attitude. On its centenary in 1980, Radio 3 relayed a studio performance of *Prometheus*, describing it – both in the *Radio Times* and in the spoken introduction – as the work which 'one hundred years ago, marked an epoch in British music'. Radio 3's music staff had not realised that the (proudly announced!) fact that they were presenting a broadcasting premiere undermined any claim for its importance, musical or historical (Anon. *RT*: 240980).

Parry's *Prometheus* remained firmly bound to his rock, while propaganda assured the nation that he was free to visit and inspire its composers. In all its inscription, the composition of 'serious' music was identified with a discourse of broadly radical pretensions. Themes of 'liberty', 'progress' and even 'protest' became standard. This was fully in step with evolutionary trends elsewhere in British institutional life, and hardly uncharacteristic of British society in general. In a remark which reflected a similar spirit to Gramsci's theory of 'cultural ensemble', Rutland Boughton (1934: 78) said that 'the master-class [have] learned how to use even expressions of revolt as a brake on rebellion'. Indeed, the discourse itself was a thoroughly sanitised one, and, if retaining undertones of the Left, its overtones were 'national' and even patriotic. It was rarely allowed to become genuinely subversive, to pose a challenge to the positions of those who directed the movement, or to the preconceptions of the concert-going subscriber. In this, Parry's music also sounded the right chord, for few would regard *Prometheus* as being 'modern', even for its time. Its harmonic language would not have been found offensive by Beethoven, leave alone Wagner. Moreover, its livelier choruses remind the listener irresistibly of the Savoy Operas of Sir Arthur Sullivan.

Sir Arthur Sullivan's crime

For a bizarre minority of Renaissance memorialists, Sullivan himself was the true founder, whose place Parry has usurped. Percy Young once took 1862, date of the domestic premiere of Sullivan's incidental music to *The Tempest*, as a more appropriate overture to the revival of English composition (Young 1972: HMV ESD 7057). Sullivan, too, had carefully selected his text. Shakespeare at that time did not occupy quite the supreme position in English culture to which he would subsequently be elevated, but the play's concerns with the potency of art and the necessity of empire were suited to the atmosphere of the 1860s. The Crystal Palace concert evoked a strong response: 'Here was something [wrote one reviewer] that indicated an original composer ... On the whole we are inclined to think that Mr Sullivan has made the most promising debut of any English composer for some years past ... We English can no longer be called 'an unmusical people' (*Cornhill Magazine* 1862: 408–9).

Sullivan's only 'grand opera', *Ivanhoe*, was premiered many years later, in 1891. By now, the craze for the mock-medieval was at its height. Themes associated with crusade and chivalry constituted an obsession among the upper classes. Knighthood was accepted at its

Romantic valuation, as a condition instituted for the protection of the weak and downtrodden, and the overthrow of injustice (Girouard 1981). Sir Hubert Parry himself was under the spell of the Gothic. He called his new home in Sussex 'Knight's Croft', and his only opera, written at a time when the avocation of Avalon was ubiquitous, was entitled *Guenever*.

However, while Parry's opera – even today – has never reached the stage, Sullivan's was a sensational success. A business consortium built a new opera house in the West End, intended to display a series of such epics. The backers of Sullivan and his Goodly House banked not only on his Savoy Opera fame but on his possession of an artistic genius at least as profound as Wagner's. In the record books, at least, Sullivan surpasses Wagner in one respect: not one but two theatres were specifically constructed as showcases for his work. Sullivan's career had certainly been impressive. He made admirers as a student at Mendelssohn's Leipzig conservatoire. He was associated with Sir George Grove as a research scholar, especially in their rediscovery of Schubert (e.g. finding the holograph of the *'Unfinished' Symphony* in Vienna). A charming personality, his social connections led to his gaining the affectionate patronage of Queen Victoria. *Ivanhoe* – to the Queen's delight – ran for a gratifying 155 consecutive performances. The mould was broken, along with the perceived curse on the production of 'serious' English opera (Jacobs 1984: 320–33).

It is passing strange to recall that the Palace Theatre in Cambridge Circus, now an outlet for Lloyd Webber rather than von Weber, was originally designed as the English Bayreuth (Plate 10). The whole idea of an English Musical Renaissance generated by grand opera and the reputation of Sullivan seems counter-factual, and therefore absurd. But the main reason for this lies not so much in the music as in the fact that the men who mattered were not prepared to 'recognise' the phenomenon. In English music history, Sullivan is not seen as a 'serious' composer; or rather – an even worse fate – figures as the exemplar of the failed genius, a perfect parable of the wasted talents. For all his fame, and despite the support of Windsor Castle, he was *persona non grata* to the mandarins of South Kensington, who were now powerful enough to resist his bid for 'recognition'. Years earlier, Sullivan had turned his back on the whole process of the Renaissance, rejecting Grove's offer of a chair at the RCM, and thereafter accepting other 'team' chores only grudgingly. *Ivanhoe* was a belated act of atonement, an obeisance to the 'higher'

10 *Ivanhoe*'s castle in Cambridge Circus: the Royal English Opera House
(1890), later the Palace Theatre

demands of his vocation, but its popular success could not reverse
his isolation from the mainstream. The prodigal son – subject of Sullivan's previous large-scale 'serious' work (1869) – found the door
locked and barred. His offences were too many and too obstinate to
be forgiven.

Sir Arthur's mortal sin was the prostitution of his genius to the
profits of an 'inferior' and suspect trade. Though many of Sullivan's
critics themselves derived comfortable livings from the expanding
production and consumption structures created by the Renaissance,
they felt superior enough to regard his relationship with D'Oyly
Carte, which made him an immensely wealthy man, as disreputable.
Even a century later, Sullivan's tendency to seek fame and fortune is
commonly identified as the root cause of his failure in the allegedly
higher reaches of music (Wolfson BBC R3: 220490). He was not a
suitable figurehead – indeed, hardly even a gentleman. These trans-
gressions were compounded by the fact that in the Savoy Operas the

attitudes of the estate which Sullivan had abjured were ridiculed as pompous, even spurious. In *The Mikado*, biggest hit of the Gilbert and Sullivan series (1885), 'the piano organist' is placed on the Lord High Executioner's list of people who would never be missed, alongside 'the banjo singer'; while the music-hall performer is sentenced to fugues and masses and ops by Bach and Beethoven. Sullivan underlined Gilbert's wit by including a mock madrigal, while irreverent swipes at Bach can be detected in his stylised recitatives. The vicarious embarrassment felt by many when the company took this work to Germany was, if anything, intensified by the fact of its dismal failure in that enterprise.

At a time when every effort was being made to lift the moral and social profile of music onto a higher plane, Sullivan's proclivities were seen as perversely unhelpful. Accordingly, the punishment was made to fit the crime. Like the naughty boy who gave cheek to his betters, Sullivan was made to stand outside the main galleries of the pantheon, in the open portico of the Goodly House. Neither his opera nor the later cantata *The Golden Legend* was allowed a place in the Renaissance canon. The process was not smooth, for Sullivan had powerful supporters who could draw on a reservoir of popular feeling. In 1893, one writer apostrophised *The Golden Legend* as 'one of the greatest creations of this century', and saw merit even in the Savoy Operas – though admitting that progress in English Music was inconceivable without the leadership of Hubert Parry (Willeby 1893: 50, 86, 257–8). Finally, Fuller Maitland assumed the role of Lord High Executioner, and turned the tables on the jester by contributing a damning obituary on Sullivan to the *Cornhill Magazine*:

> The oratorios are lamentable examples of uninspired and really uncongenial work ... It was the spirit of compromise that did more than anything else to lower Sullivan's standard ... [*Ivanhoe*] a work that ought to have raised him to the highest plane of his life's achievement was spoiled out of deference to the taste of the multitude ... The great renaissance of English music, which took place in the last quarter of the nineteenth century, accomplished itself without any help or encouragement from Sullivan. (Fuller Maitland 1901: 300–9)

In a more considered assessment, the same critic later finished off his victim, stating categorically that Sullivan 'took no part whatever in the work of the renaissance' (Fuller Maitland 1902b: 170). Accordingly, Ernest Walker's influential study (1907: 292–5) included a demolition of Sullivan's claims to greatness. In 1924, a BBC hack ridiculed a listener's question – 'I should be much obliged if you would express an opinion as to whom you consider the more classical composer, Wagner or Sullivan' – as something which 'could not be beaten for unconscious humour' (Tristram, *RT*: 070324: 417).

Ivanhoe was the first 'serious' opera by an Englishman to be genuinely popular with a paying audience, but it was an evanescent triumph. It was resuscitated by Beecham in 1910, and lasted for only two nights; and, in 1929, a performance was mounted and broadcast by the BBC (Klein, *RT*: 220329). Sixty years later, Radio 3 carried a programme intended (apparently) to reconsider Sir Arthur's reputation as a 'serious' composer. We include the parenthetic rider here, since the intention was frustrated by the very title – 'Sullivan without Gilbert' – which provided a structured absence working against the grain of its ostensible purpose. The programme's content could hardly convince when its title inescapably confirmed Sullivan's indissoluble link with Gilbert, and thus with a subordinate dimension of creativity (Anon., BBC R3: 021189). The feature did not include an extract from *Ivanhoe*. Yet two days later Radio 3 carried a full transmission of Marschner's *Der Templer und die Jüdin*, based on the same Walter Scott novel. *Ivanhoe*'s centenary passed with no attempt at stage revival, but in 1992 a complete recording appeared. In 1995, *The Yeoman of the Guard* became the first Savoy Opera to be performed at the home of English National Opera. But a tendency in classical music fanzines to refer to Sullivan as the composer of 'operas' rather than 'operettas' was firmly contradicted when the BBC's 'Fairest Isle' firmly categorised them under the latter term; for good measure relating the anecdote that Queen Victoria once asked her proétgé 'when he was going to compose a real opera' (Fraser 1995: 64, 66). It seems Sir Arthur has still not gained release from the inferior category to which music history has condemned him, a dungeon in the castle of South Kensington – if (one suspects), by the miserable standards of most of his fellow-prisoners, a well-appointed one.

As we have seen, opera was the only major genre which aroused radically divergent views – even discord – within the upper echelons of the Renaissance Movement. Sullivan's failure to win over the High Command at South Ken was partly conditioned by this fact. Prior to 1914, a neo-puritanical spirit retained a strong influence. Parry placed himself firmly in the Roundhead camp, quietly discouraging opera in the RCM curriculum. The Cavalier Stanford, abetted by Mackenzie, opposed this and strove to improve the organisation of National Opera (Stanford 1908, 1914). With the new reign and the new century, the cause of 'serious' musical theatre was advanced by a plethora of pamphlets and books, in turn leading to the involvement of Sir Joseph Beecham and his son. Collaboration between Thomas Beecham and Percy Pitt brought financial support from the business world, and regular opera seasons with a high quality of performance and production became a feature of London's musical life.

Yet the achievement of a National Opera was crucially flawed – or so the historiography assures us – because it failed to produce a native genius. While most other genres justified the work and patronage invested in them, duly producing their masterpieces, opera languished. In general estimation, Elgar's output saw the heights scaled, in respect not only of the orchestra but of choral music. Chamber music made great strides and art-song was already flourishing. All this produced a sense of frustration that no parallel example had been found for the stage. Galloway, followed by Forsyth, Stanford and others were led to argue that private patronage, and a commercial rationale, would never suffice without major state subsidy (Galloway 1902). For the same reason, Forsyth advocated official 'recognition' of a British opera composer – it hardly mattered of whom – as a deliberate act of genius-generation, apparently predicating that if the geese were gandered, by the law of averages one of them would lay a golden egg (Forsyth 1911: 257–8). In the interwar years, London productions of the German and Italian repertoire, right up to Strauss and Puccini, received international acclaim. By now, though famous foreign singers still commanded an audience, the Renaissance had produced a native school whose leading figures were good enough for export to the celebrated international houses. As well as notable instrumental composers, Britain had produced distinguished soloists, orchestras and even conductors. On all other paths of its musical development, it seemed, watersheds had been crossed and milestones passed. The last gasp of private patronage tried a new and radical departure with the foundation of the Glyndebourne Festival. Yet still no native operatic masterpiece emerged. Then, at last, in 1945, partly with the aid of the first substantial government intervention, came Britten and *Peter Grimes*.

Analysis of the 'turning-point' represented by *Peter Grimes*, and the succesful 'recognition' of Britten as a great opera composer, lies outside the scope of the present study. We are concerned to study the failure of so many other attempts, during a half-century of intense effort. No expert on English Music has ever seriously dissented from the view that Britten's was the first masterpiece of native opera since Purcell. The nostrum is so much part of our musical lexicography that even the British Music Society, which exists to encourage the performance of neglected works, accepts it as a matter of course. Indeed, having helped to organise many performances of the canonically excluded during the course of 1985, the Society issued a publication which celebrated the rich heritage of native opera. Its cover bore a photograph of Peter Pears creating the role of Grimes (Meares 1986). As a result of this bland consensus, avowedly based on aesthetic considerations, other events which point to a course not taken by the mainstream, or stand at a divergent angle to it, can be elided in the histories, to the extent that even a need to explain them away is rarely in evidence. The complementary 'facts' of 1945, Britten and *Peter Grimes*, occupy a certain place as of right, established, assured, beyond challenge. No other explanation is conceivable: this is the significant conjuncture.

The slightly *Immortal Hour*

The orthodoxy of *Peter Grimes* also heavily overlays the story of Rutland Boughton and his opera *The Immortal Hour*. Boughton was a disciple of the 'English' socialism of William Morris and Edward Carpenter. In youth, he expressed this through a patriotic response to the organic nation. Around the time of the Boer War, he wrote the tone-poem *The Spanish Armada* and a symphony entitled *Oliver Cromwell* – regular themes of English Protestant/Populist nationalism. His musical mentality was also shaped by the ethical puritanism of Parry and Renaissance 'purists' like Fuller Maitland, and he seems almost to have designed himself as the complete opposite to Sullivan. However, critical indifference stimulated his first essay in literary polemic, the consciously ironic *Self-Advertisement for Rutland Boughton* in 1909. This flysheet, which attacked the way in which the London establishment selected some composers for attention while ignoring others, indicates both naive ambition and awareness of the political context of artistic developments (Boughton 1909).

After a spell with the 'Midlands School', on the teaching staff of the Birmingham Institute under Bantock, Boughton deliberately turned his back on bourgeois society and the prospect of earning a conventional living through music. With a group of friends, he sought the Holy Grail of an 'English operatic style' that would be direct, choral and communal, within reach of all in terms of both performance and understanding (Hurd 1962: 38–45). In 1914, their founding of a festival at Glastonbury sent shock-waves through the English musical world. Boughton gained the support of Elgar, who kept up an encouraging correspondence (BLMC A52364/74–82). No less a luminary than Beecham accepted the chairmanship of the Festival School, and another conductor, Dan Godfrey, was sympathetic. A Glastonbury appeal fund was quickly set up, in which Beecham was joined by Lena Ashwell, Granville Bantock, Edward Carpenter, John Galsworthy, Percy Grainger, Joseph Holbrooke, G. E. Moore and Landon Ronald as patrons. Critical responses could hardly have been more auspicious. E. J. Dent, the country's leading opera scholar, was enthusiastic. The first productions of *The Immortal Hour* brought a detailed appreciation from the noted choral trainer C. K. Scott in the *Musical Standard* and, after the second festival a year later, the *Musical Times* seconded this opinion.

The following years saw consolidation. England's leading Wagnerites, Ernest Newman and G. B. Shaw, visited the festival, and were duly impressed. A campaign was launched for £10,000 to build a theatre in Glastonbury, with the support of Henry Hadow, Thomas Hardy, John Drinkwater and Sir Edward Elgar (Hurd 1962: 46–75). The last of these had by now pronounced *The Immortal Hour* to be 'a work of genius' (Hurd 1984: Hyperion A6610/12). A contrasting source of opinion thoroughly agreed with Sir Edward. The critic of *The Sackbut*, a radical new music review which was busily debunking the reputations of the great and good, asserted: '[T]hat it will live I have no doubt, [but] it will always be performed in queer out-of-the-way places' (Lorenz 1920: 109–11). As it turned out, this fashionable organ proved to be spectacularly wrong on both counts.

Up to this point, the prominent figures in British artistic life who had not declared in favour of Boughton must have been in a minority. The fact that a powerful Glastonbury lobby built up so rapidly is an indication of the receptivity which existed in musical circles. Timing was of the essence. The festival had answered a craving whose power could never have been suspected by its founders. Moreover, instead of hampering it, the circumstances created by the war assisted its amplification and dissemination on many levels – heightened feelings of national chauvinism, the contrast Glastonbury posed to the wartime society of the industrial cities and the magical escapism of the operas themselves. Boughton had provided the ideal 'alternative conjuncture'. In any case, on the mundane practical level, the musical press had no alternative. In 1914–18, there was nowhere else for it to go – all over Europe the lights of the great opera-houses had been extinguished.

A hard core of Glastonbury pilgrims were attracted by the overtly political aims (and the covert implications) of the festival. G. B. Shaw felt sympathy for Boughton's objectives, despite having previously disparaged his creative pretensions (BLMC A52365/6: 020112). Shaw's patronage was earned partly by the sheer energy and musicality which drove the enterprise, and partly by the sociopolitical dimension of its Wagnerian spirit (Laurence 1989: III, 682–6). These ambient factors gradually converted him to Boughton's music. In an essay published in the fourth edition of *The Perfect Wagnerite* (1922), 'The Music of the Future', Shaw hailed Boughton as one of only two outstanding composers (the other being Bantock) belonging to the post-Elgar generation (Laurence 1989: III, 534). But for Shaw 'recognition' that an authentic national opera movement had taken root in an obscure provincial corner also provided a useful stave with which to beat his old adversaries, the metropolitan mandarins of the Musical Renaissance.

> Glastonbury, steeped in traditions which make it holy ground … still has no theatre, no electric light, no convenience for Wagnerian drama that every village does not possess. Yet it is here that the Wagnerist Dream has been best realised in England. That dream, truly interpreted, did not mean that the English soil should bring forth performances of Wagner's music copied from those at Bayreuth. It meant that the English soil should produce English music and English drama, and that English people should perform them in their own way. (pp. 542–5)

Here one suspects that Shaw's 'recognition', published in *The Nation*, was inspired by the Forsyth formula. The 'organic' language which saturates it also suggests the influence of the Nationalist Movement led by Sharp and Vaughan Williams – a process surely catalysed by the Great War.

At any rate, London was softened up for *The Immortal Hour* long before its professional debut in 1922. Dent and Newman, as well as Shaw, had trumpeted the arrival of a native operatic school, and negotiations for the production were the result of a public campaign not unlike that which accompanied the 'breakthrough' of Elgar a generation earlier. Boughton was roughly the same age as Elgar had been at the premiere of the *Enigma Variations*; his modest social origins and provincial orientation were other points of comparison. Elgar himself was currently writing music for Binyon's stage presentation of *King Arthur*, while his young protégé had already begun a projected cycle of 'choral dramas' intended to present a radical version of the Arthurian legends. It seemed that Boughton was about to draw the sword from the stone, and to receive the acclaim of the assembled chivalry of the English Renaissance. An element of 'destiny' was perhaps consciously involved in the composer's management of the affair. For reasons of principle, Boughton was unwilling to permit the innocence of *The Immortal Hour* to be sullied by the great metropolis. This prevarication forced up the asking price, increasing the anticipation and publicity surrounding the premiere. Yet Boughton's forename, as well as giving an agreeable impression of rural England, suggests that he may have been aware of a providential element in his forthcoming triumph in the capital. The earliest English operas had been staged at Rutland House in London in the 1650s; it seems more than coincidence that at Glastonbury Boughton and his team staged revivals of several of these works (Dent 1940/49: 158, 189).

In October 1922 *The Immortal Hour* began its phenomenal run. Less than two years later it had chalked up nearly 400 performances, and a 1926 revival took the figure over 500. This remains a record for the maiden production of any example in the history of the oldest major musical genre. If performances at Glastonbury and elsewhere are taken into account (largely amateur productions with piano accompaniment) the total exceeds 1,000 within a dozen years of its premiere. These statistics suggest a reception at least as impressive as that given to Elgar's *Symphony No. 1* – and, therefore, that the opera-house had at last emulated the achievement of the concert-hall. The man and *The Immortal Hour* had met. The London production fulfilled many times over the expectations aroused by critics and impresarios. Even when comparatively indifferent to its charms, witnesses admitted it to have a sufficient number of satisfying tunes to sustain a work of its length. Use of the chorus, both in sung ensembles and in the *mise en scène* was striking and seductive. Its aesthetic ideas, so antipathetic to everything represented by the modern metropolis, were irresistible. The rich, the well-born and the famous flocked to see it, led by several royals – Princess Marie Louise, the King's sister, attended fifty-two performances. For these, and for thousands of anonymous middle-class Londoners, *The Immortal Hour* provided a genuinely multidimensional artistic experience.

The libretto was based on the writings of 'Fiona Macleod', a sequence of 'Celtic' mythological narratives as spurious as the *nom de plume* of their author William Sharp. The counter-cultural attractions of the Celtic Twilight had spread from the esoteric circles that had nurtured it before the war into a more popular area of interest. It provided a modest quota of mysticism, like a home-brewed version of the oriental – Bantock, for example, had exploited both species of exotica. The topographical setting of *The Immortal Hour* is legendary Ireland, and the score makes use of 'Gaelic' folk-tunes arranged by Marjorie Kennedy-Fraser, a north-British equivalent of the English Sharp. Its success encouraged composers and critics to a belief that a 'Celtic' milieu was establishing a dominance over the national operatic medium. Joseph Holbrooke's *Mabinogion* trilogy enjoyed brief attention; and a hopeful of the younger generation like George Lloyd – more Celtic in origin than Boughton or Holbrooke – gave his first opera a similar provenance (*Iernin*, 1932). All these works were destined to pass into oblivion – a fate which seemed unlikely, even unthinkable, in 1926, when Boughton enjoyed a reputation among 'serious' English musicians comparable only to that of Elgar at the time of his first London festival. Another full-length 'choral drama', *Alkestis*, had already been produced in 1924 by the British National Opera under Percy Pitt. This became the subject of the first live broadcast of an English opera by the BBC – an event surrounded by much further publicity (Pitt *RT*: 040124). The Christmas opera *Bethlehem*, described by Shaw as 'a great success', had become widely popular among amateur and semi-professional groups, also registering hundreds of performances in the early 1920s (BLMC A52365/18: 211223).

Yet a crucial difference existed between the Elgar of 1904 and the Boughton of twenty years later. The former had already established a strong position abroad, especially in Germany. E. J. Dent identified this weakness in Boughton's case and sought to remedy it (BLMC A52364/44–6: 150123). Dent was more influential on the Continent than any previous English musicologist. Meanwhile the Finnish musician Järnefelt, brother-in-law of Sibelius, saw *The Immortal*

Hour and wrote: 'The music was wonderful, and I shall write to Sibelius about Rutland Boughton in order to transmit my enthusiasm. I wonder why this great composer is not wider known abroad' (BLMC A52364/144: 220226). Despite this, and despite the fact that German opera-houses were anxious to rebuild contacts with England, no contract was forthcoming. In 1926 the opera opened in New York and was given a poor reception. The London triumph had convinced Boughton's backers that he would win over the American public, too, and they persevered for four disastrous weeks. No further performance ever took place outside Great Britain. Dent remained loyal to Boughton, or at least to his most famous work. After a moderately successful revival in 1932, he assured the composer that it was 'now pretty well established as a classic'; later adding that 'I really begin to think it is one of the best operas ever written' (BLMC A52364/48, 62v: 210533, 161246). In 1949, the second edition of Dent's standard book on opera, while acknowledging the greatness of *Grimes*, refused to change its encomium to Boughton and the Glastonbury movement. All the same, the author felt obliged to admit that '*The Immortal Hour* can hardly be said to have passed into the standard repertory' (Dent 1940/49: 190).

The fact was that *The Immortal Hour* had simply passed. Excalibur, grasped in a mysterious hand, disappeared into the misty waters. As early as 1937, Bantock wrote to Boughton, in terms which were probably not disingenuous, that 'it may be some consolation to feel that a future generation will re-discover and appreciate all you have done for a national British opera' (BLMC A52364/10: 200137). By 1942, the critic Eric Blom found himself unable to explain how the work had ever impressed so many people (Blom 1942: 193). Two or three numbers from the opera remained favourites among a core of initiates. This brought frequent requests for radio hearings down to the 1950s, and few 'classical' music buffs born before the Second World War would fail to recognise the *Faery Song*. But this was never enough to arouse the interest of a new generation. In retrospect, *The Immortal Hour* came to be seen as merely an immoral moment. The grass-roots activist Christopher Le Fleming recalled (1982:37) – or rather, confessed – that 'there was a good deal of pentatonic as well as modal nostalgia in the air at the time'. Two mainstream texts with the title *The English Musical Renaissance* are dismissive of the whole immortal hour (Howes 1966: 314; Pirie 1979: 112). A third makes no attempt to answer his own deadly question about Boughton: 'how important was he as a composer?' (Trend 1985: 61–72).

As the above illustrates, Boughton was of massive importance in the history of English Music, and should remain so, if we are to understand it better. A more apposite rhetorical question, therefore, than Trend's is: if nothing fails like success, then what price success?

Archaeology lesson

Though it is the most spectacular lost monument of our musical past, *The Immortal Hour* is by no means alone. The resourceful rambler can find others which offer perplexities and puzzles, and many readers could report on rewarding examples which we have overlooked in this book. Even in the immediate vicinity of Boughton's opera there are other remains which repay the archaeologist. Indeed, the years following 1918 seem to have been fecund in failed experiments – strong evidence that it was an intense period in the struggle for supremacy in English musical culture.

It is certainly true that the hegemony established by the Pastoral School did not happen overnight. In 1912, Landon Ronald – a year younger than Vaughan Williams – was the junior among eight composers approached by the Philharmonic Society to provide works for its centenary concerts (BLMC L48–13–38/24). Only with the war, and with *The Lark Ascending* and *A Pastoral Symphony*, did RVW's central role become evident. 'Recognition' took time to filter downwards, and public reception of the folklorists remained a comparatively low-key affair. None of its exponents achieved Boughton's audience or critical acclaim. This is especially important, since both Holst and RVW were committed to opera and made significant investments in the genre. A similar point could be made about 'serious' theatre music. Contemporaneously with *The Immortal Hour*, Delius's score for *Hassan* – an entertainment based on James Elroy Flecker – achieved 'an instant and fashionable success, and was to have one of the longest runs in the history of the West End Theatre' (Carley 1988: 278–81). Compared to these works, operas like *The Perfect Fool* (Holst, 1922) and *Hugh the Drover* (Vaughan Williams, 1924) reached only an esoteric minority.

But, above all, the new leaders of style and taste failed to register popular success even in the area accepted as culturally germane – the major choral forms. The reliable audiences for choral and orchestral concerts which existed before the war were now melting away. Worship of Handel and Mendelssohn had been officially discouraged, but – apart from *The Golden Legend* and *Gerontius*, neither being an *echt*-Renaissance work – little had emerged to take their place in the regional festivals and competitions. *The Hymn of Jesus* (Holst, 1917) and *Sancta Civitas* (Vaughan Williams, 1926) may have elicited approval from the critical cognoscenti, but they failed to make the repertoire of the choral societies. In contrast, two other works made a genuinely popular impact in the 1920s – Samuel Coleridge-Taylor's *The Song of Hiawatha* and *The World Requiem* of John Foulds.

First heard in 1898, *Hiawatha's Wedding Feast* made its composer famous. For a few months, just before the triumph of the *Enigma Variations*, Coleridge-Taylor was hailed as the nation's promise. Indeed, Elgar himself concurred with Stanford, Parry and others in this opinion. The full version of the cantata was heard on the same day as the premiere of *The Dream of Gerontius* (1900), and created the more favourable impression. The subject matter was of topical interest, since Indian tribes had recently ceased to be a threat to the white population of the American West. Their history could now safely become myth, and the colonisation process, history (with F. J. Turner's 'frontier thesis', 1897). Coleridge-Taylor's meteoric rise saw him invited to the USA in the same year as Elgar was accorded a London festival (1904). He participated in a three-day festival of his own works, held concurrently in Washington and Baltimore, and met President Roosevelt at the White House. While Elgar was by no means the first English composer to succeed in Germany, Coleridge-Taylor was certainly the first to achieve fame on both sides of the Atlantic (Sayers 1915: 106–9).

Hiawatha's Wedding Feast became a choral society staple, and within four years of its premiere had registered 200 performances. As in the case of *The Immortal Hour*, this constitutes an achievement fully comparable to that recorded by Elgar's *Symphony No. 1*. However, its great fame was yet to come. In 1924, over a decade after Coleridge-Taylor's death, *Hiawatha* sprang back into national prominence when the impresario T. C. Fairbairn mounted a costumed production at the Albert Hall. The cantata was turned into a semi-opera, with immense scenic backdrops, dramatic lighting effects and (what was deemed to be) ethnically appropriate dancing by the chorus. The production became a jamboree, a hardy perennial of London life for the rest of the interwar period.

For two weeks every summer all roads to the hall were thronged with capacity audiences and close on a thousand 'Red Indian' performers. These 'braves' and 'squaws' came not from the 'Land of the Dakotahs' but from the concrete wigwams of Wapping, Tooting, Penge, Chearn and Coleridge-Taylor's own village of Croydon – in fact any village that could send singing braves and squaws to the great 'Pow-Wow' in the Albert Hall Arena under the Great Chief of Music Dr Malcolm Sargent. (Alwyn 1991: Argo 430–356–2)

The success of *Hiawatha* offers parallels with that of *The Immortal Hour*. In political and aesthetic terms, both are founded on the choral base. The mixture of representational, choreographic and musical media, along with an exotic setting, suggests a similar escapist appeal. In 1925, the enterprise was taken over by the Royal Choral Society. On the management committee, Sargent sat alongside a bevy of titled ladies. His gifts of showmanship helped to guarantee the success of the event, and even in the early years of the Depression it regularly returned substantial profits (Reid 1968: 15–63).

Like Boughton, and also somewhat accidentally, Coleridge-Taylor had sparked off a fashionable craze. The specific 'conjuncture' relates to its transatlantic subject matter. Public interest in things American had become intense. In 1917, the USA's entry into the war stimulated great pro-American feeling. The Armistice was followed by Woodrow Wilson's official visit – the first by an American president – which was received with great enthusiasm (1919). Simultaneously, the first shock-waves of American culture – jazz music and the feature movie – were hitting British cities. In the aftermath of the Treaty of Versailles, and the widespread reaction against war fostered by Wilson's statesmanship, Longfellow's tale of an earlier, wise and peace-loving, American leader had an irresistible appeal. All this was complemented by the impact of D. W. Griffith and William S. Hart – the rise of the 'Western' – on the popular imagination.

Thankfully, the organisers of the 'great Pow-Wow' had the decency to restrict their vulgar intrusion into South Kensington to the period of the summer vacation. The nearby control-centre of the English Musical Renaissance – along with the select world of musical journalism – were thus more easily able to ignore it. The performances attracted no more critical attention than would the weekly Albert Hall coruscation of Tchaikovsky's *1812 Overture* with military band and 'real cannon' in the 1960s. Yet this remarkable feature of London's musical life only lapsed with the outbreak of war in

1939. Thereafter, it was gently elided by 'official' history. By the time of Howes's book, *Hiawatha* called for merely a passing mention, although it had commanded a dimensionally greater following than any comparable work of Vaughan Williams to which this author devoted so much attention (Howes 1966: 307). Not even a nod was necessary when Pirie came to write his book (1979). Not until Trend's survey (1985: 51–61) was Coleridge-Taylor's career accorded a coverage in any way commensurate with its contemporary fame. Like many other significant works of the English musical past, the complete version of *Hiawatha* was not recorded commercially until the 1980s, and little else of Coleridge-Taylor's considerable output has survived in the repertoire.

In the years immediately prior to *Hiawatha*'s success, the Albert Hall was the scene of another choral success by an English composer. John Foulds, Manchester-born, began his career in the Hallé Orchestra under Richter. In 1922, he wrote *The World Requiem* to honour Britain's war dead. Pronounced 'worthy of performance on a national occasion' by the British Music Society, in 1923 it was taken up by the British Legion for Armistice Day performance (Foreman 1987: 166). For some years, it formed part of the Festival of Remembrance, an occasion presided over by royalty, and which quickly became the central ritual of the nation. The work's impact has been compared to that of Britten's *War Requiem* (Foreman 1987: 299). At a truly sensational premiere in 1923, its mixture of 'Celtic' pentatonalism and 'oriental' modes, made an effect similar to that of *The Immortal Hour*: 'The audience was ecstatic, many of them in tears' (MacDonald 1975: 29). Sir Henry Wood had already premiered some of Foulds's pieces, and in this same year he played the *Keltic Suite* at the Proms. This, and some other –'lighter' – pieces, were taken up by the BBC. Then Shaw chose Foulds to write the incidental music for *St Joan*. He enjoyed great success with a score which Vaughan Williams did not overlook when writing his music for *Scott of the Antartic*. For a time, Foulds was in demand as a composer for the theatre. Meanwhile, however, the *Requiem* was dropped from the Armistice Day schedule, which soon became the almost exclusive preserve of Elgar and Vaughan Williams. In 1927, just when he seemed to be building a reputation, Foulds left London and settled in Paris. He found work as an arranger and copyist, but later he was reduced to being a cinema accompanist. He returned to England in the early 1930s, but by then he had fallen by the wayside, and his attempts to canvass Boult and the BBC for performances were fruitless. In 1935, he left for India, where he died four years later (McDonald 1975: 29–33; Foreman 1987: 166–7).

The disappearance (literal and metaphorical) of John Foulds was both complete and perplexing, perhaps more so than those of Brian, Boughton or Scott – to name a few other victims at random. His failure to achieve a profile in the mainstream documentation of the Musical Renaissance is a demonstration of its capacity to write-off and write-out. In the official history of the Promenade Concerts, his first performances are omitted from the index of 'significant premieres', where even those of Brian (for example) are not (Cox 1980: 263, 266, 271). For Howes (1966), he never existed, and Pirie (despite his preference for the 'modernist' school to which Foulds belonged) dismisses The World Requiem with contempt (1979: 112). In the 1970s, his biographer suggested that Erie Blom's scathing paragraph about Foulds in the fifth edition of Grove's Dictionary might be replaced with something more charitable. This initative was rejected, and Blom's piece reprinted in 1981 (Sadie 1981: VI, 733). Foulds failed to gain admittance to Trend's elite division of thirty-five featured composers, and only turns up in Gerald Norris's exhaustive compilation (1981: 202) as one line in the entry for the city of his birth.

In 1982, in a bizarre counter-factual ploy, a group of enthusiasts promoted Foulds to the status of one of the 'Masters of the English Musical Renaissance'. The occasion followed publication of a biography by Malcolm MacDonald, and took the form of a pioneer LP recording made by Radio Luxembourg (presumably with private philanthropic support) of works by Parry, Brian and Foulds, in which the latter two were characterised as 'after Vaughan Williams, really the true heirs to Parry and Elgar's legacy' (Benoliel and Roberts 1981: Forlane UM 3529–3531). Such promotionism, even when motives are of the highest, rarely achieves its object. A further decade elapsed before any of Foulds's major works – in this case the Dynamic Triptych for piano and orchestra – obtained a Radio 3 premiere. As for The World Requiem, it resteth yet in peace.

Even in the field of 'light music', to which the BBC relegated him, Foulds's reputation pales beside that of another who is emphatically not part of the Musical Renaissance as it presently perceives itself. We refer to Albert W. Ketèlby, who became in the 1920s the best-known and the biggest earner of any composer since Sullivan and

German. For millions of cinema-goers – that is, all except a minority, estimated in single percentile figures, whose main leisure pursuit was music rather than movies – the works of Ketèlby, quite simply, represented 'serious' music. There were good reasons for this. They are melodious well-scored pieces of ideal duration, mostly arranged in a clear ABAB form, providing a painless induction to Art Music. Yet academic determination to cast them into a subordinate and distantly related sphere (abetted by the less academic determination of the marvellous music-hall act 'Wilson, Keppel and Betty') was absolute. Ketèlby fails to figure in any of the mainstream textbooks, and is apparently beneath even the disdain reserved for others who are seen (at least) as honest rivals of the 'great' national composers. Yet his melodic gift and sinuous rhythms infected thousands of the otherwise untouchable with an interest in 'serious' music. It seems to us that *In A Monastery Garden* created more 'music lovers' than any other English composition of its period; one expert reckons that *In a Persian Market*, Ketèlby's original hit of 1916, 'probably received more performances than any other work in the history of English music' (Ehrlich, in Banfield 1995: 47).

Ketèlby was a son of Birmingham, and matured in the period when Bantock presided over the only centre of English music which held out against the colonialism of South Kensington. Bantock compiled enormous works on pseudo-oriental subjects – such as his complete setting of *The Rubaiyat of Omar Khayyam* – which rarely achieved more than one performance. In contrast, Ketèlby turned out short seductive pieces of orientalia like *In A Persian Market*. These were more suited to Birmingham's industrial *locus geni*, mass production of widely distributed small-scale consumables, exotic bric-à-brac with east-of-Suez overtones. The label 'Made in Birmingham', once slightingly attached to Bantock, seems to adhere more suitably, and without intended slur, to Ketèlby. The huge success of Ketèlby's music, as with that of Boughton, Coleridge-Taylor and Foulds, was due to the broad cultural context of its time. His primary medium was not the concert-hall but the cinema; and without the imperial experience his career would be as inconceivable as Elgar's. *In A Persian Market* was produced at the time when Persia and its oil resources were becoming crucial to Britain's imperial strategy. *With Honour Crowned* is a full-fledged Elgarian march, and *Jungle Drums* turns into a raucous military parade. At the same time Ketèlby did not ignore indigenous climes, and pieces like *The Cockney Suite*, though following RVW, arguably rested also on 'folk-music'. By the early 1930s, he was probably the best-known English composer, and the only one apart from Elgar to conduct concerts of his own music on the wireless – at peak listening hour! (Anon., *RT*: 28073 1). Yet unlike Eric Coates's – the 'recognised' English Johann Strauss-figure of the interwar years ('uncrowned king of light music') – Ketèlby's constituency was evidently beyond the pale. His populist appeal was simply too embarrassing for him to be granted any kind of 'recognition'. He never obtained entry to Grove's *Dictionary* during his lifetime, and twenty years after his death was not even represented in the *Gramophone Classical LP Catalogue* (Day 1978). The final accolade came on 30 November 1999, when he was entered as 'Alfred' Ketèlby in the *Radio Times*'s schedule for Radio 3.

Neither in the Grove nor the groove, the once-ubiquitous sounds of Albert W. Ketèlby have now faded away. His popular impact was similar to that of Coleridge-Taylor, Boughton and Foulds; like theirs, his music was seen as merely escapist or exotic (he wrote *A Fairy Suite* and *A Prelude to a Japanese Play*). But there is a striking difference. Uniquely among the composers we deal with in this book, Ketèlby nurtured no ambitions to be a Great Artist. His monetary rewards, beyond the wildest dreams of most 'serious' composers, helped ensure that such a destiny never overtook him (Ehrlich 1989: 164). Places in the Pantheon of Immortality were reserved for those who demonstrated loyalty to a given and ever-narrowing ideal of 'national music'.

Political pathology and Professor Plum

> Some in the tumult are lost;
> Baffled, bewilder'd, they stray.
> Some as prisoners draw breath.
> Others – the bravest – are cross'd,
> On the height of their bold-followed way,
> By the swift-rushing missile of Death.
>
> Hardly, hardly shall one
> Come, with countenance bright,
> O'er the cloud-wrapt, perilous plain:
> His Master's errand well done,
> Safe through the smoke of the fight,
> Back to his Master again.
>
> (Arnold, *Men of Genius*)

We are confident that, having examined the evidence presented above, few of the jury will feel able to eliminate suspicion of foul play. Indeed, it seems to the prosecution that a serial killer has been at work on the perilous plain. Unsuspected by the cloud-wrapt readers above, the library basement is a kind of morgue where our artistically undead are stored, like examples of species rendered extinct by the evolution of normative types. We submit that their extinction was not brought about by an act of violence; no ritual knife or candlestick silenced the sacrificial lambs. The preferred procedure was to 'disappear' the intended victim, followed by silent suffocation, the ether of anonymity and disposal as recorded above.

Our indictment is not of murder – not even the murder most prosaic of the who-dunnit – but damage to artistic reputations, in which (at worst) something analogous to character assassination is involved. The victims have been deprived not of their mortal lives but of a perceived immortal destiny. Nonetheless, in a cultural climate where 'Genius' and the halo of the 'Great Artist' were dominant tropes of social intercourse, an infinitely desirable condition endowing its possessor with superhuman status as well as material comfort, failure was an unenviable fate for any who once had aspired. For some, its penalties were real and prolonged, a mental more than a physical agony (if sometimes both), and ultimately commensurate – one might suppose – with the scale of individual ambition or self-delusion. Even where the latter was to the fore, our murderous analogy should not be lightly dismissed as fantastic or self-indulgent. In one case, as many of his biographers agree, it was above all the bitter frustration of the rejected artist which produced the most appalling perpetrator of vengeance in world history, a man passionately convinced of his own 'genius', and deeply moved by 'serious' music (Hitler 1926/69: 32, 65).

In terms of the cultural politics which dominated our period, the possession of 'genius' brought power with it – in the same way as do other forms of ownership. For this reason, the question of 'recognition' was a critical one. The need to control potentially maverick sources of influence produced methods of assessment designed more to exclude than to admit. The principles evoked had been laid down by Mozart in *The Magic Flute*, and brought to a high degree of contemporary relevance by Wagner in *Die Meistersinger*. One of the founders of the Musical Renaissance described himself in appropriately Masonic fashion, in the title of his autobiography, as *A Door-Keeper of Music*. We have examined the process by which

Fuller Maitland admitted Parry to the pantheon and excluded Sullivan, thus canonising one and marginalising the other. We contend
that the guilty men were the professional writers, critics and teachers, those who literally 'authorised' the Renaissance. Their capital
crimes metaphorically resemble those of the once-popular 'who-
dunnit' board game 'Cluedo', which always took place in one of the
rooms of the same Goodly House, and were often committed by
'Professor Plum'. Their principles were aesthetical, their methods
academical and their motives political.

    We can now reveal the written confession of an agent–accomplice
to these ritual proceedings. Though not (perhaps) guilty in the first
degree, he was one of their principal beneficiaries, and condoned
their operation. He did so according to the ideological imperatives
of the 1930s, in terms of what W. H. Auden was to call 'the necessary murder': 'The business of finding a nation's soul is a long and
slow one at the best and a great many prophets must be slain in the
course of it. Perhaps when we have slain enough prophets future
generations will begin to build their tombs (Vaughan Williams
1934/87: 72).

    With this exhibit before us, we return to (arguably) the outstand-
ing case among the mysteries discussed in this chapter. Rutland
Boughton's is a patent example of a musical career dominated by
political considerations. He was an active socialist long before the
success of *The Immortal Hour*. He imbibed his Marx via the potent
herbal preparations of Morris, and his affiliations to Proudhon,
Fichte and Schopenhauer (likewise imbibed at second-hand, via
Wagnerian exegesis) were potentially disturbing to many supporters
– with the exception of Shaw. Indeed, in 1914 his politics were close
to those of RVW and Holst – a heavily Anglicised socialism, with a
reassuring dimension of patriotism. Such ideas were regarded as
native in origin and non-revolutionary in essence. Boughton's music
complemented this impression, for it never strayed outside the limits of the acceptable in style or content. Finally, the social manifestations of his early radicalism, if not without consequences, were not
serious enough (in the wake of Wagner and Wilde) to destroy the
parameters of the relationship between bohemian producer and
bourgeois patron/consumer. But Boughton refused to develop along
prescribed lines, and did so in a sense which even the proud and
obstinate Elgar had never contemplated. What distinguished him
from other artists of his time was a rigorously objective notion of

genius, one which worked against the dominant subjective mode by which it was presented in society. His formulations increasingly tended to the Leninist. He published music criticism which saw the primary role of art as inspiring apocalyptic social change. He went politically off the rails at exactly the time that *The Immortal Hour*'s success made him the hottest property in the country's musical life.

By the 1920s, experience of conscription had increased Boughton's hatred of traditional authority and deepened his sense of common suffering and injustice. In the wake of the Bolshevik Revolution, as his middle-class constituency entered its most frenetic 'Red Nightmare' phase, the composer moved in the opposite direction. When communist leaders were jailed in 1926, he reacted by joining the Party. The decision attracted press comment and was accompanied by Boughton's published apologia. A little earlier, in the year of the first Labour Government and the Zinoviev Letter scare, the British National Opera Company planned a production of *Alkestis*. The producer, Frederic Austin, took fright at Boughton's activities and addressed him like a naughty child:

> I've just read an article in the *Sunday Chronicle* commenting sharply on one of your own ... We are again involved in controversial matters. This we are doing our best to avoid ... Do help us in this, and keep us away as far as possible from aspects of a political or chauvinistic [sic] kind ... I personally feel strongly that the only justification or the only plea for artistic work is its excellence. (BLMC E3305/2: 140524)

The sentiment expressed in the last sentence quoted constituted a kind of warning. Throughout his career, Boughton was to receive similar admonishments from a variety of well-wishers – fellow-composers, performers, music lovers, public figures and even political soul-mates (BLMC A52362–71). All expressed the feeling that if only the composer would lower his political profile, nothing could prevent his artistic work from taking its rightful place at the centre of English musical culture. As late as 1956, Vaughan Williams addressed Boughton in this sense after the Soviet suppression of the Hungarian revolt, when communists were less popular than for some time past (Vaughan Williams 1964: 378). The obvious sincerity of this advice illustrates the conviction, common to its authors, that a causal relationship existed between the composer's communism and the decline of his career after 1926. Further, by implication it rejected Austin's dictum, suggesting that politics – or rather their assumed/overt absence – was a necessary, if not sufficient, index of the value of any music.

Indeed, Boughton himself could not validly object to this principle. Maturity had strengthened his belief that a work of art is valuable only insofar as it is useful to the achievement of a proper (socialist) society. Effectively, therefore, his position was identical to that of the establishment which first attempted to embrace, and then ruthlessly rejected, his 'genius'. If, after some hypothetical domestic revolution, Boughton had become the British Lunacharsky – Lenin's state commissar for the arts – his policy would have been based on principles impossible to differentiate from those which (if more covertly) inspired the controllers of music under the obtaining capitalist dispensation. Therefore, Boughton had no consistent cause for complaint; rather he should have welcomed his personal fate as a demonstrative sacrifice laid down by the dialectic he embraced as given truth.

It was also perfectly consistent that Boughton should use his fame to proselytise indefatigably for the Comintern. To 1926, that year of fear and ferment, belong his only works that are revolutionary on a primary level of signification – settings of *The Internationale* and *The Red Flag*, and a ballet entitled *May Day*. In that age, with a ruling class trembling at the wholesale *trahison des clercs*, Boughton was a loyal and assiduous member of the Party intelligentsia. Those who contacted him in connection with his music received in return unsolicited ideological exhortations, either holograph and impromptu or in the form of printed propaganda. Having made a surprising convert in Thomas Hardy's wife, Florence (BLMC A52364/99: 290624), Boughton did not blanch from assaults on even hardier targets, like Dames Clara Butt and Ethel Smyth. The latter roundly retorted: '[Y]ou know what I think of socialism – that it's dead unsocial' (BLMC A52366/18v.: 100326). Boughton was indeed unsocial in his unremitting pursuit of politics, and often succeeded in alienating his supporters – like the well-disposed Edward Clark at the BBC, who, following a misunderstanding which was entirely the composer's fault, found himself being insulted and traduced as a hired assassin of the workers (BLMC A52256/72–5v.: 160634). Boughton's attack on his old teacher Walford Davies, then Master of the King's Musick, was less gratuitous but probably no less counterproductive (BLMC A52364/38: 310535).

Boughton's career was produced by conventional capitalist modes – operating in his case *a fortiori*. His original patron was one 'Cecil

Barth', the alias of a music agent who had inherited a fortune. His subsequent RCM education was paid for by the local MP, a member of the Rothschild family! After bourgeois social taboos deprived him of his Birmingham post, he was taken up by a new patron, the rich dilettante Frederick Jackson – on the recommendation of Shaw. The Glastonbury Festival attracted financial support from the Clark (Footwear Ltd) family of nearby Street. However, the *pièce de resistance* was still to come. Among the admirers of *The Immortal Hour* none was more extravagant than Edith, Marchioness of Londonderry. She first approached Boughton with a fan letter couched in an ecstatic language that was doubtless already familiar to him – but with an added ingredient:

> I have been countless times ... I was fortunate enough to get Mr Heseltine to come and sing some of it the night the King and Queen dined with us – and I told the Queen she ought to hear it & support an entirely British opera. I believe you do not often come to London but if you do I hope you will give me the great pleasure of coming to see me at Londonderry House. (BLMC A52366/33: 040323)

There followed what seems, at first dash, a dialogue of the deaf, conducted with an utter absence of understanding on both levels of discourse, artistic and political. Though a genuine friendship ultimately developed, at first the relationship ran on a mutually exploitative dynamic. Lady Londonderry was a person of pronounced right-wing views, another object of her admiration being Benito Mussolini. She was known in society's higher reaches as 'Circe', the hostess of a private salon to which many public figures on the Right – including Winston Churchill, hammer of the general strikers – pseudonymously belonged. When the 1930s arrived, she became a stalwart of the Anglo-German Fellowship Society and advocate of something more than mere appeasement of Hitler.

As if this were not enough, her husband, the marquess, was the epitome of everything Boughton despised – one of the largest absentee landowners in Ireland, one of the greatest mine-owners in England, and a personal friend of Hermann Goering. Far from spurning Circe's advances, however, Boughton cultivated them. The marchioness supported his attempts to found a new festival, even offering the use of her country home in Ulster. She lobbied her friends (including, through Lady Cunard, Beecham) on his behalf, and put on private performances of his works. On at least one of these occasions the guest-list was drawn up by Boughton himself (A52366/50: 080130). As in this detail, so in the general relation-ship, the composer was acting for, and in the manner recommended by, his political masters. The Communist Party sought the exposure of ideologically sound art and artists to the ruling class, which, since it hastened the twin processes of intrinsic decay and mass desertion from its ranks, was to be accomplished by any means.

But it is difficult to believe that either of these political sophisti-cates was ignorant of the true horror of the other's commitment. Lady Londonderry, like others related to the world of High Art, firmly believed in 'national music' as a cement of patriotism and sol-vent for class hatred. She could detect nothing in Boughton's cre-ative universe which even remotely threatened the status quo, and much which solidly confirmed it. She saw *The Immortal Hour* in Carlyle's terms and not those of Morris. For her, it was a celebration of an ineluctable elite, even a defence of it against the anarchic lower hordes, which at that juncture seemed more frightening than ever. Boughton remonstrated by letter (more courteously than he was wont); and in the interests of his Higher Truth, connived at the per-petuation of one of the social evils identified by Morris – domina-tion of art by the plutocracy. However, while the miners were still out at Christmas 1926, and the patroness sighed for an ancient world of Lost Content, the protégé mounted a production of his opera *Bethlehem* in which the Saviour was born in a miner's cottage and Herod was portrayed as a fat-cat capitalist (Hurd 1962: 96–8).

As this incident reveals, Boughton remained a Christian socialist. In this respect, his fundamental convictions remained in tune with those of many others on the British Left. This attracted a residual sympathy; he became a conscience of the artistic Left, adopting the role of his aristocratic hero Count Leo Tolstoy. Intermittently, for more than thirty years his voice was heard from a smallholding on the edge of the Forest of Dean. The respect accorded him was shown by an major obituary in the *Observer* (1963) celebrating a composer whose name was unknown to the vast majority of its readership. Many admirers believed that Boughton had always shunned con-ventional fame. His biographer supports this impression, but the extant evidence will not bear it out. No fewer than three volumes of correspondence with the Society of Authors (BLMC A56671–3) illustrate a constant search for 'recognition', and a stout defence of financial interests. On one occasion, he challenged the right of

William Sharp's widow to derive any benefit from the 'mechanical reproduction' of his setting of the *Faery Song*. 'Please do not think that I personally have any grievance', he asked the secretary of the Society: 'I have already secured myself (coming of a business family)' (BLMC A 56671/63–5: 140623).

John Foulds failed to secure himself even to Boughton's extent, and surely for reasons which were not unadjacent. He was – though his scrupulous biographer refuses to state the appalling facts outright – a socialist and a freethinker. His wife and ruling influence Maud McCarthy was a suffragist and advocate of Indian philosophy; the couple developed connections with Shaw and other notable Fabians during the Great War. As MacDonald (1975: 27–31) concedes, the savaging that *The World Requiem* received from the London critics was carried out with rare unanimity – 'there was certainly an intrigue against Foulds'. Shaw evidently patronised Foulds for the same reasons as he supported Boughton. The motives of Foulds's enemies were likewise politically inspired, like those of the 'distinguished member of the British Music Society committee' – which had originally sponsored the *Requiem* – who was instrumental in destroying its prospects behind the scenes. Foulds's sudden departure for France remains unexplained, but its timing (early 1927) might be indicative – in the wake of the General Strike, the defeat of the miners and the collapse of the workers' cause. It seems unlikely to have been enforced by economic logic, and nothing suggests that Foulds felt an aesthetic compulsion to acquire 'a little French polish'.

The obvious explanation for the vanishing act performed by Coleridge-Taylor's reputation – that he was the half-caste son of an African – is too simplistic. It seems unlikely that racial prejudice in itself impeded his rise to fame. In youth he attracted considerable patronage, and made a sensational impact while a student at the RCM. Favoured by Stanford, he became the first in that famous pedagogue's brood of successful pupils, only much later to be emulated by RVW, Holst and others (Sayers 1915: 52). But there his progress ended, despite no (quantitative) diminution in his powers of composition. He obtained none of the honours showered upon Elgar. He was not invited to teach in the key institutions or to join the important committees. Of course, Coleridge-Taylor was much younger than Elgar, and died before reaching the maturity at which the latter achieved fame. He was obliged to accept a life of middle-level teaching in London and competition-adjudicating in the provinces. The evidence suggests that he had been excluded from the Renaissance. A recent attempt to prove that he was a truly 'English' artist – based largely on the proposition that he was descended from the writer Coleridge – is surely misconceived (Butterworth 1989).

Boughton was isolated because of a contemptuous refusal to conform: the problem resided not in his politics themselves but in their unremitting expression. Similarly, more important than Coleridge-Taylor's racial origins was his identification with Black causes. While always comporting himself within the bounds of propriety (or, if you like, deference), he campaigned for Black rights, and gently drew attention to the evils of colonialism – this in the most rabidly imperialistic decade of our history. During the Boer War he was elected delegate to a Pan–African Congress held in London to draw attention to the condition of colonised peoples, while 'coloured Americans had long since discovered him as the rising star of their race in the artistic heavens' (Sayers 1915: 108). The American Festival of 1904 was an exclusively Black affair, based on Black choral societies and an organisation allied to Booker T. Washington's Negro Movement. Coleridge-Taylor became friendly with both Washington and Dubois, and was eulogised in a poem, sung to the tune of *America* (to other ears, *God Save the King*). Around this time, moreover, moderate influences were being overtaken by a more assertive phase of Black activism, stressing the cultural connections between American Blacks and those of other Atlantic communities. In 1904, Coleridge-Taylor wrote to the treasurer of the Society named after him in the USA: 'As for prejudice, I am well-prepared for it. Surely that which you and many others have lived in for so many years will not quite kill me ... I am a great believer in my race, and I will never lose an opportunity of letting my white friends here know it' (quoted in A. Coleridge-Taylor 1979: 52).

When the composer died in 1912, his white friends passed the hat around for his family, and a memorial concert – held, prophetically, in the Royal Albert Hall – raised £1,200. Sir Hubert Parry's tribute in the *Musical Times* (1912) speaks volumes for its period: 'Like his half-brothers of primitive race, he loved plenty of sound, plenty of colour, simple and definite rhythms, and above all things, plenty of tune.' His tombstone in Croydon carries an evocative protest:

He lives while Music lives
Too young to die

His great simplicity
His happy courage in an alien world
His gentleness
Made all who knew him love him.

Much of the musical and extra-musical content of Coleridge-
Taylor's compositions was derived from African or other aboriginal
sources. He often used African and Caribbean rhythms; in his
orchestral works, he selected as heroes the Haitian slave revolutionary Toussaint L'Ouverture, or Shakespeare's Othello. In *The Song
of Hiawatha*, Longfellow stresses the heroic endurance of a free
people, arguing that colonisation and cultural extinction are synonymous. The European invaders are greeted with stoic acceptance.
Preaching of the Christian message – a miniature Passion adumbrat-
ing the coming passion of the Indian – is presented in an ironic vein.
Stylistically, Coleridge-Taylor's music for *Hiawatha* leans heavily on
Dvořák, then very popular in England. Dvořák was a Czech composer of peasant origins and oddly African appearance, who had
recently used 'negro spirituals' in music composed in America –
including a string quartet which once shamelessly sported the title
'Nigger'. At the time of *Hiawatha*'s composition, Dvořák was a
model for the master, Stanford, and an idol for the pupil. *The Song
of Hiawatha* insinuated an anti-colonial and (mildly) anti-white message. It summoned up, not the comforting landscape of England but
the breathtaking horizons of the New World. It also suggested that
the captains celebrated by Whitman and Vaughan Williams should
take themselves back across the Big Sea Water. Its political dynamic
praised a chosen people who were decidedly not the English. Via the
bourgeois 'Pow-Wows' at the Albert Hall, Coleridge-Taylor's work
stimulated the sympathy of the middle classes for dangerous causes.
With the aid of hindsight, it seems likely that *Hiawatha* had too
much in common with Mahatma Gandhi or even Marcus Garvey.

We have dealt above with a few selected events, linked to composers who achieved substantial success in English musical life. But
legion were the prophets slain. Many other candidates imagined
themselves as victims of the sacrificial process. The violin virtuoso
Tamsin Little recently went to Florida in search of a love-child,
allegedly the result of Delius's liaison with a Black slave girl; and to
her own satisfaction (at least) tracked down his descendants ('The
Works', BBC2 TV: 260697). Equally a slave to Delius, in a sense
bearer of his children, was his amanuensis Eric Fenby, without

whom the late flowering of the composer's output would have been impossible. In old age, Fenby told Ken Russell that 'he was never really given a chance as a composer', because obliged to live out his career in Delius's shadow ('Music Matters' BBC R3: 230297). As an example of a different kind of 'conjuncture', consider the career of Benjamin Britten. The young star aroused envy by his first successes in the 1930s. His own ex-teacher John Ireland was one of many resentful observers (BL A52256/193: 010338). But even Britten's sensational success with *Peter Grimes*, did not guarantee his present status. In the 1950s, interest in his work stalled. In 1959 he was overlooked in a Proms series devoted to 'Masters of the Twentieth Century' (which included RVW, Holst and Walton) and had only one work performed in the entire season (Ayre 1968: 145). Then, in that same year, William Glock took over at the BBC – and created the history we now take for granted. Meanwhile, for fifty years, Britten's almost exact contemporary Raymond Francome carried on composing liturgical music in Bristol, while earning his living as a jobbing gardener. Until a journalist uncovered his story in 1991, he had never heard a note of his own work (BBC1 TV West: 300391). He died shortly afterwards, at the age of 80.

The images presented by history's 'murdered' victims – real or imagined – are now sadly faded. Their sacrifice is based on lofty principles of aesthetics, perfectly intangible, yet perfectly objective, like the ways of God. Yet, surely, some applicants for immortality founded their hopes on something more than self-delusion? Their destiny was decided by a selection process in which something less abstract than aesthetic judgement was involved.

7

Becoming transfigured

Eternal longings

One evening in August 1914, having made a momentous speech in the House of Commons, Sir Edward Grey went to a dinner party. After the meal, Foreign Secretary Grey sat in his host's drawing-room to hear a performance of Beethoven's 'Waldstein' Sonata. According to an account given many years later, 'at a moment in the first movement a sudden illumination came to him. If, he thought, Beethoven could write music such as this, then, ultimately, everything, *everything*, must come right' (Le Fleming 1982: 96–7). The emphasis presumably referred to the coming ordeal to which Grey's speech had committed the nation. In this hour of darkness, music was apprehended as an inextinguishable Promethean spark, capable of illuminating statesmen, and ultimately, of re-igniting the lamps of Europe.

Five years later, after a war which had exhausted both the material and the spiritual capital of Europe, Harold Nicolson attended the peace conference at Versailles as a Foreign Office representative. There he met a prominent Polish aristocrat, and they talked about Ignacy Paderewski, president of the newly-independent state of Poland. Nobody could better personify the role of music in the forging of national identity. Through this universal medium, the famous virtuoso communicated his nation's aspirations to the international political classes. He seemed the epitome of the philosopher–king adumbrated by Plato and the eighteenth-century *philosophes*. He occupied a niche in the new Olympus, carved out as part of the very formation of the civilised world. Such places were reserved for the artistic messengers of the Messiah, hieratic healers and statesmen, preachers of peace and national self-determination through the language of music.

Paderewski's fame rivalled that of President Wilson, sole begetter of the great conference that would make a new heaven and a new earth (Hadden 1913: 49–62). But to Nicolson's interlocutor, Paderewski had a flaw which was ineradicable – he was not a member of the *schlachta*. 'Do you realise that he was born in one of my own villages? And yet, when I speak to him, I have absolutely the impression of conversing with an equal' (Roberts 1972: 453).

Here spoke a desperate man, clinging to a withered branch of the tree of genealogical privilege, now uprooted by the storm and hacked at from all sides. Paderewski may not have been born to the ermine, but he was a symbol of a more valued elite – let us call it the *artistocracy*. No longer the quasi-anonymous artisan of a past age, the uniformed court flunkey sitting below the salt, artists and, above all, musicians, with their polyglot voice, had come to constitute another estate. The artistocracy were the new *état soignée*, more at home in Versailles' *galerie des glaces* than were the representatives of the *ancien régime*. Perhaps, for most, Paderewski's triumph lacked the significance of the Bolshevik Revolution in Russia (1917), which seemed a greater threat to established society. Maybe, for men of affairs like Nicolson, it was not as notable as the pressure to concede the female franchise, or the equally alarming need to grant recognition to Irish nationalism. In the grand scheme of historical materialism, its importance seems overshadowed by the sensational visit of the Original Dixieland Jazz Band to Britain in 1919, and by the return of Charlie Chaplin to London two years later,when 73,000 messages and gifts of welcome awaited him at his hotel (LeMahieu 1988: 53). But, even if not equal in degree, the rise of Art Music was similarly antithetical in nature, given its historical conjuncture of multiform revolution, to the old order of things.

Like the range of 'national' emotions which it encouraged, Art Music had achieved this profile through the dissemination of court culture during the previous century. Through it, as Molière had anticipated, the *haute bourgeoisie* aimed to acquire a mark of nobility, more fitted to urban society than hunting, and, furthermore, susceptible to the economics of mass consumption. Yet although music had exchanged the patronage of the prince for that of the middle-class chauvinist, it was developing features which would place it – in the estimation of millions – in a position immeasurably superior to all considerations of politics. More and more consciously, Art Music was assuming mediation of the divine, while its exponents rose accordingly in the scale of social esteem. The Great War, in which the English Musical Renaissance had 'done its bit' for the cause, had contributed insidiously to this process. While the armies on the Western Front were destroying each other, ostensibly in an attempt to save the old values, the spiritual and social assault of music made rapid progress toward its targets. If not quite identical, these things developed *pari passu*, and to some extent must be treated accordingly.

A welcome insight from one music historian explains:

> If we find it impossible to understand why, for instance, decorous Victorians treated theatrical or operatic musicians as stars yet refused to regard them as socially acceptable, or why Delius's father, an intelligent, ex-German Bradford wool merchant, who enjoyed playing in amateur string quartets and fostered musical events for his community, should have disowned his son once he decided to make music his livelihood, it is because we have treated music as an absolute value rather than as a variable in the cultural equation. (Banfield 1981a: 13)

This passage effectively describes the mode of perception within which music lovers have been conditioned to operate. It is a good starting-point for a more radical departure. The term 'music lover' came into critical usage in the 1920s, the period when music – which previously had provided an accompaniment, occasion or context of emotion – became in itself an object of romantic aspiration, or, if you like, desire. Music was invested with the emotional and spiritual appurtenances of Romantic Love, a construct which was coming to dominate public apprehension of life and meaning. For its 'lovers', music became a privileged medium of the objectively eternal verities, or even something which had subjectively expropriated them. Precisely because of its alleged immaterial character, like the object of Romantic Love, and unlike other forms of expensive High Art (painting, etc.), it could not be physically owned. Yet since its pleasures were potentially unlimited, music's material rewards were incalculable. One purpose of this chapter is to explain the processes at work in moulding these angelic apprehensions.

Let us begin with the unoriginal observation that during this period, in many hearts and homes, Art Music became a pursuit which supplanted religious belief and observance. As early as the 1840s, expression of the analogy between religious and musical experience was beginning to ignore the laws of blasphemy. Sterndale

Bennett referred to the Crystal Palace, in its second manifestion as a concert-hall, as a refuge for 'a band of worshippers having one faith and one soul ... It seemed to us that the shining glass house at Sydenham had become the Temple of a new and gracious gospel' (Oliver, BBC R3: 060876). Like all new religions, however, music had to undergo the fires of persecution before entering its inheritance. In the mid-Victorian period, the number of 'believers' was still small, and music's gospel widely distrusted. Indeed, most middle-class families saw music not as a religion but rather as something utterly antipathetic to it. Moreover, so far from being taken as a road to social improvement, music could not escape identification with varieties of immoral public behaviour. Music was a constant feature of the low life of Mayhew's London – drunkenness, violence, and the free expression of 'emotions' (that is, sexual licence). The raucous songs of public-houses and music-halls made these places morally indistinguishable, dens of iniquity to the respectable classes. Moreover, in the streets of London and other cities, music was associated with begging. Thus, all music outside a place of worship seemed to offer ample evidence of the Calvinist dialectic. General Booth may have believed that the devil had all the best tunes, but Mayhew pointed out that even the lowest categories of street musician were 'remarkable for the religious cast of their thoughts, and the comparative refinement of their tastes and feelings' (quoted in Quennel 1984: 149, 514).

Despite this, music 'lived a life below stairs in the social context', and its practitioners enjoyed incomes to match (Banfield 1981a: 17). When the present authors were taught music in primary school, it added to the verisimilitude of things that almost every 'Great Composer' – a striking exception was Mozart – appeared to have been lumbered with parents who were determined to stifle his genius. Delius, defying parental prohibition in order to follow his vocation, was a typical case. Here, the problem was exacerbated by experience: on the one hand, of the father, who was well-acquainted with members of this menial trade; and, on the other, of the son, whose behaviour in Paris confirmed such damning suspicions about the music profession. Delius was saved only by the personal intervention of his friend and mentor Edvard Grieg (Carley and Threlfall 1977: 18). The kind of prejudice displayed by Delius senior was countered in the 1870s by a public campaign, led by the Royal Family. It was important to give the Renaissance a splendid architectural base, a conspicuously Goodly House. At the RCM, the student's name for the concert-hall built in the 1890s – 'the tin tabernacle' – was revealing (Scholes 1947: I, 129). Apart from aesthetic and economic considerations, the new academies, concert-halls and opera-houses offered some assurance of the public propriety of a pastime often suspected of being a private occasion of sin. The expensive apparatus of South Kensington was also designed to help transform working musician into genteel professional. The curriculum set standards in every relevant social and intellectual area. Teachers in the provinces began to organise themselves, seeking to campaign for 'professional' status – the standard of aspiration being the 'gentle' professions of Army and Church. By the 1880s, the Incorporated Society of Musicians was flourishing, and had shifted its headquarters to London (Ehrlich 1989).

During the Great War, Lena Ashwell, inventor of 'concert parties', attempted to enlist governmental support. She saw the war as an opportunity for Whitehall to lead the way in demonstrating that prejudice against musical entertainment was not only absurd but unpatriotic. She formed a committee where bishops and generals sat alongside 'artists', and travelled the country persuading public figures that the boys at the Front should be exposed to 'good' music. Ashwell's efforts were rewarded in 1915 when the War Office gave them formal recognition (Ashwell 1922: 5–7). Not all musicians agreed with her methods, and in Manchester she encountered stiff opposition to her ideas. But no less a figure than Sir Edward Elgar, eager to contribute to the war-effort, was a willing collaborator with Miss Ashwell and many other war-related organisations.

The Kingdom

Delius's early difficulties were of one kind, Elgar's of another, but both reflected an inflexible social order. The latter's unconventional background (religious and provincial as well as social) was the main element in his character-formation. His relationship with the mainstream Renaissance movement was always ambivalent. By upbringing and instinct, Elgar was conservative, an English royalist and Tory patriot. Yet he always felt marked with original sin, as the son of a shopkeeping family – even if it was a music shop. Elgar was born into the music business in an actuarial sense which many of his future associates in the profession would find embarrassing. As a young man he earned a living as an executant musician. One account has him avoiding carrying around a violin case so as not to draw attention to his lowly occupation (Hughes 1989). In a transfiguration noticed by none of his biographers, Elgar's career as an artist – his 'genius' – took him from the Worcester Lunatic Asylum to the London Athenaeum, cynosure club of the nation's intelligentsia.

Elgar was well-placed to see that service to the 'nation', largely constituted by the expanded middle classes, was an indispensable condition of music's material progress. In his Birmingham lectures (1905) he advocated cultivation of a 'sixpenny audience', bringing this burgeoning mass into the fold. At the same time, it was important that consumers–believers should be conscious of the grace they were about to receive. Elgar's personal struggles, above all the bitterness of occasional failure, intensified his contemplation of his own genius and the ineffable glories of its medium. What he represented had a transcendental value that put the establishment, even the nation, in its shade. Such feelings were accentuated by (and possibly responsible for) the gradual fading of Elgar's Catholicism, which placed even greater emphasis upon the spiritual attributes of his art. He saw 'the composer' (or 'bard') as serving the nation in the capacity of a hieratic caste – in the 'chivalric' sense of a knight's service to king and a priest's to God.

In order to create a new musical nation, the old one had to be galvanised. Elgar duly addressed it with two large-scale works which set out his basic propositions. Deliberately cast in the traditional 'English' oratorio form for soloists, chorus and orchestra, they were intended for performance at the regional festivals. *The Apostles*, written at the unprecedented dizzy height of Elgar's fame, came first (1903). Three years later, thousands packed into Birmingham Town Hall for the premiere of the second part of the cycle, *The Kingdom*. Those lucky enough to obtain seats were paying forty-two times over the humble tanner that Elgar had recently itemised. The occasion was auspicious, for the Birmingham Temple – a replica of the Parthenon – had seen some of the significant premieres of the recent past, including Mendelssohn's *Elijah*, Dvořák's *Requiem* and *The Dream of Gerontius* (Plate 11).

The new work's title was redolent of the aspirations Elgar and others nurtured for the progress of music. On the subjective level, Elgar's was the kingdom. In *The Apostles*, among the beatitudes of Christ, are set the lines:

11 The Midlands Parthenon – a temple of the oratorio cult: the Town Hall, Birmingham (built 1843)

> Blessed are those which are persecuted for righteousness' sake:
> For theirs is the kingdom of heaven.

After the premiere of *The Kingdom*, the baritone David Ffrangcon-Davies, who sang Christ in the first part of the (intended) trilogy and Peter in the second, wrote to Elgar: 'Now, for the days that are to come! Soar, dear Friend – from planet to planet, the universe is yours' (Ffrangcon-Davies 1938: 44–5). The genius who had struggled for half a lifetime against prejudice and persecution had finally arrived at the pinnacle – literally so, according to the words intoned by the chorus at the opening of the final section of *The Kingdom*:

> The voice of joy
> Is in the dwelling of the righteous
> The stone which the builders rejected
> Is become the head of the corner [of the Temple].

More objectively, all the performers were also entering an inheritance, for *theirs was the kingdom* who were the makers of music. From the platform in Birmingham Town Hall they had only to look around to see that they had entered a munificent room of the Father's mansion – English Music was a popular and financial success. The promoters of the Musical Renaissance were hardly lacking in righteousness, for they accepted, even sought, the sanctions bestowed on their mission by analogy with the origins of Christianity. 'Whatsoever thou shalt bind on earth shall be bound in heaven: and whatsoever thou shalt loose shall be loosed in heaven' (Matt. 16:19). Perhaps the *Apostles*' metaphor helps to explain why Hubert Parry, small supporter of revealed religion or the established Church, based so many of his choral works on biblical narrative.

In *The Kingdom*, St Peter invokes Christ's name and powers in the miraculous cure of a lame man: 'Silver and gold I have none, but what I have I give thee.' Possession of the cure was to bring Elgar silver and gold in abundance, not to mention a series of official honours which he coveted at least equally. Yet he remained hypersensitive to failure, and suspicious that full recognition was being withheld. In 1912, following a period when his new works had been coolly received, he produced another grandiose assertion of the sublime ethical and political value of music. But *The Music Makers* – also written for Birmingham – goes further than this. It represents an assertion of its composer's personal greatness, expressed in blatant terms at which even Richard Strauss may have balked. On this occasion, the music shared the burden with the text, for every major pronouncement of the latter is accompanied by a self-quotation from the Elgarian canon. The political powers of music are represented by the opening March from his *Symphony No. 1*:

> One man with a dream at pleasure
> Shall go forth and conquer a crown;
> And three with a new song's measure
> Can trample a kingdom down.

O'Shaughnessy's text (1874) adumbrates several of the dynamic ideas of the Musical Renaissance.

> Bring us hither your sun and your summers,
> And renew our world as of yore;
> You shall teach us your song's new numbers,
> And things that we dreamed not before.

In particular, the poet glimpses a musical prophet who at the moment of crisis becomes the repository of truth and leadership. The following extract from the ode is introduced by the main theme of the *Enigma Variations*, carefully prepared by an ecstatic modulation on harp and strings. During its course, this music yields place, first to 'Nimrod' from the same work, and then to the so-called 'Windflower' theme from the *Violin Concerto*:

> [O]n one man's soul it hath broken
> A light that doth not depart _
> Oh Men! It must ever be
> That we dwell in our dreaming and singing
> A little apart from ye.

Elgar thus laid claim to the headship of the *illuminati*, demanding 'recognition' as the custodian of the Ark of the Covenant. In one of his 1905 lectures he had looked forward to the day when English music produced the great genius to compare with the glories of the past (Young 1968: 79ff.). He could hardly have renounced this affectation of modesty more completely than with *The Music Makers*. The journalist who covered the first Bristol performance in December 1912 chose to ignore its aspects of outrageous self-promotion. He confined himself to the sceptical but accurate enough comment that 'the idea seems to be that the music makers and dreamers are really the creators and inspirers of men, and their deeds the true makers of history ... Cities and Empires and the death of Empires are their work. Soldier, King and peasant are their instruments' (BRBC DM: 433).

Elgar's egoism was as sacred in its way as that of Delius. Yet neither was he alone in seeking to define ideas about music via images which are metaphysical and miraculous. The works discussed above are examples of a sequence, spanning its chronological history, possessing a profound significance in the self-definition of the Renaissance. It is important to grasp the liturgical character of the meaning at work. It represents not simply a finished, enclosed, historical event, but a continuing communion. It provides a performing tradition which is a ritual revitalisation of Renaissance. The audacious personal element in *The Music Makers* ensured that it was rarely heard – it went into the musical equivalent of the Royal Academy's basement – but other examples of its genre exercised a more lasting influence.

One of these arose from Vaughan Williams's obsession with *Pilgrim's Progress*. RVW returned over and again during his creative life to Bunyan's text: it was a dense source of his aspirations for national music. In 1942, a provisional opera version, broadcast by the BBC, featured Christian's search for 'an inheritance incorruptible, undefiled, and which fadeth not away' – a search illustrated and consummated by music. The composer espied the Delectable Mountains as the homeland of music. Indeed, the vision of 'an endless kingdom to be inhabited' is accompanied by quotation of the composer's own arrangement of the melody in the *Fanatasia on a Theme of Thomas Tallis*. While avoiding the blatant egoism of Elgar, RVW made immanent the link with his earlier years, and vividly endorsed the sanction of communion. But the link extends further back, almost to the origins of the Renaissance. In 1887, Parry produced a work which is prophetic of more than the mere accidentals of the Elgarian style. *Blest Pair of Sirens* is a setting of the poem *At a Solemn Musick*, in which Milton equates discord with the Fall, and the restoration of right harmony with Salvation – a perfect metaphor for the composer who was taken as the dividing line between the pre-Renaissance chaos and the new order. Like his patron Grove, Parry was keen to emphasise music's capacity for moral instruction, and endorsed Milton's prayer

> That we on Earth, with undiscording voice
> May rightly answer that melodious noise;
> As once we did, till disproportion'd sin
> Jarr'd against nature's chime, and with harsh din
> Broke the fair music that all creatures made
> To their great Lord, whose love their motion sway'd
> In perfect Diapason, whilst they stood
> In first obedience, and their state of good.
> O may we soon again renew that Song
> And keep in tune with Heav'n, till God ere long
> To his celestial consort us unite
> To live with Him, and sing in endless morn of light.

The ethical precepts of many Parry works helped to guide RVW to a fuller vision. (*Blest Pair of Sirens* remained the latter's favourite among the former's enormous output.) In his early days a follower of Morris's 'English socialism', RVW and many *fin de siècle* contemporaries believed that Victorian England – like the Restoration England of Milton – had allowed its robust spiritual essence to be overlaid with materialism and the soulless demands of the business world. Most of these young radicals were from aristocratic, academic or business backgrounds – RVW himself derived from all three. They aspired towards an art of ideas, posing a moral challenge to the nation and presenting themes which would be critical in terms of its daily life.

Like Elgar, Vaughan Williams defined his task in music of conventional form aimed at the conservative public of the choral festivals. Indeed, his work incorporated elements of homage to both Parry and Elgar. Yet the message was in deliberate contrast to its medium of delivery. The texts were by Walt Whitman, poet of 'The New World' – then regarded as a wild iconoclast. In *Toward the Unknown Region* (1907) RVW challenged his audience to set out on a journey of self-discovery. This time, the analogy is not with Christian theology, but with the contemporary craze for exploration in the remotest and most hostile regions of the globe. The music assumes the form of a large-scale march; if broader and more flexible, not unlike the ceremonial style of Parry and Elgar, but with more adventurous political overtones. As surely as the march-hymns of Berlioz or Shostakovich, the music strides towards a climax of revolution and revelation.

> Till when the ties loosen,
> All but the ties eternal of time and space,
> Nor darkness, gravitation, sense, nor any bounds bounding us.
>
> Then we burst forth, we float,
> In time and space, O soul, prepared for them,
> Equal, equipt at last …

On the surface, Vaughan Williams's definition of 'renaissance' and of 'national music' seems anti-elitist. It is a kingdom, certainly – but one without a king, an aristocracy or a hierarchy, instinct with the democratic spirit which composer and poet shared.

Wider still and wider

The decade before 1914 saw the frantic culmination of European imperialism, when inhabited parts of the globe, until then relatively undisturbed, became dominated by competing colonial systems. The process absorbed much of the energy and attention of 'advanced' nations. It also gave rise to an epiphenomenon which, despite the fame it brought its participants, proved to be somewhat outside the mainstream of history: the movement of polar exploration. RVW's interest in this subject was not specifically formulated until much later, in music for the film of Scott's final expedition. But in *A Sea Symphony*, written at the time of the famous expeditions, the metaphor of exploration is already developed, and begins to express an imperialism which pertains to the world of music itself. As with any mission, the progress of National Music demanded leadership as well as ideology. Although we are dealing with the same composer and the same poet, the democratic moment of *Toward the Unknown Region* had passed. The extended central climax of *A Sea Symphony*'s finale ('The Explorers') proclaims, in Whitman's lines:

> After the seas are all crossed,
> After the great captains have accomplished their work,
> After the noble inventors,
> Finally shall come the poet worthy that name,
> The true son of God shall come singing his songs.

Grandiose switches of harmonic direction – orchestral *tutti* with cymbal clashes – unfold on the words 'poet' and 'God'. The calm which follows projects the experienced ear forward to RVW's characteristic utterance – music probably inserted during a later revision. The heroism of exploration is only a metaphor for a more transcendental pronouncement. The true hero is the composer–poet, greeted as a kind of messiah – but one who exists in a dimension light years away from the vision vouchsafed to Handel. We are near, instead, to the supremacist Nietzsche of *Zarathustra*. The questions are posed: 'Whither, unsatisfied soul? Whither O mocking life?' – nothing other than the so-called 'World Riddle'. If not expressed in Nietzsche's words, it is the same message as relayed by Strauss and Delius: 'God is dead: long live the Artist!' The Genius arises to lead the 'myriad progeny' of humanity, 'soothing the feverish children' with the Holy Oil of music. As with Elgar, if with a less vulgar display of the ego, RVW seems to apostrophise a new oligarchy, among whom musicians will naturally take priority – an Artistocracy of Genius.

As *A Sea Symphony* was being composed, RVW's Cambridge contemporary E. M. Forster mused on the problems posed by Mammon and the motor-car in his novel *Howard's End*.

> We reach in desperation beyond the fog, beyond the very stars, the voids of the universe are ransacked to justify the monster, and stamped with a human face. London is religion's opportunity – not the deco-

rous religion of theologians, but anthropomorphic, crude. Yes, the
continuous flow would be tolerable if a man of our own sort – not anyone pompous or tearful – were caring for us up in the sky. (Forster
1910/83: 16)

Although the musical world was not lacking in pomp and tears, its
claim remained powerful even for Forster. The *Pomp and Circumstance March No. 1* plays a key role in the politics of Forster's novel.
The words of A. C. Benson – son of an Archbishop of Canterbury –
set to Elgar's famous tune, can be heard as applying not only to the
King–Emperor and the British Empire, but also to the empire of
music itself.

Wider still and wider
Shall thy bounds be set.

In the same year as *Howard's End* appeared and the first performance of *A Sea Symphony* was given, a great captain sailed the
uncharted seas to conquer man's final terrestrial frontier. With R. F.
Scott's last expedition, the internal combustion engine reached the
most distant continent. But the mechanical sleds manufactured in
England failed to win the race against Amundsen's Danish dogs. A
few weeks after Scott and company died in their tent, another leader
of British industrial achievement, the liner *Titanic* – a kind of float-
ing London – also expired on the ice. The much-vaunted promises
of urbanisation and technology were beginning to be exposed as
false even before they were terminally undermined by the trenches
of the Western Front. Alongside disastrous first performances, such
as those given by the motor-sled and the unsinkable liner, the
premiere of *A Sea Symphony* offered its audience a different and
better kind of hope for the future.

That future arrived in 1938, in the European crisis which was the
prelude to another great war. At exactly the point in *A Sea Symphony* described above – the appearance of 'the true son of God' –
a subsidiary theme can be heard (*mf* brass chords, then strings). It
was taken from an abortive earlier work, *The Solent*, and it remained
a fixation for the composer (Kennedy 1964). For RVW, the melody
represented some elemental reality about music and nation, and he
used it again in his last works – *The England of Elizabeth* and *Symphony No. 9*. It also crops up, however, in the *Serenade to Music*,
connecting these works across the half-century which contained
their creation. The origins of the *Serenade* reveal much about the

imperialist agenda of the Musical Renaissance. Ostensibly, it was a
thank-offering to Sir Henry Wood, master of the Promenade Concerts, who in 1938 completed fifty years as a conductor. Wood
planned a celebration concert, and approached RVW, as the country's leading composer, for a new piece. 'I should love to write – to
have the honour of writing – a piece in your praise if I can manage
it', came the reply. 'Is there any poet you can suggest who could
write some words appropriate to the occasion? How about asking
the Poet Laureate?' (BLMC A56422/139: 240138).

Demanding the attention of the Poet Laureate, a major musical
jubilee was now seen as equivalent in status to a royal one. Indeed,
the sanctions of music supervened those of monarchy. Wood's
concert was a charity occasion, helping a hospital ward for sick
musicians. He was anxious to obtain the services of the world's
greatest composer–virtuoso, Rachmaninov, playing the concerto
which at that time was (arguably) the most popular piece of 'High
Art' in existence. Wood wrote to Rachmaninov in August 1937, to
book him for St Cecilia's Day (22 November) the following year.
But he was already committed to begin his annual USA tour in mid-
October. 'If you can possibly rearrange your plans', Rachmaninov
offered, 'so that the concert can take place the first week of October 1938 … I will be prepared to make a special journey to London'
(A56421/99: 280837). However, a serious objection to this proposal arose. If the date were altered, members of the Royal Family,
whose attendance was to dignify the occasion, would still be on holiday at Balmoral. In the event, the royal dignity had to yield to that
of the artistocracy (in fact, Rachmaninov, like Vaughan Williams,
had aristocratic connections). Rachmaninov's condition was met
and the concert set for 5 October 1938 – to take place not in Wood's
own stamping-ground of the Queen's Hall, but at the performing
centre of the English Musical Renaissance, the Royal Albert Hall in
South Kensington (A56421/103: 020138).

The *Serenade to Music* operates at a much deeper level than that
demanded by its commission. The title places it at once on a metaphysical plane. As a hymn to Music it seeks the exalted company of
Schubert's *An die Musik*, Mahler's *Symphony No. 4* or Parry's *Invocation to Music*. But by 1938 RVW was the spokesman of national
music, and his statement was (and is) to be heard in that capacity.
The Poet Laureate did not contribute, but RVW upstaged any potential rival by enlisting Shakespeare, whose lines from *The Merchant of*

Venice seem to have anticipated the political triumph of music in even more striking terms than those of O'Shaughnessy. The score itself marks the culmination of the Pastoral Style, which had for a generation been the orthodox idiom of national music. It was written for performance by British artists – no fewer than sixteen (nominated) solo singers, the BBC Symphony Orchestra, with Wood, the dedicatee, conducting. In it, the unique bond between music and nation is described and praised. Each soloist is allocated at least one discrete sentence or phrase from the text, and each (at a given point) sings an independent musical line in the polyphonic web, a texture referring back across the destiny-laden centuries to Tallis and the Tudors. Yet the singers also unite to speak with one voice – the chorus of the English community, the organic union of people and song. Nation is a fusion of individual, society and art. Anyone who does not respond to music is explicitly condemned – in a passage which is both minor in key and minatory in effect – as somehow not part of society, a type of heretic or pariah. The last line of the quotation which follows is sung in sombre unison:

> The man that hath no music in himself,
> Nor is not moved with concord of sweet sounds,
> Is fit for treasons, stratagems and spoils:
> The motions of his spirit are dull as night,
> And his affections dark as Erebus:
> Let no such man be trusted.

The minds of many in the audience must indeed have been full of stratagems and treason. At that particular moment in the nation's destiny, the attention of most of the world was focused not on music but on Munich (Shepherd 1988: 204–50). The *Serenade* required careful rehearsal during the last week of September, and a newsreel item shows RVW sitting alongside conductor and performers at one session in the Albert Hall. Meanwhile, a very different kind of rehearsal was taking place outside the building. Across the road, trenches were being dug in Hyde Park; gas masks were handed out; evacuation of children from the metropolis was beginning. The ultimatum given by the world's best-known music lover, Adolf Hitler, to Czechoslovakia, was due to expire on 1 October. On Wednesday 28 September – a week before the concert – Mr Chamberlain announced his response to an invitation from Signor Mussolini. He would fly to Germany in order to make a final effort to avert war.

The premiere of the *Serenade* thus took place in the atmosphere of intense public relief – not unclouded with shame – which followed the Munich Agreement. That very day Churchill condemned the agreement, during a debate in the House of Commons, and German troops began to occupy the Sudetenland. The programme of Wood's Jubilee Concert resonated in sympathy with the conflicting emotions in its listeners' hearts. Beethoven's *Egmont Overture* evoked the struggle of smaller nations to be free from the domination of the greater. Wagner's *Ride of the Valkyries* surely evoked for some a vision of aeroplanes: the consequences of supporting Czechoslavakia might be a London sky turned black with Luftwaffe bombers. Choruses from Handel's *Israel in Egypt*, supported by Bax's *London Pageant* – and (of course) the *Pomp and Circumstance March No. 1* – reassured others that the chosen people might yet survive the threat of extinction. But the essence of consolation was conveyed by the *Serenade*, which calmed tensions and smoothed away fears of war and defeat. Rachmaninov himself, doubtless in a mood of receptivity heightened by recent events, was overcome, and arriving back at his hotel immediately wrote to Wood asking him to give Vaughan Williams his congratulations (BLMC A56421/117: 061038).

The Munich Crisis was the climax not only of a summer of mounting dread but of a decade of economic depression, potential class war, actual ideological conflict and accumulating international danger. The listener to the *Serenade*, however, escapes the pressures of politics, and experiences a privileged glimpse into the other-worldly.

Look how the floor of heaven
Is thick inlaid with patines of bright gold:
There's not the smallest orb which thou behold'st
But in his motion like an angel sings
[...]
Such harmony is in immortal souls
But whilst this muddy vesture of decay
Doth grossly close us in we cannot hear it.

Hitler may have successfully claimed the Sudetenland, but the empire of music is the soul, and the ultimate destination of all souls. What we hear on earth – such is the implication of the *Serenade* – is only a foretaste of the consummation to come once we have shuffled off our mortal coil.

Promised Lands

The visionary element in the music treated here was interpreted by its contemporaries in both metaphorical and literal terms. For many, its worldly aspect was manifested in their party-political lives, and/or in some philanthropic duty to counter cultural deprivation ('And was Jerusalem builded here?'). Holst and RVW regarded themselves as heirs to the socialist tradition of William Morris (Harrison in Norris 1989). Promised Lands lie about us in the English music of the interwar years. They were variously organic, arcadian or Arthurian, but all were lands fit for heroes. They were Utopias, filling the spiritual vacuum made by disillusionment and depression in ways which only music could. In some cases, they were also material constructs, reflecting a deliberately antithetical relationship to those of South Kensington.

During the Great War, the singer–composer Frederic Austin visited the new arts festival which Boughton had established in Glastonbury, Somerset. 'Dear Rutland', he wrote on his return, 'Home again – to realities! Business London – the old whirl! Well, it has been an enormous inner refreshment to get a glimpse of what the life of an artist may be, when he is able to live without a thought beyond his work ... I've set my heart upon entering the Promised Land' (BLMC A52364/1:?0815).

On one level, the Glastonbury commune was a conscious attempt at an English Bayreuth. Boughton and his common-law wife, the designer and choreographer Christina Walshe, along with a literary collaborator, Reginald Buckley, were the founders. They saw themselves as social progressives with an ideological message, and aimed at a theatrical *Gesamstkunstwerk*. But, in contrast to Wagner, the collective was intended to dominate over the subjective genius of the individual. English music–drama was to be 'choral' and participatory, and thus democratic; and the enterprise (ostensibly) free of princely patronage. Boughton and his associates were 'freethinkers', who dared to follow a path only discreetly indicated by predecessors like Parry and Sharp. If, from any perspective this side of the 1960s, their society seems hardly less pastel in tone than the Pre-Raphaelite groups from whom they lineally descend, its socially and sexually libertarian aspects attracted many. Glastonbury itself was well chosen, to reflect the myths of Celticism and Christianity, Arthur and Aramithea, of which it was a matchless shrine. It was also

physically close to the Cotswolds' refuge of the arts and crafts movement founded by disciples of Morris and Ruskin. Membership of the
festival school demanded extended training periods in new techniques of dance and drama, along with meticulous rehearsal of
works which included Purcell's and Gluck's as well as Boughton's
own operas. The inaugural festival coincided exactly with the outbreak of war in August 1914. However, wartime conditions helped
Glastonbury's success, for young ladies flocked to its biannual ses-
sions, seeking escape from home-front duties like knitting the socks
and nursing the wounded.

As a potential focus for creative English opera, Glastonbury also
represented a challenge to the dominance of London and the choral-
based provincial festivals, ecclesiastical and civic (Hurd 1962: 40ff.).
Above all, Boughton's prototype 'choral drama' *The Immortal Hour*
attracted widespread interest. Within ten years of its premiere in the
medieval town-hall of Glastonbury, it became the most popular 'serious' stage work of the whole period covered in this book. Early converts were followed by a substantial slice of the London intelligentsia
and polite society. Austin's 'Business London – the old whirl' was
captivated by Boughton's 'Promised Land'. Moreover, after two
astounding runs of *The Immortal Hour* in London, even RVW and
Holst, each of whom had strained to produce an opera that was both
'English' and 'great', felt obliged to recognise that another had
stolen the palm. It was as if Moses and Aaron had acknowledged the
co-leadership of a third brother–prophet. The opera, with its atmos-
pheric score of folkish pentatonic chords, and assisted by the elfin
beauty of Gwen Ffrangcon-Davies (daughter of Elgar's apostle),
was set in a mystic land of eternal youth and love. For thousands of
devotees – often women of a certain age and station who attended
on a regular basis – it evoked 'the land of lost content'. Its immortal
hero Midir, Prince of 'the Lordly Ones', gave them a paranormal
glimpse of the sons, husbands and lovers taken from them by war,
providing many griefs with not so much spiritual as spiritualist consolation. Such expensive therapy was not Boughton's actual purpose. Though his militant communism had a Christian tinge, his
utopia was a mainly materialist one. It was despite rather than
because of its author that the opera seemed to catch the post-war
mood. Meanwhile, Boughton worked on an enormous cycle of
Arthurian choral dramas, intended to glamorise a different Promised
Land – a classless England of pre-industrial fellowship, to which

dialectical communism – led, perhaps, by 'King' Arthur Horner – could return his people.

The Great War's horrors of mass-produced death gave utopianism a new lease of life. William Blake became an icon of the Left, a prophet who discerned the fate of England at the outset of the Industrial Revolution. 'Oh pray for the Peace of Jerusalem', sings the chorus in Parry's coronation anthem *I Was Glad* (1902), and his setting of Blake's *Jerusalem*, composed in the year of the Somme, inspired many not to cease from mental strife. The folklorists sought to recapture an 'organic', rural, non-capitalist past, somewhere before the pollution of motor-car, motorised sled and ocean liner. With *The Lark Ascending* and *A Pastoral Symphony*, Vaughan Williams planted the Promised Land firmly in the English countryside. The unknown region dreamed and dared in 1907 turned out, through the catalyst of total war, to be the familiar rural idyll, nothing other than England's green and pleasant land. So much for radicalism and progress.

In the 1920s, RVW's favourite pupil Gerald Finzi began work on his *Dies Natalis*, contemplating an English Eden – 'everything at rest, free and immortal' – in music which represents for many the purest of all expressions of the Pastoral Style. But Promised Lands were often specifically topographical, Elysian fields with local habitations and names, as well as landscapes of the mind. In the 1920s it seemed as though every place of natural beauty in England would sooner or later achieve its musical consummation. The high places were the most evocative. For Delius they were summits of Nietzschean superiority; to Bax they were repositories of Celtic magic. E. J. Moeran's *In The Mountain Country* and Patrick Hadley's *The Hills*, works by wounded veterans of the Western Front, sought descriptive musical utopias that were physically elevated: the exact reverse of the trenches, rarified places where the songs of birds replaced the scurrying of rats. Remote and high are the places of the gods, and the hills are alive with the sound of their music. As *The Immortal Hour*'s famous number puts it:

> How beautiful they are
> The Lordly Ones
> Who dwell in the hills
> In the hollow hills.

Apostles and disciples

Music in England shared aspects of its development with other national communities. In this period 'serious' music became accepted by the 'civilised world' not only as an indispensable badge of national membership but as a pyschological balm for the stresses of modern life, and the transcendental discourse of the afterlife. As Anthony Burgess remarks: 'During the nineteenth century the Beethovenians, like Sir George Grove in England, had no doubt of the moral content of the great instrumental works ... The view of the composer as the sublime custodian of ultimate values was sustained well into our own century' (Burgess 1982: 82).

This understates the case. Not only composers but even their interpreters were touched with transfiguration. Basil Maine complained in the 1930s that 'the sanctification of the conductor is a sign of the age. The power that he has assumed enables him to parley with rulers and princes and sometimes dabble in the affairs of State' (Maine 1945: 103). Moreover, the purveyors of Art Music came to realise that they had something eminently marketable. Ultimate values are the most valuable of values – though, of course, we must never say so. Edwin Evans informed *Daily Mail* readers shortly after the Armistice that a well-known medical consultant, 'addressing the British Association, has instanced some remarkable effects of music as a "divine healer" in shell-shock cases' (Evans 1924: 66). No one could ask – apropos of Ivor Gurney – why did the physician not heal himself? Frank Howes could hardly have been unaware of Gurney's fate. Yet he resorted in 1948 to a variety of magazine blurb which seems to advertise Sir Thomas Beecham's family business rather than his chosen profession.

> The appetite for music was unquestionably sharpened by the mental stress of war. Under the psychological strain of war people needed relief, solace, and the heartening reassurance that beyond the intolerable present the eternal values remained unimpaired. Organised religion ... no longer satisfied ... What was needed was a creedless revelation of the eternal, which is what music is. (Howes 1948: 174)

The commodity was widely accepted at this valuation. During the Second World War, in response to an insistent musical lobby, the celebrated National Gallery concerts were organised. During the 'darkest days', harassed civil servants and forces' personnel on leave, passed through the monument to Trafalgar on their way to ingest an analogous message of consolation and reassurance, but in a different medium. In the feature-film *The Cruel Sea* (1952) England is a warship fighting the U-boat menace. Its commanders have already had one vessel sunk under them. On shore-leave, the First Mate explains his feelings to his girl:

> When you lose a ship it's like losing a part of yourself. I went to one of those concerts in the National Gallery. Listening to the music I found I was crying and couldn't stop. Later I found I could think of the *Compass Rose* and the men who died in her without crying or being upset.

Successful communication of such nostrums sustained the inexorable growth of the Art Music establishment. As a result, the great singers, instrumental virtuosi, impresarios, conductors and some notable survivors of the late-Romantic school of composition, took on the aspects of a lofty caste, dispensers of a life-enhancing elixir of endless resources and boundless properties. Beneath their benign rule was a series of subordinate layers of acolyte functionaries. These, in turn, were supported on an expanding base of middle-class consumers, who looked upon the great ones with an awe often not far removed from idolatry.

Art Music continued to be a minority interest in the grand scheme of things (LeMahieu 1988: 187). All the same, by the 1930s the Musical Renaissance had generated a mass following, including an inner core of what (in a neighbouring cultural context) might be called 'groupies'. One morning, in 1942, a middle-class housewife was busy with her ironing when she heard music from Vaughan Williams's *Symphony No. 4* broadcast on the BBC. She instantly 'recognised' this as more meaningful than anything else she had ever encountered, and devoted the rest of her leisure-time to studying the composer, about whom she eventually produced a book. She describes the moment of conversion in words similar to those used by religious zealots of an earlier age. The music

> struck me a stunning blow in whatever region lies the seat of the affections, a blow from which, more than a decade later, I am dizzy still. Music assaulted and transported me; music I did not understand but which, instead of forbidding by its strangeness, filled me with a desperate longing for more and more: music which, for all its unfamiliarity, had a puzzling and elusive echo as if of something I had forgotten but had once known intimately. (Pakenham 1957: 1)

After an Introduction in which she 'confesses' that her pursuit of RVW is 'the history of an obsession ... the shocking personal revelations of a secret music addict', the author opens her main discussion with the bald assertion: 'Ralph Vaughan Williams is a composer who walks in heaven ... The key is in his pocket and he ascends there for his refreshment and ours when he is tired of wandering the lowlands of the English countryside, or exhausted by his frequent battles with the powers of darkness' (p. 14).

The sublime experience is shared by celebrant and communicant. As Michael Kennedy recently said of the same composer: 'he was there with you, but in a sense he was in that other kingdom inhabited by Great Artists, an area where you would never trespass' (in Oliver, BBC R3: 080392). This is not far away from the conviction articulated by Cecil Gray (1948/85: 143), that High Art is the only redeeming feature of our world: 'I believe in the possibility of the salvation of humanity through the medium of art.' Such are the giddy notions about music's redemptive power which result from the heavy dropping of philosophers' stones on the heads of music inscribers by German thinkers from Hoffman to Adorno.

At much the same time as RVW revealed himself to Mrs Pakenham, another middle-class housewife, Mrs Tessa Bradley, attended a meeting of the Proms Circle – a support group of the Promenade Concerts – to hear Moiseiwitsch introduce some of his gramophone recordings. Not daring to approach the great pianist directly, she expressed her appreciation to the Hon. Sec., concluding that 'there is nothing we poor mortals can do in return but place on record our gratitude' (BLMC A56425/7: 291241). On both these occasions, the divine being had no need to demonstrate his powers in person, like Chopin or Liszt before him, but appeared (as it were) ethereally via the new media of radio and gramophone. Indeed, broadcasting, recording and film were quick to realise the potential of music's emotional content. In June 1935, Jack Westrup wrote of Toscanini's broadcast performance of Beethoven's *Symphony No. 7* with the BBC Symphony Orchestra that 'anyone listening realises that music is a fortress of the spirit against a brutish, earthy world' (BBC R3: 171190). Such an encomium would have been of little interest to Beethoven, but was of surpassing interest to Toscanini and the BBC. A few years earlier, Gustav Holst was approached to write music for 'a sound-film ... of Irving's famous play "The Bells"'. He was offered £200 – perhaps £8,000 today – for recording and reproduction rights. Holst wrote what was required, and received thanks from the Company Secretary, Mr Nolbandov.

> We unfortunate film people are always accustomed to be regarded as somewhat lowbrow and vulgar in all our tendencies, and that is why we sometimes are a bit frightened to work with people who are not accustomed to our ways. But in you we found not only a musician who has done great work for us but someone who has been very tolerant of all our weaknesses. (BLMC A56726/72: 040831)

Thus the medium which in the future was to dictate the world's cultural parameters abased itself before another, which in the past had also been despised by 'society'. (In the event, Nolbandov's self-disparagement proved amply justifed, since his firm defaulted on payment of Holst's fee! [BLMC A56726/74–8].) Things were already different in Hollywood, where the new patrons of art stepped brazenly into the buckled footwear of princes and prelates, with no hang-ups about spiritual inferiority. Darryl F. Zanuck kept Max Steiner locked in a hotel suite, with a supply of Benzadrine and a team of copyists, in order to be on schedule with the score for *Gone With the Wind* (Anon., BBC R3: 121288). When Schoenberg asked $55,000 (*c.* £500,000 today) for a Hollywood score – commenting 'If I'm going to commit suicide I want to be as comfortable as possible afterwards' – his offer was rejected with non-deferential amusement (Siegmann, BBC R3: 100191).

In fact, the arrival of 'sound-film' had the effect of depreciating the cultural currency of music. The latter arguably reached its peak in the silent era, the absence of sound dialogue allowing music to play a privileged role in the emotional suggestion communicated to audiences. In the twenty years after 1910, the wide dissemination of silent pictures was a major reason for the growing interest in Art Music. Ernest Irving, who later joined Ealing Studios as musical director, recalled that each cinema

> received with the film a list of music suggested for it ... The opening of the Schubert 'Unfinished' Symphony was in the catalogue as a light flowing agitato, and the Beethoven 'Coriolanus' overture was recommended for hewing down trees. Any number of people made their first acquaintance with the classics by being compelled to listen to them in this way. (Irving 1959: 161)

Irving's career illustrates cultural changes stimulated by the developing film industry, as well as the values now entrenched in the mindset of English Music. Born into the lower middle class, he started work in musical theatre – an entertainment which evolved in the late nineteenth century from a fusion of music-hall and operetta. Irving became a highly paid professional, but always knew his place, regarding himself as being in show business rather than the art business. He admired composers who did not disdain work in the commercial theatre – Edward German, Norman O'Neill and William Walton. Yet his real veneration was reserved for RVW, whom he persuaded to compose for several films, including *Scott of the Antarctic* (1949) (Irving 1959: 161–3, 174–6).

For all his awe of the great man, Irving did not hesitate to accuse RVW of 'over-valuing the composer's work' when it came to the aesthetics of film. The title of his autobiography, *Cue for Music*, is refreshingly precise about his working priorities. RVW – here, at least, no differently from Schoenberg – maintained that the screenplay should be subordinate to the demands of the music. As ruling patriarch of the Renaissance, he was obliged to defend the exalted status that Art Music had attained. Irving argued that since the music 'is not being played at a concert, its principal effect should be upon the subconscious mind, and if the film is a good film, the music will be felt rather than listened to' (1959: 163; see Vaughan Williams 1964: 280). The composer later exacted his revenge, in the manner of an English gentleman, by manufacturing a symphony out of his *Scott* score, and dedicating it to Irving. Indeed, Irving's principal motive had all along been – according to his own account – to provide the great composer with fee-income to facilitate the production of 'serious' music.

Irving's influence over lucrative commissions, and the professional advice he was able to give to 'serious' composers, brought its rewards from the High Priesthood. He was invited to join the committee of the Royal Philharmonic Society, and at his death in 1953 was the only British member of that Olympian body, fellow of Cortot, Stravinsky, Toscanini, Stokowski, Sibelius and Casals. He expressed his astonishment at this development in his career, 'humbly equipped as I am for the service of great music' (Irving 1959: 182). Irving's humility was not out of place in the eyes of many. Doubtless because of his 'entertainment' background, he failed to gain notice in the early editions of the *Who's Who in Music*, edited by Sir Landon Ronald in the 1930s (Ronald 1937), and had no entry in the dictionary *British Music* produced by Russell Palmer in 1947, at the height of his influence.

Composers became involved in the film business not only as music providers but as (fictional) screen protagonists. 'Classical' music became an area of dense romantic associations, as Hollywood producers discovered the 'biopic' appeal of Schubert, Chopin *et al*. The history of music and its contemporary profile was celebrated by the British branch of the industry. In *While I Live* (1947) the creative process itself was the object of fascinated attention: a female composer is tormented by a tune that she cannot fully formulate – which turns out to be *The Dream of Olwen*. *The Women's Angle* (1952) featured a concert pianist as a Don Juan-type swashbuckler, with music which became known – with no covert signifying intention – as the 'Mansell Concerto'. Similarly, *Dangerous Moonlight* (1941) concerned a composer–pianist who joined the most glamorous group of Second World War heroes, expatriate Polish fighter-pilots. After being shot down, he loses his memory (i.e. identity) until he stumbles upon a piano and begins to render Addinsell's *Warsaw Concerto*. Such films fell into the category of women's entertainment, and it is notable that women remained a majority among 'music lovers' until the 1960s. The phenomenon reached a peak with *Brief Encounter* (1945), where Rachmaninov's music is the only area in which the lovers actually succeed in making love – a reference clearly intended to be understood by the audience in the sense described (above) by Ernest Irving. What a BBC scriptwriter in the 1930s once neatly referred to as 'tabloids' of the great Romantic piano concertos – versions of Grieg or Tchaikovsky, abridged to fit on a 78 rpm record – began to appear in many a working-class parlour, stacked beside the wind-up phonograph, and enjoyed mainly for their cinematic associations (Anon., BBC R3: 04–081289).

The critic and failed composer Cecil Gray deplored such 'vulgar' appeal. Gray is a case study in marked contrast to that of Irving. An unashamed elitist, his psyche was permanently inflated by the conviction that association with music made him effortlessly superior and wonderful. A typical example of the new priesthood, he lived a life of ease and conspicuous consumption on the proceeds of his father's metallurgical factories in Scotland. Not surprisingly, he was one of a vociferous minority of English critics who admired Delius (Stradling 1989). With Delius, Gray believed High Art to be the repository of everything worth having and knowing, all else being mundane, sordid, even despicable. It hardly occurred to him that even some of his 'sophisticated' readers might be offended when, for example, he described his first sight of Bartók: 'He stood out against the dim, circumambient mass of negligible humanity' (Gray 1948/85: 180). Gray's 300-page autobiography has no other reference to the non-artistic citizen, those who had endured a generation of poverty and war, while he sported with mutual-admiration societies like the Fitzrovia literati. Neither do the writings of this apostle contain one word of appreciation of the helot class of teachers and players who made the music on which his ego battened. Indeed, Gray makes no substantive comment on the material fabric of English musical life, clearly a subject beneath the attention of the true aesthete. Property and breeding no longer in themselves justified class distinctions, at least to many intellectuals. Instead contact with High Art served at a subconscious level to legitimise the continuance of modes of caste exclusivism.

If it would hardly be an insult to his memory to describe Gray as quasi-fascist, beatific attitudes about music can also be traced on the other side of the ideological fence. An example of the latter was Thomas Russell – a communist who started as one of those players unworthy of gentleman Gray's notice. Russell was lead viola player of Beecham's London Philharmonic, later becoming its manager. In 1942 he produced a best-selling 'collective autobiography'entitled *Philharmonic*. The book radiates the conviction that Art Music elevates its initiates above the common rout. It deplores the fact that the Depression had forced so many orchestral players into areas like those presided over by Ernest Irving, or (even worse) into jazz- and dance-bands, obtaining 'incomes in inverse order to the musical value of the works they performed': 'Too often such players end by regarding music as a job like any other, thus revealing a lamentable frame of mind ... If we are to have the finest possible orchestras these men must be brought in before they have been spoiled by the purely commercial side of life' (Russell 1942/53: 88–9).

It is hardly surprising to find Russell asserting that 'art is the highest expression of mankind'; and that (as in the USSR) Art Music should be supported entirely from public funds. In a passage containing a metaphor recurrent in music literature, he went on to suggest: 'To leave a concert hall after a vital experience and fight for a seat in a bus or a train, to jostle for a place in a crowded cafe, surrounded by people *not blessed with the same experience*, is to become aware of an anti-climax' (p. 119; our emphasis). When commentators as politically diverse as Gray and Russell agree on the metaphysical essentials, it helps us understand how Art Music was accepted as *the* apolitical discourse, a highly desirable commodity in a hyper-political age.

Unlike Gray, Russell wanted all citizens to be blessed, and in their own interests rather than those of his corporation. Similar feelings inspired Arthur Bliss when he visited the south Wales' valleys in 1935 as part of a nationwide survey – 'A Musical Pilgrimage of Britain' – commissioned by the BBC's *Listener* magazine. He noted with satisfaction that unemployed miners each paid one shilling and sixpence towards hire of music 'for the privilege of playing in the Brahms *Requiem* or the Bach *B Minor Mass* ... the masterpiece which will sustain him through the winter' (Bliss 1991: 114). We may char-itably suppose the blissful artist had no way of knowing that only scragging for coal sustained many miners and their families that win-ter. But as this incident suggests, experience of Art Music was already 'traditional' in the lower reaches of society in some areas. By the 1900s, it was perceived as a socially improving medium, a ladder which those of lesser birth and means might climb to rub shoulders with their betters. Arnold, Ruskin and Pater had not been entirely without success in the struggle against mid-Victorian philis-tinism. Literary popularisers of 'great composers and their music', often shamelessly plundering Grove's *Dictionary*, rushed into print. The market was provided by the newly literate classes called into being by Forster's Education Act; and it was the educational reformer's namesake who created its fictional representative in Leonard Bast. The character is a stereotype of the lowly consumer of High Art, and is perceived as such by the loftier characters of *Howard's End*. Bast, who 'stood at the extreme verge of gentility' grasps that knowledge of 'good' books and music will help him to move away from the abyss.

> Leonard listened to [the voice of Art] with reverence. He felt that he was being done good to, and that if he kept on with Ruskin and the Queen's Hall concerts, and some pictures by Watts, he would one day push his head out of the grey waters and see the universe ... One guessed him as the third generation, grandson to the shepherd or ploughboy whom civilization had sucked into the town; as one of the thousands who have lost the life of the body and failed to reach the life of the spirit ... [Margaret] knew this type very well – the vague aspi-rations, the mental dishonesty, the familiarity with the outsides of books. (Forster 1910/83: 62, 122–3)

The new genre of cheap guides to Art Music produced in these years were like missals or bibles which nervous initiates tucked under their arms on the way to concerts. One example was F. J. Crowest's *The Story of Music* (1902), a copy of which (in our possession) has an entry pencilled by its original owner in a fly-leaf: 'Order & Dates of the high tone musicians'. He was evidently a dutiful disciple of the Renaissance. His list comprises the names and dates of eight Austro-German composers from J. S. Bach to Schumann, painstakingly transcribed. A separate entry notes that the 'Operatic Composers' – not quite 'high-tone' – were Weber and Wagner. The volume could have belonged to Leonard Bast, a founding member of the 'sixpenny audience' which Elgar, himself born not all that far from the grey waters, hoped to create.

The tone of these textbooks now seems squirmingly patronising. Readers were made aware of being introduced to an infinitely superior world which they could never hope to understand. If approached, at least metaphorically, on one's knees, they would reward the humble neophyte with instruction and improvement. A well-known mediator of the divine was Percy Scholes, whose *Listener's Guide to Music* was introduced by Sir Henry Hadow as being 'addressed not to students and connoisseurs, but to plain simple people who like music but are a little bewildered by its complexity'. Secure in the belief that his clients were difficult to insult, Scholes claimed to be satisfying 'the need of the ordinary listener – the *quite ordinary, humble-minded, so-called "unmusical" person*' (Scholes 1922: v–vi, 2, our emphasis). Similarly, a publication which explained the practicalities of establishing a local music club was 'Dedicated to the Great Ones who wrote and the Little Ones who listen' (Henriques 1934). Between the wars, Walford Davies became a species of Radio Doctor, presenting a durable series of broadcast chats on music. In 1939, a BBC series entitled 'This Symphony Business' adopted the ploy of having an actor portray a philistine member of the public, who was gradually and grudgingly enlightened by a smooth-tongued critic. 'Hundreds of people wrote to say that they postponed, or interrupted, their evening meal on Sunday to listen to it' (Graves and Hodge 1940/63: 374). On the eve of the war which was to be aurally symbolised for all time by a free sample from one of its famous products, the symphony business was showing a healthy profit. Book titles such as *The Musical Pilgrim* or *The Music-Lover's Catechism* pullulated, and Malcolm Sargent referred with perfect naturalness to the 'happy band of ordinary musical pilgrims' (Palmer 1947: 8). However, in the social-democratic atmosphere of post-1945 Britain, some critics had become less insensitive. In introducing the *Penguin Music Magazine*, Ralph Hill (1946: 7–8) assured his readers that articles would be written 'by intelligent musicians who can write simply and interestingly and can show the newcomers the way about music without condescension or pedantry'.

Eternal verities

During her attempts to bring serious music to the wounded troops behind the lines of the Western Front, Lena Ashwell discovered not only a great thirst for the truth but great confusion about where true revelation lay. At Abbeville in 1916, her troupe performed some Mozart songs:

> [A] colonel urged the advisability of a higher standard ... and mentioned 'The Perfect Day', 'The Old-Fashioned Town', 'Donegal', 'Roses in Picardy'. Apparently everybody had a different idea as to the meaning of the word 'classic'. One YMCA leader ... urged the necessity for a high standard of classical music, and begged me to send immediately for the Fisk trio. They were the noted coloured singers of negro melodies ... (Ashwell 1922: 136–7)

Thus the work of the proselytisers in the 'training of taste' had more than one dimension. In the 1920s, Percy Scholes devoted a weekly column in the *Radio Times* to 'urging the necessity for a higher standard', pointing out how much better it was to be a 'Highbrow' than a 'Lowbrow' – terms which he seems to have invented – and drawing aesthetic boundaries which were evidently as necessary as those being drawn by political commissions in Ireland or the Balkans (Carpenter 1996: 3–5). But the irresistible drive of crude demand was never doubted. Much of our material has been derived from the era of total war, our argument stimulated by its effects on English society. It underlines one of our fundamental propositions. Art Music was approached as therapy for, even as prophylactic against, the sufferings and stresses of 'modern life'. Thus some took it for a medium of the eternal; others, as an aspirin. Either way, it was regarded as not only above politics, but as actually the antithesis of politics, a refuge from the threatening, the competitive, the unstable, the ephemeral.

This was an age when the X-ray of science had exposed to public gaze the skeleton of religion in the body of politics. The mordantly agnostic conclusions of the intelligentsia were now being transmitted to the millions via vulgarised versions of Marx, Nietzsche, Max Weber and Freud. Beside the compromised status of organised religion, music was increasingly seen as a purer condition towards which – to paraphrase Pater – all people and things could aspire. 'Music is the greatest of all spiritual forces', in the blasphemous assertion of *The Cambridgeshire Report* (Dent 1933: 9). 'It is the strongest fortress of spiritual values', echoed the nearby offices of *Scrutiny* (Mellers 1947/76: 196). The problem was that its advocates lacked a verbal discourse, and found themselves obliged to adapt for their purpose a vocabulary inherited from the centuries of Christian worship and contemplation. We may observe the twin processes of semantic transference and philosophical osmosis.

In 1924, Professor C. Sanford Terry argued in a radio talk that the BBC had a mission to campaign against all kinds of bad music – he meant music of the popular (and American) variety. Jazz was 'a musical literature which for vapidity, blatancy, unreality and reckless levity is without parallel ... [a] dismal declension from musical grace'. He refrained from use of the word 'sinful', but insisted that listeners must be exposed to – what he could not resist calling – 'salvation'. Under the heading 'A Woman's Conversion' – perhaps inserted by a pious compositor – Terry went on to tell a parable of the times.

> A book has just been published which points my argument. Its author, a woman, not merely was indifferent to but actually disliked, music, regarding musicians of every degree as vexatious babblers in a futile idiom. She had passed her thirtieth birthday, when she was taken reluctantly to hear Busoni, the greatest of living pianists. Her conversion was sudden and absolute. (Terry, *RT*: 250424)

The evangelist concluded by thanking the BBC for providing his 'pulpit', and expressing his relief that BBC policy was beyond criticism. Even where no explicit religious discourse was involved, the language of musicologists was often one of moral or emotional hyperbole. An example of *moral* hype came in 1935, when R. S. Thatcher addressed the annual conference of the Royal College of Organists on 'Music and Education'. He attacked jazz in virulent terms, contending that 'it would be nonsense to pretend that that music is a medium immune from prostitution ... This type of music

... would alone justify the need for a musical censor – just as much as a film censor' (Royal College of Organists 1935–36: 213–14). Thatcher, a teacher at Harrow, was soon appointed as the BBC's deputy music director (Foreman 1987: 307). An example of *emotional* hype comes from the critic Eric Blom, when relating how Cardinal Newman had attempted to persuade Dvořák to make a setting of *The Dream of Gerontius*: 'It is almost terrifying for many people to reflect that this very nearly deprived them of a masterpiece' (Blom 1942: 170).

A litany of hyperbole is provided by Victor Gollancz, for whom music was:

joy inexpressible
Such high hour of visitation from the living God,
Rapt into still communion, blessedness and love [after Wordsworth]
inevitable rightness
revealed reality
existent in another dimension
spiritual blessedness

Listening to music is an act of communion, but 'communion is also a recognition ... one greets it with a "Yes, this is it: this is what I know it to be, must ever know it to be, must ever have known it to be"'. The trance of Gollancz comes to an end with the unequivocal admission: 'There has been awe: one has bent the knee' (Gollancz 1964: 29–32).

Gollancz, radical left-wing publishing millionaire and music lover, gave many a music critic his first publishing break. In 1934 he inspired the production of *The Musical Companion*, an inexpensive compendium of history and criticism which became a best-seller. In a subsequent edition, Eric Blom sermonised on the theme of high seriousness which Gollancz believed all initiates should respect. Music, he adjured his readers, must never be cheapened by excessive quantity or familiarity. The listener must decide 'quite firmly never to have the radio on unless [he or she] means to listen'. The record-collector is reminded that 'if Beethoven's B flat major Trio were available in a performance by the Archangels Gabriel, Michael and Raphael, it should still be bought for the sake of Beethoven' (Bacharach and Pearce 1934/77: 735–6). We are back at revealed religion; and fifty years later an emphatically agnostic composer like Tippett had to be wrapped in priestly vestments, the better to present celebrations of his ninetieth birthday to the public. 'Visions of Paradise', as the series of concerts was called, was explained by Anthony Burton as 'having no religious significance [but as] appropriate to describe the moments of transcendental ecstasy towards which much of Tippett's music strives' (BBC R3: 110295). Thus Tippett is the legitimate and apostolic heir of RVW, 'a true son of God [who] will come singing his songs'.

Such an attempt by Art Music promoters to compete with the mind-blowing instant metaphysics of the Lizard Kings of Pop, crawling into skins which have long since been shed, is hardly a novel trend. In the early 1900s, the composer–pianist Cyril Scott trailed long hair, clouds of glory and Debussy's praise home from his education on the Continent. His biographer presented him as a secular saint: Scott was portrayed as an angelic being, dispensing light and delight to all who approached him, a philosopher–poet 'a hundred years ahead of his time'. 'There is a power within him which gives impulse … the joyful welling forth of music itself as a natural force' (Hull c. 1918: 179). Reams of publicity in this vein were turned out by music publishers, attempting to stimulate a market for the works of the composers in their stables. Some did indeed achieve high-profile fame. Promoters' hopes were fulfilled in ways dictated both by the pace of socio-cultural change and by the need to proselytise. In the 1930s, two series of cigarette-card caricatures were issued by W. D. & H. O. Wills presenting 'serious' musicians alongside other entertainment celebrities and sportspersons. Among the former was the Master of the King's Musick, Sir Walford Davies (CBSO Archive: Documents 1930s). The reaction of this high-minded and ultra-serious musical mandarin to finding himself in company with Gracie Fields and Stanley Matthews is not recorded. Most likely it would have been 'better me than Duke Ellington' – that other-track artistocrat.

We do not suggest that any of these refinements of an imperialist discourse, whether mundane or eschatological, were patented by the English Musical Renaissance. Tropes of comparison between music and the divine – ideas of music as consolation, salvation, and even paradise itself – were articulated as early as the sixteenth century. Satisfactory exploration of its cultural significance in terms of our civilisation would demand another book. But in view of the teleology we have traced above, it is possible to argue that the pretensions of Music in England to a unique spiritual authority were developed and advanced with a conscious purpose. 'The Goodly House' achieved the status among growing numbers of believers – in Sterndale Bennett's word – of a 'temple'. It is not surprising that Britten's overture *The Building of the House* should have followed Beethoven's *Consecration of the House* at the start of the Aldeburgh Festival in 1965, celebrating as it does the transmutation of Maltings into music. Of course, each music lover understood the liturgical aspect of what took place in conservatoire, concert-hall or opera-house somewhat differently according to temperament or occasion. But the ideal was to have the main ingredients of devotion more or less in balance with each other – love of country, of an immanent God and of 'music itself', the essential intermediary.

Conclusion

With the end of the Second World War, appreciation of the English Musical Renaissance understandably reached a high point. The phenomenon was widely perceived as contributing to national self-confidence and morale at a very profound level of collective psychology. The nation had been through an unprecedented test which, for the majority of its population, represented a continuous and unitary experience stretching back to 1914. Like the working masses, who had borne the brunt of the war's physical privations, and were now to benefit from a range of social welfare reforms, the bourgeois arts were also to receive their reward. The claim that High Culture deserved structured support from the State was finally conceded and the Arts Council evolved into today's Olympian dispensatrix of taxpayers' money. Thus, as Beveridge worked in his Cambridge study to re-weave the fabric of British society, so Boult, Thatcher and Bliss at Broadcasting House laid down the basic principles of post-war music policy in Board Paper G28/42 (1942).

> Creative Principle: Music is an ennobling spiritual force which should influence the life of every listener.
> Practical Interpretation: Inexorably to continue and expand the principle of great music as an ultimate value, indeed a justification of life… Physically and mentally to stimulate, cheer, and soothe tired bodies and worn nerves.
> [...]
> Statement of Policy: 1(d) The BBC regards it as a matter of the first importance to develop a strong sense of pride in British music in order to exorcise the long-standing national sense of inferiority in music and rid music of its status as a foreign art. (Quoted in Foreman 1987: 273)

With the era of the Third Programme and the Arts Council, Nation and Renaissance became one at last. As far as most of the travellers were concerned, the 'great trek' had arrived at the sunlit uplands. Retrospective anthologies polished the Pantheon of the Goodly House.

> Elgar's 'Enigma' Variations constitute the first great landmark in the British renaissance. They inaugurate a period whose musical richness and variety, fully sustained at the present day, surpass that of any other country between 1899 and 1944. This claim demands statement with unrepentant vigour. (Hull 1944: 9)

> Britain is now leading the world in every branch of serious music-making, and unless someone is prepared to lay out the facts in support of this claim ... the world will never fully appreciate the tremendous progress we have made ... We are able to see the skill of British composers shining across the musical universe like a beam of light. (Palmer 1947: 10–13)

> It is permissible to ask, without being chauvinistic, whether any other single country can claim so strong a school of native composers. (Frank 1953: 8)

As late as the 1948–49 season, a quarter of all works played by domestic orchestras were native in origin. Nearly half of these were by three composers – Elgar, Delius and Vaughan Williams: these priorities have on the whole proved lasting (Potts 1950: 53–5). 'Values in modern English music have become stabilised. We have at last established some sort of hierarchy', announced one critic. A comprehensive and popular Penguin survey, *British Music of Our Time*, placed in a 'premiership division' fifteen composers, to each of whom a chapter was allocated. All fifteen were, in fact, English – or at least 'English' when the term is opposed to 'British'. None of the rest 'has a place sufficiently important in the mainstream of English [sic] music to warrant a full-length study' (Lockspeiser 1946: 185). Forty years later, over half the membership of this league had been relegated to the nether regions, and a kind of 'super league', comprising Elgar, Delius, Vaughan Williams, Holst, Walton, Tippett and Britten, was instituted. These are the canon, and form the group which figures in Macmillan's *Twentieth Century English Masters* (McVeagh 1986) – selected from the eighteen volumes of the 'New Grove'. This elite survived more or less intact at the Barbican jamboree of British Music ('A Theme with Variations') held in 1988 and at several similar subsequent events in the 1990s – though, it seems, any digest of the latest Grove would be likely to add Birtwhistle – born in the watershed year of 1934 – Tavener and Maxwell Davies.

The whole issue of 'English' versus 'British' in the discourse of the 'national music' is as thorny a thicket as it is in the realm of national politics. Almost any consistent usage is impossible, and every instant usage offends against some deeply held principle of Britain's nation-alisms. We have tried, broadly, and perhaps not without error, to use 'England' and 'English' when referring to the spheres of ideas, cul-ture and cultural politics; and 'Britain' and 'British' when speaking of the collective history and institutions of the greater part of these islands. We believe that this is how the overwhelming majority of those who took part in, and wrote about, the English Musical Renaissance preconceived matters. Indeed, the most notable and more or less demonstrable exceptions occurred during the two World Wars, when the inscribers and broadcasters were very careful not to transgress the received trope of a 'Britain' socially, ethnically and culturally united in its struggle for survival.

Moreover, we are aware that the overall title we have selected may tend (in the opinion of some) to work against the grain of our intention. In fact, as much of the argument above demonstrates, there was never any truly homogeneous Musical Renaissance. Although it constantly aimed at collective values and identity, at no time did it achieve this ideal. Like any institution it proceeded by adaptation. At times its strategies were inclusive, at others rigorously exclusive. This brought success in many aspects: it produced a vast expansion of music, music-making and music-listening, which achieved (by all accounts) ever increasing standards until the 1970s. In this sense it may be said: If you seek its monument, look about you at the Goodly Houses and their occupants – concert-halls, opera-houses, conservatoires, university departments, the musical press and so on.

In the late 1940s, Bayreuth was still under ban, and music in Europe was devastated. Yet, despite the Anglo-Saxon liberation of western Europe, and subsequent military occupation of much of it, continental gratitude stopped short of our music. It was reported in a popular British musical periodical, with obvious resentment:

> In a recent issue of the R. C. M. Magazine an ex-student, who has been staying in Paris, wrote: 'No English works have yet found their way

into the repertoire. I heard exactly two English works during six months in Paris. The first was at a restaurant in Montmartre where the singer, as a compliment to a friend and myself, sang *Arbres*. For the benefit of those who do not know it, this is a popular ballad ... The other work was *Colonel Bogey* played by a military band on the Champs Elysées.' (R. Hill 1949: 9)

This situation has altered very little to date. In 1970 when the celebrated teacher, scholar and *Parisienne* Nadia Boulanger was told of Delius's *Paris – Song of a Great City*, it was the first she had heard of the composer, leave alone the work (Palmer 1976: 190). A few years ago the same composer's *Violin Concerto* was performed for the first time in Leipzig – the city where he spent the most formative years of his musical life. Before 1914, major English premieres – Stanford, Elgar, Delius, Butterworth – were given by the great German conductors, and even in the 1920s Holbrooke and Scott secured prestigious operatic premieres in Germany. Sixty years later, Alexander Goehr's opera *Behold the Sun* was shabbily treated by producers and audience on its debut in Germany (Williams 1989). Many foreign conductors have failed to evince interest in British works, even when contracted to Britain's major musical institutions. The relatively infrequent exceptions in the careers of Toscanini, Karajan, Mitropoulos, Bernstein, Haitink and Solti – among other lesser luminaries – seem sufficiently tokenist to prove this point. Despite the worldwide reputation of British executants, English music arguably receives less attention from European musicians today than it did a century ago. In the 1970s, Piérre Boulez managed to avoid the native muse altogether during his tenure as chief conductor of the BBC Symphony Orchestra. Sir Simon Rattle's appointment in 1999 as chief conductor of the Berlin Philharmonic was apparently secured by his commitment to a 'modernist' repertoire. But in the 1990s' TV series 'Coming Home', which was devoted to introducing the outstanding composers of this repertoire, Rattle himself lamented the fact that from his native tradition he could include only Britten – and even that by employing a certain partisan latitude. It remains to be seen whether his tenure at Berlin will help to broaden the European appeal of English music. During the BBC's 'Fairest Isle' year (see below) several contributors to the series 'As Others See Us' revealed surprising ignorance of the 'English canon' in the conservatoires of our major European partners. The English Musical Renaissance has nothing like the profile, for example, in Czechoslovakia or Spain, that theirs have in Britain.

But we have little ground for complaint, since the Renaissance has left a domestic legacy which is both exiguous and equivocal. For example, no full native production of an opera written by any British composer before 1945 has ever been presented on national television. A substantial fraction of the works we have discussed in the text were first broadcast and/or recorded during the actual period of research and writing. This goes for almost the whole symphonic output of both Parry and Stanford; in particular, when the latter's *Symphony No. 6* received its first broadcast performance, in 1988, the BBC Radio 3 researchers had failed to track down a single rendering since the work's premiere in 1906! Several orchestral works by Stanford's ostensibly 'celebrated' pupil Herbert Howells were given their first hearings during a Radio 3 'Composer of the Week' series in 1989. Constant Lambert's ballet *Horoscope* was not performed uncut on Radio 3 until it was more than 50 years old. This situation is by no means limited to those composers who are regarded variously as 'minor' or – to use a cliché of aesthetic partisanship – 'unjustly neglected'. Many of the lesser-known works of Elgar (a substantial fraction of the whole) were given premiere recordings at this time. For some years – approximately 1985–95 – there was almost a performance culture of what might be called 'foundation' works of the Musical Renaissance, and relevant recording activity was intense. Yet, at the start of the twenty-first century, only a tiny proportion of the output of the elite group named above – whatever their canonical significance – could seriously be regarded as repertoire pieces. Among most 'serious' music followers, composers representative of the English School of the period we have discussed are regarded as marginal to a centre still occupied by their German, Russian, French, Scandinavian or east-European contemporaries.

We point up this catalogue of omission because it reflects on the disparity between the public claims and the real priorities of the Renaissance, a disparity illustrated in the partisan and arbitrary use of the resources stored up in its Goodly House. For us, this is a matter of historical record. We are not among those who believe – or even hope – that the world would be a better place if things were otherwise. 'We should blow our own trumpet' was the phrase chosen by Mr Renton in 1992 to herald 'National Music Day'. But who are 'we'? And do we have only one trumpet – a National Music for National Music Day? If otherwise, which of our trumpets are we to blow? And can we be sure that they will sound a certain note?

Postlude

In 1893, Charles Willeby published his *Masters of English Music*, an early critical assessment of the musical composition produced by the Renaissance project. The music publishing house of Novello took fright, believing that Willeby's generally negative attitude to some of the composers in their stable would have an adverse effect on sales figures. They issued a writ against the author and turned to the influential and widely respected Herbert Thompson, music critic of the *Yorkshire Post*, to provide expert witness of Willeby's error. He was asked to read the book with the express intention of 'picking as many holes as possible for the purpose of fortifying our evidence ... defects of all sorts ... whether they be sins of commission or omission ... We will of course pay you any reasonable fee you may ask' (H. Clayton to Thompson 020893: LUBC 361/49).

A century after Mr Willeby's chastening experience, the first edition of the present book, titled *The English Musical Renaissance, 1860–1940: Construction and Deconstruction* (hereafter *EMR1*), was widely reviewed. Substantial notices appeared in the national daily and Sunday newspapers as well as in several literary journals, music periodicals, and the specialist history press. The critics fell into two very distinct camps: a minority, who thought the book a major work of music and cultural history; and the majority, who held it to be at best a flawed account of the English Musical Renaissance, at worst a denial of music itself. For or against, the critical reception of *EMR1* nevertheless provided a useful index of the debates which were swirling around musicology and cultural history in the 1990s.

EMR1 was praised for its pioneering and even iconoclastic approach to the role of national music in forging an English (and, by extension, British) national identity in the nineteenth and twentieth centuries. Many of our critics acknowledged that the book had finally brought English Music out of the ghetto of musicology–music history and into the arena of mainstream political and cultural history. Some of the fiercest among them even agreed with a central tenet of the book – that the English Musical Renaissance was the conscious production of an intellectual and social elite.

Criticism of *EMR1* concentrated on its methodology and, to a lesser degree, on certain aspects of its content. Several critics felt deeply uncomfortable with a methodology which insisted that music is subjected to the forces of history just like every other aspect of life. The book insisted that the 'life and works' approach to music history has had its day, and that a new way of looking at the subject was absolutely essential to its future vitality. Yet this was the starting-point of the project – to write a work of history about the evolution of English Music. Eight years on, the authors remain convinced that an English music history that is anchored in the 'life and works' paradigm is intellectually exhausted. In this respect, musicology as a discipline has much to do to catch up with other cognate disciplines – most especially literature, film and the fine arts.

Several reviewers were keen to question our fundamental attitude towards music. Many remarked on our too 'dispassionate' approach to our subject, criticising us for not loving the music, nor revering the composers, enough. We were also called to account for our 'undue' emphasis on composers' politics and a more general preoccupation with politico-cultural values. In *EMR1*, it was said, social and economic considerations were foregrounded at the expense of music and musicians. But we reject the notion that a love of music is a necessary precondition of writing about music. For us, too much musicology–music history is riddled with the subjectivity of 'loving the subject'; far better to seek to place music in a broader social and political context. Music history, in our view, is still being written with too much 'music' and too little 'history'. We welcomed the fact that *EMR1* outraged so many of the fundamental orthodoxies of musicology–music history since for far too long these disciplines have been mired in outmoded discourses and tired values. Yet, even in 1993, a bright new world of musicology was already in existence, heralded by later editions of Joseph Kerman's fundamental introduction to the discipline, and adorned by names like Susan McLary, Lydia Goehr, Larry Kramer, Cyril Ehrlich and Edward Said, and responsive to the resonances of history, sociology, linguistics and politics in the production and prioritising of musical works.

The reader of the second edition might find it instructive to sample the flavour of the reception given to *EMR1*, if only as an index of how English music sees itself at the beginning of the new millenium. We start with the *Guardian* which, in its annual selection of Christmas books (261193), recommended *EMR1* as a choice which 'will interest (and amuse) anyone who enjoys a good polemical read'. Since it had appeared back in the July of 1993, and Richard Gott had apparently compiled the list in person, we were naturally delighted. The *Guardian*'s intervention was perhaps mainly responsible for the fact that the book sold out well within a year of publication, despite its discouraging retail price of £40. But perhaps our delight was premature. In Gott's opinion, the book had received 'short shrift from music critics'. The original meaning of 'short shrift' refers to a hasty last confession before execution. As it happened, *The Times*'s reviewer had issued a peremptory decree that the book should be 'pulped' – as it were by the Lord High Executioner – as an intolerable offence to the musical nation (Heffer, *The Times* 090893). Since Routledge had hedged its bets by printing a mere 650 copies, carrying out Simon Heffer's sentence would not have been a difficult task. Doubtless, the ghost of Charles Willeby would have looked on stoically. In any case, our publisher soon stopped hedging, got off the fence, and firmly kicked the book into the long grass by quietly dropping the idea of a paperback edition. Consequently, 'this controversial, revisionist book' (as Gott had called it) was studiously ignored by the academic establishment.

This fate is voluble testimony to the fact that the cow which stares over the fence remains a sacred cow. Nothing irritated reviewers from the 'musicology' camp more than our attempt to assess and interpret the cultural heritage of the Pastoral School from a postmodernist perspective. A context of discussion which seemed less than worshipful of 'national music' – particularly when it came to the symbolic–mythological role of 'Uncle Ralph' Vaughan Williams and the cultural profile of his output – was deeply upsetting to many. It should be emphasised that the consequent reaction, clearly that of an intellectual elite invincibly assured of the greatness of Vaughan Williams's music, was directed against a book which had meticulously refrained from offering any opinion on this subject. Yet thirty years earlier no less an authority than Donald Mitchell had dismissed the whole 'creative' achievement of the English Musical Renaissance, *tout court*, in a single footnote to his book *The Language of Modern Music*. Here RVW was placed firmly in the company of Kodaly rather than that of Bartók. But, Mitchell added,

> Vaughan Williams was not so fortunate [as Bartók], even if one leaves on one side all question of comparative talent. In England there was not, as there was in Europe, an emerging tradition concerned with the New ... On the contrary the musical scene in England after the turn of the [twentieth] century possessed all the immobility of a waxworks stacked with dummy composers and the effigies that they passed off as compositions ... No one would wish to deny or diminish the importance of Vaughan Williams's act of rehabilitation, which restored an identity to English music and gave English composers a much-needed boost. But it is difficult to escape the conclusion that he became in some sense a victim of his own achievement: encircled by the past, not freed by it. His attempts to widen his scope – e.g., the fourth symphony – suggest that he was intermittently conscious of the prison bars. (1963: 109–10)

While Vaughan Williams is at least what Mitchell's namesake Tovey used to refer to as 'an interesting historical figure', Elgar is not even important enough to be noticed by name among the waxwork dummies. It is surely pertinent to ask, in view of this and a dozen other similar dicta issued since 1940 by musicologists of international repute: why are so many sensibilities still so raw? Equally pertinently, reviewers in the specialist history journals seemed not to share this paranoid anxiety to protect the musical treasures of the nation. For example, Keith Robbins welcomed 'a striking contribution to the cultural history of music and its role in forging and sustaining national identity'; while John Ramsden commended a book 'remarkable especially for its wealth of cultural cross-reference ... an invaluable correction to all that has gone before' (*History* 0294: 165; *English Historical Review* 0496: 520–1).

What emerged even more ominously from the reviews was that English cultural identity and the canon of 'classical' music that represents it are no laughing matters. Sacred cows cannot be laughing cows. We freely admit that our book was (and is) offered partly in the spirit of the Last Night of the Proms. The youthful audience who contribute so much anarchy to this event are rarely thereby accused of not enjoying (or even of not 'appreciating') the music. Their irreverence is aimed at its performance context: a context of reverent patriotism based on historical tradition and cultural formation – rightly so, and in all good humour. Of course, as Welshmen we cannot deny that our cultural identity stands at an awkward angle to that which prevails in the Albert Hall on those September evenings. Not long ago, the Welsh baritone Bryn Terfel, appearing at the Last Night, wore a Wales team shirt and kicked a rugby ball into the packed promenaders. The *Radio Times* (07–130899) later explained that 'it was his way of connecting fully with the audience'. If the response of musicologists to our book is a reliable guide, then the impact of its landing has left a bruise too painful to permit any positive connection.

In the intellectual context, humour and satire, parody and pastiche have always been seen as legitimate – that is to say, serious – modes of critical approach to cultural hegemony or political correctness. Composers (Couperin, Rossini, Berlioz, Saint Saëns, Weill, Shostakovich, Britten) have utilised these subversive modes fully as much as have writers. A key motive in writing the book was to spark dialogue and debate, above all between musicologists and cultural historians. That no such conference was ever likely to take place was signalled by the distinguished musicologist Malcolm MacDonald, who was deeply wounded by many of our opinions and expressions. In the *TLS* (051193) he made no attempt to dissemble his anger, reaching an inarticulate climax which represented a comprehensive exposure of sensitivity: 'I believe a sufficiently measured response would be: Balls.' At this point, the fastidious reader may be assured that MacDonald was not referring to rugby, but rather to the apparent seat of his own physical discomfort. His only answer to our challenge in the *TLS* correspondence columns was to commission an almost equally savage review for *Tempo* (January 1994: 27–8), the magazine he edits. Like the definitive final chords of Sibelius's *Symphony No. 5*, the guild of musicologists closed its ears, mind, heart, mouth, and (finally) its doors to further debate. To the extent that this was our fault we regret it, but to say this is not the same as to say: 'Sorry, we were only joking.' We were certainly not 'only joking'.

That music criticism should be so unbiddable is all the more ironic since a major intention of our book was to suggest that music critics should be a suitable case for scholarly treatment. Fully fifty years ago a pioneer cultural historian, Jacques Barzun, in his path-breaking study *Berlioz and the Romantic Century*, expressed the need for study of music criticism 'as an element of general culture' (1951: 9).

As William Weber (1996) has more recently shown, the influence of criticism became an axiom in the political context of composition and performance during the era of Roger North, the earliest accredited English musicologist who flourished in the early eighteenth century. Indeed it was our fundamental contention that critics have at least as much importance in modern music history as do composers or performers. Sibelius dealt with this transgressive notion in words as emphatic as any symphonic coda: 'there has never been a statue set up in honour of a critic' (quoted in Watson 1991: 382). For our part, we are no more inclined to support subscriptions for such a purpose than we would subscribe to any campaign to rehabilitate individual 'unjustly neglected' composers. Yet the fact that several reviewers seemed to conclude that the only wholly laudable aspect of our book was its advocacy of such victims – at times citing with approval our treatment of their particular unsung hero – is an even more delicious irony. English music critics are, it seems, a deferential profession, perennially happy to cling to their status in the Goodly House as mere hand-servants of genius. The current *Grove Dictionary*'s entries on 'Criticism', and 'Musicology', as well as its vignettes of individual English critics from the founder himself down to Frank Howes, reflect the profound assumptions of the pecking order. Music writers have 'responsibilities' and need 'qualifications': little is offered in terms of the historical hermeneutics of criticism, and no hint is ever dropped that both the existence and the survival of individual composers and works in the canon owe anything to their influence. Given the defensive complaisance of the guild, we were not surprised when a highly qualified friend of ours commented wryly that the corpus of English musicology was an easy target for the deconstructive historian, but that we should find a tussle with the likes of Schenker, Adorno, Dahlhaus or Kerman a more challenging experience.

During the same period, a 'New Musicology' has risen to prominence across the Atlantic, exciting tremendous intellectual ferment, demolishing disciplinary frontiers and creating vast new dimensions of understanding in the relationship and application of politics, philosophy, sociology, linguistics and cultural theory to musicology. In Britain, embarrassed silence prevailed. Only in very recent years have signs emerged of a willingness among British music specialists to open negotiation with other disciplines. In general, instead of self-examination self-celebration remained the order of the day, less clangorous, perhaps, but more ubiquitous even than that of Last Night of the Proms. We refer (chiefly) to 'Fairest Isle', the BBC's year-long celebration of English Music, ostensibly inspired by the Purcell anniversary which occurred in 1995. National Music Day, inaugurated confidently as an annual event in 1992, withered so rapidly that three years later even the BBC virtually ignored it. Yet Radio 3's then controller, Nicholas Kenyon, introduced 'Fairest Isle' in identically chauvinistic language to that used by a succession of arts ministers: 'Let us rejoice: we are not *ohne musik*, but on the contrary, have at times led the world in music', was Kenyon's keynote (*Daily Telegraph* 031294). Nothing could have more firmly underlined the fact that the carefully scripted farce of the Last Night is the BBC's permitted joke, which it offers as a tiresome necessity, an annual sop to the sceptics, and a clumsy example of what Gramsci categorised as 'cultural ensemble'. In reality little has changed since John Reith, its first director, was finally forced in the 1930s to allow the broadcasting of 'jazz music' – 'this filthy product of modernity', as he called it in his private diary (quoted, *Sunday Times* 290893). Self-congratulation made up the staple fare of Radio 3's programme under the 'Fairest Isle' rubric. It was a spirit that was almost relentlessly ethnic, since Scottish, Irish and Welsh composers made little more than wanly token appearances in the schedules.

Not – we hasten to add – that we subscribe to any brief for Welsh composers (whatever they are). At the level of personal evaluation, both of us retain the preferences we had in 1993. RS can now reveal his conviction that one day Havergal Brian will be seen as greater than Elgar (an opinion arrived at by reading and re-reading Malcolm MacDonald's magisterial study in conjunction with listening to recordings of the symphonies), while MH remains equally convinced that, were this ever to happen, it would not be saying very much. We plead in our defence the nostrum of Friedrich Hegel, who maintained that it was perfectly valid to admire subjectively a thing which one might objectively reject from the historical or philosophical perspective (thus the love of Wagner's music by a venerable succession of Jewish musicians and thinkers). As historians, we make no apology for surveying the vast landscape of music-related historical evidence from the vantage-point mainly of our own discipline. For this, we may cite another authority, Edward Said, who insists on invoking history as an indispensable analytical tool and referent in the hermeneutics of music (elucidated, e.g., in his extended TV interview with Tariq Ali, broadcast on Channel 4 in 1995). Moreover, as regards our 'methodology', Said's 'Introduction' to his seminal essay *Musical Elaborations* cannot be improved upon as a statement of the broad intellectual motives and objectives to which this book of ours aspires.

> [Scholars] have already started to avail themselves, without any loss in musical accuracy or scholarship, of what deconstruction, cultural history, narratology, and feminist theory have to offer ... Things are changing, but, in the main, professional musicology is like any other field in that it has a corporate or guild consensus to maintain, which sometimes required keeping things as they are, not admitting new or outlandish ideas, maintaining boundaries and enclosures ... I am struck by how much does not receive their critical attention, and by how little is actually done by fine scholars who, for example, in studying a composer's notebooks or the structure of classical form, fail to connect those things to ideology, or social space, or power, or to the formation of an individual (and by no means sovereign) ego. (Said 1992: xii–xiii)

Of course, our matrix discipline is itself, as Said implies, neither intellectually autonomous nor immune from the effects of cultural change. Such changes are themselves in their turn, as Gramsci saw, socially constructed and reflect the dynamics of existing power relationships. Thus our intrusion has no implications of aggrandisement, any more than the use of historical materials and research techniques by musicologists suggests an equally imperialist ambition. All the same, in the last analysis, we remain historians. In preference to any musicological lobby, therefore, we should rather endorse the opinion of Roger North's contemporary, the eminent English historian Thomas Carte, who appealed for public subscription to his forthcoming *History of England*, at the rate of £10 from a gentleman and £20 from a member of the nobility. This represented, he claimed, little more than a season's subscription to Handel's opera, which 'serves only for the transient amusement of some winter evenings to particular persons, whereas a good history ... will be a lasting benefit to the public' (1737).

References

Abbreviations

BBC	British Broadcasting Corporation
BBC R3	BBC Radio 3
BBC R4	BBC Radio 4
BBCC	BBC Written Archives Centre, Caversham
BLMC	British Library Manuscripts Collection
BLMC A	British Library Manuscripts Collection, Additional Manuscripts
BLMC E	British Library Manuscripts Collection, Egerton Manuscripts
BLMC L	British Library Manuscripts Collection, Loan Collection
BNOC	British National Opera Company
BRBC	Bristol University Barter Collection
BRBC DM	Bristol University Barter Collection, box no.
BUBM	Birmingham University Bantock Manuscritpts
BUBM F	Birmingham University Bantock Manuscripts, file no.
CBSO	City of Birmingham Symphony Orchestra
DNB	*Dictionary of National Biography*
EBCB	Elgar Birthplace Collection, Broadheath
FWLC	Fiztwilliam Library, Cambridge
FWLC BS	Fiztwilliam Library, Cambridge, Barclay Squire Papers
HWRO	Hereford and Worcester Record Office, Worcester
ISCM	International Society for Contemporary Music
LPO	London Philharmonic Orchestra
LUBC	Leeds University Brotherton Collection
MT	*Musical Times*
NTS	National Training School
Oxf.Bod	Bodleian Library, Oxford
Oxf.Bod. EL	Bodleian Library, Oxford, English Letters
PROK	Public Record Office, Kew

PROK PREM   Public Record Office, Kew, Prime Ministers' Papers
RAM   Royal Academy of Music
RAMA   Royal Academy of Music Archives
RAMA PAM   Royal Academy of Music Archives, Pamphlet Collection
RCM   Royal College of Music
RCMA   Royal College of Music Archives
RCMA NTS   Royal College of Music Archives, National Training School
            Minutes
RCMA PAM   Royal College of Music Archives, Pamphlet
RMCM   Royal Manchester College of Music
RNCM   Royal Northern College of Music
RPS   Royal Philharmonic Society
RT   *Radio Times*

Unpublished archival sources

* indicates selected volumes only

The British Library
Additional 41570–41574: F. G. Edwards
Additional 49600–49603: The Musical League (1908–12)
Additional 50529, 52364–52366: Rutland Boughton
Additional 52256–52257: Edward Clark
Additional 54793: Macmillan Company Papers
Additional 56419–56443 & 56464–56466: Sir Henry Wood*
Additional 56575–57264: Papers of the Society of Authors*
Additional 59814: Papers of the McNachten Concerts Society
Additional 60498–60503: Sir Adrian Boult*
Additional 61882–61886: Ernest Chapman*

Egerton 3090–3097: F G Edwards
Egerton 3301–3306: Percy Pitt

Loan 48: Royal Philharmonic Society*

Royal College of Music
Sir George Grove's personal library deposit
Pamphlets Collection
National Training School Minute-Books (1873–82)
Grove's correspondence (1882–1900)

Royal Academy of Music
Sir Alexander Mackenzie's papers
Minute-Books of the Council (1886–75)

BBC Archives (Caversham Park)
Composer's Files: Elgar, Delius, Bax, Mackenzie and Holbrooke
Commissioned Music Files
Minutes of the Music Advisory Committee
Memoranda of Boult, Clark and other officials

(FWLC) FitzWilliam Library (Cambridge)
William Barclay Squire, correspondence with Arthur Goring Thomas
  (1881–91)

(Oxf.Bod) Bodleian Library (Oxford)
Correspondence between Sir H. Parry and Edward Dannreuther (1878–
  1905)

(HWRO) Hereford and Worcester Record Office (Worcester)
Elgar's correspondence and Lady Elgar's diary

(EBCB) Elgar Birthplace Museum (Broadheath)
Elgar's papers and personal library

Barber Institute (Birmingham University Library)
Sir Granville Bantock's correspondence with Joseph Holbrooke (1908–46)

(BRBC) Bristol University Manuscripts Collection
DM 433: Records of the Bristol Concerts Society, 1905–61*

*(CBSO) City of Birmingham Symphony Orchestra Archives (Birmingham
  Conservatoire)*
Letters, newspaper cuttings, concert programmes and other memorabilia
  relating to the orchestra's history

(RNCMA) Royal Northern College of Music Archives (Manchester)
Papers of Sir Charles Hallé and Adolph Brodsky (1874–1910)

(TP) Thompson Papers (Brotherton Library, University of Leeds)
Letters and other memorabilia of Herbert Thompson

Radio and TV programmes

(Writer/producer, date, subject or title)

BBC Radio 3
Anon, 060486, Ethel Smyth, *Mass in D*

— 121288, Composers of the Week: Hollywood Films
— 021189, 'Sullivan Without Gilbert'
— 021289, Composers of the Week: British Films
— 100191, 'Schönberg in America'
— 200491, 'Music Weekly' on Stanford
Hindmarsh, P., 290788, Composer of the Week: Frank Bridge
Hughes, M., 260790, 'Elgar and the English Class System'
— 210791, 'Elgar and Academe'
— 030792, 'Elgar and his Patrons'
— 200195, 'Elgar and the Press'
Johnson, S., 171090, 'Vaughan Williams and the BBC'
MacLaren, C., 200885, 'Broomhouse Reach'
Oliver, M., 060876, Music at the Crystal Palace
— 080392, 'Soundings' on Vaughan Williams
Spicer, P., 230489, Composer of the Week: Howells
Spiegl, F., 010188, 'The Land Without Music'
Wolfson, S., 220490, Sullivan

BBC Radio 4
Anon., 301289, 'Nymphs and Shepherds of 1929'
Semper, C., 180589, Parry's *Jerusalem*

TV programmes
Russell, K., ITV, 020488, 'ABC of British Music'
Scruton, R., BBC2, 221091, 'England's Green and Pleasant Land'

Disc 'liner notes'

(Author, year, label, composer: work)

LP sleeve-notes
Demuth, N. (?1954), HMV BLP 10001; Vaughan Williams: *Symphony No. 6*
Guyatt, A. (1979), Unicorn–Kanchana 8000; Goossens: *Symphony*
Hall, D. (?1964), World Record Club, WRC T144; Vaughan Williams: *Symphony No. 9*
Hurd, M. (1984), Hyperion A66101/2; Boughton: *The Immortal Hour*
Kennedy, M. (1984), HMV EL 7 49558 1; Ireland: *These Things Shall Be*
Palmer, C. (1975), Lyrita SRCS 68; Howells: *Chamber Music*
Wimbush, R. (1968), Columbia ASD 2400; Smyth: *The Wreckers*
Young, P. (1972), HMV ESD 7057; Sullivan: *The Tempest*

CD inserts
Alwyn W., 1991, Argo 430–356–2; Coleridge-Taylor: *Hiawatha*

Foreman L., 1990, Chandos 8884; Stanford: *Symphony No. 4*
— 1988, Chandos 8627; Stanford: *Symphony No. 6*
Palmer C., 1986, Unicorn–Kanchana UKCD 2013; Dyson: *In Honour of the City*

Published sources

Items from the Radio Times
Anon., 130325, 'A Great Enterprise Develops'
Anon., 130325, 'A Great Enterprise Develops'
— 241126, 'Annotated Programmes: A New Feature of the *Radio Times*'
— 280731, Ketèlby Programme (London Regional)
— 140733, 'The Broadcasting of Music: The BBC Replies to Recent Criticism' (1)
— 210733, 'The BBC Replies ...' (2)
— 280733, 'The BBC Replies ...' (3)
— 291233, Ethel Smyth *The Prison*
— 240980, C. H. Parry's *Prometheus*
— 220788, Frank Bridge (quotation)
— 300490, La Bruyère (quotation)
Cohen, A., 140733, 'This Englishness: Does it Exist in Art?'
Einstein, A., 050134, 'No Longer a "Land Without Music"'
Evans, E., 260735, 'The Great Schism'
Hadow, W. H., 040227, 'The Choice of Broadcast Music'
— 110227, 'The Choice ...' (continued)
Klein, H., 220329, '*Ivanhoe* – An Introduction'
— 050134, 'Modern British Music in the Making'
Moiseiwitsch, B., 061125, 'Radio to Make Us Musical'
Pitt, P., 040124, 'Why Opera Should Be Broadcast'
Scholes, P., 040124, 'Rutland Boughton's *Alkestis*'
— 080525, 'Joseph Parry's *Blodwen*'
— 200826, 'Our Second National Anthem?' (*Jerusalem*)
— 091227, 'Is Bartók Mad – Or Are We?'
— 180528, 'The Music of Today'
— 050134, 'British Music in Our Century'
Terry, C. S., 250424, 'The Way to Like Good Music'
Tristram, C., 070324, 'Hope for British Music'

Items from the Musical Times
Anon., Dec. 1906, 'A Folk-Song Discussion'
— July 1915, 'The Music Profession and the War: An Appeal'
— Mar. 1924, 'A Talk With Sir Alexander Mackenzie'
Bennett, J., July 1877, 'The Influence of Handel on Music in England'

Broadwood, L., Oct. 1904, 'Hints to Collectors of Folk-Music'
Colles, H. C., Jan. 1923, 'Review of Vaughan Williams's *Mass in G Minor*
Edwards, F. G., Nov. 1898, 'Frederic Hymen Cowen'
Evans, E., Jan. 1919, 'Modern British Composers' [Series]
Grace, H., April 1933, 'The Musical Profession and the BBC'
Hull, R. H., Aug. 1929, 'The Folk-Song Movement'
Jaeger, A., June 1902, 'The Lower Rhenish Musical Festival'
Lessmann, Jan. 1901, 'Review of *The Dream of Gerontius*'
Newman, E., Aug. 1914, 'Russian Opera and Russian "Nationalism"'
— Sept. 1914a, 'The War and the Future of Music'
— May 1916, 'The Spirit of England: Edward Elgar's New Choral Work'
Sharp, C., Nov. 1915, 'English Folk Dance: The Country Dance'

Books, articles and essays
Place of publication is London unless otherwise entered.

Ackroyd, P. (1992) *English Music* (Hamish Hamilton).
Allen, H. P. (1922) 'Director's Address', *RCM Magazine*, 18(2).
Anderson, R. (1993) *Elgar* (Dent).
Andrews, H. (1948) *Westminster Retrospect: A Memoir of Sir Richard Terry* (Oxford, Oxford University Press).
Anon. (1848) 'Dr Felix Mendelssohn-Bartholdy', *Musical Times*, ii (1 January): 153–9.
Ashwell, L. (1922) *Modern Troubadors: A Record of Concerts at the Front* (Copenhagen, Oslo and London, Gyldenhal).
Ayre, L. (1968) *The Proms* (Leslie Frewin).
Bacharach, A. L. (ed.) (1946) *British Music of Our Time* (Harmondsworth, Penguin Books).
— and Pearce, R. R. (eds) (1934/77) *The Musical Companion* (Gollancz).
Bailey, C. (1948) *Hugh Percy Allen* (Oxford, Oxford University Press).
Baily, L. (1966) *The Gilbert & Sullivan Book* (Spring Books).
Banfield, S. (1981a) 'The Artist and Society', in Temperley: 11–28.
— (1981b) 'Aesthetics and Criticism', in Temperley: 455–73.
— (1985) *Sensibility and English Song: Critical Studies of the Early Twentieth Century*, 2 vols (Cambridge, Cambridge University Press).
— (1993/94) 'England, 1918–45', in Morgan.
— (ed.) (1995) *Music in Britain in the Twentieth Century* (Oxford, Blackwell).
Banister, H. (ed.) (1937) *Josef Holbrooke: Various Appreciations by Many Hands* (London).
Barclay Squire, W. (1912) 'Catalogue of Printed Music Published Between 1487 and 1800 Now in the British Museum', 2 vols (British Museum Trustees).
Baring-Gould, S. (1889) *Songs and Ballads of the West* (Methuen).

Barker, E. (ed.) (1947) *The Character of England* (Oxford, Oxford University Press).

Barlow, M. and Barnett, R. (1991) 'Stanley Bate – Forgotten International Composer', *British Music* 13: 16–36.

Barrington, J. (*c.* 1948) *And Master of None* (Walter Edwards).

Barty-King, H. (1980) *GSMD* [Guildhall School of Music and Dance]*: A Hundred Years of Performance* (Stainer & Bell).

Bax, A. (1943) *Farewell My Youth* (Longman Green).

Bax, C. (1925) *Inland Far* (Heinemann).

BBC (1998) 'BBC Proms' (BBC booklet).

Beecham, T. (1944) *A Mingled Chime* (Hutchinson).

Beedell, A.(1992)*: Decline of the English Musician.* (Oxford, Oxford University Press).

Behrman, C. F. (1977) *Victorian Myths of the Sea* (Ohio, Ohio University Press).

Benedict, J. (1850) *Sketch of the Life and Works of the Late Felix Mendelssohn-Bartholdy* (Murray)

Bennett, J. R. S. (1907) *The Life of William Sterndale Bennett* (Cambridge, Cambridge University Press).

Benson, A. C. (1906) *Walter Pater* (Macmillan).

Berlioz, H. (1852/1963) *Evenings in the Orchestra*, ed. D. Cairns (Harmondsworth, Penguin).

— (1860/1969) *The Memoirs of Hector Berlioz*, tr. and ed. D. Cairns (Gollancz).

Binns, P. L. (1959) *A Hundred Years of Military Music: Being the Story of the Royal Military School of Music Kneller Hall* (Gillingham, Blackmore Press).

Bledsoe, R. T. (1998) *Henry Fothergill Chorley: Victorian Journalist* (Aldershot, Ashgate).

Bliss, A. (1970) *As I Remember* (Faber).

— (1991) *Bliss on Music: Selected Writings of Sir Arthur Bliss, 1920–1975*, ed. G. Roscow (Oxford, Oxford University Press).

Blom, E. (1942) *Music in England* (Harmondsworth, Penguin).

— (ed.) (1954) *The New Grove Dictionary*, 9 vols, 5th edn (Macmillan).

Boughton, R. (1909) *Self-Advertisement for Rutland Boughton* (Birmingham, Harries).

— (1934) *The Reality of Music* (Kegan Paul).

Boyes, G. (1993): *The Imagined Village: Culture, Ideology and the English Folk Revival* (Manchester, Manchester University Press).

Bridge, F. (1921) *A Westminster Pilgrim* (Novello).

Broadwood, J. (1847) *Old English Songs* (London).

Brown, J. D. and Stratton, S. S. (1897/1977) *British Musical Biography: A Dictionary of Musical Artists, Authors and Composers Born in Britain and its Colonies* (Da Capo Press).

Burckhardt, J. (1860) *The Civilization of the Period of the Renaissance in Italy*, English trans. 1878, 2 vols (Kegan Paul).

Burgess, A. (1982) *This Man and Music* (Hutchinson).

Butterworth, S. (1989) 'Coleridge-Taylor: New Facts for Old Fiction', *Musical Times*: 202–4.

Byron, M. (*c.* 1925) *A Day with John Sebastian Bach* (Hodder & Stoughton).

Calvocoressi, M. D. (1925) *Musical Taste and How To Form It* (Oxford, Oxford University Press).

Cardus, N. (1961) *Sir Thomas Beecham* (Collins).

Carley, L. (ed.) (1983) *Delius: A Life in Letters*, vol. 1 (Scolar).

— (ed.) (1988) *Delius: A Life in Letters*, vol. 2 (Scolar).

— and Threlfall, R. (1977) *Delius – A Life in Pictures* (Oxford, Oxford University Press).

Carlyle, T. (1843/1909) *Past and Present* (Oxford, Henry Frowde).

Carpenter, H. (1996) *The Envy of the World: Fifty Years of the BBC Third Programme and Radio 3* (Phoenix).

Carte, T. (1737) *A Collection of Several Papers and Essays*.

Cazelet, W. W. (1854) *The History of the Royal Academy of Music* (Bosworth).

Chadwick, O. (1966) *The Victorian Church* (Black).

Chorley, H. F. (1836) 'The Liverpool Musical Festival: Mendelssohn's New Oratorio', *Athenaeum* (15 October): 739.

—– (1842) 'Contemporary Musical Composers: Felix Mendelssohn-Bartholdy', *Athenaeum* (29 January): 116.

— (1842a) 'Philharmonic Society', *Athenaeum* (16 June): 549.

—– (1846) 'Birmingham Music Festival: Dr Mendelssohn's *Elijah*', *Athenaeum* (29 August): 891–2.

— (1847) 'Dr Felix Mendelssohn-Bartholdy', *Athenaeum* (13 November): 1178–9.

— (1854) *Modern German Music: Recollections and Criticisms*, 2 vols (Smith & Elder).

— (1860) '*Elijah* at the Crystal Palace', *Athenaeum (12 May): 656*.

— (1880) *The National Music of the World*, ed. H.G. Hewlett (Sampson Low).

Clayre, A. (ed.) (1977) *Nature and Industrialization* (Oxford, Oxford University Press).

Cole, H. (1884) *Fifty Years of Public Work*, 2 vols (Bell).

Coleridge-Taylor, A. (1979) *The Heritage of Samuel Coleridge-Taylor* (Dobson).

Colles, H. C. (ed.) (1927–28) The *Grove Dictionary of Music and Musicians*, 3rd edn, 5 vols (Macmillan).

— (1933) *The Royal College of Music: A Jubilee Record, 1883–1933* (RCM).

— (1942) *Walford Davies* (Oxford, Oxford University Press).

— (1945) *Essays and Lectures* (Oxford, Oxford University Press).

Colls, R. and Dodd, P. (eds) (1986) *Englishness, Politics and Culture, 1880–1940* (Croom Helm).

Cooke, D. (1982) *Vindications: Essays on Romantic Music* (Faber).

Cooper, M. (ed.) (1974) *The New Oxford History of Music*, vol. X: *The Modern Age, 1890–1960* (Oxford, Oxford University Press).

Corder, F. (1922) *A History of the Royal Academy of Music from 1822 to 1922* (Corder).

Cowen, F. H. (1913) *My Art and My Friends* (Arnold).

Cox, D. (1980) *The Henry Wood Proms* (BBC).

Crowest, F. J. (1902) *The Story of Music* (Newnes).

Crump, J. (1986) 'The Identity of English Music: The Reception of Elgar, 1898–1935', in Colls and Dodd: 164–90.

Dahlhaus, C. (1989) *Between Romanticism and Modernism* (Berkeley and Los Angeles, University of California Press).

Dakers, C. (1987) *The Countryside at War, 1914–18* (Constable).

Dannatt, G. (1947) 'Concerts in London', *Penguin Music Magazine*, 2: 79–85.

Darnton, C. (1940) *You and Music* (Harmondsworth, Penguin).

Davison, J. W. (1847) 'Death of Dr Felix Mendelssohn-Bartholdy', *Musical World*, xxii (13 November): 718–20.

Day, C. (ed.) (1978) *Gramophone Classical LP Catalogue* (June).

Day, J. (1998) *Vaughan Williams* (series: 'Master Musicians', Oxford, Oxford University Press).

Deathridge, J. (1991) 'German Music and Germany's "Special Path"', paper presented at the Conference of the Royal Music Association, London, 6 April.

Dennis, D. B. (1993) *Beethoven in German Politics, 1870–1989* (New Haven, CT, and London, Yale University Press).

Dent, E. J. (ed.) (1933) *Music and the Community: The Cambridgeshire Report on the Teaching of Music* (Cambridge, Cambridge University Press).

— (1940/1949) *Opera* (Harmondsworth, Penguin).

Donohue, B. and Jones, G. W. (1973) *Herbert Morrison – A Life* (Weidenfeld & Nicolson).

Dyson, G. (1915) *Grenade Warfare* (Sifton, Praed).

— (1938) 'Director's Address', *RCM Magazine*, 34(1).

Eastaugh, K. (1976) *Havergal Brian: The Making of a Composer* (Harrap).

Edwards F. G. (1896): *The History of Mendelssohn's 'Elijah'* (Macmillan).

Ehrlich, C. (1976) *The Piano: A History* (Dent).

— (1989) *The Music Profession in England Since the Eighteenth Century* (Oxford, Oxford University Press).

— (1990) *Harmonious Alliance: A History of the Performing Rights Society*

(Oxford, Oxford University Press).

— (1995) *First Philharmonic: A History of the Royal Philharmonic Society* (Oxford, Clarendon).

— and Russell, D. (1998): 'Victorian Music: A Perspective', *Journal of Victorian Culture*, iii: 111–22.

Engel, C. (1862) 'A Norwegian Musician – Ole Bull', *Cornhill Magazine*, vi: 514–27.

— (1866) *An Introduction to the Study of National Music* (Longman).

— (1879) *The Literature of National Music* (Novello).

Engler, B. (1992) 'Shakespeare in the Trenches', in S. Wells (ed.), *Shakespeare Survey: An Annual Survey of Shakespeare Studies and Production*, vol. 44 (Cambridge, Cambridge University Press): 105–11.

Enright, D. J. (1990) *Selected Poems* (Oxford, Oxford University Press).

Evans, E. (1924) *The Margin of Music, Oxford Musical Essay* (Humphrey Milford for Oxford University Press).

Fellowes, E. H. (1913–24) *The English Madrigal School*, 36 vols (Stainer & Bell).

Ffrangcon-Davies, M. (1938) *David Ffrangcon-Davies: His Life and Book* (Lane).

Finkelstein, S. (1960/89) *Composer and Nation: The Folk Heritage in Music* (New York, International Publishers).

Foreman, L. (1972) 'The British Musical Renaissance – A Guide to Research', 3 vols, unpublished FLA thesis, London.

— (ed.) (1987) *From Parry to Britten: British Music in Letters, 1900–1945* (Batsford).

— (1988) *Arnold Bax: A Composer and His Times*, 2nd edn (Scolar).

— (ed.) (1998) *Vaughan Williams in Perspective* (Aldershot, Ashgate).

— Payne, A. and Bishop, J. (1976) *The Music of Frank Bridge* (Thames).

Forster, E. M. (1910/83) *Howard's End*, ed. O. Stallybrass (Penguin).

Forsyth, C. (1911) *Music and Nationalism* (Macmillan).

Foss, H. (1950) *Ralph Vaughan Williams* (Harrap).

Foulds, J. (1934) *Music Today: Its Heritage from the Past, and Legacy to the Future* (Nicholson & Watson).

Fox-Strangways, A. H. (1936/68) *Music Observed* (New York, Books for Libraries Press).

Frank, A. (1953) *Modern British Composers* (Dennis Dobson).

Fraser, D. (ed.) (1995) *Fairest Isle: BBC Radio 3 Book of British Music* (BBC).

Fuller Maitland, J. A. (1901) 'Sir Arthur Sullivan', *Cornhill Magazine* (March): 300–9.

— (1902a) *The Age of Bach and Handel* [vol. 4 of *The Oxford History of Music*] (Oxford, Oxford University Press).

— (1902b) *English Music in the Nineteenth Century* (Grant Richards).

— (ed.) (1904–10) *The Grove Dictionary of Music and Musicians*, 2nd edn,

5 vols (Macmillan).

— (1929) *A Door-Keeper of Music* (Murray).

— and Broadwood, L. (1893) *English Country Songs* (Leaderhall Press).

Fussell, P. (1975) *The Great War and Modern Memory* (Oxford, Oxford University Press).

Galloway, W. J. (1902) *The Operatic Problem* (Long).

Gatens W. J. (1986): *Victorian Church Music in Theory and Practice* (Cambridge, Cambridge University Press).

Gatie, J. (1836): 'English Music', *Musical World*, ii (2 September): 177–83.

Geissmar, B. (1944) *The Baton and the Jackboot: Recollections of Musical Life* (Hamish Hamilton).

Gibbons, S. (1991) *Collect British Stamps*, 42nd edn (Stanley Gibbons Publications).

Gibbs, J. A. (1898/1983) *A Cotswold Village, or Country Life and Pursuits in Gloucestershire* (Hemel Hempstead, Dog Ear Books).

Girouard, M. (1981) *The Return to Camelot: Chivalry and the English Gentleman* (New Haven, CT, and London, Yale University Press).

Glock, W. (1963) *The BBC's Music Policy* (BBC).

— (1991) *Notes in Advance* (Oxford, Oxford University Press).

Goddard, S. (1946) 'The Roots and the Soil: Nineteenth Century Origins', in Bacharach: 11–29.

Gollancz, V. (1964) *Journey Towards Music: A Memoir* (Gollancz).

Gordon, A. (1847) *Lighthouses of the British Colonies and Possessions Abroad* (Barclay).

Graeme, E. (ed.) (1870) *Beethoven: A Memoir* (Griffin).

Graves, C. L. (1903) *The Life and Letters of Sir George Grove* (Macmillan).

— (1926) *Hubert Parry: His Life and Works*, 2 vols (Macmillan).

Graves, R. (1929/73) *Goodbye to All That* (Harmondsworth, Penguin).

— and Hodge, A. (1940/63) *The Long Week-End: A Social History of Great Britain, 1918–1939* (New York, Norton).

Gray, C. (1924) *Survey of Contemporary Music* (Humphrey Milford).

— (1934) *Peter Warlock: A Memoir of Philip Heseltine* (Cape).

— (1936) *Predicaments* (Oxford, Oxford University Press).

— (1948/85) *Musical Chairs*, 2nd edn (Hogarth Press).

Greene, H. P. (1935) *Sir Charles Villiers Stamford* (Arnold).

Grosvenor, P. and McMillan, J. (1973) *The British Genius* (Hodder).

Grove, G. (ed.) (1879–89) *A Dictionary of Music and Musicians, 1450–1889*, 4 vols (Macmillan).

— (1883) *The Royal College of Music* (Clowes).

— (1890) 'Handel', entry in *Chambers' Encyclopaedia: A Dictionary of Universal Knowledge*, new edn, vol. 5 (London and Edinburgh, William & Robert Chambers): 541–3.

Guerdon, G. (1892) 'Street Musicians', *The Strand Magazine*, 13(3): 64–72.

Hadden, J. C. (1884) 'The National Music of Scotland', *Cassells' Magazine*: 222–3.

— (1913) *Modern Musicians: A Book for Players, Singers and Listeners* (Foulis).

Hadow, W. H. (ed.) (1901–5) *The Oxford History of Music* (Oxford, Oxford University Press).

— (1931) *English Music* (Longman).

Haldane, J. B. (1918) *Report of the Royal Commission on University Education in Wales* (Cd 8991).

Harker, D. (1985) *Fakesong: The Manufacture of British 'Folksong', 1700 to the Present Day* (Milton Keynes, Open University Press).

Harries, M. and Harries, S. (1989) *A Pilgrim Soul: The Life and Work of Elizabeth Lutyens* (Michael Joseph).

Harrington, P. (1989) 'Holst and Vaughan Williams: Radical Pastoral', in C. Norris: 106–27.

Haweis, H. R. (1871) *Music and Morals* (Strahan).

Henriques, R. L. (1934) *The Approach to Club Music: Suggestions for the Use of Club Workers with Little Musical Training* (Humphrey Milford for Oxford University Press).

Heseltine, P. and Gray, C. (eds) (1920–22) *The Sackbut*, vols 1–4.

Hill, R. (1946) 'Through the Looking-Glass', *Penguin Music Magazine*, 1: 7–12.

— (1949) 'Through the Looking-Glass', *Penguin Music Magazine*, 8: 7–13.

— and Hinrichsen, M. (eds) (1944) *Hinrichsen's Year Book, 1944: Music of Our Time* (Hinrichsen Editions).

Hill, S. (1971) *Strange Meeting* (Hamish Hamilton).

Hiller, F. (1870) 'Quasi Fantasia', in Graeme.

Hitler, A. (1926/69) *Mein Kampf*, ed. D. C. Watt (Hutchinson).

Holbrooke, J. (1925) *Contemporary British Composers* (Cecil Palmer).

Holst, I. (1938/69) *Gustav Holst – A Biography* (Oxford, Oxford University Press).

Houghton, W.E. (1957) *The Victorian Frame of Mind* (New Haven, CT, Yale University Press).

Howes, F. (1948) *Man, Mind and Music* (Secker & Warburg).

— (1966) *The English Musical Renaissance* (Secker & Warburg).

Howkins, A. (1986) 'The Discovery of Rural England', in Colls and Dodd: 62–88.

Hudson, D. (1945) *Norman O'Neill: A Life of Music* (Quality Press).

Hueffer, F. (1874) *Richard Wagner and the Music of the Future* (Chapman & Hall).

— (1879) 'The Chances of English Opera', *Macmillan's Magazine*, 40 (May–October): 57–65.

— (1880) *Musical Studies* (Edinburgh, Adam & Black).

— (1889) *Half a Century of Music in England (1837–1887): Essays towards a History* (Chapman & Hall).

Hughes, M. (2001) *The English Musical Renaissance and the Press, 1850–1914: 'Watchmen of Music'* (Ashgate).

— (1989) 'The Duc d'Elgar – Making a Composer Gentleman', in C. Norris: 41–68.

— (1997) '"The Lucifer of Music": Rossini and German Music Nationalism in the Nineteenth Century', in Stradling *et al.* (eds).

Hull, A. E. (*c.* 1918) *Cyril Scott: The Man and His Works* (Waverley Book Co.).

Hull, R. (1944) 'Music of Our Time: From Elgar to Britten', in Hill and Hinrichsen: 9–17.

Hullah, F. R. (1886) *Life of John Hullah* (Longman).

Hurd, M. (1962) *Immortal Hour: The Life and Period of Rutland Boughton* (Routledge & Kegan Paul).

— (1981) *Vincent Novello – And Company* (Novello).

Hyatt King, A. (1957) *W. Barclay Squire: Music Librarian* (Bibliographical Society).

Irving, D. (1978) *The War Path: Hitler's Germany, 1933–39* (Viking).

Irving, E. (1959) *Cue For Music* (Dobson).

Jackson, H. (1913) *The Eighteen-Nineties* (Grant Richards).

Jacobs, A. (1984) *Sir Arthur Sullivan: A Victorian Musician* (Oxford, Oxford University Press).

Jefferson, A. (1979) *Sir Thomas Beecham – A Centenary Tribute* (MacDonald & Jane's).

Johnstone, A. (1905) *Musical Criticism* (Manchester, Manchester University Press).

Jones, F. A. (1894) 'How Composers Work', *The Strand Magazine*, 7(38): 206–11.

Karpeles, M. (1967) *Cecil Sharp: His Life and Work* (Routledge & Kegan Paul).

— (1973/87) *An Introduction to English Folk Song* (Oxford, Oxford University Press).

Kemp, I. (1991) 'The "Teaching Piece" in the Weimar Republic', paper presented at the Conference of the Royal Music Association, London, 6 April.

Kennedy, M. (1964) 'Vaughan Williams, Whitman, and Parry', *The Listener*, 12 November: 778.

— (1964/71) *The Works of Ralph Vaughan Williams* (Oxford, Oxford University Press).

— (1968/82) *Portrait of Elgar* (Oxford, Oxford University Press).

— (1970) *Elgar's Orchestral Music* (BBC).

— (1971) *The History of the Royal Manchester College of Music,*

1893–1972 (Manchester, Manchester University Press).

— (1987/89) *Adrian Boult* (Macmillan).

— (1991) 'Hugh Wood', Music on Radio 3 April (BBC).

Kerman, J. (1962) *The Elizabethan Madrigal: A Comparative Study* (New York, American Musicological Society).

— (1985) *Musicology* (Collins).

Kidson, F. (1891) *Traditional Tunes* (Oxford, Taphouse).

King-Smith, B. (1970) *1920–1970 – The First Fifty Years: A History of the City of Birmingham Symphony Orchestra* (Birmingham, CBSO).

Klein, H. (1903) *Thirty Years of Musical Life in London, 1870–1900* (Heinemann).

Klingemann, K. (1836): 'Account of the Musical Festival at Dusseldorf: Mendelssohn's New Oratorio *St Paul*', *Musical World*, ii (17 June): 1–6.

Krause, E. (1964) *Richard Strauss: The Man and His Work* (Colletts).

Lahr, J. (1992) *Dame Edna Everage and the Rise of Western Civilization* (Flamingo–HarperCollins).

Lambert, C. (1934/85) *Music Ho! A Study of Music in Decline* (Hogarth).

Latham, M. (1890) *The Renaissance of Music* (Stott).

Laurence, D. H. (ed.) (1989) *Shaw's Music: The Complete Musical Criticism of Bernard Shaw*, 3 vols, 2nd edn (Bodley Head).

Le Fleming, C. (1982) *Journey into Music: By the Slow Train* (Bristol, Redcliffe).

Legge, R. and Hansell, W. E. (1896) *Annals of the Norfolk and Norwich Triennial Music Festivals, 1824–1893* (Jarrold).

LeMahieu, D. L. (1988) *A Culture for Democracy: Mass Communication and the Cultivated Mind in Britain Between the Wars* (Oxford, Oxford University Press).

Leyshon, A. *et al.* (eds) (1998) *The Place of Music* (New York and London, Guilford Press).

Linsay, D. A. E. (Lord Crawford) (1926) *Broadcasting Committee Report* (HMG Cmd 2599).

Lloyd, S. (1984) *H. Balfour Gardiner* (Cambridge, Cambridge University Press).

Lluna, J. E. (1998) 'La Musica de las Islas', in *Impresiones: Trimestral de the British Council en Espana: Verano 12–13* (Madrid, British Council).

Lockspeiser, E. (1946) 'Mixed Gallery', in Bacharach: 185–96.

Lorenz, R. (1920) 'Review of Boughton's *Immortal Hour*', *The Sackbut*: 109–11.

Lunn, H. (1854) *Musings of a Musician* (Cocks).

MacDonald, M. (1974–83) *The Symphonies of Havergal Brian*, 3 vols (Kahn & Averill).

— (1975) *John Foulds* (Rickmansworth, Triad).

MacDougall, H. A. (1982) *Racial Myth in English History: Trojans, Teutons and Anglo-Saxons* (Hanover and London, University Press of New England).

Macfarren, G. A. (1842) 'Symphony in A Minor', *Musical World* xvii (16 June): 185–7.

Mackerness, E. D. (1964) *A Social History of English Music* (Routledge & Kegan Paul).

McVeagh, D. (1986) *Twentieth-Century English Masters* (Macmillan).

Maine, B. (1933) *Elgar: His Life and Works*, 2 vols (Bell).

— (1945) *Basil Maine on Music* (John Westhouse).

Mann, T. (1947/68) *Doctor Faustus: The Life of the German Composer Adrian Leverkühn as Told by a Friend*, tr. H. Lowe-Porter (Harmondsworth, Penguin).

Marek, G. (1967) *Richard Strauss: The Life of a Non-Hero* (Gollancz).

Marsden, G. (ed) (1990): *Victorian Values: Personalities and Perspectives in Nineteenth-Century History* (Longman).

Marshall, H. E. (*c.* 1955) *Our Island's Story* (Nelson).

Mason, A. (1980) *Association Football and English Society, 1863–1915* (Brighton, Harvester).

Mayer, R. (1979) *My First Hundred Years* (Van Duren).

Mayhew, H. (1861/1984) *Mayhew's London*, ed. P. Quennel (Bracken Books).

Meares, S. (ed.) (1986) *British Opera in Retrospect* (British Music Society).

Mellers, W. (1936a) 'Tight-Ropes to Parnassus: A Note on Contemporary Music', *Scrutiny*, 5(2): 150–7.

— (1936b) 'Bernard Van Dieren: Musical Intelligence and "The New Language"', *Scrutiny*, 5(3): 263–76.

— (1937) 'Rubbra's New Symphony', *Scrutiny*, 6(1): 75–6.

— (1939) 'Edmund Rubbra and Symphonic Form', *Scrutiny*, 8(2): 56–71.

— (1947/76) *Studies in Contemporary Music* (Greenwood Press).

— (1989) *Vaughan Williams and the Vision of Albion* (Barrie & Jenkins).

Middleton, J. A. (1911) 'Introduction', in E. S. Sheppard, *Charles Auchester* (Dent).

Middleton, R. (1978) *From Liszt to Music Hall* (Milton Keynes, Open University Press).

Moore, J. N. (1984) *Edward Elgar – A Creative Life* (Oxford, Oxford University Press).

— (ed.) (1987) *Elgar and His Publishers: Letters of a Creative Life*, 2 vols (Oxford, Oxford University Press).

Morgan, R. P. (ed.) (1993/94) *Music and Society: Modern Times, from World War I to the Present* (Macmillan [1993]; Englewood Cliffs, NJ, Prentice-Hall [1994]).

Morris, A. J. A. (1984) *The Scaremongers: The Advocacy of War and Rearmament, 1896–1914* (Routledge).

Motion, A. (1986) *The Lamberts* (Chatto & Windus).

Mulhern, F. (1979) *The Moment of Scrutiny* (NLB; distributed by Schocken Books, New York).

Murdoch, W. G. B . (1911) *The Renaissance of the Nineties* (Moring).

Nettel, R. (1945/76) *Havergal Brian and His Music*, rev. version of *Ordeal by Music* (Dobson).

— (1948) *The Orchestra in England: A Social History* (Cape).

Newman, E. (1902/37) 'A Young English Composer', in Banister 1937: 35–41.

— (1926a) 'The World of Music: Sir Hubert Parry', *Sunday Times*, 4 April.

— (1926b) 'The World of Music: Sir Hubert Parry', *Sunday Times*, 11 April.

Newton, C. S. S. and Porter, D. (1988) *Modernization Frustrated: The Politics of Industrial Decline in Britain Since 1900* (Unwin Hyman).

Norris, C. (ed.) (1989) *Music and the Politics of Culture* (Lawrence & Wishart).

Norris, G. (1981) *A Musical Gazetteer of Great Britain and Ireland* (David & Charles).

Norris, M. (1989) 'Stalking the English Folk Song', *Sunday Correspondent*, 24 September.

Orwell, S. and Angus, I. (eds) (1970) *The Collected Essays, Journalism and Letters of George Orwell*, vol. 1 (Harmondsworth, Penguin).

Ottoway, H. (1966) *Vaughan Williams* (Novello).

— (1974) *Vaughan Williams' Symphonies* (BBC).

Pakenham, S. (1957) *Ralph Vaughan Williams: A Discovery of His Music* (Macmillan).

Palmer, C. (1976) *Delius: Portrait of a Cosmopolitan* (Duckworth).

— (1984) *George Dyson: A Centenary Appreciation* (Sevenoaks, Kent, Novello).

Palmer, R. (1947) *British Music* (Skelton Robinson).

— (ed.) (1983) *Folk-Songs Collected by Ralph Vaughan Williams* (Dent).

Parrott, I. (*c.* 1969) *The Spiritual Pilgrims* (privately published).

— (1971) Elgar (Dent).

Parry, C. H. (1887/1950) *Studies of the Great Composers*, 21st edn (Routledge).

— (1893) *The Art of Music* (Kegan Paul).

— (1902) *Music of the Seventeenth Century* [vol. 3 of the *Oxford History of Music*] (Oxford, Oxford University Press).

— (1905) *Summary of the History and Development of Medieval and Modern Music* (Novello).

(1909) *Johann Sebastian Bach: The Story of the Development of a Great Personality* (Putnam).

(1920) *College Addresses Delivered to the Pupils of the Royal College of Music*, ed. H. C. Colles (Macmillan).

Pater, W. (1873) *Studies in the History of the Renaissance* (Macmillan).

Pattinson, B. (1934) 'Music and the Community: A Review of *The Cambridgeshire Report*', *Scrutiny*, 2(4): 399–404.

— (1935) 'Musical History', *Scrutiny*, 3(4): 369–77.

Pirie, P. (1979) *The English Musical Renaissance* (Gollancz).

Potts, J. E. (1950) 'Analysis of 1948–9 Orchestral Programmes', in R. Hill (ed.), *Music 1950* (Harmondsworth, Penguin): 49–60.

Pound, R. (1969) *Sir Henry Wood* (Cassell).

Proctor, D. (1992) *Music of the Sea* (HMSO).

Quennel, P. (ed.) (1984) *Mayhew's London* (Bracken Books).

Radcliffe P. (1990) *Mendelssohn* (Dent)

Rapaport, P. (1985), 'Havergal Brian and His Gothic Symphony', in *Six Composers from Northern Europe* (Kahn & Averill): 77–109.

Reece, H. and Elton, O. (1905) *Musical Criticism of Arthur Johnstone* (Manchester, Manchester University Press).

Reeves, J. (ed.) (1962) *Georgian Poetry* (Harmondsworth, Penguin).

Reich, W. (1971) *Schoenberg – A Critical Biography*, trans. L. Black (Longman).

Reid, C. (1962) *Thomas Beecham: An Independent Biography* (Gollancz).

— (1968) *Malcolm Sargent* (Hamish Hamilton).

— (1984) *The Music Monster: A Biography of James William Davison* (Quartet).

Revill, G. (1991) '*The Lark Ascending*: Monument to a Radical Pastoral', *Landscape Research*, 161(2): 25–30.

— (1995) 'Hiawatha and Pan-Africanism: Samuel Coleridge-Taylor (1875–1912), a Black Composer in Suburban London', *Ecumene: A Journal of Environment, Culture, Meaning*, 2: 247–66.

— (1998) 'Samuel Coleridge-Taylor's Geography of Disappointment: Hybridity, Identity, and Networks of Musical Meaning', in Leyshon *et al.*: 197–221.

Rich, P. (1989) 'The Rise of English Nationalism', *History Today*, 37: 24–30.

Richards, J. (1988) 'Elgar, Kipling and Edwardian Imperialism', unpublished typescript, University of Lancaster.

Rigby, C. (1948) *John Barbirolli: A Biographical Sketch* (Altrincham, John Sherratt & Son).

Roberts, J. M. (1972) *Modern Europe, 1880–1945* (Longman).

Ronald, L. (ed.) (1937) *Who's Who in Music*, 2nd edn (Shaw).

Rouville, H. de (1986) *La Musique Anglaise* (Paris, Presses Universitaires de France).

Royal College of Organists (1935–6) *Calendar, Proceedings and Report*

(Milner).

Royal Society of Arts (1867) *First Report of the Committee Appointed to Enquire Into and Report On the State of Musical Education at Home and Abroad* (Bell & Daldy).

Ruskin, J. (1869) *Queen of the Air: Being a Study of the Greek Myths of Cloud and Storm* (Smith & Elder).

— (1877) 'Preface' to 'Rock Honeycomb: Broken Pieces of Sir Philip Sidney's *Psalter*' Bibliotheca Pastorum (Ellis & White).

Russell, T. (1942/53) *Philharmonic* (Harmondsworth, Penguin).

Sadie, S. (ed.) (1981) *The New Grove Dictionary*, 6th edn, 18 vols (Macmillan).

Said, E. (1992) *Musical Elaborations* (Vintage).

Salmon, E. (1894) 'How Brass Bands Are Made', *The Strand Magazine*, 47–8 (November): 542.

Sayers, W. C. B. (1915) *Samuel Coleridge-Taylor: His Life and Letters* (Cassell).

Schacht, H. (1947) *The Trial of the German Major War Criminals: Proceedings*, part 12 (HMSO).

Schmitz, O. A. H. (1914/26) *The Land Without Music* (originally published 1914, revised 1918, in Germany); English trans. (1926) by H. Herzl (Jarrolds).

Scholes, P. A. (1922) *The Listener's Guide to Music* (Oxford, Oxford University Press).

— (ed.) (1947) *The Mirror of Music, 1844–1944: A Century of Musical Life in Britain as Reflected in the Pages of the* Musical Times, 2 vols (Novello/Oxford University Press).

Searle, M. V. (1979) *John Ireland: The Man and His Music* (Tunbridge Wells, Midas Books).

Sharp, C. (1907/65) *English Folk Song: Some Conclusions*, 4th edn, ed. and rev. M. Karpeles (EP Publishing).

Shepherd, R. (1988) *A Class Divided: Appeasement and the Road to Munich* (Macmillan).

Sheppard, E. S. (1853) *Charles Auchester: A Memorial*, 3 vols (Hurst & Blackett).

Sheppard, F. W. H. (1975) *The Museums' Area of South Kensington and Westminster* [vol. 38 of the *Survey of London*] (Athlone).

Short, M. (1991) *Gustav Holst – The Man and His Music* (Oxford, Oxford University Press).

Speyer, E. (1937) *My Life and Friends* (Cobden-Sanderson).

Stanford, C. V. (1908) *Studies and Memories* (Constable).

— (1914) *Pages From an Unwritten Diary* (Arnold).

— (1922) *Interludes, Records and Reflections* (Murray).

— and Forsyth, C. (1916) *A History of Music* (Macmillan).

Stradling, R. (1989) 'On Shearing the Black Sheep in Spring: The Repatriation of Frederick Delius', in Norris: 69–105.

— et al. (eds) (1997) Conflict and Coexistence: Nationalism and Democracy in Modern Europe – Essays in Honour of Harry Hearder (Cardiff, University of Wales Press).

— (1998) 'England's Glory: Sensibilities of Place in English Music, 1900–1950', in Leyshon et al.: 176–96.

Sullivan, A. (ed.) (1984) British Literary Magazines: The Victorian and Edwardian Age, 1837–1913 (Westport, MA, Greenwood Press).

Talmon, J. L. (1967) Romanticism and Revolt: Europe 1815–1848 (Thames & Hudson).

Tapert, A. (ed.) (1984) Despatches From the Heart: An Anthology of Letters From the Front During the First and Second World Wars (Hamish Hamilton).

Taylor, A. J. P. (1948/64) The Habsburg Monarchy (Harmondsworth, Penguin Books).

— (1976) A Personal History (Hamish Hamilton).

Temperley, N. (1962) 'Mendelssohn's Influence on English Music', Music & Letters, xliii (July): 224–33.

— (ed.) (1981) Blackwell's History of Music in Britain: The Romantic Age, 1800–1914 (Athlone).

Thomas, P. (1998) 'The Anglicisation of Bach', unpublished MA dissertation, University of Wales at Cardiff.

Thompson, K. (1986) Beliefs and Ideology (Chichester, Ellis Horwood).

Thornton, R. K. R. (ed.) (1984) Ivor Gurney War Letters – A Selection (Hogarth).

Tippett, M. (1959/74) Moving Into Aquarius (Paladin).

Tischler, B. L. (1986) An American Music: The Search for an American Musical Identity (Oxford, Oxford University Press).

Tomlinson, E. (1976) Warlock and Delius (Thames).

Tovey, D. and Parratt, G. (1941) Walter Parratt: Master of the Musick (Oxford, Oxford University Press).

Trend, M. (1985) The Music Makers: The English Musical Renaissance From Elgar to Britten (Weidenfeld & Nicolson).

Trollope, J. (1988/92) The Choir (Black Swan).

Turner, W. J. (1928) Musical Meanderings (Methuen).

Vamplew, W. (1988) Play Up and Play the Game: Professional Sport in Britain, 1875–1914 (Cambridge, Cambridge University Press).

Van Dieren, B. (1935) Down Among the Dead Men and Other Essays (Humphrey Milford for Oxford University Press).

Vaughan Williams, R. (ed.) (1905) Welcome Odes, vol. 1 (Novello).

— (ed.) (1906) The English Hymnal With Tunes (Oxford, Oxford University Press).

— (ed.) (1910) *Welcome Odes*, vol. 2 (Novello).

— (1950) 'Who Wants the English Composer' [1912], in Foss.

— (ed.) (1925) *Songs of Praise* (Oxford, Oxford University Press).

— (1931) 'Introduction', in Hadow (1931).

— (1934/87) *National Music and Other Essays* (Oxford, Oxford University Press).

— (1950) 'Musical Autobiography', in Foss: 18–38.

— and Holst, G. (1959) *Heirs and Rebels – Letters Written to Each Other and Occasional Writings on Music*, ed. U. Vaughan Williams and I. Holst (Oxford, Oxford University Press).

— and Shaw, M. (eds) (1928) *The Oxford Book of Carols* (Oxford, Oxford University Press).

Vaughan Williams, U. (1964) *RVW: A Biography of Ralph Vaughan Williams* (Oxford, Oxford University Press).

Wakefield, A. M. (ed.) (1894) *Ruskin on Music* (Allen).

Walker, A. (1970) *Stardom: The Hollywood Phenomenon* (Michael Joseph).

— (1989) *Walter Carroll: The Children's Musician* (Forsyth).

Walker, E. (1907) *A History of Music in England* (Humphrey Milford for Oxford University Press).

Weber, W. (1975) *Music and the Middle Class* (Croom-Helm)

— (1996) *The Rise of Musical Classics in Eighteenth-Century England: A Study in Canon, Ritual and Ideology* (Oxford, Oxford University Press).

Wesley S. S. (1836) 'A Sketch of the State of the Music in England', *Musical World*, 18(i) (March): 1–5.

Westrup, J. (1947) 'Music', in Barker: 397–407.

Wheeler, H. (*c.* 1936) *How Much Do You Know? A Book of Fascinating Questions and Answers on Every Subject* (Odhams).

Wiener, M. (1985) *English Culture and the Decline of the Industrial Spirit, 1850–1980* (Harmondsworth, Penguin).

Willeby, F. (1893) *Masters of English Music* (Osgood, McIlvaner).

Williams, N. (1989) 'Behold the Sun: The Politics of Musical Production', in C. Norris: 150–71.

Winter, G. (1973) *A Country Camera, 1844–1914* (Harmondsworth, Penguin).

Wood, H. J. (1938) *My Life in Music* (Gollancz).

Young, P. M. (ed.) (1956) *Letters of Edward Elgar* (Bles).

— (ed.) (1965) *Letters to Nimrod* (Dobson).

— (ed.) (1968) *A Future for English Music and Other Lectures by Sir Edward Elgar* (Dobson).

— (1980) *George Grove (1820–1900): A Biography* (Macmillan).

Zon, B. (ed.) (1999) *Nineteenth-Century British Music Studies*, vol. 1 (Aldershot, Ashgate).

Index